D1566839

THE ROLE OF MONARCHY IN MODERN DEMOCRACY

Volume 27 in the series Hart Studies in Comparative Public Law

How much power does a monarch really have? How much autonomy do monarchs enjoy? Who regulates the size of the royal family, their finances, the rules of succession? These are some of the questions considered in this edited collection on the monarchies of Europe.

The book is written by experts from Belgium, Denmark, Luxembourg, the Netherlands, Norway, Spain, Sweden and the UK. It considers the constitutional and political role of monarchy, its powers and functions, how it is defined and regulated, the laws of succession and royal finances, relations with the media and the popularity of the monarchy.

No new political theory on this topic has been developed since Bagehot wrote about the monarchy in *The English Constitution* (1867). The same is true of the other European monarchies. 150 years on, with their formal powers greatly reduced, how has this ancient, hereditary institution managed to survive and what is a modern monarch's role? What is the role of monarchy in advanced democracies, and what lessons can the different European monarchies learn from each other?

The public look to the monarchy to represent continuity, stability and tradition, but also want it to be modern, to reflect modern values and be a focus for national identity. The whole institution is shot through with contradictions, myths and misunderstandings. This book should lead to a more realistic debate about our expectations of the monarchy, its role and its future.

Hart Studies in Comparative Public Law

Recent titles in this series:

The Role of Monarchy in Modern Democracy

European Monarchies Compared

Edited by
Robert Hazell
and
Bob Morris

·HART·
OXFORD · LONDON · NEW YORK · NEW DELHI · SYDNEY

HART PUBLISHING

Bloomsbury Publishing Plc

Kemp House, Chawley Park, Cumnor Hill, Oxford, OX2 9PH, UK

1385 Broadway, New York, NY 10018, USA

HART PUBLISHING, the Hart/Stag logo, BLOOMSBURY and the Diana logo are
trademarks of Bloomsbury Publishing Plc

First published in Great Britain 2020

A catalogue record for this book is available from the British Library.

Library of Congress Cataloging-in-Publication data

Names: Hazell, Robert, editor. | Morris, R. M. editor.
Title: The role of monarchy in modern democracy : European monarchies compared /
edited by Robert Hazell and Bob Morris.
Description: Oxford ; New York : Hart, 2020. | Series: Hart studies in comparative public law ;
volume 27 | Includes bibliographical references and index.
Identifiers: LCCN 2020012026 (print) | LCCN 2020012027 (ebook) | ISBN 9781509931019 (hardcover) |
ISBN 9781509931026 (ePub)
Subjects: LCSH: Monarchy—Europe, Western. | Constitutional law—Europe, Western. |
Europe, Western—Politics and government.
Classification: LCC KJC5408 .R65 2020 (print) | LCC KJC5408 (ebook) | DDC 342.4/062—dc23
LC record available at https://lccn.loc.gov/2020012026
LC ebook record available at https://lccn.loc.gov/2020012027

ISBN: HB: 978-1-50993-101-9
        ePDF: 978-1-50993-103-3
        ePub: 978-1-50993-102-6

Typeset by Compuscript Ltd, Shannon

To find out more about our authors and books visit www.hartpublishing.co.uk.
Here you will find extracts, author information, details of forthcoming events
and the option to sign up for our newsletters.

Foreword

THE CONSTITUTION UNIT has long done work on church and state in the UK, led by Bob Morris, but our interest in doing work directly on the monarchy is more recent. It began with a report on the role and future of the monarchy, published to coincide with the 90th birthday of Queen Elizabeth II in 2016. That led on to a couple of reports on the Accession and Coronation oaths, published in 2018. That initial work tickled our interest in other monarchies, for two reasons: first, that there is very little academic writing about the monarchy; second, that it is an institution full of paradoxes and contradictions, which made us want to explore it further. The essential paradox is that this ancient hereditary institution continues to play a central role in some of the most advanced democracies in the world. It is too glib to dismiss it as a medieval hangover, emblematic of everything that is wrong with a backward-looking Britain that is stuck in the past. How does that explain the survival of monarchy in countries like Denmark, Sweden or the Netherlands? Or are they different, and if so, in what ways?

That sparked our interest in the other monarchies of Europe. To learn more about them we asked a series of research volunteers to help compile an annotated bibliography of the literature on those monarchies, which can be found on the monarchy pages of the Constitution Unit website. It enabled us to identify the leading experts, whom we then invited to a two-day conference in London, together with representatives from some of the royal households. The conference was held in March 2019 at the Royal Foundation of St Katharine in Limehouse. St Katharine's was a suitable venue for our project, having been founded by Queen Matilda in 1147, with over 800 years of royal patronage, the current patron being Queen Elizabeth II. Twenty-five papers were written for the conference and they have been woven into the ten chapters of this book.

We are very grateful to our European colleagues for coming to the conference to share their expertise and for agreeing to their papers being segmented across the different chapters of the book. It would have been easier simply to have separate chapters on the monarchy in each country; but it makes for a stronger analytical approach and sharper comparison to have chapters on the different functions, and that is the structure to which the contributors kindly agreed.

A long-running project like this incurs many debts of thanks. First, we should thank all our research volunteers who helped to compile the bibliography, and with the background research for our own chapters: Georgina Hill, Nazenin Kukukcan, Lorenzo Leoni, Alex Lanucci, Ailsa McNeil, James Moore, Laetitia Nakache. We should also thank the researchers who helped to prepare for the conference: Olivia Hepsworth and Sarah Kennedy-Good. And we should thank the volunteers who helped with the final editing and preparation of chapters for this book: Nabila Roukhamieh-McKenna and Harrison Shaylor.

Next, we should thank all those who attended the conference. In addition to the contributors to this book, they included Christian Behrendt (Belgium), Jes Fabricius Møller (Denmark), Jan Versteeg from the Netherlands and Robert Blackburn and vi *Foreword*

Caroline Creer from the UK. We thank the contributors for their conference papers and for their persistence in commenting on successive drafts as their papers were turned into chapters for the book. Finally, we should thank Kate Whetter, our editor at Hart, and her assistant Rosie Mearns. They have shown great patience in answering our many questions and have turned our complicated manuscript into a beautiful book with Hart's usual speed and efficiency.

Robert Hazell
The Constitution Unit

Bob Morris
School of Public Policy, University College London
January 2020

Contents

List of Contributors

Rudy Anderweg, Emeritus Professor of Political Science, Leiden University

Paul Bovend'Eert, Professor of Constitutional Law, Radboud University, Nijmegen

Ian Bradley, Emeritus Professor of Cultural and Spiritual History, University of St Andrews

Axel Calissendorff, Partner, Calissendorff Swarting, Stockholm, Solicitor to the King since 2009

Frank Cranmer, Honorary Research Fellow, Centre for Law and Religion, Cardiff University

Robert Hazell, Professor of Government and the Constitution, Constitution Unit, University College London

Olivia Hepsworth, formerly Research Volunteer, Constitution Unit, University College London

Luc Heuschling, Professor of Constitutional and Administrative Law

Helle Krunke, Professor of Constitutional Law, University of Copenhagen

RM (Bob) Morris, Honorary Senior Research Associate, Constitution Unit, University College London

Roger Mortimore, Professor of Public Opinion and Political Analysis, Department of Political Economy, King's College, London

Philip Murphy, Professor of British and Commonwealth History, Institute of Commonwealth Studies, University of London

Lennart Nilsson, Senior Researcher at the SOM Institute, University of Gothenburg

Quentin Pironnet, Lecturer in Public and Constitutional Law, University of Liège

Bart van Poelgeest, Deputy Secretary General, Ministry of General Affairs, The Netherlands

Charles Powell, Professor in Contemporary History, San Pablo-CEU University (Madrid) and Director of the Elcano Royal Institute

Frank Prochaska, Senior Research Fellow, Somerville College, University of Oxford

Jean Seaton, Professor of Media History, University of Westminster

Eivind Smith, Professor of Public Law, University of Oslo, Norway

Henrik Wenander, Professor of Public Law, Lund University

List of Figures and Tables

Figures

Tables

Part I

Defining the Project

1

Genesis of the Book

PROFESSOR ROBERT HAZELL AND DR BOB MORRIS,
THE CONSTITUTION UNIT, UNIVERSITY COLLEGE LONDON

WE DECIDED TO embark on this project to fill a serious gap in the literature: and not just a gap, but a gaping void. Lots of popular books are written about the monarchy; and lots of history books, both popular and academic. But in the academic disciplines of law and politics, monarchy is almost non-existent as a subject. In constitutional law books, the Crown or the sovereign typically rates just a few pages; in politics, the topic is ignored. Yet to the general public the monarchy commands a loyalty and fascination which politicians would die for, with opinion poll ratings in the European monarchies showing that between 60 and 80 per cent of the people wish to retain the monarchy. Details of the opinion polling in each country are given in Chapter 9.

Political science has devoted extensive studies to the other institutions of the state, including the presidency in republics, but has a blind spot about monarchy. This is not the place to speculate on the reasons why. Suffice it to say that 44 countries around the world are monarchies, with a dozen of them to be found in Europe. We have chosen European monarchies for this comparative study, because they are amongst the most advanced democracies in the world: one of the issues we wish to explore is the paradox of an ancient, hereditary institution surviving as a central part of modern democracies.

Our primary purpose is academic, but the topic also attracts great public interest. The monarchy is the subject of endless fascination and media speculation, but also subject to myths and misunderstandings. The public tend to attribute more power and autonomy to monarchs and royal families than in fact they possess: whether it involves the formation of new governments, opening parliament or giving assent to laws, the choice of state visits, or the award of honours. Another paradox is that the public look to the monarchy to represent continuity, stability and tradition, but also want it to be modern and to reflect modern values. The whole institution of monarchy is shot through with contradictions and unrealistic expectations. Our wider purpose in this study is to help to develop a better informed public debate about our expectations of the monarchy, its role and its future. In that task we hope to widen the insular British debates about the monarchy by including European perspectives supplied by our European counterparts.

SURVIVAL OF MONARCHIES IN EUROPE

Monarchy has a long history in Europe, being the predominant form of government from the Middle Ages until the French Revolution. That led to some states becoming republics under French influence during the Napoleonic wars, but after the Congress of Vienna in 1815 they reverted to being monarchies. Despite the revolutions of 1848, at the turn of the twentieth century every country in Europe was a monarchy with just three exceptions: France, Switzerland and San Marino. The abolition of the monarchy in most European countries during the twentieth century occurred mainly as a result of defeat in war, sometimes accompanied by a revolution. The First World War led to the collapse of three very large monarchies, in the Austro-Hungarian, German and Russian empires; the Second World War resulted in the disappearance of the monarchy in Italy and five other countries in Central and Eastern Europe. By the turn of the twenty-first century, most European countries had ceased to be monarchies, and three quarters of the member states of the European Union (21 out of 28) are now republics. That has led to a teleological assumption that in time most advanced democracies will become republics, as the highest form of democratic government.

But there is a stubborn group of countries in Western Europe which defy that assumption, and they include some of the most advanced democracies in the world. There are many different indices compiled by academics and NGOs to judge the state of democracy, judged by human rights, economic freedom, press freedom, free elections and so on. To take just one, the Democracy Index compiled by the Economist Intelligence Unit, in their 2018 survey four out of the top five democracies in the world were monarchies, and nine out of the top 15. They include six of the countries in this study: Norway, Sweden, Denmark, the Netherlands, Luxembourg and the UK.

Of the 12 surviving monarchies in Europe, we decided to focus on these six countries, plus Belgium and Spain. We have excluded the remaining four European monarchies (Andorra, Liechtenstein, Monaco, the Vatican) mainly on grounds of size, but also because they are not constitutional monarchies in the same sense as the eight larger countries. It is the strictly limited role of the monarch, either under the law and the constitution, or in political practice by the parliament and the government, which characterises the eight larger European monarchies. Given their strictly limited role, we wanted to ask what constitutional and political functions they still perform; how much autonomy, if any, they still enjoy; and if they have no political power, what is the point of these modern monarchies – what other purposes do they serve?

NO NEW THEORY OF MONARCHY SINCE BAGEHOT

Another reason for embarking on this study is that no new political theory has been developed in the UK since Bagehot wrote about the monarchy in *The English Constitution* (1867). And not just in the UK: Bagehot holds sway in much of Europe as well, and is still widely quoted in countries like Belgium, Luxembourg and the Netherlands. He distinguished between the dignified and the efficient constitution, and suggested that the monarch has three rights: to be consulted, to encourage and to warn. But a lot has changed since Bagehot's day; even in the dignified part of the constitution, Queen Victoria had far greater discretion in the exercise of her formal powers than does Queen Elizabeth II. The same is true of the other European monarchies. 150 years on, with their formal powers greatly reduced, what is the role of the modern monarchy in advanced democracies?

To answer that question we invited the leading experts on the monarchies of Western Europe to a conference in London, held in March 2019, and their conference papers have provided the basis for this book. In writing their papers, we asked them to address the following questions.

- What is the monarch's constitutional and political role? How is this exercised in practice: what are the main day-to-day functions?
- How much power does the monarch have? How much autonomy in the exercise of their different functions?
- How is the monarchy defined, and regulated? What are the laws of succession? The limits to the size of the royal family, and their finances?
- What are the limits on their travel, marriage, religion, choice of career, freedom of speech?
- What explains the survival of the monarchy in these eight European countries? What lessons can the different European monarchies learn from each other?

The monarchies themselves are not entirely uniform. They fall into three groups: the older monarchies of Denmark, Norway, Sweden and the UK; the post-Napoleonic settlement monarchies of Belgium, Luxembourg and the Netherlands; and the monarchy of Spain restored in 1976, after almost half a century of authoritarian rule. Following Besselink (2010), we can also divide them into countries with evolutionary, and those with revolutionary constitutions. An evolutionary constitution is incremental, adapting to political changes and weaving the outcomes into an overall longer term constitution that codifies rather than modifies. The prototype is the British Constitution. The Scandinavian constitutions, though not uniformly, are also varieties of the evolutionary type; as is the Constitution of the Netherlands. The counterpoint is a constitution which represents a clean break, a radical departure from the previous system of government: the archetype in our sample would be the Spanish constitution of 1978, designed to lay the foundations for a fresh start after 40 years of dictatorship under General Franco.

One feature the monarchies do share, however, is that succession is determined by primogeniture. Although it involves a step back to an earlier age, it is worth taking a little time to explain how European monarchies became hereditary. In the early Middle Ages, many of them were elective, or contained persistent elective elements. Writing about medieval Germanic monarchies, Kern says 'The part played by the people or their representatives in the elevation of the monarch fluctuated between genuine election and mere recognition (or acceptance) of a king already designated' (Kern 1948: 12). The Holy Roman Empire remained elective until the fifteenth century, and in England primogeniture did not become firmly established until the thirteenth century: of the six kings who followed William the Conqueror, only Richard I succeeded in accordance with the strict rules of hereditary succession (Pool 1951: 3).

To the modern mind election appears preferable, to choose the ruler best suited to be the successor, rather than rely on the lottery of heredity. But these were autocratic rulers, and warrior kings, and in autocracies arranging the succession is difficult. If the autocrat designates a successor, that person might be tempted to depose the autocrat and take power. If the autocrat fails to appoint a successor, the elite have few incentives to remain loyal when he grows old. Tullock (1987) has argued that succession based on primogeniture offers a solution to the dilemma. It provides the autocrat with an heir, who can afford to wait to inherit power peacefully; and it provides the elite with assurance that the regime will live on, and continue to reward their loyalty.

The counter-intuitive theory that primogeniture might be a preferable order of succession, despite the risk of producing incompetent rulers, was tested recently by Kokonnen and Sundell (2014). They compiled a dataset covering 961 monarchs ruling 42 European states between 1000 and 1800, and found that fewer monarchs were deposed in states practising primogeniture than in states with alternative orders of succession. Primogeniture also contributed to building strong states: by 1801 all European monarchies had adopted primogeniture or succumbed to foreign enemies.

As mentioned above, while in 1900 every country in Europe was a hereditary monarchy, with just three exceptions, during the twentieth century most of those monarchies disappeared, after the First and Second World Wars. That has led to the teleological assumption that in time most advanced democracies will become republics. But this assumption is challenged by the continued existence of the group of eight European monarchies which form the subject of this book, and which include some of the most advanced democracies in the world.

The secret of their survival has been continuous adaptation to the needs of modern democracy. All these monarchies, ancient and modern, have witnessed a growing gap between the formal political power conferred on them by the constitution, and the actual power they wield in reality. Sweden is the only country to amend the Constitution to match the political reality, in the new Instrument of Government adopted in 1974 which reduced the monarchy to a purely ceremonial role. In the other countries changes in conventions and in political practice, accompanied occasionally by changes in the law, have seen the monarch retaining a constitutional role, but in practice enjoying little or no discretion in how their formal powers are exercised. Allowing their political power to shrink virtually to zero has been the key to their continuation. And as their political power has shrunk, new roles and new expressions of old roles have emerged to re-legitimate their existence.

THE STRUCTURE OF THIS BOOK

The book is divided into four parts. The first part is very short, consisting simply of this chapter and chapter 2, which summarises the position of the monarchy in the different constitutional texts. What is striking in reading the different texts is how central the monarchy is in each country's constitution: in terms of the prominence given to the monarchy, which often appears very early; and in terms of the space given to it, which is extensive. To take the most extreme example, just under half of the 110 articles in the Norwegian Constitution of 1814 are devoted to the role and powers of the monarchy, or mention the King. The other striking thing is how similar are the powers of modern constitutional monarchs in Europe (again, with the exception of Sweden), and how in many of the constitutional texts, they are specified in near identical terms.

The second part of the book opens with Chapter 3 on the constitutional functions of the monarchy, followed by Chapter 4 on the political functions. The constitutional functions are the power to appoint and dismiss ministers, and so to form new governments, and to bring them to an end; the power to summon and dissolve parliament; and the power to give royal assent to laws and decrees. Chapter 4 on the day-to-day political functions covers working with the prime minister, with other ministers, and with senior officials; chairing the Council of State; countersigning government decisions and decrees; and the appointment of senior officials and judges. In all countries both the constitutional and political functions of the monarchy have become tightly circumscribed by convention, and in some cases regulated by law, so that the monarch is left with little or no discretion.

Chapter 5 looks at the ceremonial functions of the monarchy, including its links to religion, which are stronger in the UK and Scandinavia than in the other four monarchies. It explores the monarch's wider role as head of the nation as opposed to head of state, and asks how far monarchical ceremonial contributes to support for the legitimacy of the state and its political system. Chapter 6 then looks at other softer roles of the monarchy in supporting public service and other welfare and charitable activities, through patronage and through royal visits, with analysis of the royal calendar in the different countries. We then move on in the second part of Chapter 6 to study foreign state visits, incoming and outgoing, their use in the promotion of trade, and how the reputation of the monarchy can thereby be put at risk.

The third part of the book is about the regulation of the monarchy. Chapter 7 discusses how the line of succession was changed between 1979 and 2013 in all countries (except Spain) to introduce gender equality. The size of the royal family is also regulated, in some countries by law, in others by the reigning monarch; it is normally limited to those royals who carry out public duties, as is public funding for those duties. Size varies in part with the size of the country: the UK, with the largest population, has 15 royals performing public duties, while Norway has five. Chapter 8 then looks at regulation of the individual behaviour of the monarch and other members of the royal family, finding that they are severely constrained in terms of their freedom of speech, freedom to travel, freedom to marry, freedom of religion, free choice of career, and the right to privacy and family life.

The final part of the book is about the popularity of the monarchy, and its legitimacy as an institution. Chapter 9 suggests that new legitimisation arguments have been developed: that the monarchy is a neutral protector and guardian of democracy; a symbol of continuity and stability; a contributor to society, through royal visits and patronage, and to the economy, as a tourist attraction. To demonstrate its contribution to society, the monarchy is heavily dependent on the media, who can hold the monarchy to account, and also frame perceptions of the monarchy through commissioning opinion polls. These do more than simply measure public opinion; they also help to frame the terms of debate about the monarchy and its future.

Chapter 10 concludes with further reflections on legitimation. Formal legitimation in some countries derives historically from referendums: in the twentieth century 18 referendums were held on the future of the monarchy in nine different European countries, including five of the countries studied in this book. Monarchies survive only with the continuing support of government and the people. Governments support a hereditary monarchy because it has popular support; it lends legitimacy to the other institutions of the state; it is likely to be less interfering than an elected or appointed president. Public support for the monarchy depends more on the roles performed as head of nation rather than head of state, the ceremonial roles, speaking to and for the nation at times of crisis and of celebration, bringing glamour and stardust to national and local events.

Monarchy may be ancient, but it has proved adaptable in response to enormous social and political change. Five of the eight monarchies were occupied during the Second World War, and came through even that experience. As we showed at the start of this chapter, many of the previous monarchies in Europe disappeared following defeat in war. In the chapters which follow, we hope to show how the eight monarchies which remain have survived through tight regulation and controls on their behaviour, combined with gradual changes in their constitutional, political, ceremonial and other functions.

2

Monarchy in the Constitutional Texts

PROFESSOR ROBERT HAZELL,
THE CONSTITUTION UNIT, UNIVERSITY COLLEGE LONDON

INTRODUCTION

T
HIS CHAPTER SUMMARISES the main provisions about the monarchy in the
constitutions of the eight countries surveyed in this volume. The constitutions
vary, in terms of their age, the prominence given in the constitution to the
monarchy, and the degree of detail in which the powers and functions of the monarch
are specified; but overall the similarities are much greater than the differences. This is
especially the case with regard to the powers of the monarch: not only are the powers
of modern constitutional monarchs in Europe more or less identical; but in many of the
constitutional texts, they are specified in near identical terms. That is a reflection not
simply of a coincidence of ideas about the limited role of the monarch in a parliamentary democracy; it also reflects direct and indirect copying by those drafting or revising
their constitutions. None of these constitutions developed in isolation; the draftsmen
were able to draw upon the American and French and Polish Constitutions, and they
also referred to the constitutions of the other European monarchies. Let us give just two
examples. The main source for the Constitution of the new Belgian state in 1831 was
the British example of a constitutional monarch with limited powers (see Chapter 3.6).
And in the next decade, the sources of inspiration for the Danish Constitution of 1849
included the Norwegian Constitution of 1814, and the Belgian Constitution of 1831.

'Constitution' in this chapter refers to the codified constitution of each country, with
two exceptions: Sweden and the UK. In Sweden the main provisions of the Constitution
are to be found in four fundamental laws, which are much harder to amend than ordinary
laws: the basic laws regulating the monarchy are two of these four laws, the Instrument of
Government, and the Act of Succession. In the UK there is no formal distinction between
constitutional laws and ordinary laws: the main provisions of the Constitution are to
be found in a dozen or so Acts of Parliament, and important constitutional conventions
affecting the monarchy have recently been codified in the Cabinet Manual (Cabinet Office
2011). There have also been independent initiatives to codify the British Constitution:
one undertaken by Professors Vernon Bogdanor and Stefan Vogenauer and their students
(Bogdanor and Vogenauer 2007); and a second commissioned by a parliamentary committee from Professor Robert Blackburn (Blackburn 2014). So for the UK and for Sweden,
when we refer to the constitutional text, we are referring to several different texts, which
in combination provide the text of the constitution.

CENTRALITY OF THE MONARCHY IN THE CONSTITUTION

It is striking when reading the different constitutional texts how central is the monarchy in each country's constitution. It is central in terms of the prominence given to the monarchy, which often appears very early, as a focal point of the constitution; in the section about the institutions of government, the Crown or the King comes first (the one exception being Belgium, where the parliament comes first). The monarchy is also central in terms of the space given to it. As a crude generalisation, the older the constitution, the more central is the monarchy within it. An extreme example is the Norwegian Constitution, the oldest in our sample: dating from 1814, it is the second oldest written constitution in the world. In a constitution of 110 articles, just under one half are about the role and powers of the monarchy, or mention the King. The longest section, in Title B, about the King and the royal family and the executive power, runs to 43 articles. Anyone reading the Constitution would be given the impression that the King governs the country:

Article 3   The Executive power is vested in the King

Article 12   The King himself chooses a Council ... This Council shall consist of a Prime Minister and at least seven other members. The King apportions the business among the members of the Council as he deems appropriate.

Article 13   During his travels within the realm, the King may delegate the administration of the realm to the Council of State.

Article 21   The King shall choose and appoint, after consultation with his Council of State, all senior civil and military officials.

Similarly the constitutions of Denmark (which originated in 1815) and the Netherlands (which also goes back to 1815) and Luxembourg (1868) all devote long sections to the monarchy: 30 out of 96 articles in the Danish Constitution, 25 out of 142 in the Dutch, 30 out of 140 in Luxembourg. In Denmark and Luxembourg the monarchy appears very early, right at the start of the Constitution. By contrast in the most recent codified constitution, the Spanish Constitution of 1978, the monarchy appears lower down, and gets shorter treatment, just ten articles out of 169. That may reflect greater ambivalence about the monarchy in Spain; or it may simply reflect a concern to emphasise rights and freedoms, and give them more space, in the opening sections of the post-Franco Constitution. The Dutch Constitution similarly opens with a catalogue of fundamental rights, before turning to the institutions of government, starting with the King.

POWERS OF THE MONARCH

With the exception of Sweden, the monarch has a common set of constitutional functions and powers in almost all the constitutions in our sample:

- To summon and dissolve Parliament;
- To appoint and dismiss ministers, including the Prime Minister;

- To give Royal Assent to laws passed by Parliament;
- To make war, and peace;
- To be commander-in-chief of the armed forces.

The executive power is formally vested in the monarch, but several constitutions provide that responsibility rests with ministers, and decisions of the monarch must be counter-signed by the relevant minister. The monarch typically also has some lesser powers in the constitution:

- To issue the currency;
- To provide for the collection of taxes;
- To grant pardons, under the prerogative of mercy;
- To grant honours.

Examples of these powers are illustrated in the following extracts from the Danish Constitution, which goes back to 1849, but was substantially revised in 1953:

Article 3   The legislative power shall be vested in the King and the Folketing conjointly. The executive power shall be vested in the King.

Article 12   [T]he King shall have the supreme authority in all the affairs of the Realm, and he shall exercise such supreme authority through the ministers.

Article 14   The King shall appoint and dismiss the Prime Minister and the other ministers ... The signature of the King to resolutions relating to legislation and government shall make such resolutions valid, provided that [it] is accompanied by the signature ... of one or more ministers. A minister who has signed a resolution shall be responsible for the resolution.

Article 17   The body of ministers shall form the Council of State ... The Council of State shall be presided over by the King.

Article 19   The King shall act on behalf of the realm in international affairs.

Article 22   A Bill passed by the *Folketing* shall become law if it receives the Royal Assent ... The King shall order the promulgation of statutes and shall see to it that they are carried into effect.

Article 24   The King shall have the prerogative of mercy and of granting amnesty.

Article 26   The King may cause money to be coined as provided by statute.

Similar powers can be found in the Belgian Constitution, which dates originally from 1831, and last underwent major revision in 1993:

Article 37   The federal executive power, as regulated by the Constitution, belongs to the King.

Article 44   The Houses [of Parliament] meet by right each year [in October], unless they have been convened prior to this by the King. The King pronounces the closing of the session.

Article 45   The King can adjourn the Houses ... for [not] longer than one month.

Article 46   The King has the right to dissolve the House of Representatives [in the event of a vote of no confidence, or resignation of the government]

Article 88   The King's person is inviolable: his ministers are accountable.

Article 96   The King appoints and dismisses his ministers.

Article 106 No act of the King can take effect without the countersignature of a minister, who, in doing so, assumes responsibility for it.

Article 107 The King bestows ranks within the army. He appoints civil servants to positions in the general and foreign affairs administrations of the state.

Article 108 The King makes decrees and regulations required for the execution of laws.

Article 109 The King sanctions and promulgates laws.

Article 110 The King has the right to remit or to reduce sentences passed by judges.

Article 112 The King may mint money, in execution of the law.

With varying degrees of detail, the same catalogue of powers can be found in all the constitutions, except for Sweden. An outsider could be given the impression that the monarch has wide ranging and significant political power. The Dutch Constitution, in its section on the King and the ministers, is the most explicit in stating that the ministers are responsible for the government, and not the King.

Sweden is an important exception. Under the 1809 Instrument of Government, the King had powers similar to those in the other monarchies. But in a major revision in 1974 the monarch lost all formal executive power, and was reduced to a purely ceremonial and representative role. The Prime Minister is no longer appointed by the King, but elected by the Riksdag. The Speaker became responsible for nominating and dismissing the Prime Minister; and the Prime Minister appoints and dismisses the other ministers. Bills passed by the Riksdag become law without royal assent, and the King is no longer commander-in-chief of the armed forces.

REGULATION OF THE LINE OF SUCCESSION

These are all hereditary monarchies. All constitutions regulate the line of succession, defining carefully who is the heir to the throne, and how subsequent monarchs will be identified. They define the age of majority for the monarch (typically 18); they make provision for a regency, if the monarch is a minor, or is incapacitated; and they make provision for the throne becoming vacant, if the line of succession dies out. In that event, the constitution normally provides that the parliament will appoint a new monarch.

Acts of succession vary in the degree of detail they provide, but fairly typical are these provisions from the Spanish Constitution:

Section 57.1 The Crown of Spain shall be inherited by the successors of HM Juan Carlos I de Borbón, the legitimate heir of the historic dynasty. Succession to the throne shall follow the regular order of primogeniture and representation, the first line always having precedence over subsequent line ... within the same grade, the male over the female; and in the same sex, the elder over the younger.

Section 57.3 Should all the lines designated by law become extinct, the Cortes Generales shall provide for succession to the Crown in the manner most suitable to the interests of Spain.

Section 57.4 Those persons with a right of succession to the throne who marry against the express prohibition of the King and the Cortes Generales, shall be excluded from succession to the Crown, as shall their descendants.

Section 59.1 In the event of the King being under age, the King's father or mother or ... the oldest relative ... who is nearest in succession ... shall immediately assume the office of Regent.

Section 59.2 If the King becomes unfit for the exercise of his authority ... the Crown Prince shall immediately assume the Regency, if he is of age.

In one respect the Spanish Constitution is atypical, in providing that male children take precedence over females. That was the rule in all the constitutions in our sample, but with growing gender equality male primogeniture has now been abolished in all countries except for Spain. Sweden was the first, changing the law in 1980, and displacing Crown Prince Carl Philip in favour of Princess Victoria. The UK was the most recent, changing the rules in the Succession to the Crown Act 2013, but not affecting any existing claims, because the eldest children in direct line of succession were all male.

RESTRICTIONS ON THE MONARCHY

The main restrictions on the monarchy which are prescribed in the constitution relate to marriage, religion, acceptance of a foreign crown, and foreign travel. All the constitutions in our sample impose tight controls on royal marriages. Those in the line of succession typically need to obtain the consent of the monarch, the government or parliament before they can marry. Section 57.4 of the Spanish Constitution (above) expresses this in negative terms, of marrying against a prohibition; more common is a positive requirement for consent, like this provision from the Swedish Act of Succession:

Article 5 A prince or princess of the Royal House may not marry unless the government has given its consent thereto upon an application from the King. Should a prince or princess marry without such consent, that prince or princess forfeits the right of succession ...

In Britain the Royal Marriages Act 1772 provided that no descendant of George II could marry without consent of the reigning monarch. Any marriage contracted without consent was null and void. The Act was replaced by the Succession to the Crown Act 2013, which now provides that only the first six people in line of succession require royal consent before they can marry.

The three Scandinavian constitutions and the UK also impose a religious requirement. In the UK this requirement goes back to the Bill of Rights 1688, when William (of Orange) and Mary were invited to assume the English throne following the deposition of the Catholic King James II, and required to take an oath that they were Protestants. In the modern form of the oath prescribed in the Accession Declaration Act 1910, the monarch upon accession must swear to be a faithful Protestant, and to uphold the laws which secure the Protestant succession to the throne. Under section 3 of the Act of Settlement 1700 the monarch must also be in communion with the Church of England; and the Coronation Oath Act 1688 requires the monarch at his coronation to swear to maintain the settlement of the Church of England, and its doctrine, rights and privileges (Hazell and Morris 2018).

The restrictions in the Scandinavian countries are no less strict, and in Sweden little less elaborate. The relevant provisions from their constitutions are as follows:

Denmark, article 5   The King shall be a member of the Evangelical Lutheran Church.

Norway, article 4   The King shall at all times profess the Evangelical-Lutheran religion.

Sweden, article 4   [T]he King shall always profess the pure evangelical faith, as adopted and explained in the unaltered Confession of Augsburg and in the Resolution of the Uppsala Meeting of the year 1593, princes and princesses of the Royal House shall be brought up in that same faith and within the realm. Any member of the Royal Family not professing this faith shall be excluded from all rights of succession.

All constitutions require an oath to be taken by a new monarch on acceding the throne, and most prescribe the text of the oath in the constitution. The oaths are shorter and simpler than the accession and coronation oaths required in the UK. Typical is the oath in Belgium, 'I swear to observe the Constitution and the laws of the Belgian people, to preserve the country's national independence and its territorial integrity'. The monarch in Belgium only accedes to the throne after having sworn the oath before Parliament (article 91). In Denmark, the monarch is required to sign a written declaration that he will adhere to the Constitution (article 8). Apart from the UK, the only country to include a religious element in the oath is Norway: 'I promise and swear that I will govern the Kingdom of Norway in accordance with its Constitution and Laws: so help me God, the Almighty and Omniscient' (article 9).

The Scandinavian constitutions also all contain a requirement that the monarch may not accept any other crown without the consent of the Parliament (Denmark article 5, Norway article 11, Sweden article 8 of Act of Succession). The Belgian Constitution has a similar requirement (article 87). Such a restriction might appear strange in the UK, where because of Britain's imperial past the monarch is also head of state in 15 other countries, including Australia, Canada, New Zealand, and Jamaica, and other smaller countries in the Caribbean and the Pacific. But the Westminster Parliament over time has consented to this multiplicity of crowns, because one by one it enacted the independence constitutions of all these former colonies which have retained the British Crown.

Restrictions on foreign travel apply to the monarch, and in some cases the heir, such as these provisions in Sweden:

Instrument of Government, chapter 5, article 2	The Head of State shall consult the Prime Minister before undertaking travel abroad
Act of Succession, article 7	The heir to the throne may not undertake travel abroad without the knowledge and consent of the King.

Finally it is worth mentioning some exceptional provisions in the Dutch Constitution. The first allows Parliament to exclude individuals from the hereditary succession 'if exceptional circumstances necessitate' (article 29.1). The second allows the Cabinet and Parliament to remove the King from the throne if they are of the opinion that he 'is unable to exercise the royal prerogative' (article 35). The third permits the King to 'temporarily relinquish the exercise of the royal prerogative and resume the exercise thereof pursuant to Act of Parliament' (article 36). Although these provisions were designed to facilitate a regency, and have never been used in the Netherlands to resolve conflict between the monarch and the government, such a provision could have been helpful in Belgium and Luxembourg when the monarch was unwilling to grant Royal Assent to legislation because of conscientious objections (see Chapter 4).

INVIOLABILITY, AND AUTONOMY

All the constitutions provide for the monarch to enjoy civil and criminal immunity. In Norway the Constitution states 'The King's person cannot be censured or accused' (article 5). In Spain the equivalent provision states 'The person of the King is inviolable and shall not be held accountable' (section 56.3). In Denmark the Constitution provides 'The King shall not be answerable for his actions; his person shall be sacrosanct' (article 13).

Finally it is worth mentioning a provision found in several of the constitutions, which is designed to protect the autonomy of the monarchy. This is that the monarch is in charge of the royal household, and can appoint his own officials and advisers. An example is article 24 of the Norwegian Constitution: 'The King chooses and dismisses, at his own discretion, his royal household and court officials'. Similar provisions are to be found in Spain, and the Netherlands.

Part II

Monarchical Functions

3

Constitutional Functions of the Monarchy

Contents

3.1. INTRODUCTION

Professor Robert Hazell, The Constitution Unit, University College London

THIS CHAPTER IS about the monarch's constitutional role. In all the countries under review, except for Sweden, the monarch retains important prerogative powers. These are summarised in Table 3.1, with the relevant provisions from each country's constitution. They are the power to appoint and dismiss ministers, and so to form new governments, and bring them to an end; the power to summon and dissolve parliament; and the power to give royal assent to laws and decrees. In all the countries these powers have become tightly circumscribed by convention, and in some cases regulated by law, so that the monarch is left with little or no discretion in exercising these powers.

One question to be explored is whether the monarch is left with any real power in exercising these constitutional functions. How much discretion is left to the monarch in the process of government formation, or summoning or dissolving parliament? And should the monarch retain discretionary powers; or should they be removed, as in Sweden? Another question is to ask how much difference there is between Sweden, where formally the King has no role; and Denmark or Norway, where the constitution prescribes a role, but in practice there is none.

A third set of questions asks whether it still makes sense, on a precautionary basis, for the monarch to retain deep reserve powers, even if they might never be exercised. What does it mean, for the monarch to be the ultimate guardian of the constitution? In a constitutional crisis, would the monarch still have effective powers? In what circumstances would they be exercised? These questions are debated amongst constitutional scholars, and receive different answers in the different countries surveyed below.

Table 3.1 Main constitutional functions of the monarchy

Country	Appoint and dismiss ministers	Summon and dissolve parliament	Royal Assent to legislation	Immunity of monarch, accountability of ministers	Oath to observe the Constitution
Belgium	Article 96	Articles 44 and 46	Article 109	Article 88	Article 91
Denmark	Article 14. Constitutional convention of *Dronningerunden*	Article 32	Article 14	Article 13	Article 8
Luxembourg	Article 77.	Articles 72 and 74	No: Article 34 amended in 2009 to remove Royal Assent	Articles 4 and 78: ministers are responsible	Article 5
Netherlands	Articles 43 (general provision), 44 (departments, ministers), 48 (prime minister)	Article 64 (dissolution by royal decree: requires ministerial countersignature)	Articles 47 and 87 (legislation requires consent of parliament and King, counter signed by a minister)	Article 42.2 for immunity of the king and accountability of ministers	Article 32 for the king, Article 37.4 for the Regent

(continued)

Table 3.1 (*Continued*)

Country	Appoint and dismiss ministers	Summon and dissolve parliament	Royal Assent to legislation	Immunity of monarch, account-ability of ministers	Oath to observe the Constitution
Norway	By the King in Council. Article 12 (appointment), Article 22 (dismissal)	Article 69: King can summon parliament during vaca-tions etc. Parliament cannot be dissolved	By the King in Council. Articles 77 to 81	Article 5	Article 9
Spain	Section 62.d, 62.e	Section 62.b	Section 62.a	Section 56.3	Section 61
Sweden	No. Speaker appoints the prime minister on behalf of the Riksdag. 1974 Instr of Gov, Ch 6 Art 6	No	No	Criminal immunity. 1974 Instr of Govt, Ch 5 Art 8	New monarch is expected to give declara-tion of office before the Riksdag
UK	Yes. Cabinet Manual paras 2.7–2.20	Power to dissolve rests with Parliament itself, under Fixed Term Parliaments Act 2011. Monarch summons Parliament on ministerial advice	Royal Assent last withheld in 1708. Monarch would only refuse Royal Assent on ministerial advice	Civil and criminal immunity at common law	Coronation oath includes promise to govern the peoples of the UK and realms according to their respec-tive laws and customs

Note: The Table records the formal position, as set out in each country's constitution. In practice, many of the functions are exercised only on the advice of the government: for details, see the text on each country below.

3.2. CONSTITUTIONAL FUNCTIONS OF THE MONARCHY IN THE UK

Professor Robert Hazell, The Constitution Unit, University College London

INTRODUCTION: THE LOSS OF THE MONARCH'S RESERVE POWERS

All of the important prerogative powers remaining in the hands of the monarch in the UK have been removed or diluted in recent years. In particular the power to choose a Prime Minister, and the power to dissolve Parliament have been significantly curtailed.

Most prerogative powers are now exercised directly by government ministers. But the Queen still exercises some prerogative powers herself, known variously as her reserve powers, constitutional powers, or the personal prerogatives (a term first coined by Jennings, 1959). The most important powers are:

- To appoint and dismiss ministers, in particular the Prime Minister;
- To summon, prorogue and dissolve Parliament;
- To give royal assent to bills passed by Parliament.

The sections which follow demonstrate that in exercising these powers the monarch no longer has any effective discretion. This introduction summarises the overall argument.

The constitutional conventions about the appointment of the Prime Minister have been codified in the 2011 Cabinet Manual, which explains that it is for the parties in Parliament to determine who is best placed to command the confidence of the House of Commons, and communicate that clearly to the monarch.

The prerogative power of dissolution was abolished by the Fixed Term Parliaments Act 2011. Parliament is now dissolved automatically after five years, or earlier if two thirds of the House of Commons vote for an early election, or the government loses a no confidence motion and no alternative government can be formed. The power of prorogation was exercised in 2019 to close down Parliament for five weeks, an order subsequently declared to be unlawful. Following that judgement, future prime ministers who wish to prorogue Parliament for more than a few days will have to provide good reasons.

Royal assent to a bill has not been refused since 1708. It would only be withheld now (as then) on the advice of ministers. That might happen with a minority government which could not otherwise prevent the passage of legislation against its wishes, but it would be very controversial.

The Queen might still have to exercise discretion in very exceptional circumstances: for example, if the Prime Minister suddenly died, or refused to resign following a formal vote of no confidence. So the monarch remains the ultimate constitutional longstop.

The Appointment of the Prime Minister

The appointment and dismissal of ministers is made on the advice of the Prime Minister. The last time a Prime Minister was dismissed was in 1834: few would maintain that the power could be exercised today, save as a deep reserve power (Blackburn 2004: 551; Twomey 2018 ch 4).[1] As the Cabinet Manual records:

> Historically, the Sovereign has made use of reserve powers to dismiss a Prime Minister or to make a personal choice of successor, although this was last used in 1834 and was regarded as

---

[1] Blackburn, in an article aimed at restricting any discretionary use of the monarch's personal prerogatives, suggested that 'A monarch is duty bound to reject prime ministerial advice, and dismiss the Prime Minister from office, when the Prime Minister is acting in manifest breach of convention'. The example he gave was if a Prime Minister, after a successful no confidence motion, refused to resign or call a general election. The consequence of no confidence motions is now regulated by the Fixed Term Parliaments Act 2011.

having undermined the Sovereign (Cabinet Office 2011:14. The episode was King William IV's dismissal of Lord Melbourne and replacement by Sir Robert Peel).

Until 2010, the conventions governing the appointment of a Prime Minister were to be found only in the academic literature, as in Denmark (see 3.3 below). But they have now been codified in the Cabinet Manual. It states that when a party wins an overall majority in a general election the result is clear, and the Queen appoints the party's leader as Prime Minister. When the result is unclear because no party has an overall majority, the Queen will appoint that person who is most likely to command the confidence of the House of Commons.

The key paragraphs in the Cabinet Manual about a hung parliament are as follows:

Parliaments with No Overall Majority in the House of Commons

2.12 Where an election does not result in an overall majority for a single party, the incumbent government remains in office unless and until the Prime Minister tenders his or her resignation and the Government's resignation to the Sovereign. An incumbent government is entitled to wait until the new Parliament has met to see if it can command the confidence of the House of Commons, but is expected to resign if it becomes clear that it is unlikely to be able to command that confidence and there is a clear alternative.

2.13 Where a range of different administrations could potentially be formed, political parties may wish to hold discussions to establish who is best able to command the confidence of the House of Commons and should form the next government. The Sovereign would not expect to become involved in any negotiations, although there are responsibilities on those involved in the process to keep the Palace informed.

The Cabinet Manual goes on to describe what happens if the Prime Minister resigns mid-term, stating that it is for the party or parties in government to identify who can be chosen as the successor (paragraph 2.18). So the monarch is left with no discretion in any circumstances in which she may be required to appoint a Prime Minister, whether post-election or mid-term. Indeed the Cabinet Manual makes clear that the whole purpose is to remove any residual discretion:

> In modern times the convention has been that the Sovereign should not be drawn into party politics, and if there is doubt it is the responsibility of those involved in the political process, and in particular the parties represented in Parliament, to seek to determine and communicate clearly to the Sovereign who is best placed to be able to command the confidence of the House of Commons (para 2.9).

One further reform which has been advocated would be to hold an investiture vote on the floor of the House of Commons as the first piece of business after an election, to determine who commands the confidence of the new parliament (Commons Political and Constitutional Reform Committee 2015: paras 62-63). This is the practice followed in Scotland and Wales, under section 46 of the Scotland Act 1998, and section 47 of the Government of Wales Act 2006. It would help clearly to distance the monarch from the political process; but it has not yet found favour with the government at Westminster (Schleiter et al 2016).

The Power to Summon and Dissolve Parliament

The summoning and dissolution of Parliament has also been done by the personal prerogative. By convention, it has been the constitutional right of the Prime Minister to determine the timing of a dissolution and hence of the next election, and to advise the monarch accordingly. The majority view amongst constitutional experts has been that the monarch could refuse an untimely request for dissolution, even though there has been no refusal in modern times (Blackburn 2004: 554–61; Brazier 2005: 45–47). But any doubt or dispute is now academic, because the prerogative power of dissolution has been abolished by the Fixed Term Parliaments Act 2011. Dissolution in the UK is now regulated by statute not the prerogative; and it is a matter for Parliament, not the executive.

The Fixed Term Parliaments Act 2011 provides for five year parliaments, with automatic dissolution 17 working days before the next election. Section 3(2) states boldly, 'Parliament cannot otherwise be dissolved'. There is provision for mid-term dissolution in section 2, but again by statute not under the prerogative. Section 2 allows for a midterm dissolution in only two circumstances: if two thirds of all MPs vote for an early general election; or if the House passes a formal no confidence motion 'that this House has no confidence in Her Majesty's Government', and no alternative government which can command confidence is formed within 14 days. The procedure for forming an alternative government has not yet been tested. It might require exercise of the Queen's powers to appoint or dismiss a Prime Minister. She might be called on to appoint a new Prime Minister, if it appears that there is an alternative Prime Minister who could command confidence. She might also be called on to dismiss the incumbent Prime Minister, if there is a successful no confidence motion, but the Prime Minister refuses to resign (Howarth 2018; but see Laws 2019).

The Power to Prorogue Parliament

The prerogative power to prorogue Parliament remains. Prorogation happens at the end of a parliamentary session (normally each year); dissolution happens at the end of a Parliament, to dissolve Parliament before an election. The Cabinet Manual explains prorogation as follows:

> 2.24 Prorogation brings a parliamentary session to an end. It is the Sovereign who prorogues Parliament on the advice of his or her ministers. The normal procedure is for commissioners appointed by the Sovereign to prorogue Parliament in accordance with an Order in Council. The commissioners also declare Royal Assent to the Bills that have passed both Houses, so that they become Acts, and then they announce the prorogation to both Houses in the House of Lords.

Until 2019 prorogation had generally been exercised without the kind of controversy which has occurred in Canada (Russell and Sossin 2009). That changed dramatically when in August 2019 the new Prime Minister Boris Johnson advised the Queen to prorogue Parliament for five weeks, leading to accusations that he was closing down

Parliament in order to avoid scrutiny of his Brexit plans. A successful court challenge led the Supreme Court to declare not merely that the advice to prorogue for such a lengthy period was unlawful, but that the prorogation order itself was null and void (*R (Miller)* v *The Prime Minister* [2019] UKSC 41). The subsequent prorogation to end the session in October was for just three sitting days. In future Prime Ministers who wish to prorogue Parliament for more than a few days will have to provide good reasons, which may be scrutinised by the Palace in the light of the principles laid down by the Supreme Court: neither the monarch nor the Prime Minister will want any future prorogation to be declared unlawful. But post-Brexit, legislation may be introduced to require parliamentary consent to prorogation, or to remove the power from the Prime Minister and hand it to the House of Commons – as has happened with the power of dissolution.

Giving Royal Assent to Bills

Royal assent to a bill was last refused in 1708, when Queen Anne, on the advice of her ministers, withheld royal assent to a bill to arm the Scottish militia. In 1914, King George V nearly withheld his assent to the Irish Home Rule Bill but was persuaded not to, again on ministerial advice. It is inconceivable that the monarch would withhold royal assent today, save on the advice of ministers. Robert Blackburn suggests that the monarch's role is limited to one of due process, and royal assent is a certificate that the bill has passed through all its established parliamentary procedures (Blackburn 2004: 554). Rodney Brazier has argued that a monarch might still veto a bill which sought to subvert the democratic basis of the constitution, but accepts that this leads to grave difficulties of definition. Mike Bartlett's play *King Charles III* (2014) is predicated on the new King Charles refusing royal assent to a bill restricting the freedom of the press. Even in such an extreme case, Brazier would prefer the monarch to find a means other than withholding royal assent to express his concerns (Brazier 2005: 47).

The only circumstance in which it is conceivable that royal assent might be withheld is if a bill had been passed by both Houses against the wishes of the government, and it afforded the government a last ditch means of preventing the bill from becoming law. That might happen with a minority government which could not prevent the passage of legislation by the opposition majority, but did not wish to see it enacted. Brexit has now provided such a circumstance. In January 2019 the *Daily Telegraph* reported that 'a senior government minister confirmed that one option was for the Queen to be asked not to give royal assent to any backbench legislation' designed to frustrate Brexit (Hope 2019).

This raises the question whether royal assent is a legislative power that is triggered by successful passage of a bill through the two Houses of Parliament, or an executive power effectively in the hands of the government. Recent precedent suggests that it is an executive power. Anne Twomey records that the 'Sovereign has … frequently and recently refused assent to bills passed by the legislatures of British colonies'. This includes former colonies: in 1980 the UK government prepared to advise the Queen to refuse royal assent for a bill from New South Wales, which forced the New South Wales government to let it lapse to prevent a formal refusal (Twomey 2018: 638).

Writing about the application of these precedents to blocking Brexit legislation, Robert Craig concluded

> [t]he better view is probably that [the Queen] must follow the ministerial advice. The Queen could not legitimately be criticised for following the advice of a Government that has the confidence of Parliament. All criticism ought to be directed at her Government which is democratically accountable to Parliament and whose constitutional role is to absorb such criticism instead of the monarch (Craig 2019).

So if the Queen is advised to withhold royal assent, she would have to follow the government's advice. The remedy for parliamentarians frustrated at their legislation being blocked would be to put down a motion of no confidence, and seek to remove the government.

The Retention of a Deep Reserve Power

So to conclude, the monarch's personal prerogative powers contain no real political power. The Queen has no effective discretion in deciding whom to appoint as Prime Minister; in deciding whether to summon, dissolve or prorogue Parliament; or to grant royal assent to bills. It is true that the monarch might, in very exceptional circumstances, still have to exercise a choice: for example if the Prime Minister were killed, or suddenly died. In that event, there would be no time to hold a vote of the party membership. An interim prime minister would need to be appointed until the party had elected a new leader; the monarch would look to the Cabinet to nominate the caretaker (Norton 2016). Other hypothetical examples are possible: if the Prime Minister refused to resign after a successful no confidence motion, even though the House of Commons had voted confidence in an alternative; or if the Prime Minister sought an unduly long prorogation, or a sudden prorogation in order to avoid a parliamentary vote of no confidence (Twomey 2018: ch 8). In such circumstances the monarch retains a deep reserve power to dismiss the Prime Minister; or, strengthened by the judgement of the Supreme Court in *Miller*, to refuse or to modify an improper request for prorogation.

The monarch is the ultimate constitutional longstop. In 2016 I wrote, in a paper to mark the Queen's 90th birthday just before the Brexit referendum, that 'in Britain's political culture, it is hard at present to see those longstop powers ever needing to be exercised' (Hazell and Morris 2016: 9). That judgement now seems complacent, and premature. The fevered politics of Brexit have seen conventions being stretched to the limit, and beyond. Conventional wisdom is that reserve powers should remain in the background, never needing to be deployed because politicians will not wish to push the boundaries, and will certainly want to avoid dragging the Queen into politics. But Brexit has smashed that wisdom, and those certainties. In October 2019 the Sunday Times had the histrionic headline, 'Sack me if you dare', Boris Johnson will tell the Queen' (Shipman and Wheeler 2019). It is hard to believe the Prime Minister would really defy the Queen in this way; but Brexit has challenged so much conventional wisdom about the constitution, it could yet yield more surprises.

3.3. THE MONARCH'S CONSTITUTIONAL FUNCTIONS IN DENMARK

Helle Krunke, Professor of Law, University of Copenhagen

Introduction

In Denmark, the King is the head of state while the Prime Minister is the head of government. A foreign reader of the present Danish Constitution with no knowledge of Danish constitutional law might get the impression that the monarch plays an important role in the governing of Denmark. The 'King' is mentioned in many articles concerning constitutional powers. For instance, in article 3 it states 'Legislative authority shall be vested in the King and the Folketing, the Danish Parliament, jointly. Executive authority shall be vested in the King'. Other examples are prerogatives like the foreign affairs prerogative in article 19: 'The King shall act on behalf of the Realm in international affairs'. In most of the articles in the Constitution, the 'King' is contemporarily interpreted as the government (including article 3 and article 19). The former royal prerogatives are nowadays governmental prerogatives. There are in fact only a few important constitutional competences left for the King personally. These competences will be discussed below.

The Council of State is Presided over by the King

The Council of State has its legal basis in article 17 of the Constitution. The body of ministers form the Council of State. The Council of State is presided over by the King (article 17, part 1). It has given rise to discussion whether the King has the right to vote in the Council like the members. The King cannot be considered a member of the Council (Andersen 1954: 180-81). The King's role in the Council of State is discussed in more detail in Chapter 4.3.

The King Signs Resolutions Relating to Legislation and Government

The King signs resolutions relating to legislation and government (for instance the appointment of ministers) according to article 14, third sentence: 'The signature of the King to resolutions relating to legislation and government shall make such resolutions valid, provided that the signature of the King is accompanied by the signature or signatures of one or more ministers'.

Whereas many articles in the Constitution, which only mention the term 'King' can today easily be interpreted as meaning the 'government', article 14 mentions both the King and the government (ministers). A distinction is made between the King and the government. The reason for this is that article 14 stems from the 1849 Constitution and has survived several revisions of the Constitution.

A constitutional convention has emerged according to which the King can sign resolutions outside the Council of State and the Council can then give its approval to the resolution at a following meeting (Zahle 2006: 173).

Article 14 gives rise to two related questions: can the King refuse to sign a bill? And is a bill, which is not signed by the King, valid?

Generally, it is unthinkable that the King should refuse to sign a bill. In contemporary constitutional theory it has been argued that the monarch does not have the right to decline to sign a bill laid before him. According to the constitutional scholar Zahle (2001: 301), this 'corresponds to the Monarch's non-political position and practice'. Apparently, Zahle refers to article 13 according to which 'the King shall not be answerable for his actions; his person shall be sacrosanct. The ministers shall be responsible for the conduct of government; their responsibility shall be defined by statute'. This means that the monarch acts on the responsibility of a minister and in this way has no independent political role to play.

If article 13 is interpreted as containing an obligation for the King to act according to the wishes of the ministers (Andersen 1954: 97), the King violates the Constitution by not signing a bill.[2] Thus, he would violate the solemn declaration that he signed before the Council of State prior to his accession to the throne. According to article 8, the King must declare that he will faithfully adhere to the Constitutional Act. On the other hand, if the King refuses to sign a bill because he finds that the bill violates the Constitution, he would partly be true to his own solemn declaration. The King might have the support of the people in such a situation. The Constitution does not give the government and Parliament a specific right to depose the King from his throne, but if he violates the Constitution, the precondition for his right to reign has lapsed.

The refusal to sign a bill would without doubt create a political crisis. The King would be under substantial political pressure if he refused to sign a bill; this pressure would almost certainly lead to his resignation. In practice, the monarch always signs legislation laid before him.[3]

The second question – whether a bill that is not signed by the King would be valid – is also of great significance. One might argue that by not signing a bill laid before him the King violates the whole idea of parliamentary government, which is an essential constitutional principle. This principle was established in 1901 when the King accepted that it is Parliament and not the King that decides who should be in government. The legal basis for this principle was a constitutional convention until 1953, when it was then codified in article 15 of the Constitution:

(1)   A Minister shall not remain in office after the *Folketing* has approved a vote of no confidence in him.

(2)   When the *Folketing* passes a vote of no confidence in the Prime Minister, he shall ask for the dismissal of the Ministry unless writs are to be issued for a general election.

---

[2] According to Andersen, it follows from article 13 of the Constitution that the King normally has an obligation to act according to the wishes of the ministers.

[3] An instruction from the Ministry of State states how the Queen should be addressed in the Council of State when asked to sign a bill, which the government is going to introduce, or to give royal assent to a bill passed by Parliament. Interestingly, terms like 'petition/request' and 'it may please your Majesty to approve' are used. See Vejledning om ekspedition af statsrådssager, 14 January 2002.

Where a vote of censure has been passed on a Ministry, or it has asked for its dismissal, it shall continue in office until a new Ministry has been appointed. Ministers who remain in office as previously mentioned shall perform only what may be necessary to ensure the uninterrupted conduct of official business.

If article 14 is read and interpreted against the principle of parliamentary government, it seems that the King's signature cannot be mandatory in a modern democracy for a bill to become valid. Otherwise, the King would be able to block bills adopted by the legislature (Parliament and government), which is elected by the people.

However, there exists a very interesting case, which supports the proposition that bills actually need the monarch's signature in order to be valid. On 26 June 1998, a bill, which amended another bill on social pensions, was adopted in the Danish Parliament (L 109, 26 June 1998, session 1997-98). According to article 22 of the Constitution, a bill must receive royal assent not later than 30 days after it was finally passed. This royal assent is carried out as described in article 14. The King and a minister sign the bill. By mistake, the Ministry of Social Affairs did not manage to get the Queen's signature on the bill within 30 days. The bill was then introduced once more before Parliament on 13 November 1998 (L 85, 13 November 1998, session 1998-99). The explanatory notes said the following:

> The bill is an unchanged introduction of bill no L 109, parliamentary session 1997-98, which was adopted by the Parliament on 26 June 1998. Due to a mistake in the Ministry of Social Affairs the bill did not receive Royal Assent and thus it lapsed.

Under the (very short) discussion of the bill in the Danish Parliament it was accepted by representatives from several political parties that the bill needed the Queen's signature in order to become valid.[4] Additionally, the Minister of Social Affairs expressed the necessity of the second introduction of the bill (and thereby of the Queen's signature). This precedent suggests that it would seem incorrect to claim that a bill can be valid without the King's signature. It is interesting to see this in connection with the first question on whether the King can refuse to sign a bill. If we follow this line of thought, the King might have a constitutional obligation to sign bills; but if he disagrees with the content of a bill and fails to sign it, it might not be valid. If this is the case, it seems to place the King in a powerful position, if he does not want to sign a bill.

Treaties

According to article 19 of the Constitution, the King acts on behalf of the state in international affairs. Today the 'King' is interpreted as the 'government'. Nevertheless, the King still signs international agreements of importance. The Prime Minister or the Minister of Foreign Affairs countersigns such agreements and the King signs under the

---

[4] See the discussion in Parliament regarding the re-introduction of the bill on 13 November 1998. Most clear is the comment from *Fremskridtspartiet*, but in their comments other parties as *Venstre, SocialistiskFolkeparti*, and *Dansk Folkeparti* also seem to consent in the necessity of a new introduction of the bill. *Enhedslisten* also seemed to recognise the necessity, but the party spokesman added the following: '... but I have to say that if one could quit the little silly formality which rests in this signature and if one could change the conditions so that it was the parliamentary majority which decided when the adoption of a bill was definite/final, then we would not have needed this farce'.

responsibility of the minister (article 14). In practice, the Minister of Foreign Affairs (or other ministers) sign the less important international agreements without involving the King.

The King Dismisses and Appoints the Members of the Government

The King appoints and dismisses the members of the government. The Constitution does not describe the departure of an old government and the formation of a new government in detail. Two articles in the Constitution are important: article 14, first sentence: 'The King shall appoint and dismiss the Prime Minister and the other ministers', and article 15: 'A minister shall not remain in office after the *Folketing* has approved a vote of no confidence in him'.

When reading these two articles one might get the impression that they are inconsistent. Article 14 originates from the first Danish Constitution from 1849. Article 15 originates from 1953, but the parliamentary principle actually goes back to 1901. The King's competence in article 14 has a formal character, in practice. The King dismisses the government when it tenders its resignation to the King.[5] The King signs off the resignation which is counter-signed by the Prime Minister.[6] The King does not decide when the government should resign. The last time the King dismissed a government without its consent and appointed a new government by his own choice was during the Easter Crisis of 1920. King Christian X ordered the Prime Minister to include Central Schleswig in a programme of re-unification with Denmark, even though 80 per cent of the population had voted to remain part of Germany. The Prime Minister resigned, and the King dismissed the rest of the government and appointed a caretaker Cabinet. But the dismissal caused an almost revolutionary atmosphere in Denmark, and threatened the future of the monarchy. After a few days, the King had to dismiss the new government he had appointed.

An interesting situation would occur if the Prime Minister refused to tender his government's resignation to the King after Parliament had approved a vote of no confidence in him (and he did not call an election as described in article 15, part 2), or if he did not call a general election before the expiration of the period for which the Parliament has been elected (four years according to article 32, part 1). The latter is the duty of the Prime Minister according to article 32, part 3. No doubt it would result in a constitutional crisis, but would the King in this situation have competence to dismiss the Prime Minister on the King's own initiative? In practice the King's involvement in the dismissal of the government has a formal character, but does this practice also have a legal character? In the situation of a vote of no confidence, the action of the King would protect the parliamentary principle in article 15, and he would be safeguarding the Constitution. According to article 8 of the Constitution, the King must, prior to his accession to the

---

[5] An ordinary minister has to resign after a vote of no confidence. When the Prime Minister receives a vote of no confidence, the whole government must resign unless the Prime Minister calls for an election. See article 15 of the Constitution.

[6] The government will remain in office until a new government has been appointed. However, the ministers may only perform what may be necessary to ensure the uninterrupted conduct of official business. See article 15, part 2, of the Constitution.

throne, make a solemn declaration in writing before the Council of State that he will faithfully adhere to the Constitutional Act. In the case described, the King's dismissal of the government would probably not be condemned by the Parliament and the public because the King would actually be supporting the democratic process by dismissing the government. The King is still an actor on the political scene and he might play a role especially in a state of emergency. Nevertheless, the democratic process would of course be even more secured if Parliament succeeded in forcing the government to tender its resignation (Zahle 2001: 205).[7]

The situation draws close to a constitutional emergency, if the Prime Minister refuses to tender his resignation after Parliament has approved a vote of no confidence. One could therefore argue that the King can dismiss the Prime Minister on this ground (Zahle 2001: 207). However, by accepting the constitutional emergency argument one accepts a space for the King to act without any other legal basis than emergency. Then it becomes important that the King is still an actor on the constitutional scene even though his powers are mostly (or normally) of a limited substantive nature. Under these specific circumstances, the King's role can change quickly from an insignificant player to an active, powerful political player. Accepting article 15 combined with article 8 as the legal basis of the King's ability to dismiss the Prime Minister in such a situation would be less controversial.

The King still plays a part in the formation of a new government. In Danish, the formation of a new government is called *dronningerunden* (*Dronning* meaning 'Queen' and *runde* meaning 'session/round'). This is not described in detail in the Constitution. However, some guidelines have developed in practice. They are characterised by their origin in concrete situations and of course the political course of events may vary from time to time (Zahle 2001: 209, and 2006: 157). The normal procedure is as follows. The King consults with representatives from the political parties in Parliament. According to the current Cabinet Secretary, Henning Foged, the sequence follows the number of votes each party has received in the election starting with the party with the most votes. The representatives bring two copies of their considerations on which parties should form a new government, one copy for the King and one for the Cabinet Secretary (Matzon 2019:53). After all the consultations, the Cabinet Secretary together with the Head of the Ministry of State write an analysis of who has the most support to form a new government. On the basis of the consultations, a leader of the subsequent negotiations is selected and this will be the person with the best chance of forming a government. This person is given a mandate by the King to negotiate with the political parties in order to examine the possibilities of forming a government. On the basis of these inquiries, the leader of negotiations may form a government or a new leader of negotiations may be selected. A majority government must be preferred to a minority government (Zahle 2001: 210).

This might be a difficult process because the King may receive conflicting advice given by the different political parties. If the situation becomes difficult to solve, the King should not decide the further developments of the case by himself, he should follow the advice of the retiring Prime Minister. At least, this is the clear starting point (Zahle 2006: 157). The King's actions are throughout the process carried out on the

---

[7] Zahle is under the impression that a minister who does not tender his resignation after Parliament has approved a vote of no confidence in him can be dismissed. However, Zahle does not clarify who dismisses him and on what legal basis.

responsibility of the retiring Prime Minister. At the end of the process, the King appoints a new Prime Minister, as well as new ministers. In 1988, it turned out to be very difficult to form a new government. Four *dronningerunder* were needed in order to reach an agreement. Some of the mandates were broader than just finding a leader of the negotiations and forming a new government. All things being equal, the broader the mandates are, the more the King will be involved in the political process (Hansen 1988).[8]

The legal status of the guidelines just described is unclear and they may vary dependent on the concrete parliamentary situation (Zahle 2006: 157). Some constitutional theorists argue that the guidelines are legally binding (Zahle 2001: 207 ff, 214 ff).[9] Others argue that the guidelines only have a political status (Christensen 1990: 197 ff; Jensen 1997: 84 ff). The unclear state of the law seems to provide the King with a certain flexibility when forming a new government, at least from a legal point of view. Especially, in a situation where a majority government cannot be established and there is more than one possibility of minority governments, there appears to be a certain room for manoeuvre (Ross 1983: 430). However, as mentioned earlier in practice there is a close cooperation between the Cabinet Secretary and the Head of the Ministry of State.

3.4. THE KING AND PUBLIC POWER IN THE MINIMALIST MONARCHY OF SWEDEN

Henrik Wenander, Professor of Public Law, Lund University

Introduction

Under the current Swedish Constitution, the distribution of powers to the monarch is based on one overarching principle, namely that the monarch shall have no formal power. This principle is based on the political compromise that formed the basis for the adoption of the current central fundamental law, the 1974 *Regeringsform* (Instrument of Government). In international comparison, Sweden stands out as formally limiting the role of the monarch to an extent that has made at least one foreign commentator question Sweden's status as a monarchy (Smith 2017: 215).

From the 1809 Instrument of Government to Constitutional Reform in 1974

The immediate predecessor to the current central fundamental law was the 1809 Instrument of Government. This fundamental law stated that the Realm should be governed by a King as a hereditary monarchy (article 1). He should govern the Realm alone, albeit for the most part on the advice of his counsellors (articles 4 and 7), then acting as *Kungl. Ma:jt i statsrådet* (Royal Majesty in the Council of State). The Council

---

[8] In the article, Hansen describes the process of forming a new government.
[9] According to Zahle, the parliamentary principle entails that the political parties play an important role in the appointment of a new government, see also Zahle 2001: 210, 34.

of State met in the weekly *konselj* (cf French 'conseil'). In some duties, the King acted by personal power. This was the case for his role as the Commander-in-Chief (article 14) and as head of the royal court (article 48).

The overall structure of the 1809 Instrument of Government grew ever more obsolete over the decades. Without constitutional amendments, the Council of State developed from being the King's counsellors to a government, accepted by a majority in the Riksdag. In this way, parliamentary rule was established around 1918. According to constitutional convention, the King from now on always followed the advice of his ministers (Herlitz 1969: 99).

In the general modernisation of Swedish society, a constitutional reform project started in 1954. One central question was whether Sweden should remain a monarchy. The Social Democratic Party wanted Sweden to become a republic, while the more conservative parties wanted to retain the monarchy. The work of a cross-party committee of inquiry, supported by legal and political experts, ended in the so-called Torekov Compromise in 1971, named after a bathing resort in southern Sweden where the inquiry convened (Åse 2009: 29 ff).

This compromise meant that Sweden should remain a monarchy, but that the King should be stripped of all his constitutional functions, leaving a purely ceremonial and symbolic role. The formal legislative and political powers vested in the monarch under the 1809 Instrument of Government should be transferred to other constitutional actors. Under the leading principle of popular sovereignty, the new constitutional body of the *Regering* (government), consisting of the prime minister and the other ministers, should replace Royal Majesty in the Council of State. Other features of Swedish monarchy, not directly related to the exercise of public power, were to remain as they were, notably the legal status of the royal court as a special body under the direct and individual leadership of the king (SOU 1972:15, 80).

The proposal of the drafting committee meant a total constitutional reform with a new Instrument of Government to replace the 1809 Instrument. The proposal was for the most part accepted by the government, which proposed a government bill to the Riksdag (Prop. 1973:90). The Committee on the Constitution accepted the proposal without further comments on the role of the monarch (Bet. KU 1973:26, 29 ff). The new Instrument of Government was adopted by the Riksdag in 1974 and entered into force in 1975.

The Current Role of the King

Under the 1974 Instrument of Government, the King or Queen occupying the throne in accordance with the Act of Succession is the head of state (Chapter 1, article 5). If the King or Queen is unable to perform his or her duties, the member of the royal house in line of succession shall assume the duties of head of state as regent *ad interim* (Chapter 5c, article 4). Although the text of the Instrument of Government uses the term head of state, for simplicity we refer to the King in what follows.

The fundamental role of the King is regulated in the written constitution by the absence of formal powers (Warnling Conradson et al 2018: 110). Thus, the Swedish King neither signs new legislation, nor does he appoint the government (Nyman 1982: 182).

Also, the remaining tasks of the King are to a large extent left unregulated in the fundamental laws. Some clarity, however, is offered by the legislative materials to the 1974 Instrument of Government. The government bill makes rather vague references to the King's role according to custom and public international law. It especially mentions the King's state visits to other countries, his tasks relating to foreign and Swedish ambassadors and other representative tasks. The King's public activities 'shall be characterised by his role of representing the nation as a whole' (Prop. 1973:90, 173 ff, Nyman 1982: 183).

Relating to this latter role, the King may act as a unifying symbol in times of crisis. In this way, the King in January 2005 made a televised speech at a memorial ceremony for over 500 Swedish victims of the tsunami in Asia a few days earlier. The speech was very favourably received by public opinion (Åse 2009: 133 ff).

The legislative materials underline that the King may not give the impression of tensions between the monarch and the political branches of government. He should furthermore avoid taking part in activities that concern controversial social issues (SOU 1972:15, 139; Prop. 1973:90, 174; Nyman 1982: 183).

On some occasions, the King's public statements have given rise to debates relating to his neutrality. This was the case in 1989, when a televised documentary film on the brutal hunting of seal pups in Norway raised general indignation in Sweden. The King commented critically on the role of the Norwegian Prime Minister. This in turn spurred criticism from both Norway and political leaders in Sweden (Ögren 2006: 85; Åse 2009: 40).

There is no form of legal or political control of the King's actions. Further, the King cannot be prosecuted for his actions (chapter 5, article 7 of the 1974 Instrument of Government). This criminal immunity applies to both the official and the private capacity of the King's actions. However, this provision does not prevent Sweden from fulfilling its obligations towards the International Criminal Court or other such courts (chapter 10 article 14). The absence of criminal sanctions, however, does not imply that the King is above the law (Nyman 1982: 184).

The King shall also under the current constitutional order act as the head of *Kungliga Hovstaterna* (the royal court) and the royal family (Prop. 1973:90, 172 ff). The latter role is reflected in the provisions of the Act of Succession on marriage and travel abroad (see Calissendorff in chapter 8).

The King, acting within *Kungl. Maj:ts Orden* (The Order of his Majesty the King), may decide on royal orders according to *Ordenskungörelsen* (The Ordinance on Orders, 1974:768). A further competence – not regulated in any piece of legislation – is the possibility to award the status of *Kunglig hovleverantör* (purveyor to the royal court) (Föreskrifter rörande hovleverantörskap 2015).

Strömberg (2001-02: 723 ff) identifies a number of other tasks of the King, including participation in public festivities such as the award of the Nobel Prizes in Stockholm as well as acting as a patron of various private and quasi-public organisations. A special debate relating to this latter function concerned the King's role as patron of the Swedish Academy, founded in 1786 as a Royal Academy. Following a scandal in the Academy in 2018, the question arose whether the King had the power to amend the statutes. The King held the view that the statutes adopted by his predecessor King Gustav III were at his disposal, and decided on an amendment. The decision was legally founded on the view that the King as patron had retained this competence over this quasi-public body ever since 1786, and that nothing in the 1974 Instrument of Government meant that the government had taken over this function (Sunnqvist and Wenander 2018: 570 ff). It is plausible that the government, concerned about the reputational damage to Sweden, and uncertain about the scope of its own legal authority, was content for the King to act. But in the ensuing debate, critics remarked that this could be seen as an attempt to strengthen royal power, which would be at odds with the principles behind the Torekov Compromise (eg Gustafsson 2018).

The King and the Riksdag

Under the principle of popular sovereignty underlying the 1974 Instrument of Government, all public power shall proceed from the people with the Riksdag as the people's foremost representative (chapter 1 articles 1 and 4). The 1974 Instrument of Government therefore has limited the King's role to a minimum (Nyman 1982: 182). Still, the constitutional relationship between the King and the Riksdag is not entirely clear (Bull and Sterzel 2015: 144). Not least, the written Constitution is silent on the scope for adopting further legislation on the King and the royal court. Sterzel (2009: 153) concludes that the Riksdag could only regulate the King's duties and status by constitutional amendments.

However, the Riksdag may regulate the King's activities indirectly, since it decides on the national budget, including the public funding of the royal court (Bull and Sterzel 2015: 144). This has opened up parliamentary discussions on the royal court's use of resources and on requirements of transparency (Bet. 2013/14: KU1, 12 ff). However, this is complicated by the partially unclear boundaries between public property and the private possessions of the King and the royal family (Sterzel 2009: 161 ff): see also Chapter 7. *Riksrevisionen* (The National Audit Office), an independent administrative authority under the Riksdag, may audit parts of the royal court, viz *Kungliga Slottsstaten* (the Palace Administration) and *Kungliga Djurgårdens Förvaltning* (the Royal Djurgården Administration) (article 2 of *lagen* [2002:1022] *om revision av statligverksamhet m.m.*, the Act on Audit of State Activities).

When a new King or Queen accedes the throne, he or she may give an *ämbetsförklaring* (declaration of office) before the Riksdag (chapter 6, article 17 of the 2014 Riksdag Act; Prop. 1973:90, 270). Since there has been no succession to the throne under the current Instrument of Government, this provision has not yet been applied.

The King and the Government

How the King works with the government is described in Chapter 4.6. A new government takes office at a special Council of State before the King, in the presence of the Speaker of the Riksdag. The latter issues a letter of appointment on behalf of the Riksdag (Chapter 6, article 6 of the 1974 Instrument of Government). According to convention, the King concludes that a new government has taken office. After this, behind closed doors, the Prime Minister informs the King on the programme of the new government (Holmberg et al 2012: 310).

The Constitution contains an unusual provision if Sweden is at war, which may stem from Sweden's observation of what happened in Denmark and Norway during World War Two. In the event of war, the King shall accompany the government. Should the King be on occupied territory, or be separated from the government, he shall be considered unable to carry out his duties (chapter 15, article 10 of the 1974 Instrument of Government). The reason for this is the risk of an occupying power trying to use the symbol of the King for its own purposes (Prop. 1973:90, 462).

Conclusions

To conclude, the overall impression of the constitutional framework for the Swedish monarchy is that the Torekov Compromise has been carried out effectively. The scope for a King or reigning Queen to legally interfere with the work of the Riksdag or the government, or to take any formal political role is very limited. A special case is the curious legal status of the Swedish Academy, where the King actually made a formal decision in a much-debated matter. It is highly unlikely that there are other such hidden competences in the Swedish public or, in this case, quasi-public, sector.

Equally important are the more 'soft' constitutional powers of the King. The recurrent contacts with the Prime Minister may establish a certain scope for informal influence. The core of the constitutional role of the King is, however, his role as a symbol of the whole nation. A concrete example of this function is the King's speech at the memorial ceremony for the victims of the tsunami catastrophe. This is further reflected in the provisions on the King's role in situations of war.

The Swedish monarchy, resting on the 1971 Compromise, is an idiosyncratic model founded on a political compromise. Whereas certain aspects are indeed stretching the understanding of the concept of a constitutional monarchy, it also retains some archaic features which have not been changed by the 1974 Instrument of Government. In the latter category we find the role of the King as the head of the royal court and the royal family. The King's status outside of the constitutional structure based on the idea of popular sovereignty, the interplay between modern and archaic features and the combination of written and of unwritten law makes the constitutional role of the Swedish King partially unclear.

3.5A. CONSTITUTIONAL FUNCTIONS IN THE NETHERLANDS

Rudy Andeweg, Professor of Political Science, Leiden University

Introduction

The Netherlands is one of the few states that transformed from a republic into a monarchy, and this transformation was largely imposed on the Dutch by France and the United Kingdom. In 1806, the Emperor Napoleon created a Kingdom of Holland with his brother on the throne, but after only four years Louis Bonaparte was forced to abdicate and the Netherlands were annexed outright by France. The monarchical experiment had no lasting effects, except for the fact that a few years later King William I did fall back on some of the arrangements of 1806-10. The British contribution may have been more important. On his return to the Netherlands after the Napoleonic period, in 1813, the Prince of Orange was accompanied and advised by Lord Clancarty, who saw himself as the midwife and guardian of the new Dutch state. A few patricians, acting of their own accord and without any legitimate basis, offered the Prince the sovereignty of the country: he became Sovereign Prince, and the Netherlands became a monarchy in all but name. The name and legitimation came on 12 February 1815 when the Congress of Vienna, acting on a British proposal, created the Kingdom of the Netherlands, comprising both the former Republic of the Seven United Provinces and the Austrian Netherlands, now known as Belgium. There are several theories about the British motivation for setting up this Kingdom, ranging from a geopolitical desire to have a strong buffer state north of France, to giving the Prince of Orange satisfaction for the fact that the English Princess had broken off their engagement. Although 'The Dutch monarchy is no home-grown product' (Cramer 1980), a return to republican government has never been proposed in earnest, except for a half-hearted attempt at a socialist revolution in 1918.

The eight monarchs since 1815 (four Kings and four Queens) have gradually seen their political functions reduced: in 1840 the ministerial countersignature on all bills and decrees was introduced; in 1848 ministerial responsibility was introduced; in 1866–68 it became clear that the confidence of a parliamentary majority in the government trumped the confidence of the monarch; in 1904 the royal throne was removed from the Second Chamber of Parliament; in 1939 the immediate dismissal by Parliament of a government formed by the monarch alone signaled a reduction of the role of the monarch in the formation of coalition cabinets; in 1983 the royal appointment of Speakers of Parliament was abolished; in 2003 the Office of the Queen (now of the King) was brought under the responsibility of the Prime Minister; and in 2012 the Second Chamber ended the involvement of the monarch in coalition formation.

This contribution starts with the role of the monarch in forming a government coalition. The abolition of that role is too recent to conclude that it may never return.

Coalition Formation

The constitutional basis of the monarch's involvement in the formation of a government is the provision that the King appoints the ministers. The current wording stipulates merely that the Prime Minister and the other ministers are appointed and dismissed by royal decree, but until 1983 the Constitution read that the King appoints and dismisses ministers 'at his pleasure'. Actually, that had already been a dead letter since the incident in 1939, mentioned above, when a government appointed by Queen Wilhelmina entirely at her pleasure, was censured by Parliament immediately after the royal appointment. Since then, the practice developed that the monarch's role was more to initiate and oversee the process of government formation by the party leaders. As no political party has ever controlled a majority of the seats in the Second Chamber of Parliament, the formation of a government includes more than just the appointment of individual heads of ministerial departments: it involves first the choice of political parties to make up the coalition, the drawing up of a coalition agreement spelling out the coalition's policy plans, and the allocation of ministerial portfolios to the prospective governing parties. The most important instrument of the monarch was the appointment of one or more individuals who chaired the negotiations. Originally, such an individual was called a *formateur* but since 1951 the term *informateur* was used as well. The distinction between *formateurs* and *informateurs* is of little significance. In practice, it is now customary for *informateurs* to leave only the recruitment of new ministers to a *formateur*, who is the Prime Minister designate.

Before appointing an *informateur*, the monarch would consult all parliamentary party leaders after the election results had become known, or after an incumbent government had collapsed prematurely. If a likely coalition emerged from these consultations the monarch would follow the advice of the party leaders and appoint a politician from one of the potential governing parties, usually the largest one. If the political situation was more complicated, she would first appoint a less partisan politician such as the vice-president of the Council of State as *informateur* to explore which combination of parties was most likely to succeed in forming a coalition. If trust between the potential governing parties was too low for them to accept an *informateur* from one of the parties, a duo or troika would be appointed. In this way the monarch sought to avoid making politically controversial decisions. Nevertheless, as soon as the appointment was made public, the appointee's past was scrutinised like the entrails of a sacrificial beast by Roman augurs for any sign of a royal coalition preference.

In exceptional cases the monarch has been known to intervene personally. During the coalition formation of 1981, for example, an elder statesman from the Christian Democratic Party appeared on television to criticise his own party leader for refusing to accept the political reality that the coalition that had made up the outgoing government no longer had a parliamentary majority. The next day Queen Beatrix appointed him as *informateur* against the advice of the party leaders. In 1994, a three-party coalition was needed for a majority government, but each potential combination was vetoed by one of the party leaders. When this impasse was reported to Queen Beatrix by the *informateur*, she publicly ignored his advice and appointed the leader of the Labour Party as the new *informateur*, the only one who had not yet vetoed any combination. The monarchs probably saw it as their role to ensure that the process of forming a new government was not unduly delayed, but such personal interventions were inevitably criticised as revealing personal political preferences.

This was certainly the case in 2010 when negotiations were initiated to form a minority Cabinet of Liberals and Christian Democrats, supported in Parliament by a majority coalition comprising these parties and the populist Freedom Party. The cooperation with the populists created considerable controversy within the Christian Democratic Party, and when Freedom Party leader Geert Wilders estimated that division within the Christian Democratic Party would deprive the coalition of its parliamentary majority, the *informateur* reported to Queen Beatrix that the attempt had failed. While the Queen was still considering her next move, the leaders of the three parties suddenly decided to resume their negotiations. The Queen was not amused and appointed the vice-president of the Council of State (and a member of the Labour Party, which was opposed to this prospective coalition) as *informateur* to see if the negotiators were now serious. In contrast to the monarch's general role, this intervention actually delayed the formation process, and was interpreted as a sign of the Queen's personal displeasure regarding the inclusion of Mr Wilders – a staunch critic of her televised Christmas messages – in a governing coalition.

It may be no coincidence that soon after this episode Parliament restricted the monarch's role in the formation of a new government to the swearing in of the new ministers. The King is kept informed of the progress of the negotiations, but the Second Chamber appoints the *(in)formateurs* after some consultations by the Speaker. This procedure had actually been approved by Parliament in a resolution in 1971, but a parliamentary majority was not able to converge on a choice of *(in)formateur*. Sceptics point out that the increasing electoral fragmentation may well lead to a future failure to find a majority for a choice of *informateur*, and that the monarch's role will have to be revived. The fact that the new procedure has produced a result twice (in 2012, and 2017) provides no guarantee for future success.

Royal Assent to Bills

The Constitution stipulates that all Acts of Parliaments and Royal Decrees must be signed by the King and by one or more ministers. There is no provision in the Constitution for the resolution of a conflict between monarch and ministers leading to the refusal of the monarch to sign a bill. Such a refusal is 'the nuclear option' in such a conflict. The few cases of such a conflict that have become known all date back to the reign of Queen Juliana. After the Second World War the death penalty had been reintroduced for war criminals. The Queen, however, was a strong opponent of the death penalty. She refused to sign the death sentences of several German war criminals and the government avoided a constitutional crisis by commuting the death sentences to life imprisonment. The most famous case of a conflict between monarch and ministers is the attempt by the Biesheuvel I Cabinet (1971–72) to legislate for a reduction in the number of members of the royal family for whom the ministers would be responsible. Queen Juliana feared the introduction of first and second-rank Princes and Princesses. According to then Home Secretary Geertsema:

> I had to deal with the Queen because it was my task to draft a bill on membership of the royal house. The Queen and I had completely different views on that issue. Eventually, the Prime Minister and I had a final meeting with her in which we reached the conclusion that the Queen did not want what we wanted, and that we definitely did not want what the Queen wanted. [Former Prime Minister and Vice-President of the Council of State] Beel made an attempt to mediate, but when that failed we put the legislation on hold .... If the Queen said 'If you get that bill through Parliament I will not sign it', and that happened once in a blue moon, you had a constitutional crisis for which our constitution offers no solution. In such cases you may have to stop the legislative process, although it is extremely difficult because you cannot openly explain why you do so (interview by the author).

3.5B. THE NETHERLANDS: FROM PERSONAL REGIME TO LIMITED ROLE

Dr Paul Bovend'Eert, Professor of Constitutional Law, Radboud University Nijmegen

Introduction

This contribution discusses the position of the King in the constitutional monarchy and parliamentary democracy of the Netherlands. It specifically focuses on the development of the (prerogative) powers of the King within the government, his role in the process of government formation and termination, and his position in case of a political conflict ending up in a dissolution of parliament. The Dutch Constitution only uses the term 'King'. In the history of the Dutch constitutional monarchy successive Queens (Queen regent Emma 1879-90, Queen Wilhelmina 1890-1948, Queen Juliana 1948-80, Queen Beatrix 1980-2013) have exercised powers in government for more years than Kings (King William I 1814-40, King William II 1840-49, King William III 1849-79, King Willem-Alexander 2013-). Nevertheless, we will use the constitutional term King, applying to the King as well as the Queen.

We first examine briefly the development of the King's governmental powers and position in general since 1814. We then separately address the position of the King in the government, his role in the formation of a new Cabinet, and in a dissolution of parliament. Lastly, we examine the changing role of the King in the Dutch system of government.

The Dutch Constitutional Monarchy Since 1814

The initial period of the constitutional monarchy (1814-48), after the adoption of the Constitution of 1814, was marked by a strong position of the King within the governmental system. The King appointed and dismissed his Cabinet ministers 'as he pleased'. And he made ample use of this power (Kranenburg 1928: 139). In addition, he exerted significant influence on the composition of the two Houses of the States General. King William I conducted a personal regime during his period of government (1814-1840). His ministers were subordinate public officials who carried out his orders. The King used to have meetings together with his ministers, called the Cabinet Council. But all matters of any importance the King eventually decided autonomously (Oud 1967: 251).

The constitutional reforms of 1840 and 1848 changed the intergovernmental relationships drastically (Besselink 2014: 1193). The introduction of the ministerial countersignature for royal decrees (government decrees) as part of the constitutional revision of 1840 led to the removal of the King's power to take governmental decisions on his own, without the involvement of his Cabinet ministers. Meetings between the King and his ministers in the so called Cabinet Council became a rare phenomenon. As a result, the King lost his central position in the government, although a general awareness that the King was no longer head of the government did not penetrate the political reality until much later.

The adoption of ministerial responsibility (1848) and the unwritten rule of confidence (1868), the rise of political parties at the end of the nineteenth century, and the introduction of general suffrage in the early twentieth century (1917) led to the establishment of fully-fledged parliamentary democracy in the Netherlands. This no longer allowed room for a leading position for the King as head of the government. Instead of the King, it was the Council of Ministers, and in its wake the Prime Minister, that played a leading role as the twentieth century progressed. At the end of the 1960s, there was even talk in constitutional theory of 'the dominion of the Council of Ministers' (Van Maarseveen 1968). For a long time, Cabinet ministers were still inclined to refer to themselves as 'servants of the Crown', but in fact, they had become servants of a majority in Parliament. The King was increasingly forced to the background.

The Role of the King in a Modern Parliamentary Democracy

It is certainly remarkable that the position of the King in the Dutch government remained so strong for such a relatively long time after the establishment of a fully-fledged parliamentary democracy early in the twentieth century. Queen Wilhelmina (1898-1948) kept a dominant position in government although the political coalition between the Cabinet and the majority in Parliament had become the primary foundation of government policy. The Queen nevertheless participated actively in the decision making process within the government. She had a special interest in foreign affairs and matters concerning the Dutch armed forces. On several occasions she personally prepared government policy notes and discussed them with the ministers in a Cabinet Council, the last examples of these meetings between Queen and Cabinet ministers in Dutch constitutional history. She also refused to sign government decrees on several occasions.

Queen Wilhelmina can be considered the last Dutch monarch with a strong position in government in the Netherlands. Her successor Queen Juliana (1948-80) did not take an active part any more in the decision making process within the government. A modern constitutional monarchy within a system of a parliamentary democracy was eventually established during the reign of Queen Juliana. In this modern concept of a monarchy the role of the King in the government is limited to what Bagehot described for the British King: the rights to be consulted, to encourage and to warn.

This limited role of the King in the government however did not exclude occasional exceptions in constitutional practice. Apparently it was accepted by the ministers in this concept of a modern monarchy that in exceptional circumstances the King was allowed to put aside his limited role in government and take up his traditional position to take joint decisions with his ministers. Queen Juliana refused on repeated occasions to grant her cooperation to government decrees proposed by ministers (see the examples cited by Andeweg above). In particular, Queen Juliana actively participated in government decisions concerning the monarchy. She played a predominant role in establishing new legislation on the funding of the monarchy (Van Baalen, Bovend'Eert et al 1972). And she refused to sign an Act of Parliament concerning (limitations on) membership of the Royal House. Nevertheless, these interventions of Queen Juliana were, as far as we know, incidental and exceptional.

As for Queen Beatrix (1980-2013), there are still no official documents available to analyse her role in government affairs. But it is likely that she continued to take up a limited role in the government as well.

These altered relationships between King and ministers within the government were for the first time reflected in the general revision of the Dutch Constitution of 1983. With this revision, the Constitution lost its strongly monarchical character. Significant attention was given, both in the text of the new Constitution of 1983 and in the explanatory notes, to the position of the King and his relation to the Cabinet members. According to the new article 42, paragraph 1, of the Constitution ('The government shall comprise the King and the ministers') the King is a constituent part of the Dutch government, not head of the government. This means that all the government decisions, referred to in article 47 of the Constitution as 'royal decrees', shall be co-signed by the King and one or more Cabinet ministers. The limited role of the King in the government is addressed in the explanatory notes to article 42 and article 47 of the Constitution. In these notes it is finally clearly explained by the government that the King shall confine himself to the exercise of 'the rights to be consulted, to encourage, to warn' as formulated by Bagehot for the British monarch (Tweede Kamer den Staten-Generaal, Kamerstukken II 1980/1981, 16035, 8: 2). In Chapter 4 we will address further this limited role of the King in government, when we discuss the day to day political functions of the monarchy.

The King and the Formation of Government

Until 1848 the King personally decided on the appointment and dismissal of 'his' ministers, and for quite some time after 1848 the King continued to play an important role in the composition of the Cabinet. Nonetheless, in the new era after 1848 he increasingly took into account the majority positions in the Parliament, in particular with the directly elected majority in the Second Chamber (Lower House). This development, of growing parliamentary influence on the formation of Cabinets, accelerated because of the adoption of the rule of confidence in the parliamentary system (1866-68). Regarding the formation of a new government, the practice developed wherein the King appointed a *formateur* (one of the political leaders in the Parliament or the Cabinet) to form a Cabinet following elections (or, in case of a Cabinet crisis, between elections) that could count on the support of a parliamentary majority. The *formateur* would then hold consultations with the leaders of the various political parties in the Parliament in order to establish a majority coalition. The involvement of the Parliament in the formation of a new government increased over time. As from 1946, it became standard practice for the King to consult all party leaders from the Lower House at the start of the formation process. Based on the recommendations of the majority, the King next appointed one or more *formateurs* or *informateurs* to conduct coalition negotiations with the political leaders in the Parliament. In the multi-party system that characterises the Dutch Parliament, involving an electoral system of proportional representation, it is often a cumbersome exercise to form a majority coalition after a general election. Quite intensive negotiations between political leaders, sometimes lasting for months, are needed to form a Cabinet. In this new formation practice, the King continued to be closely involved in the complicated formation process, as he would appoint, at the start of the proceedings or in case the coalition negotiations reach a deadlock, one or more *formateurs* or *informateurs* based on the advice of the leaders of the parties constituting a majority (Van Baalen and Van Kessel 2012). The King fulfilled a key – but altogether neutral – role in the formation process. In this role, he acted as an independent head of state. On a few occasions involving the appointment of a *formateur* or *informateur*, the King's personal preference turned out to be decisive, in particular when the party leaders were heavily divided about the direction that the Cabinet formation should take.

The formation process thus grew out of organically developed practices, as the Constitution simply provides that Cabinet ministers are to be appointed and dismissed by royal decree, with the Prime Minister and the King together signing the decrees (articles 43 and 48 of the Constitution). The rule of confidence is of decisive importance, in that it requires that a Cabinet must be able to count on the support of a parliamentary majority.

The year 2012 saw an abrupt change in the formation proceedings that had developed over time. The Second Chamber adopted in its Standing Orders a regulation for new formation proceedings (article 139a of the Standing Orders of the Second Chamber), which set out that the Second Chamber must appoint *informateurs* or *formateurs* itself after elections (or between elections in case of a cabinet crisis), who are charged with the formation of a (new) Cabinet (Bovend'Eert, Van Baalen and Van Kessel 2015). This new regulation made the involvement of Parliament in the formation process even more explicit. For the first time, the Netherlands had a written rule of procedure, in which the Second Chamber assigned itself the principal role. The King was removed from his role in the formation process. He no longer needed to appoint *formateurs* or *informateurs* based on consultation with the political leaders.

This new rule of procedure was first applied during the formation of the Rutte II Cabinet (2012-2017), following the elections of September 2012, and it turned out that the Second Chamber was quite capable of forming a new Cabinet without the intermediary role of the King. Various parties expected that the politicians would ultimately crawl back to His Majesty, for him to take the lead again. But in fact the formation of 2012 went rather smoothly, and it was not clear what role (if any) the King could still have fulfilled. Some parties wanted to keep the King away from the process, and not even to keep him informed. Others considered it appropriate to keep the King involved under the new procedure as well. In the end, the King was hardly kept up to date about the progress of Cabinet formation in 2012. An evaluation committee later advised the Second Chamber to keep the King better informed in future. After all, the King is still a constitutive element of the government; and he must place his signature under the appointment decrees for the new ministers and the dismissal decrees for the departing ministers (Bovend'Eert, Van Baalen and Van Kessel 2015). The Second Chamber accepted this advice, and during the Cabinet formation of 2017, the longest in Dutch history, the King was kept informed on a regular basis.

Since 2012 the King has lost his role due to the introduction of a new procedure by the Second Chamber. That is a remarkable development considering that until recently the 'monitoring' role of the King was in general much appreciated. After the Cabinet formation that followed the general election of 2010, this view faltered among various political parties, partly because Queen Beatrix was accused – rightly or not – of having made personal choices regarding the appointment of specific *informateurs*. A parliamentary majority subsequently introduced a new rule of procedure in the Standing Orders, making the King's role redundant.

However, despite the growing involvement of the Parliament in government formation, the government is not to be regarded as a committee of the Parliament. The Cabinet is a separate state authority, and the Prime Minister and the cabinet members are not appointed by the Parliament. They are appointed by royal decree, with the signature of the Prime Minister and the King. In this constellation, it is logical and wise that the King continues to fulfil a certain role in the formation process and that he is kept sufficiently informed.

The King and the Dissolution of Parliament

The Constitution of 1848 gave the government the power to dissolve each of the two Houses of Parliament. The introduction of the power of dissolution was closely linked to the enhancement of the position of the Parliament through the constitutional revision of that same year. As of 1848, the government was much more dependent on the cooperation of Parliament for the execution of its political programme. Should an unbridgeable gap arise between government and Parliament, new elections could resolve the situation (Bovend'Eert and Kummeling 2017: 450).

In the first three dissolutions of Parliament after 1848, the King still played a leading role. The first dissolution of the Second Chamber (in 1853) was the direct result of an internal conflict in the government between King William III and the Thorbecke Cabinet concerning a religious issue. The Cabinet ministers offered their resignation. Since a majority in the Parliament supported the Thorbecke Cabinet, the government (the King plus the new ministers) decided to dissolve the Parliament.

The dissolutions of Parliament in 1866 and 1868 had special significance since a battle of principle between the government and the Parliament was fought and decided, regarding the question whether not only the approval of the King but also the approval of a parliamentary majority was needed for the Cabinet ministers to stay on. King William III initially refused to bend to the Parliament. He proceeded to dissolve the Second Chamber and, in 1868, even went so far as to call upon the citizenry in a personal proclamation to support his government in the elections. But it turned out that a majority of the newly elected Second Chamber rejected the government's policy as well. King William III considered dissolving the Second Chamber a second time, but ultimately yielded to parliamentary pressure.

After 1868, the King no longer played a central role in dissolutions of Parliament. During the course of the twentieth century the practice arose that, in case of a serious political conflict with the Parliament, the Cabinet ministers would first offer their resignation. This was then followed by an attempt to re-form a government, to see whether the party leaders could lend it their support, or whether a dissolution of Parliament was the only way to resolve the crisis. In such a crisis, the King fulfilled a similar role as in government formation after elections, described by Andeweg above. Based on the majority advice of the party leaders he would then appoint a *formateur* or *informateur* to find a way out of the crisis.

The current rule of procedure in the Standing Orders of the Second Chamber (article 139a) provides that also in case of a mid-term loss of confidence, it is not the King, but the Second Chamber which itself appoints a *formateur* or *informateur* to resolve the crisis.

Conclusion

In a modern parliamentary democracy it is unacceptable that the King would have a leading position in the government, in the formation of a government or in the dissolution of parliament. The power to make governmental decisions lies with the ministers who are responsible to the Parliament and require the confidence of a parliamentary majority. Over the years the Parliament has gained a dominant position. The King no longer has effective powers when it comes to government formation and the dissolution of Parliament. His role within the government has also changed drastically. In general, the King now only holds an advisory role.

3.6. CONSTITUTIONAL FUNCTIONS IN BELGIUM

Quentin Pironnet, Lecturer in Public Law, University of Liège

Introduction

Belgium has been a monarchy since its independence in 1830 (although the first King was crowned on 21 July 1831). However, this regime was not pre-ordained. A majority of the members of the National Congress in 1830 wanted Belgium to be a republic; but they worried the new state would not be recognised. The Netherlands did not recognise the breakaway state, and the Belgians feared that Britain, France, Germany and Russia would not recognise them either. After agonised debates in the assembly, the monarchists won by 174 to 13. The argument also had a theoretical turn, based in particular on the work of Montesquieu and Burke, and reflected a pragmatic conservatism (de Dijn 2002: 244). But in the end, a monarchy was seen as more stable.

Given the republican sentiment, it is unsurprising that the assembly chose a weak model of monarchy. The King's powers would be curtailed by the supreme text and his government would be accountable to Parliament. Inspired by the Westminster model, the founding fathers of the Kingdom of Belgium imagined their country as a parliamentary system in which ministers are fully accountable to the House of Representatives (article 101 Belgian Constitution).

On 3 February 1831, the Belgian National Congress presented the Crown to the Duke of Nemours, the second son of the French King Louis-Philippe. Faced with numerous international pressures, mainly British, Louis-Philippe declined the throne for his son on 17 February 1831. It was not until 4 June 1831 that Congress agreed to offer the Crown to Prince Leopold of Saxe-Coburg and Gotha, who was notably uncle of Queen Victoria of England. He was sworn in on 21 July 1831.

The constitutional functions of the King are not transferred to him at the time of the death or abdication of his predecessor, but on the day of the swearing of an oath before the assembled legislative chambers, pursuant to article 91 of the Belgian Constitution. During the interregnum, it is the 'ministers meeting in Council' who, jointly, are the recipients of the sovereign's powers.

These constitutional functions are of several kinds, and have been interpreted differently throughout Belgian history. First, it should be noted that the King has no purely personal power, since a minister must always take responsibility for his own actions. This is the primary rule of ministerial countersignature (article 106). The King is also inviolable (article 88), which led Joseph Lebeau, one of the founding fathers of the Kingdom, to conclude early on that royalty was not a real power (Senelle 2006: 55).

Since the conclusions of the Soenens Committee in 1949, the King has been restricted in his constitutional power, and ministerial responsibility is absolute. The rise of political parties and predominantly coalition governments have now constricted the King's real power(Velaers 2019, 2: 447), so that when one talks about the King's constitutional prerogatives, a word still used in the Constitution, these powers in practice are exercised by the government.

The principle of the Belgian constitutional monarchy assumes that, according to article 105 of the Constitution, 'The King has no powers other than those formally attributed to him by the Constitution and by specific laws passed by virtue of the Constitution itself'. Thus, only the Constitution grants a number of constitutional functions to the King of the Belgians (and not the King *of Belgium*, since the dynasty had been chosen by the elected representatives themselves (Delpérée 2017: 2122).

If the executive power is fully vested in the King (article 37), with ministerial countersignature, the sovereign is also part of the legislative branch, as the third actor alongside the House of Representatives and the Senate pursuant to article 36 of the Constitution. As such, the King is notably competent to give assent to bills, as confirmed by article 109 of the Constitution.

Royal Assent to Bills

The royal assent is the last step in the process of law making by the legislative branch; it marks the agreement of the King and the government on the text submitted, and is carried out by a signature of the King with the countersignature of a minister (or, to a lesser extent, a secretary of state, a kind of deputy minister). The King, head of state, by sanctioning a bill, attests to the regularity of its adoption process (Behrendt & Vrancken 2019: 198). As the King is politically irresponsible, he is in principle required to sign and has no discretionary power in that matter, except, according to some legal scholars, in the case of manifest fraud.

However, Belgium has a famous exception. In 1990, Parliament passed a bill that decriminalised, under certain conditions, the practice of abortion. King Baudouin informed the Prime Minister of his unwillingness to sign, though his signature was necessary to give the bill its force of law (Ergec 1990: 265-67). Baudouin insisted that he did not oppose the democratic will expressed in parliament; rather, it was a 'case of conscience' of the sovereign, who was deeply Catholic. Prime Minister Wilfried Martens' office, therefore, found an ingenious legal solution. This consisted of making use of article 93 of the Constitution and finding that the King was – for reasons of conscience – unable to rule. This provision, directly inspired by British constitutional law and the experience of the 'mad King' George III, was not originally intended for this purpose, and had only been applied once in the history of the kingdom, for King Leopold III then a prisoner in Germany in 1944 (when his brother Charles was appointed as Regent). It was the Council of Ministers which was consequently able to exercise the royal prerogatives and gave assent to the law on abortion on 3 April 1990. Two days later, both the House and the Senate lifted the ruling on Baudouin's *'impossibilité de régner'*.

Appointment and Dismissal of Ministers/Dissolution of Parliament

The two most important powers attributed to the King by the Constitution are undoubtedly the power to appoint and dismiss ministers (article 96) and to dissolve Parliament (article 46).

The King appoints and dismisses his ministers by simple royal decree, which must be countersigned by a minister. Beyond the constitutional rule, it was quickly understood by the sovereign, notably Leopold I, that the way in which governments were to be formed was entirely undefined. Chapter 4 will further discuss how governments have historically been formed in Belgium. This is indeed a more political aspect of the Belgian sovereign's power. However, we should already note the existence of the use of the 'countersignature of courtesy', which traditionally requires that, when a new government is inaugurated, the outgoing prime minister countersigns the order appointing his successor, who in turn countersigns his predecessor's resignation (Behrendt & Vrancken 2019: 282). However, this practice is not mandatory, so it is legally possible for the King, in the event of a deadlock, to appoint a new Prime Minister who will countersign both his own appointment and the resignation of his predecessor. In any event, this new Prime Minister will be accountable to the House of Representatives and will be required to face a vote of confidence.

The dissolution of Parliament is another important constitutional prerogative of the King, or at least it has been. In the early days of the kingdom's history, dissolution was considered, in the words of MP Paul Devaux, as a 'right of royal prerogative' (Stengers 2008: 79). It was accepted that the King could decide to summon the voting population if he considered that the Chambers no longer reflected the political forces of the moment. Article 46 of the Constitution has since been substantially revised in 1993 with the introduction of a 'rationalised parliamentary system' (see Velaers 2019, 2: 165-71). Dissolution now requires the approval of the House of Representatives, either directly (article 46 §3) or indirectly when a vote of no confidence is passed (and no successor to the prime minister is proposed) or a vote of confidence is rejected (article 46 §1). However, when an early dissolution happens nowadays, most of the time it is triggered by the process of constitutional amendment, which requires the dissolution of both chambers (article 195).[10]

With regard to the parliamentary session, articles 44 and 45 of the Constitution, which literally allow the King to convene or adjourn the two chambers, have fallen into disuse (Belmessieri 2008: 803). The King no longer has any personal power in matters of summoning and adjourning parliament; nor does the government use these powers. Indeed, parliamentary sessions are most of the time automatically fixed and adjourned.

Implementation of Laws

The King has the exclusive prerogative to implement the law, whether by general authorisation (article 108), or special authorisation enshrined in a law. In practice, it is the government that does it. This consists first of all of the promulgation of the law by the same signature as the one that gives rise to assent. The laws are commenced by royal decrees, signed by the King and a minister. In principle, Belgium does not have a system

---

[10] One particularity of Belgian constitutional law, which would take too long to explain, is to revise the Constitution over two parliamentary terms. The first step, the 'declaration of revision of the Constitution', automatically leads to the dissolution of both chambers (see Velaers 2019, 3: 670-709).

of 'special powers'. However, case law has now accepted that, under certain conditions, provisions of a law may be adopted by the government alone. These are Royal Decrees of Special Powers and Extraordinary Orders of Powers in Wartime.

International Relations

The King directs international relations, which includes negotiating and signing treaties but also commanding the army in wartime. If, nowadays, the King no longer has personal power in this matter, leaving this to his government, this has not always been the case.

At the beginning of the kingdom's history, the King of the Belgians sought to exercise certain foreign policy prerogatives himself. Leopold I, with a strong European dynastic personal network, always considered international relations as his own ministry, countersignature being only a formality (Stengers 2008: 259-71). However, his independent diplomatic action was an exception in the country's history. All his successors have since taken a low-profile role, leaving this responsibility to the government.

The King's personal command of the Belgian army was considered a personal prerogative of the sovereign, without ministerial countersignature, until the end of the Second World War. Article 167 states: 'The King shall command the armed forces and declare a state of war and the end of hostilities'. As commander-in-chief of the Belgian armed forces, the King holds the highest rank in the military hierarchy. Thus, three monarchs decided the military fate of Belgium independently, communicating with their generals with very little consultation with the government, as the Prime Minister in exile during the Second World War attested (Pierlot 1947: 28-33). During the Franco-Prussian war of 1870, Leopold II placed Belgium in a state of war and mobilised the army as a preventive measure. It was then the turn of King Albert during the First World War, and Leopold III in the Second World War, to personally take over the reins of the army. Following the King's disputed choices in 1940, the Soenens Committee in 1949 definitively classified this King's personal prerogative as ancient history.

Currently, the government is responsible for international relations, including in the event of war. The King, as head of the Belgian state (and no longer only of the federal government), also ratifies mixed treaties (article 167), i.e. those that deal with both federal and federated matters.

Additional Constitutional Powers

Among the other functions entrusted to the King by the Constitution, but which are in practice exercised by the government, we can mention:

- The right of pardon (article 110);
- The right to issue coins (article 112), which has been rendered a dead letter in view of Belgium's participation in the euro zone;
- The right to confer titles of nobility (article 113);
- The right to confer military orders (article 114).

3.7. CONSTITUTIONAL FUNCTIONS IN NORWAY

Eivind Smith, Professor of Public Law, University of Oslo

Introduction

Norway has been a monarchy for a thousand years or so. From 1319, however, different dynastic accidents led to a kind of union, first with Sweden, then with Denmark. The latter lasted four centuries (until 1814). During that period, Norway gradually lost most of its central state institutions. The Napoleonic wars ended with Norway's declaration of independence and the adoption of a new Constitution in May 1814.

The story of the present constitutional monarchy thus starts with the breakaway from the absolute Danish-Norwegian monarchy that subsisted in Denmark until 1849. In 1814, the Constituent Assembly elected the resident Governor-Prince of Denmark-Norway as King of Norway by virtue of the new Constitution. In conformity with the terms of the cease-fire concluded between himself, as King of Norway, and the King of Sweden in August 1814 in the aftermath of the Swedish military attack, however, the first constitutional monarch of Norway abdicated a few months later. Instead, the country's first elected parliament elected King Carl XIII of Sweden as King Karl II of Norway. The leading political figure in the military and political manoeuvring against Norway, French Marshal Jean Baptiste Bernadotte, acted in his capacity as elected Crown Prince of Sweden. In 1818, he succeeded the childless king as King Karl XIV of Sweden and Karl III of Norway.

If the union of two Crowns remained for almost a century, the legal and political institutions of the two countries were almost entirely separate and the polities evolved in different ways. In 1905, Norway finally broke away from the personal union with Sweden by unilaterally declaring that the actual king (Oscar II) was no longer king of Norway. For present purposes, we do not need to enter the political drama, military mobilisation etc. that unfolded before Sweden finally accepted the union's dismantlement.

After the replacement of the constitutional provisions for the personal union by those initially adopted in 1814, a referendum called on his demand gave an 80 per cent majority in favour of the Danish Prince Carl as the next King of Norway. Once elected by Parliament, the King took the historic name Haakon VII, whereas his young son, renamed Olav, later became King Olav V and the father of present king Harald V. In political terms, the fact that Haakon VII's spouse (Queen Maud) was a daughter of King Edward VII was regarded as an important means for ensuring British support should Sweden create problems following the Norwegian breakaway.

Constitutional Background and Functions

Notwithstanding numerous amendments, the 1814 text remains the world's oldest constitution still in use, after that of the United States. During two centuries when its institutional environment has changed significantly, most of the provisions on the monarchy have remained relatively unchanged. The form of government remains a 'limited and hereditary monarchy' (article 1). No qualification like 'parliamentary' has appeared in the text. In fact, one had to wait until 2007 to see the core element of a parliamentary system of government: the government's obligation to demand its dismissal once Parliament has declared its loss of confidence, written into the text of the Constitution (article 15).

Within the overarching framework drawn up by article 1, the Constitution's Part B is devoted to 'The executive power, the King and the Royal Family and Religion'. The opening words of the chapter, 'The executive power is vested in the King' (article 3), should be read in contrast to article 49 according to which 'The people exercises the legislative power through the *Storting* [Parliament]', and the title of part D on 'The judicial power', namely article 88 ('The Supreme Court pronounces judgment in the final instance').

Within this classic separation of powers scheme, the monarchy represents by far the most stable element; in fact, the present King is only the third since the new dynasty arrived in 1905. Does this reflect a similar permanence in the monarch's constitutional functions?

In the constitutional text, the reader will find the word 'King' in a great number of provisions. In order to grasp the constitutional functions of the monarch, however, one needs to discern two different groups of such provisions.

A first group may be qualified as dynastic because it deals with the monarch and his family as individual persons. Examples include articles 4 ('The King shall at all times profess the Evangelical-Lutheran religion'), 5 (personal immunity), 6-11 (succession, age of majority, oath, travel), 23 (the right to bestow orders), 24 (the royal household), 34-37 (royal titles, heir, marriages, immunity for princes and princesses) and 47 (education during minority).

A second group is much more important for the understanding of the constitutional functions of the monarch as head of state and, indeed, of the executive power. Examples include the monarch's role regarding government formation (article 12), provisional legislation or decrees (article 17), pardons (article 20), appointments and dismissals of high civil servants [*embetsmenn*] (articles 21-22), military command (article 25), international relations (article 26) and legislation (articles 77-78).

In sum, the number and importance of the constitutional functions devoted to 'the King' as head of state and of the executive are impressive. In order to properly understand their significance, however, it is important to recall that both the so-called 'royal prerogatives' and other constitutional functions have to be executed by the King in Council. Composed of the King or, in his absence, the Crown Prince (if of age), on the one hand, and the members of his government (or at least half of them), on the other, this highest executive body meets every Friday at 11 am in the Palace (articles 27-31). In the King's absence, the Crown Prince acts as regent, chairs the council meetings and signs the decisions.

The necessity of deciding in Council has been in force ever since the original 1814 Constitution. This explains why there is no routine of weekly audiences with the Prime Minister, as in other countries. It does not stand in the way, however, of separate albeit less frequent meetings between the King and the Prime Minister and other senior government figures.

Even the provision requiring the Prime Minister's countersignature on 'royal resolutions' (article 31) stands since 1814. Originally seen as a mechanism for ensuring the correctness of the relevant royal resolution, however, the legal function of the Prime

Minister's countersignature changed radically by a constitutional amendment adopted in 1911, only a few years after the dynastic change in 1905. Since then, the amendment makes it explicit that the countersignature is a condition for the validity of any decision taken under the royal seal ('royal resolutions'). This way, the consent of both the monarch and the Prime Minister is required.

If we read the considerable number of constitutional provisions that refer to the monarch as head of state and of the executive in combination with those that regulate the Council, we thus see that 'the King' actually means 'the King in Council'. At the same time, the latter is the only institutional form of legally binding decision-making available to the government as a collective body. By virtue of delegation from the King in Council, the next level of formal decision-making is the individual ministers as heads of the relevant parts of central government, or decisions taken under the responsibility of the relevant minister. Today, the bulk of formal decision-making at the executive's top level belongs to this second level, with no role for the monarch.

Between the two levels of formal decision-making, a sophisticated system of government meetings has emerged. Presided over by the Prime Minister with no role for the monarch, they take place at least once a week and at a number of other occasions (related to the preparation of the annual budget, for instance) in order to discuss and, in political terms, actually decide a considerable number of political issues. Decisions that are of an overarching political character will need subsequent formalisation by the King in Council or by individual ministers. In such cases, however, the outcome will provide no surprise.

The monarch can no longer decide in his capacity as head of state and of the executive without the Prime Minister's explicit approval within the framework of formal Council meetings. In practice, approvals are not given without the support of a majority among the ministers (or – more likely – of the entire government). By consequence, what remains for the monarch is the possibility of refusing to sign, a possibility to which none of the three Kings of the present dynasty has had recourse (see further in chapter 4 on the political functions of the monarch). That situation fits well with the fundamental provision in article 5 of the Constitution that the monarch enjoys complete legal immunity ('The King's person cannot be censured or accused', whereas the 'responsibility rests with his Council').

We are now in a position to grasp key aspects of the constitutional role of the Norwegian monarch as head of state and of the executive. Reading the separate provisions on these functions in conjunction with articles 27-31, we see that it is for the King in Council – for instance – to appoint high civil and military civil servants, permanent judges included. The same goes for decisions under a number of other provisions, some of which are of great political importance. For instance, the authorisation to engage Norwegian F16 planes to bomb Libya was given by royal resolution of 23 March 2011 by virtue of article 25 on the King as supreme commander of the military forces. Those Acts of Parliament that are to become formal statutes are approved under article 78; however, the veto power has not been in use since the dynastic change in 1905. The adoption of any kind of decisions taken by the King in Council requires the monarch's personal approval. However, no decision passes without the counter-signature of the Prime Minister. That it is for the King in Council to grant royal pardons has been specified *expressis verbis* all the time since 1814 (article 20).

Even the decisions to appoint or dismiss individual ministers and the entire government (article 12) follow this scheme, as a consequence of the facts that the monarch enjoys full legal immunity (article 5) and that the country should always have a responsible government. Once the identity of a new government has been identified, the King in Council would typically meet in the morning in order to dismiss the outgoing team and to appoint the new government. The dismissal would be given effect from noon of the same day, when a new council meeting with the newcomers will gather. The new government then 'apportions the business' among its members (article 12 paragraph 2) by deciding who should be Minister of Foreign Affairs, Finance and so on. Similarly, new Secretaries of State (that are not members of the government) are appointed (article 14).

According to the text of the Constitution, the appointment of a government and the distribution of ministerial responsibilities are decided the way the King himself 'deems appropriate'. Even these provisions must be read in conjunction with article 27-31 of the Constitution, however. This implies that the monarch has no freedom to appoint ministers or to distribute the portfolios between them in a way not accepted by the government itself. On the role of the monarch during government formation, see in chapter 4 on his political role.

In political terms, therefore, we easily discern the leading political actor among the two under present day conditions: *de facto*, the monarch's role at the Council meetings is to approve and give legal effect to proposals of which the politically responsible element has already defined the substance.

The Constitution of Norway no longer leaves it to the monarch to summon Parliament. Instead, it specifies on which day of the year it shall assemble (article 68); it sits until the next session is assembled. Once the Parliament has finished the necessary internal business (such as electing its Presidents and distribution of seats in the permanent commissions), it remains for the monarch to conduct the formal opening of the annual sessions (article 74 paragraph 1). At this occasion, he even gives the speech from the throne in which Parliament shall be informed 'of the state of the realm and of the issues to which he particularly desires to call the attention of the *Storting*'. Since 1905, the Prime Minister prepares the text and hands it over to the monarch during the solemn ceremony itself.

Unlike any other parliament in parliamentary democracies, it has never been possible to dissolve the *Storting* during its four year electoral term (article 71).

3.8. LUXEMBOURG: GRAND DUKE HENRI'S REFUSAL, IN 2008, TO SIGN THE BILL LEGALISING EUTHANASIA

Professor Dr Luc Heuschling, University of Luxembourg

In his play *King Charles III*, the British author Mike Bartlett imagined how Charles, once crowned, would refuse his assent to a bill restricting press freedom. In Luxembourg, this hypothesis became real in 2008. In European 'neutralised' monarchies, where monarchs are not supposed to play any major political role (exceptions: Liechtenstein and Monaco), such refusal has become extremely rare since the end of the (long) nineteenth century.

In 1912, after decades of political abstinence of the previous Grand Dukes Adolphe and Guillaume IV, the young Grand Duchess of Luxembourg Marie-Adélaïde wished to become more involved in politics. Being a devout Catholic, she considered in 1912 refusing her assent to the bill secularising schools, but, eventually, signed it. She did refuse, however, various appointments of civil servants and mayors. In 1915, after appointing a Catholic government against the wishes of the Chamber of Deputies dominated by a coalition of liberals and socialists, she dissolved Parliament. In 1919, although she was legally covered by immunity (article 4 Constitution), Marie-Adélaïde was forced to abdicate (the main reason was her perceived support for the German occupying forces during the First World War and her previous political actions). Abroad, since the end of WWI, there are only two cases where a monarch, in a 'neutralised' European monarchy, has refused royal assent: in Belgium in 1990, with King Baudouin's famous refusal of the bill on abortion (see chapter 3.6); and in the Netherlands in 1972, when Queen Juliana resisted a bill limiting membership of the royal house, leading the government to drop the proposal (see chapter 3.5 above). Given the close links of Luxembourg to both countries, those precedents may have played an essential part in Grand Duke Henri's reasoning in 2008.

Henri's (in)action must be placed in the broader context of his reign. From the start, in a famous interview given with his wife in 2000, Henri announced his will (or even 'their' will) to reshape the monarchical tradition going back to Charlotte and Jean. He introduced a series of major changes, some of which were consensual, being in line with the Zeitgeist; others were rather startling, and others were highly controversial. These reforms, or revolutions, included the abolition, in all legal texts, of the outdated formula 'Grand Duke of Luxembourg *by God's Grace*', the much more active role of his wife Grand Duchess Maria Teresa, the more popular style of public communication, the unearthing of the totally forgotten prerogative of the Grand Duke to open, in person, the parliamentary session, the claim in 2004 of the right to vote in the referendum on the EU Constitution, the reform and publication in 2011/12 of the previously secret house laws and, in 2008, the refusal of the bill on euthanasia.

The political situation in December 2008, in the midst of the global financial crisis, was all but simple. First, in contrast to King Baudouin, Henri did not clarify, and justify, in public his own position at the crucial moment when the constitutional conflict was disclosed by Prime Minister Jean-Claude Juncker in his famous, but also short press conference of 2 December(Juncker 2008). At the time, it was public knowledge that Henri invoked *moral* grounds, based on his Catholic faith (he did not mobilise any *legal* argument such as the infringement, by the bill, of a higher legal norm such as a constitutional norm, or a European or international norm as did some citizens: Jacobs et al 2008). What was not, and even today is still not, clear, is whether he wished (a) to block, definitely, the reform on euthanasia or (b) to allow this reform to go through, but without him being involved. Whereas in Belgium Baudouin's action fell clearly under the second hypothesis, and was held in high esteem by people, in Luxembourg the first reading, put forward in the prime minister's statement to the press, largely prevailed in public opinion, which led to a major legitimacy crisis of the monarchy. The support for a republic suddenly rose to 36 per cent in an opinion poll made just after the announcement of Henri's refusal; 31 per cent wanted Henri to abdicate (Le Jeudi 2008). In his later Christmas speech of 2008, Henri presented a totally different narrative: just like Baudouin, whose words he almost literally copied, Henri asserted that he did not have, and never claimed to have, any right to veto a bill (reading (b); Grand Duke Henri 2008). But this message, which came rather late, failed to convince. Public confidence was lost. Second, by putting forward his moral scruples as a Catholic, Henri not only took sides in a highly controversial debate which risked dividing society; he also put in an uncomfortable position the Christian-Social Party, which was leading the government, but which had allowed its coalition partner (the socialists) to propose this reform and to pass it through Parliament with the help of the opposition. Third, although most people agreed to qualify Henri's action as unwise, especially against the historical backdrop of Marie-Adélaïde's tragic fate, its legal assessment was less easy.

The Tricky Distinction between the Still Vast Prerogatives of the State Organ 'Grand Duke of Luxembourg' and the Shrinking Discretion of its Main Incumbent (the Individual Monarch)

In 2008, as in most other monarchies with the famous exception of Sweden, the 1868 Constitution of Luxembourg continued to vest a long list of prerogatives, especially the so-called 'executive power', not in the Council of Government but in the state organ called 'Grand Duke of Luxembourg'. The powers to negotiate and ratify a treaty (article 37 § 1), to submit an ordinary bill or constitutional amendment to parliament (article 47; article 114), to sanction and promulgate bills and constitutional amendments (article 34; article 114), to enact regulations (article 32 § 3; article 36; article 37 § 4; article 76), to declare and implement a state of emergency (article 32 § 4), to appoint ministers and civil servants (article 77; article 35 § 1), to supervise the actions of local authorities (article 107 § 3) were all granted by the Constitution to the head of state. However, in order to get a full picture of the situation, one had to combine this first series of legal norms with other norms, either legal or non-legal, a state of affairs I have called '*normativité à deux voix*' (Heuschling 2013). The two-voices-normativity technique consists in the coexistence of two sets of contradictory norms which, together, are supposed to define what remains of the monarch's personal discretion. Classically, the first set of norms, which are all legal norms, grant a long list of state competencies to the state organ 'Grand Duke / King / Emperor', and seemingly bestow on its main or most visible incumbent (the monarch as physical person) a very large discretion: it is he, or she, who is supposed to decide how to use these powers. The aim of the second set of norms, which may be legal or even non-legal (the 'constitutional conventions' in the UK, the 'custom' and/or 'political practice' in other countries, including Luxembourg), is to reduce or even abolish this discretion by various means. A classic example in Luxembourg (article 45) and in many other continental monarchies is the rule of countersignature: a norm taken by the organ 'Grand Duke of Luxembourg' is only valid if it is signed both by the monarch and a minister (according to my theoretical understanding, the minister, in this context, should be considered as the second, less visible incumbent of the state organ 'Grand-Duke', and not as the incumbent of another state organ whose approval would be necessary to the organ 'Grand-Duke').

As a result of these contradictory norms, the legal question of whether Henri could veto a bill, was not as clear as one might have wished in 2008. At the time, article 34 of the Constitution still provided, just as in the nineteenth century: 'The Grand Duke sanctions and promulgates the laws within three months of the vote of the Chamber'. A bill adopted by the Chamber of Deputies only became a legal norm when 'sanctioned' by the state organ 'Grand Duke of Luxembourg'. In the nineteenth century, it was clear that the monarch (physical person) could refuse to sanction (he or she did not need a ministerial countersignature for withholding it). Let's call this historical model solution (a). But to what extent was this solution still valid in 2008? Did there exist any legal (or extra-legal?) norm which ran against it? If so, what was its exact content? In the abstract, one can envisage three new possible outcomes (b, c, d). Solution (b): The state organ 'Grand Duke' is still entitled to say either 'yes' or 'no', but the exercise of that discretion would need to derive from a co-decision of both incumbents, both monarch and minister having to agree freely. Solution (c): The state organ 'Grand Duke' is still entitled to veto, but it is the minister (subject to the guidelines of the government) who decides; the monarch is simply executing (his/her 'no' is not free any more). Solution (d): The Grand Duke, as state organ, has lost in law any discretion to refuse on moral or political grounds the assent to bills (the organ's answer must be 'yes'): hence, both incumbents (monarch and minister) are obliged to sign.

In the pre-2008 legal literature, the most influential scholars, who were all close to the monarchist Christian-Social party (Pierre Majerus, Pierre Pescatore and Marc Thewes; for a critical analysis see Heuschling 2013: 123 ff), considered that, according to law, notwithstanding all democratic reforms of the 1868 Constitution since 1919, the state organ 'Grand Duke' was still endowed by article 34 with an 'absolute veto right'. They did not clarify, however, whether, in law, solution (a), (b) or (c) prevailed, as they omitted to discuss the impact of article 45 (countersignature) or of any other legal norm. But, according to these scholars, it would have been politically inconceivable for the monarch to use this prerogative. In its influential commentary on the Constitution, the Council of State maintained this absolute veto right, but, in light of article 45, excluded option (a) (Conseil d'État 2006: 149 ff). Whether this implied solution (b) or (c) remained obscure. A different path had been taken by the jurist Léon Metzler who, already in 1949, stated that the veto right in article 34 had been abolished by recent customary norms, given the overall democratisation of the system (solution d; Metzler 1949: 299). But this reasoning implied that custom could abrogate written constitutional norms, a thesis which was and is highly contestable in Luxembourg (see Heuschling 2014: part 2). In 2008, one could have argued, however, that the veto power in article 34 was abrogated implicitly (solution d) not by custom, but by some new abstract provision of the constitutional text: in 1919, there was enshrined the principle of 'sovereignty of the nation' (article 32 § 1), in 1948 the principle of 'parliamentary democracy' (article 51 § 1), in 1998 the principle of 'democracy' (article 1) and the general definition of the 'symbolic' role of the head of state (article 33). Yet, in the literature, these principles were rarely quoted in relation to article 34.

In his press conference of 2 December 2008, when announcing Henri's refusal, Prime Minister Jean-Claude Juncker remained extremely vague on legal arguments: all he said was that 'constitutional practice' would argue against Henri's view (Juncker 2008; also ambiguous: Frieden 2008). Later, in 2009, the Minister of Justice Luc Frieden asserted, without further details, that the government had always defended solution (d) (Frieden 2009). Public statements of prominent socialist politicians, very critical of Henri, oscillated implicitly between theses (d), (c) and (b) (Bodry 2008; Goebbels 2008).

The Commission on the Constitution of the Chamber of Deputies put forward thesis (c), but also, ambiguously, thesis (b) (CIRC 2008: 2). The opinion of the Council of State of 9 December 2008 can be read, mostly, as a defence of solution (d), in contrast to its 2006 commentary (Conseil d'État 2008).

But none of these various arguments made Henri change his mind. Nor did the government resign in order to 'force' the monarch to comply (this classic, nineteenth century solution is totally inadequate, in case of inertia of the monarch; furthermore it punishes society, and the people, rather than the monarch). The government had even proposed to Henri: (a) to sign the bill *and* (b) to make a public statement recording his moral criticisms; yet he refused (Frieden 2009: 541).

The Outcome of the 2008 Crisis: Towards a Swedish Model in Luxembourg?

The crisis was overcome by a common decision of all political parties to amend the Constitution and to delete the term 'sanction' in article 34 of the Constitution (Loi de révision du 12 mars 2009; parl. doc. n°5967). Thereafter, the bill on euthanasia was definitively adopted by the Chamber of Deputies and was 'promulgated' by Henri. During the debate on the constitutional revision, the Council of State took the time to clarify that the state organ 'Grand Duke' had no discretion regarding 'promulgation', an issue which was not beyond all doubt (Conseil d'État 2008).

As a consequence of this crisis, the Chamber of Deputies decided, in 2009, to launch a total reform of the old 1868 Constitution, in order to adapt the largely outdated text to political reality, to establish more transparent formulations and to reform, in depth, the monarchy. The initial version of this project (Meyers 2009) opted for a radical solution: the Swedish model. The state organ called now officially 'head of state', instead of 'Grand Duke', was stripped of almost all competencies, which were vested directly in the state organ 'government'. Furthermore, the monarch as an individual person, who would still wear the title of Grand Duke or Grand Duchess, lost part of his/her immunity: in exceptional circumstances, he/she could be held accountable for 'infringement of his/her constitutional functions' by the Chamber of Deputies and be forced to abdicate by a vote of two thirds of all deputies (for a first, analogous precedent to this extremely rare solution, see French Constitution of 1791, title III, chap II, articles 5-7). Later, however, due to the pressure of the Court and of the Council of State, which were afraid that the Swedish model would ultimately lead to the introduction of a republic, the Chamber changed its mind. The Commission on the Constitution (CIRC) reintroduced largely the classic two-voices-normativity technique; yet, it still kept the new rule of accountability of the monarch, which may make things even more complicated in the future (once the monarch is personally accountable, the meaning of the provision on countersignature will change; its grip on the monarch will weaken). The text of this reform project is currently still under discussion; its future is rather uncertain, as it must be approved by the opposition which, in 2019, became increasingly reluctant to do so. At the end the reform would also be submitted to referendum. Thus, the long term consequences, on a constitutional level, of the 2008 crisis are still not settled. The Swedish model is, definitely, off the table. The question is whether Luxembourg will keep the current, and old, two-voices-normativity system or opt for a slightly new two-voices-normativity system.

In either case, the classic legal issue of the monarch's power will remain a tricky question in Luxembourg.

How Risky is it, for a Monarch, to Refuse Royal Assent? A Comparative Conclusion

On a more general, comparative, level, the study of the 'neutralised' monarchies which have recently experienced a royal veto for moral or political reasons – the Netherlands in 1972, Belgium in 1990, Luxembourg in 2008 – shows that the very frequent political and scholarly discourse, asserting that a refusal of royal assent would be highly improbable because it would inevitably lead to a crisis of the monarchy must be seriously reconsidered. The empirical data tends to prove rather the contrary. None of the three cited monarchs, not even Henri who was involved in the worst of all three scenarios, has been forced to abdicate. None of the three regimes has become a republic. In two of the three examples (Netherlands, Belgium), the veto has generated no major constitutional shift. In Luxembourg, the final outcome is still unknown: the constitutional caesura could be far less dramatic than initially foreseen, the Swedish solution being definitely discarded. Thus, for an activist monarch, to dare to veto a bill appears far less risky than is generally assumed. This conclusion may be rather uncomfortable for constitutionalists and citizens living under a system in which the royal veto may still be legal, but whose use, at the same time, is downplayed as 'unreasonable and highly improbable'. Such discourse belittles how dangerous such an outdated legal situation may be – not so much for the monarchy, but for democracy.

3.9. SPAIN: THE COUP OF FEBRUARY 1981

Charles Powell, Director of the Elcano Royal Institute, Madrid

Juan Carlos I of Spain resolutely performed his function as guardian of the Constitution during the country's turbulent transition from Francoist authoritarianism to incipient democracy between the years 1975-81. The new constitutional and democratic order was met with unrest by sections of the military, unhappy with reforms which, in their calculation, amounted to emasculation and a loss of control. This unrest found expression in a series of failed plots in the late 1970s and early 1980s, culminating in the audacious attempted coup of 1981. The King, far from oblivious to such agitation, sought to placate those figures most uneasy about what democracy in Spain meant for the military, all the while emphasising his duty and commitment to upholding the Constitution. In conversations with disgruntled military men during 1979-80, the King made this commitment clear, anticipating his response to the 1981 coup:

> I listened to them carefully, and when their arguments struck me as departing too far from reality, I tried to make them see reason. But I also made it clear that in no case could they count on me to cover up for the slightest action against a constitutional government like our own. Any such action, I told them, would be regarded by the King as a direct attack on the Crown (de Villalonga 1994: 125).

The 1981 plot was instigated by Captain General of the Valencia military region, Jaime Milans del Bosch, and General Alfonso Armada. Of the shared opinion that the then Prime Minister, Adolfo Suarez, was incapable of navigating a way through Spain's perilous economic difficulties, both men saw an increased military presence in government as not only desirable, but necessary. Interestingly, at a decisive meeting of the two in late 1980, General Armada, who was formerly head of the royal household and spoke with the King on a regular basis, led Milans del Bosch to believe that Juan Carlos himself shared their concerns about Suarez. From the outset the conspirators knew that any disruption to the democratic settlement required the King's approval, tacit or otherwise.

After canvassing support for the plot from various elements within the army, the coup, which at an operational level was to be spearheaded by Lieutenant-Colonel Antonio Tejero, finally went ahead in February 1981. By that time Suarez had already left office, replaced by Leopoldo Calvo-Sotelo, an appointment which did little to appease those intent on strengthening the military's presence within government. In the wake of Suárez's resignation, a highly influential right-wing journalist published an article encouraging the King to seize this opportunity to replace him with 'a politically blessed outsider', and suggested General Armada as the best candidate. This gave rise to fresh rumours of an imminent 'operación Armada' (a pun on 'armed solution' and 'Armada solution'). However, the fact that the King did not act on this advice suggests that, at best, he was always lukewarm about a De Gaulle/Armada solution to the crisis. In the course of the consultations that later led to the appointment of Leopoldo Calvo-Sotelo as Suárez's successor, Juan Carlos made no mention whatsoever of a possible coalition led by Armada. He confined himself, as was his constitutional duty, to listening to the spokesmen of the various parliamentary groups. At a subsequent meeting with the King, held on 13 February, Armada warned him that his prestige within the armed forces was at its lowest point since Franco's death, but failed in his efforts to make the King reconsider his support for Calvo-Sotelo and appoint him instead. Following the monarch's instructions, the General agreed to meet the Minister for Defence, who later recalled him frothing with rage, insisting that Juan Carlos was wrong to replace Suárez with another civilian.

On 23 February, at 6.23 pm, some 320 civil guards under Tejero arrived at the Parliament, and approximately half of them burst into the chamber brandishing pistols and submachine guns, effectively taking the government and all 350 deputies hostage. To lend credence to the notion that Juan Carlos was behind the coup, Tejero repeatedly shouted 'in the name of the King' as he burst in. Having secured the Parliament, Tejero telephoned Milans del Bosch, who declared a state of emergency in the Valencia region at 6:45 pm and issued a proclamation stating that 'in light of the events in the capital and the consequent vacuum of power, it is my duty to guarantee order in the military region under my command until I receive instructions from His Majesty the King'. The proclamation ordered the militarisation of all public service personnel, imposed a curfew and banned all political and trade union activity. For greater effect, tanks were rolled out to guard important public buildings.

The coup began to run into trouble when the head of the Brunete Armoured Division, General Juste Fernández, grew suspicious of the claims of his co-conspirators to the effect that the uprising enjoyed the King's full support. These suspicions were confirmed when, on telephoning La Zarzuela, the monarch's official residence, he tried to speak to Armada, only to be informed that he was not there, nor was he expected (Juan Carlos was getting ready to play squash with several friends when the Parliament was taken, another indication that he was not privy to the conspiracy). As a result, the Brunete units that were preparing to advance on Madrid quickly stood down.

The track-suited monarch and his closest advisers spent the rest of the evening trying to dismantle the coup by telephone. Given that the executive was being held hostage, Juan Carlos ordered the creation of a provisional government consisting of the Secretaries of State and Under-Secretaries of each Ministry, under the direction of Francisco Laína, Director of State Security at the Ministry of the Interior. This body later issued a statement explaining that they had 'gone into permanent session, on the instructions of His Majesty the King, to ensure the government of the country through civilian channels', and guaranteed that 'no act of violence will destroy the democratic coexistence that the people freely desire and which is enshrined in the text of the Constitution that both civilians and the military have sworn to uphold'.

Crucial to the coup's failure was the King's ability to speak to most of Spain's Captain Generals personally, only a few of whom got in touch with La Zarzuela of their own accord to reassure him of their loyalty. What these conversations revealed was that, once the King made it clear that, contrary to what the insurgents were claiming, the coup did not enjoy his support, they invariably offered him their obedience. In other words, had the King wanted the coup to succeed, as has been claimed, it would have been very easy for him to secure an outcome favourable to the insurgents. The Captain-General of Madrid, Guillermo Quintana Lacaci, would later explain to the Minister of Defence, that

> I fought in the Civil War, so you can well imagine my way of thinking. But Franco gave me the order to obey his successor and the King ordered me to stop the coup on 23 February. If he had ordered me to assault the Cortes, I would have done so.

Eventually, even Milans del Bosch, who spoke to the King on three occasions, agreed to stand down, though not until Juan Carlos sent him a telex reaffirming his determination to defend the Constitution, and a warning that 'after this message, I cannot turn back'. By this he meant that unless del Bosch obeyed immediately, he would hold him responsible for the consequences of the coup (during the subsequent trial, this text was quoted as evidence of the King's alleged hesitation). The telex also stated unequivocally that 'no coup d'état of any kind whatsoever can hide behind the King, it is against the King', and concluded: 'I swear to you that I will neither abdicate nor leave Spain'. The occupation of Parliament was also eventually abandoned, at midday on the 24th, some 18 hours after it began.

In a television message broadcast at 1.15 am on the night of the occupation, the King powerfully underlined the importance of the monarch's role as custodian of the country's fragile democracy. After announcing that he had ordered all civilian and military authorities to defend the democratic status quo, the King solemnly proclaimed that

> the Crown, symbol of the permanence and unity of the fatherland, cannot in any way tolerate the attempts of any persons, by their actions or their attitude, to interrupt by force the democratic process determined by the constitution and approved by the Spanish people by means of a referendum.

On 27 February some 3 million people demonstrated across the cities of Spain in support of democracy and the King.

3.10. CONCLUSIONS

Professor Robert Hazell, The Constitution Unit, University College London

This chapter has been about the monarch's constitutional role, in three important respects: the power to appoint and dismiss ministers, to summon and dissolve parliament, and to give royal assent to laws and decrees. In all the countries under review these powers have gradually been reduced over the last two centuries, to the point where the monarch has little or no discretion. And they are still being reduced: not just in Sweden, where the monarch lost all formal power in 1974, but in other countries we have seen further reductions, just in the last decade. In Luxembourg the Grand Duke has lost the power to assent to the laws made by the parliament; now his role is merely to promulgate them. In the Netherlands the monarch is no longer involved in the process of government formation: that role has passed to the lower house of parliament. And in the UK the prerogative power to dissolve parliament has been abolished; it is now the House of Commons which decides upon early dissolution and fresh elections.

Yet the monarch still remains the ultimate guardian of the constitution, whose role in an emergency is to safeguard democratic and constitutional values. The most dramatic illustration of that was in Spain in 1981, when King Juan Carlos helped to foil an attempted coup d'état by the Civil Guard, by going on television in uniform, declaring that the coup was illegal, and ordering the armed forces as their Commander-in-Chief to return to their barracks. And there was a similar episode in Norway, when after the German invasion of Norway in 1940 King Haakon VII told his Cabinet that although it was their decision, he would rather abdicate than accept Quisling as head of the new government. That episode is still remembered today; and in both countries the courageous example set by the King helped to reinforce the legitimacy of the monarchy as an institution.

One other circumstance where the monarch might need to act to safeguard democratic values would be if the prime minister acted in breach of the constitution, and there was no other legal or political remedy to prevent him. An example could be if there was a formal vote of no confidence in the government, but the prime minister tried to remain in office, refusing either to resign or to advise fresh elections. The only remedy then might be for the monarch to dismiss the prime minister. There was an episode which came close to this in Denmark in 1993, when the Conservative People's Party prime minister Poul Schlüter wished to retire, and hand over the leadership to a Conservative successor; but he was reminded by the Palace that the majority in parliament had shifted, and the new prime minister was appointed from the Social Democrats, reflecting the new majority. In countries like Denmark and the Netherlands where no party has an overall majority and governments are often composed of multi-party coalitions, it can be a difficult matter of judgement to determine which potential coalition is most likely to form a stable and effective government. The monarch inevitably risks being criticised when making these difficult judgements, and is sometimes accused of allowing their personal preference to affect the outcome – as happened with the accusations levelled against Queen Beatrix of the Netherlands in 2010 by politicians such as Geert Wilders and the Freedom Party.

Withholding Royal Assent could be another way in which a monarch can prevent the parliament from enacting legislation which breaches fundamental constitutional values.

But none of the recent examples has involved an attempt to safeguard the constitution. Queen Juliana's opposition to the death penalty (1952), King Baudouin's to legalising abortion (1990), and Grand Duke Henri's to euthanasia (2008) were motivated by personal conscience, not constitutional values. In Luxembourg the outcome was dramatic, with an immediate constitutional amendment removing the requirement for royal assent, and subsequent proposals for further reductions in the Grand Duke's powers.

These proposals in Luxembourg include making the monarch more accountable, and giving power to the parliament to require the monarch to abdicate. What this episode shows is that the monarch may formally be the guardian of the Constitution; but ultimately the exercise of the monarch's reserve powers depends upon popular support. This was also evident in the Easter crisis of 1920 in Denmark, when King Christian X lost his Prime Minister and dismissed the rest of the government, after he insisted upon the re-unification of Central Schleswig against the wishes of the local population, and the government. The dismissal caused demonstrations threatening the future of the monarchy, and the King was forced to back down. When deploying reserve powers against the government, a wise monarch will ensure that the people are on his side.

None of the constitutions save one contains a specific power of the kind proposed in Luxembourg, giving power to the Parliament to require the monarch to abdicate. The exception is the Netherlands, where article 35 provides that, on a proposal from the Council of Ministers, the Parliament can declare the King incapable of exercising his royal authority. But most of the constitutions require the monarch to take an oath to be faithful to the constitution. Helle Krunke has written, 'The Constitution does not give the government and Parliament a specific right to depose the King from his throne, but if he violates the Constitution, the precondition for his right to reign has lapsed' (3.3 above). The guardian of the constitution must himself observe the constitution. But it may not even require a violation of the constitution; we might broaden the principle to say, if the monarch by his conduct loses the support of the government or his people, he puts his throne at risk. We have seen four examples of this over the last century: in the abdication of Grand Duchess Marie Adélaïde of Luxembourg in 1919, of the British King Edward VIII in 1936, the Belgian King Leopold III in 1951, and the Spanish King Juan Carlos in 2014. Ultimately, the continuation of the monarch in office depends upon continuing popular support. We might even broaden that one stage further to say, ultimately the continuation of the monarchy as an institution depends upon the continuing support of the people.

4

Day-to-Day Political Functions of the Monarchy

Contents

4.1. INTRODUCTION

Professor Robert Hazell, The Constitution Unit, University College London

THE DAY-TO-DAY POLITICAL functions of the monarch are less visible than the constitutional functions. They involve working closely with the Prime Minister, with other ministers, and with senior officers of state. This is done in an endless round of meetings, public engagements, reading official papers and signing documents of all kinds, from international treaties to royal pardons. For most monarchs it also involves chairing the Council of State.

There is a summary of the main political functions of each monarch in Table 4.1. It shows for each country whether there is a weekly meeting with the prime minister, regular meetings of the Council of State, a ministerial countersignature required on royal decrees, a speech from the throne to open parliament, and whether the monarch appoints senior officials and judges, receives incoming and outgoing ambassadors, and is Commander-in-Chief of the armed forces.

The chapter opens with a fascinating account of the political functions of the Dutch monarchy. In Chapter 3.5, Paul Bovend'Eert analysed the constitutional provisions about the King's role in the business of government; in this chapter Rudy Andeweg describes what happens in practice, including examples of royal interference and influence. Helle Krunke, Robert Hazell and Eivind Smith report that the Danish, British and Norwegian monarchs appear to have less influence, so far as we know; but the difficulty facing scholars in all countries is that no records are kept of the weekly meetings between monarch and prime minister, politicians are very reluctant to talk about them, and it may suit both sides to play down the extent of any royal influence.

Running through all the contributions are two sets of questions. The first is descriptive and analytical: How much autonomy does the monarch have? How much influence and soft power? The second is normative: How much influence should the monarch have? Should other monarchies follow the example of Sweden, and reduce the monarch to a purely ceremonial role? And if the monarch remains a political actor, should that remain a closely guarded secret, in the interests of the monarchy and of the politicians?

Table 4.1 Main political functions of the monarch

Country	Weekly meeting with prime minister	Council of State	Countersignature of decrees and ministerial decisions	Throne speech at annual opening of Parliament	Appointment of senior officials and judges	Foreign policy: Treaties, Ambassadors	Commander-in-chief of armed forces
Belgium	Yes, on Mondays	Yes	Yes: Article 106		Article 107		
Denmark	Yes. The queen also meets with the Minister of Foreign Affairs.	Yes, ten times a year. Article 17	Yes: Article 14		Article 27	Article 19: with consent of the Folketing	
Luxembourg	Yes, Article 77		Yes, Article 45	Yes, revived by Grand Duke Henri. Art 72.3	Yes, Article 35	Treaties Article 37	

(continued)

Table 4.1 (*Continued*)

Country	Weekly meeting with prime minister	Council of State	Countersignature of decrees and ministerial decisions	Throne speech at annual opening of Parliament	Appointment of senior officials and judges	Foreign policy: Treaties, Ambassadors	Commander-in-chief of armed forces
Netherlands	Yes, weekly on Mondays; The king also meets other ministers separately	Article 74. King presides only at ceremonial occasions.	Yes, Article 47, 87 and 89 for all legislation and royal decrees, but not for ministerial decisions	Yes, Article 65	Article 46 State Secretaries, Art 74 Council of State, judges. Some top civil servants and military officers	Articles 90 and 100 require government (of which the king is a member) to promote an international legal order and inform parliament of military deployment abroad. Legislation based on Article 91 requires the signature of the king for consent to treaties (treaties are approved by parliament by legislation)	Article 97 (the government has supreme authority over the military; the king is a member of the government; the present king has high military ranks but is not commander-in-chief of the armed forces)
Norway	Sometimes before the Council meeting on Fridays	Yes, every week on Friday (except during the holiday seasons)	Yes, on decisions adopted by the King in Council (not on ministerial decisions by delegation from the King in Council). Article 31	Yes Article 74	Yes, by the King in Council. Article 21 (cf. Articles 3 and 27 ff)	Foreign policy/ treaties: the King in Council (or by delegation). Receiving foreign Ambassadors: the monarch. Article 26	Yes (but orders adopted by the King in Council or by delegation to the minister and to military commanders). Article 25
Spain		King presides at request of President of Government	Yes, section 64		Section 62.f	Section 63	Section 62.h
Sweden	No	Yes, around three times a year. 1974 Instr of Govt, Ch 5, Art 3	No	Yes. Riksdag Act 2014, Ch 3, Art 6	No	King chairs Advisory Council on Foreign Affairs	No, but has high military titles
UK	Yes, on Wednesday	Privy Council meets once a month	No	Yes, once a year	Yes	Yes: receives incoming and outgoing Ambassadors	Colonel-in-Chief of 15 regiments

4.2A. THE KING AND THE GOVERNMENT IN THE NETHERLANDS

Professor Dr Paul Bovend'Eert, Radboud University

The King has a unique and special place in the Dutch system of government. In a constitutional sense, the King fulfils two main state functions. In the first place, he is the head of state (Bovend'Eert and Kortmann 2018: 73). In addition, his position is predominantly determined by the fact that he constitutes, together with the Cabinet ministers, the governmental office; such is stated in the official explanatory note to the Constitution of 1983 (Tweede Kamer der Staten-Generaal 1979/80: 2). As head of state, he represents the Dutch State both within the Netherlands and abroad. Nowhere in the Constitution is it explicitly stated that the King is the head of state. In the constitutional revision of 1983, this royal function was considered to speak for itself, so that no constitutional provision was considered necessary.

The fact that the King is part of the government is not that obvious. For that reason, the Constitution expresses this function explicitly since 1983 in article 42, paragraph 1 of the Constitution: 'The Government shall comprise the King and the Ministers'.

The two functions of the King must be clearly distinguished. The King does not exercise his governmental function as head of state but as part of the government, as expressed in the explanatory note to article 42 of the Constitution (Tweede Kamer der Staten-Generaal, Handelingen II 1980/1981: 2618). A characteristic feature of the exercise of the governmental function is that the King always makes decisions jointly with one or more Cabinet ministers. Article 47 of the Constitution ('All Acts of Parliament and Royal Decrees shall be signed by the King and by one or more Ministers') establishes in this context that the decrees promulgated by the government, referred to in the Constitution in a rather misleading way as 'Royal Decrees', shall be co-signed by the King and one or more Cabinet ministers. Remarkable in this respect is that the King is no longer referred to in the constitutional revision of 1983 as 'the head of the government'. He is a constituent part of the government. The requirement of article 47 of the Constitution does not apply to his actions as head of state. In that specific capacity, he can act autonomously, although the ministers always remain responsible for the conduct of the King.

Under articles 42 and 47, the King is involved in the decision-making process for all important state affairs. His signature is required for all governmental decrees, including decrees regarding the submission of legislative propositions (article 82 of the Constitution) and the ratification of laws (article 87 of the Constitution). For the adoption of governmental decrees and laws, there is an equality and mutual dependence between King and Cabinet. The King cannot act without the Cabinet ministers. However, the Cabinet ministers always need the cooperation of the King.

Article 47 of the Constitution should not be interpreted to imply that the King is required in principle to sign every decree that is submitted to him by the ministers. It cannot be deduced from the Constitution, nor from the explanatory notes or constitutional history, nor from constitutional practice, that the involvement of the King in the government and his signature are merely a formality.

In the constitutional revision of 1983, the government presented the following viewpoint. Under article 42, paragraph 2, the King is inviolable and the ministers are responsible. By countersigning a governmental decree, a minister accepts responsibility for that decree. The King shall confine himself to the exercise of 'the rights to be consulted, to encourage, to warn', as formulated by Bagehot for the British monarch (Tweede Kamer den Staten-Generaal, Kamerstukken II 1980/1981, 16035, 8: 2). As formulated by Prime Minister Kok in 1996, 'the King takes part in the government and has in that function a personal role, which consists of ... inquiring, advising and urging other members of the government' (Eerste Kamer der Staten-Generaal: 128). This advisory function of the King is also emphasised in more recent government memoranda(Tweede Kamer der Staten-Generaal 1999/2000).

The King has a restricted task (inquiring, advising, urging), and the Cabinet takes up a dominant position. The government speaks in this regard of 'the normal practice'. In this practice, a Cabinet minister will take the initiative for a governmental decree. The King will not present proposals for government decrees to the ministers, but he can urge a minister to take an initiative.

In normal practice, the King has a limited advisory function in the government, it is more than just a strictly ceremonial role. In practice the King speaks with the Prime Minister every Monday afternoon and in addition, although less frequently, with the individual ministers.

The ensuing question is whether the King's limited advisory function is acceptable in a modern parliamentary democracy. The King lacks democratic legitimacy. He does not require the confidence of Parliament but has acquired his function through hereditary succession. The hereditary and non-responsible position of the King is difficult to reconcile with an assignment of effective governmental powers to the King.

The next question is whether it is still acceptable that the King does not limit himself in special circumstances to an advisory function. In constitutional theory, it has been argued in the past that the King may not ultimately withhold his signature from government decrees or laws. The Constitution and the related explanatory note do not establish whether it is the King or the ministers who must yield. Queen Juliana once defined her position towards Prime Minister Drees as follows: 'You may bear political responsibility, but when I sign a decree, then in a moral sense I also bear responsibility for the consequences of that decree' (Drees 1980: 150). This responsibility led Queen Juliana on occasion to refuse to sign. In 1951–52 she refused to sign royal decrees rejecting a pardon of four Nazi war criminals, who were responsible for the deportation of more than 100,000 Dutch Jews. The Queen had moral objections against the death penalty. In the end these Nazi war criminals were not executed but given lifetime sentences (Bovend'Eert 1985: 443). Queen Juliana on one occasion also objected to the appointment of a mayor in one of the larger cities in the Netherlands on moral grounds. Nevertheless, these interventions of Queen Juliana were, as far as we know, incidental and exceptional.

Viewed from the underlying constitutional principle of parliamentary democracy, the stance taken by Queen Juliana is hard to defend. It might be better in such a case, where the King harbours conscientious objections in special circumstances, that he renounces the throne (article 27 of the Constitution) – as King Baudouin temporarily did in Belgium in 1990, described in Chapter 3.6.

In recent years the proposition has also been defended in the literature that the King, based on the oath that he has taken, in which he swears allegiance to the Constitution, has a certain personal responsibility to see that the constitutional rules are adhered to (Hoeneveld 2018). It cannot be concluded from this oath of allegiance that the King has a special constitutional function to subject decisions of the government to some form of constitutional scrutiny. At the most, it may be imagined that the King would voice objections to Cabinet ministers in constitutional emergencies. In such a situation, not the oath of allegiance to the Constitution, but his power by virtue of articles 42 and 47 would be the basis for the refusal to cooperate with government decrees.

In the Netherlands, the King's role in the government is hardly disputed at this time. The populist Freedom Party (PVV) of Geert Wilders did introduce a proposal some years ago to revise the Constitution, with the intent of removing the King from any governmental role, but this proposal has not been debated in Parliament. The current King, Willem-Alexander, who has been on the throne since 2013, appears to manifest himself mainly as head of state, with a strong emphasis on his ceremonial function.

4.2B. POLITICAL FUNCTIONS OF THE DUTCH MONARCHY

Rudy Andeweg, Professor of Political Science, Leiden University

Monarch and Ministers

When, in the 1970s, Prime Minister Den Uyl referred to his Cabinet as the 'Den Uyl government', he was reportedly corrected by Queen Juliana, who argued that it was the 'Juliana government'. In practice, the monarch does not preside over, or even attend, the weekly Friday meetings of the Council of Ministers, and there is no Privy Council or other formal meeting in which monarch and ministers jointly take decisions. Instead, the Prime Minister meets the monarch informally each Monday. During the first half of the reign of Queen Juliana (1948–1980), this was a time consuming task for the Prime Minister, as the Queen lived in Soestdijk palace, at least an hour's drive from the centre of government in the Hague. Prime Minister De Jong (1967–1971) persuaded Queen Juliana that it was more practical for her to come to the Hague:

> The Queen lived at Soestdijk and it was always quite a journey to get there. In addition, I felt that she should be better informed about what went on in Cabinet. The contacts were not frequent enough. First I tried to telephone her on Saturday to tell her what had been decided in Cabinet. Then I suggested that she should come to the Hague on Monday. That way I could inform her on Monday morning, and she could invite ministers and junior ministers in the afternoon. She thought this an excellent idea. (interview by the author).

These weekly meetings are intensive and time consuming, and they are complemented by frequent telephone contacts. Prime Ministers vary considerably in their appreciation of their meetings with the monarch: 'The contacts with Queen Juliana were not very useful, a waste of time, because the Queen seemed rather muddle-headed. The conversation was all over the place' (interview with a Prime Minister by the author). Prime Minister Lubbers (1982–1994), on the other hand, has publicly said that he always looked forward to his Monday meetings with Queen Beatrix, who reigned from 1980 to 2013 (Breedveld 1992, 21). In comparison with her mother, the meetings with Queen Beatrix were more business-like and well organised.

Other ministers are invited by the monarch less frequently (two to four times a year). After the intervention by Prime Minister De Jong, such meetings with Queen Juliana would also take place at Huis ten Bosch palace near The Hague, but ministers who lived not far from Soestdijk would be invited there, usually on Saturday: 'I was on the Saturday shift because I lived near Soestdijk' (interview by the author); 'Boersma and I had to come to Soestdijk on a Saturday because we lived in the area – it was like a visit to Mother'. Queen Beatrix took up residence in The Hague, so all meetings with her took place there. Ministers interviewed estimated that the meetings with Queen Juliana lasted from one-and-a-half to over two hours, and with Queen Beatrix about an hour. Again, not all ministers enjoyed their visits; they have been described as 'an examination by the Queen' and 'a nuisance, time consuming'. 'When the director of the Queen's office telephoned, my secretary already knew that I would be abroad, or something'. 'I tried to minimise those meetings. You would be there for hours and she was a difficult conversation partner' (interviews by the author). But for most ministers the monarch still held an attractive mystique (as TeVelde 2006: 201, shows for the nineteenth century) and they readily made time to go to the Palace. Some ministers will also see the monarch on other occasions:

> As Foreign Secretary I would introduce new ambassadors when they came to offer their letters of credence to the Queen. After the ambassador had left she would ask me to stay behind for a cup of coffee or a glass of sherry (interview by the author).

Other than the wide ranging meetings with the Prime Minister, the meetings with the ministers tend to focus on the minister's own portfolio, with a few exceptions – 'it was mainly about my portfolio, but also about the position of women' (female minister, interview by the author) – or about issues in the news. Especially with Queen Juliana, the nature of the meeting would depend on the degree to which the Queen was interested in the policy area. Ministers of finance, for example, did little more than update the Queen on new developments: 'it lasted for at least two hours, but it was purely about providing information', 'it was more like giving her a lecture on macro-economics' (interviews by the author). But things were different when the Queen took an active interest: 'The Queen was very interested in my policy area (social work). The contacts were not just informative. The Queen had very articulate views and you had a hard time persuading her if you disagreed with her' (interview by the author). If the Queen took an active interest, she also kept herself informed through other channels, as another Minister of Social Work experienced: 'She was well informed about my policy area, because she was friendly with Labour Senator Martina Tjeenk Willink, who was a prominent figure in the field of social work, and who did not always agree with me' (interview by the author). With Queen Wilhelmina (who reigned from 1890 to 1948) or Queen Beatrix (1980 to 2013), there were fewer ministers who reported such differences across policy areas.

Occasionally, the monarch would use these meetings to press her own agenda, sometimes regardless of the minister's portfolio:

> I was in close contact with Queen Wilhelmina, probably because I had entered the government from the (wartime) resistance movement. She would often ask my opinion, although she did not always find my opinion agreeable. Afterwards I would always report to the Prime Minister that the Queen had received such and such information and had asked my opinion (interview by the author).

During one of my meetings when I was Minister of Economic Affairs, Queen Juliana suggested that I should organise a search for oil with divining rods. I politely ignored this, but at subsequent meetings she asked if the divining rods had already been used (interview by the author).

The Queen telephoned once to invite me for lunch on Saturday. When I arrived we were joined by a few professors who worked on concentration camp syndrome. The Queen presented a plan to create a centre for the treatment of that syndrome. I replied that this was a matter for the Minister of Public Health, not for the Minister of Defence, but she thought that I could initiate it in the Cabinet, and defend it in Cabinet meetings. I then contacted the Prime Minister and suggested to pass the matter on to ... the junior Minister of Public Health. [The junior minister] demanded to know why the Queen had contacted the Minister of Defence, but the Prime Minister replied that that was a question for the Queen. If she wanted to talk to the Minister of Defence, that was her choice. But [the junior minister] remained offended and I think this delayed the creation of that centre. When it was finally opened, I was no longer a minister; I was sitting on the second row at the opening ceremony. [The junior minister] was in the front row. When the Queen entered the room she saw me, shook my hand over [the junior minister's] head and said: 'we succeeded in the end' (interview by the author).

In 1996, Foreign Secretary Van Mierlo revealed that it was at Queen Beatrix's insistence that the Dutch government was opening an embassy in Amman. The friendship between the royal families of Jordan and the Netherlands was, reputedly, the cause of the Queen's intervention.

The monarch is reported to be particularly interested in government appointments: the vice-president of the Council of State, the King's Commissioner in the provinces, mayors in cities and towns that are relevant to the monarch, and, in the case of Queen Beatrix, ambassadors.

I would discuss appointments of Queen's Commissioner in the provinces with the Queen before tabling them in Cabinet. In those days the Queen would stay at the Commissioner's residence when visiting a province (interview by the author).

When I decided to deviate from the Queen's Commissioner's recommendation in making mayoral appointments, I would call the Commissioner to ask him to accept my choice. I could then include that in my nomination to the Queen. Otherwise you would definitely be summoned to the Palace. (interview by the author).

In 1996, the ambassador to South Africa was transferred to another posting at the request of Queen Beatrix (Van Wijnen 2000: 17–24).

Although more examples of royal interference could be provided, most of the ministers I interviewed insist that open attempts by the monarch to influence government policy are the exception rather than the rule, and that the monarch usually acts as a well-informed sparring partner rather than as a lobbyist.[1]

The Public Impartiality of the Monarch

Our knowledge of the political role of the monarch is based on anecdotal and indirect information. Publicly, the monarch is impartial and has no preferences. To avoid drawing

---

[1] There is no reason to assume that this has changed since King Willem-Alexander took the throne in 2013, but I have not interviewed any ministers from that period.

the monarchy into political conflict, those who are in contact with her are not supposed to make public what was discussed, and in particular, what the monarch said. This 'secret of the palace' even led some ministers not to discuss their meetings with the monarch amongst each other. The aforementioned incident of the Foreign Secretary revealing to journalists that the Queen influenced his decision to open a Dutch embassy in Jordan is exceptional; if the secret of the palace is violated by ministers, it is long after they have left office. However, in 1999 a member of Parliament resigned after being criticised for having breached the confidentiality of a conversation he had with the Queen.

Public impartiality is most difficult to maintain when the monarch makes public speeches. Here, a distinction is often made between speeches given as head of state on the one hand, for instance during state visits, or as a member of the government, in particular the speech from the throne at the annual opening of Parliament; and on the other hand more personal speeches such as the televised Christmas speech. All public speeches fall under ministerial responsibility, but in the case of speeches as head of state or government, the ministers, and in particular the Prime Minister or the Foreign Secretary, dominate the preparation of the texts. Prime Minister Lubbers' suggestion that he spent 'many a tenfold hour' discussing the text of a speech from the throne with Queen Beatrix (Van Baalen and Brouwer 2005: 17) may be an exaggeration. Drafts are discussed with the monarch and changes are made, but his or her influence is largely stylistic. That influence is slightly more substantive for speeches abroad. In her speech to the Knesset in 1995, for example, Queen Beatrix explicitly nuanced the image of the Netherlands as a country of courageous resistance fighters during the Nazi occupation, in line with other speeches she made in that period. This shocked many Dutchmen, but the speech was carefully prepared with civil servants and ministers (Kooistra and Koole 2000: 108). This was not the case in 1952, when Queen Juliana visited the United States and gave several speeches, including one to Congress. The Queen's pacifist leanings at the time (see below) caused great concern within the Cabinet, and the drafts of her speeches caused a major conflict between the ministers and the monarch (Daalder 2006: 40–51).

It is generally assumed that drafts of the more personal Christmas speeches are also discussed with the Prime Minister, but here the contents reflect the monarch's personal concerns. On one rare occasion, the coordination between Palace and Prime Minister appears to have failed. In 1988, the speech from the throne mentioned improvements in environmental protection, particularly in the quality of air and water. This was not only strongly challenged in Parliament, but in the Christmas speech just a few months later, Queen Beatrix painted a bleak picture of environmental pollution (Van Baalen and Brouwer 2005: 49), and this was widely interpreted as royal criticism of the ministers. However, the Christmas speeches became really controversial when they dealt with issues of multiculturalism and tolerance of minority beliefs. To some extent such messages of peace and goodwill are in the spirit of Christmas and for a long time they did not draw much attention. This changed when immigration and the integration of minorities became politically controversial in the early 1990s. Warnings against intolerance were now interpreted first as criticism of conservative-liberal leader Frits Bolkestein, and later of the populist leader Geert Wilders. This new political sensitivity also took the then Crown Princess Máxima by surprise in 2007 when, as a relatively recent arrival to the Netherlands, she publicly questioned the existence of an unequivocal Dutch identity: warm hospitality, but also offering a cup of tea with just one biscuit. So far, the Christmas speeches of King Willem-Alexander have avoided controversial topics.

(Prime) Ministers and Royal Crises

The previous sections dealt primarily with the (potential) influence of the monarch over the decisions of ministers, but occasionally the tables are turned. This is, for example, the case when the Prime Minister or the Cabinet as a whole are confronted with a crisis caused by the monarch or other members of the royal family. Two such crises have been particularly threatening to the monarchy: the Hofmans affair (1948–56), and the Lockheed affair (1960–76). In the first case, Queen Juliana, desperate to find a cure for the eye defects of her youngest daughter, came under the influence of a self-professed faith healer, Greet Hofmans. When the Queen surrounded herself with other followers of Hofmans, and when the latter's influence became not just religious and mystical, but also political and pacifist, this raised concerns within the Cabinet, for example about the Queen's public speeches during the state visit to the Unites States mentioned above. It also led to a crisis in the royal marriage, already affected by the prince consort's extramarital affairs. When Prince Bernhard confided in foreign journalists, the story eventually broke in the German weekly *Der Spiegel* portraying Prince Bernhard as being caught 'between Queen and Rasputin'. A committee of wise men was appointed to find a solution, and their report – which was only recently made public – criticised both the Queen for allowing Greet Hofmans to influence her in her role as monarch, and the Prince for talking to the media. It took yet another committee of wise men to persuade the Queen to follow the recommendation of the first committee and distance herself from Miss Hofmans and her followers. The Prime Minister at the time, Labour leader Willem Drees, is widely credited with handling the crisis prudently, publicly reassuring the people that there would be neither a divorce nor an abdication, but actually he seems to have been most reluctant to intervene in the personal domain (religion, marriage) of the monarch (Daalder 2006; Fasseur 2008). Both committees of wise men were not appointed by the government, for example, and Drees' reticence was strongly criticised in Cabinet.

This was very different in the second crisis. In 1976, the US Senate conducted an investigation into allegations of corruption by the Lockheed aircraft company. During the Senate hearings one of the examples given involved bribes totalling over a million dollars allegedly made to the Prince Consort since the 1960s, supposedly to help influence the government to buy Lockheed planes for the air force; Prince Bernhard was, among other military roles, inspector-general of the Dutch armed forces at the time. Within three days, Labour Prime Minister Den Uyl had set up an independent committee to investigate the allegations, and formed a Cabinet committee of five ministers (including the Foreign Secretary, the Home Secretary, the Minister of Finance and the Minister of Justice – the latter also being the Deputy Prime Minister, representing the Christian Democratic Parties in the governing coalition), to deal with the situation. In practice, the Cabinet committee was kept informed by the Prime Minister, but played no role in setting up the independent committee or forging a solution after the committee had found information implicating the Prince. There was one meeting of the Cabinet committee with the Queen, but some of the committee members objected to further meetings between five (male) ministers and the Queen:

> When we got home from that meeting I telephoned Den Uyl and told him that we should not continue like this. It was embarrassing. Even if she had been a man it would be embarrassing.

I advised him to do it [the discussions with the Queen] together with Van Agt [the Deputy Prime Minister and Minister of Justice] (interview by the author).

When the other ministers supported this suggestion, the Prime Minister reluctantly agreed and the Cabinet committee effectively ceased to function. The crucial issue was whether criminal proceedings should be initiated against the Prince. Apart from the question whether there was sufficient evidence to secure a conviction, it could well have endangered the monarchy: not only was it likely that Queen Juliana would then abdicate, but the Cabinet had also received information that Crown Princess Beatrix was reluctant to succeed her mother in these circumstances. Eventually the Cabinet accepted the proposal of the Prime Minister not to prosecute the Prince, but to make the report of the investigation public, to dismiss the Prince from all his military functions and to force him to end his membership of the supervisory boards of several companies, including KLM. In addition, the Cabinet made clear that the Prince should no longer wear a military uniform. Prime Minister Den Uyl was widely praised for his proactive but even handed approach to the crisis, although later it was suggested that he decided to keep secret last minute information that the Prince had also accepted bribes from another aircraft company, Northrop (Bleich 2008: 342–346; but see Van Merriënboer et al 2008: 178–79).

Royal weddings also necessitate involvement by ministers as marriages by the King and those in line of succession require permission by an Act of Parliament. Without such consent, the King is considered to have abdicated, and those in line of succession, and their children, forfeit that right. When the Cabinet is unwilling to initiate legislation approving a marriage, a public conflict between the royals and the Cabinet is avoided by the engaged couple announcing that they will not request permission. This happened, for example, when Princess Irene, younger sister of Crown Princess Beatrix, converted to Catholicism and, in 1964, announced her engagement to a Catholic Prince, Carlos Hugo de Bourbon-Parma, who at the time was a pretender to the Spanish throne. In an evening session at the palace, Prime Minister Marijnen, himself a Catholic, and three ministers representing the other Parties in the governing coalition, asked Carlos Hugo whether he was willing to give up his claims to the Spanish throne. He refused, and that same day Princess Irene announced that she would not seek consent for her marriage. On the advice of the government, no members of the royal family attended the wedding in Rome later that year. By focusing on the claims to the Spanish throne – the Netherlands had gained independence in an eighty-year war against Hapsburg Spain – the government avoided addressing the question whether a Catholic could ascend to the Dutch throne. Another sister, Princess Christina, also did not seek parliamentary approval when she became engaged to a Catholic in 1975.

Religion no longer played much of a role when Crown Prince Willem-Alexander married Máxima Zorreguieta, a Catholic woman from Argentina in 2001, although she had to agree that any children from the marriage would be raised in the Protestant faith. What did play a role, however, was that Máxima's father had been a junior minister in the Videla regime, raising questions about possible involvement in the 'disappearances' of opponents of the Argentinian junta. Labour Prime Minister Kok did not want to judge the daughter by her father's past, but also wanted to avoid undermining popular support for the monarchy. In close consultations with the Queen he secretly engaged a professor of Latin-American studies to investigate the role of Jorge Zorreguieta.

The report concluded that Máxima's father must have been aware of the 'disappearances' but that it was practically excluded that he had been involved in human rights violations himself. On that basis, the Cabinet decided that there were no objections to giving consent to the marriage, but that the presence of the father of the bride at the wedding or other state occasions would undermine popular support for the monarchy. Again, after consulting the Queen, the Prime Minister asked former Foreign Secretary Van der Stoel to travel to Argentina and persuade Jorge Zorreguieta to stay away voluntarily (Chorus 2013: 166–68).

It is ironic that in each of these episodes it fell to a Prime Minister of the Labour Party, the least monarchical of the mainstream political parties, to stave off a crisis in the monarchy. Rather than acting from personal royalist sympathies, they and most other Dutch politicians realise that any controversy about the monarchy is likely to overshadow any other political issues and sidetrack their own political agenda. As Prime Minister Den Uyl reportedly put it: 'The House of Orange is well loved by the population, and social democrats have other priorities than making an issue out of the monarchy' (Bleich 2008: 334).

4.3. DAY-TO-DAY POLITICAL FUNCTIONS OF THE MONARCH IN DENMARK

Helle Krunke, Professor of Law, University of Copenhagen

Introduction

The day-to-day political functions of the Danish monarch are closely related to his constitutional functions, especially with regard to the monarch's role in the Council of State and his royal assent to laws, which also constitute part of his day-to-day political life. Because of this overlap, what follows must be read in connection with Chapter 3.3 on constitutional functions.

The Non-Political Principle

Article 13 of the Danish Constitution states that the King is not answerable for his actions and that the ministers are responsible for the conduct of government. Article 13 is said to have the following effect: if the King wishes to make a political statement, which is not a legal act – a legal act must be countersigned by a minister (article 14, part 3) – but must be seen as part of the governing of the state, he must beforehand have the consent of a minister (see Andersen 1954: 172; Sørensen 1973: 65; Germer 1995: 39, and Zahle (ed) 2006: 153). It has also been expressed in the following way: if the King's statements might have political effect, consent from a minister is required (Germer 1995: 39). This includes actions and not just verbal statements. For his private actions the King needs no consent (see Andersen 1954: 192–93; Sørensen 1973: 65; Germer 1995: 39, and Zahle (ed) 2006: 153). However, one might suggest that in reality, if the monarch expresses political views related to his private actions, people might doubt the neutrality of his actions as part of governing the state.[2]

Article 13 is normally said to have as an indirect effect that the King's competence is only formal (see Sørensen 1973: 63–64). In parts of the constitutional literature, this is presented as an obligation for the King to act according to the wishes of the ministers (see Andersen 1954: 97). It is thus a common view in contemporary constitutional theory that the King has no real *influence* in Danish politics any more, and that the few duties and competences left for the King are only of a symbolic nature.

In practice, the monarch and the royal family have in some cases expressed political views. However, the present Queen is normally very careful about not expressing political statements in public. On the home page of the royal court, it is said that 'HM The Queen takes no part in politics and does not express any political opinions'.

The Danish version proclaims that the Queen takes no part in 'party politics'. At first glance, one might think there is a slight difference between party politics and politics, but it does not seem to be a tenable distinction. Ultimately, all political subjects are also party political subjects. In her new year's speech in 1984, the Queen urged the Danes to be more tolerant towards asylum seekers, refugees, and immigrants. This created a stir. In the book *Margrethe*, the Queen explains that she was surprised by this reaction. Today, she probably would not express such a view, though, because integration is clearly regarded as a political issue. Still, integration was already a political issue in 1984. At that time, integration was one of the most important questions for Fremskridtspartiet, a right-wing Party in Parliament. Nevertheless, the Queen touches upon a very important point: it is extremely difficult to determine which subjects are 'politics' and which are not, time and norms change and the transition is often vague.

Many questions concerning humanitarian issues that were once considered to be non-political issues are today considered political questions. This makes it difficult for the royal family because by tradition, they support and visit exposed and vulnerable groups both in Denmark and abroad and frequently are engaged in charitable activities.[3] Furthermore, involvement in art and culture in general can have political repercussions. The Danish Queen is very interested in cultural matters.[4] Cultural matters might not at first glance seem like a politically controversial subject. Yet, politics in this field has been a very important political subject area for the former Danish Prime Minister, Anders Fogh Rasmussen and his government. In an interview from 2008, he mentioned immigration politics and policy in the field of culture as, in his opinion, important political fields (Kastrup 2008). According to Anders Fogh Rasmussen, his government has, for

[2] Furthermore, as we shall see in Chapter 9, the present legitimisation of the monarchy among other things builds on its neutrality, which makes it extremely important for the Monarch to appear non-political.

[3] The present Queen's father King Frederik IX often underlined that it was part of being Danish to make sure that the weaker groups in Danish society shared in technical and material developments, see Buttenschøn and Ries (2003: 61). The present Danish Crown Prince and the Crown Princess have visited ghettos with many residents with different ethnic backgrounds many times, see also Bjørn (2001: 260–61). Moreover, it is not just the royal family but also the Danish national church which operates in a difficult field. Some vicars in their Christmas sermons have expressed concern with the conditions of asylum seekers in Denmark. This caused a political reaction from several prominent politicians.

[4] The Queen is a painter herself and her interests include literature (she has translated and illustrated several books), ballet (she has designed costumes and scenography for several ballets) and textiles (she has designed robes for the church).

instance, eliminated cultural relativism by introducing canons in almost every cultural field (literature, music, and art, for instance). The Crown Prince's involvement in the Olympic Committee is also interesting. Sports are considered part of cultural policy and with the Olympic Games taking place in China in 2008, foreign policy was also involved because of the question of China's policy in the field of human rights. A good example of the Danish royal family participating in an uncontroversial area is the Crown Princess's involvement in the attempt to eliminate bullying in Danish schools.

Thus, the potential arena for the royal house to participate in is being reduced. Areas like humanitarian issues, arts, and sports – which were formerly considered quite neutral subjects – are now controversial political subjects. This does not leave much room for the royal family to become involved, and show that they are useful to the community. As a result, it seems to have become increasingly difficult for the royal family to interact with Danish society. The political vs non-political distinction is without doubt a very difficult matter to handle for the royal house, and the distinction is getting increasingly burdensome to determine. That the royal family is in an almost impossible situation is illustrated by the logical argument that when the royal family chooses which subject areas are political and which are not, this in itself is a political statement.

This analysis of the principle of non-political behaviour in the Danish monarchy reveals the difficulties of handling the principle in practice. Thus, even though the non-political behaviour principle might at first glance seem like the perfect bridge builder between monarchy as a state form and a modern democracy, the content and application of the principle are in fact filled with grey areas. As a general rule, the Queen tries to be non-political both in her formal actions, as part of government, and in her private actions. Regardless, room for informal influence in practice still seems to exist.

Some years ago, an interesting statement could be found on the home page of the Danish Crown Prince: 'The Danish Crown Prince has been thoroughly educated in political science and military disciplines because the royal house still wants the monarch to be able to see and assess the political challenges of his country'. The statement, which has now been removed from the home page, seems to show that the royal house takes its constitutional duties seriously and that their members do not want to be mere puppets. Why is it significant that the Crown Prince is able to see and assess political challenges for Denmark if the royal house sees its constitutional role as entirely formal? One answer could be that the monarch is still a player on the constitutional scene. This provides the monarch with an opportunity to advise the government and influence political actions in Denmark. In a state of emergency, it is of great importance to be an actor on the political scene. The highly respected constitutional theorist Max Sørensen (1954: 64) declared that if a government tried to launch a coup d'état, the King might actually play a role as the guardian of the Constitution. This happened in Spain in 1981 (see Chapter 3.9). In the new version of the home page of the Crown Prince it is briefly mentioned that he has a Master's degree in Political Science. However, the main emphasis is put on his military education.

The Council of State

The body of ministers form the Council of State (article 17). The Council of State is presided over by the monarch (article 17, part 1). The Secretariat of the Royal Cabinet and the Ministry of State arrange the meetings, and the Secretariat of the Royal Cabinet calls the meetings. According to article 17, part 2, all bills and important government measures shall be discussed in the Council of State. The Constitution does not define what is meant by 'important government measures'. There exists no clear principle on which government decisions should be discussed in the Council. Bills adopted by Parliament (which need royal assent) and parliamentary decisions are put before the Council.[5] Under normal circumstances, only very few decisions apart from legislation come before the Council (see Zahle (ed) 2006: 173). Normally, no negotiation takes place. A minister introduces a bill, and the King signs it (Zahle (ed) 2006: 173).[6] According to a constitutional convention, the King can sign bills outside the Council given subsequent confirmation in the Council. A bill may be valid, even if it is not put before the Council.[7]

The fact is that the Council of State is no longer an important political forum (Zahle 2001: 211, and Germer 1995: 25, 74, note 32). Thus, the process in the Council of State is purely formal and has no real constitutional significance (Zahle (ed) 2006: 172). The average number of meetings in the Council is 10 each year (Zahle (ed) 2006: 173). Even so, the Queen drew much attention to her role in the Council of State during her recent 40 years anniversary as monarch. A few more meetings than normal were held in the Council in order for the Queen to be able to celebrate the number of her Council of State meetings reaching 500 in combination with her anniversary. Political discussion on whether the Council of State should be abolished arose. Some political parties found it unnecessary to have the meetings in the Council. Today, the important political decisions are discussed in the so-called minister-meetings.[8] However, the former Prime Minister Helle Thorning-Schmidt from Socialdemokratiet made the following statement:

> The Council of State is here to stay. It is an institution which connects the current modern democracy with past times, and in this way I think it is a good institution in the relationship between Parliament and the Royal House (Politiken 2012).

This is an interesting statement since the government, of which she was the Prime Minister, had expressed interest in a revision of the Constitution and since another political Party in that government, SocialistiskFolkeparti, is critical of the monarchy.

On the other hand, Queen Margrethe is much more active in her role as head of state than her father, King Frederik IX. Former Prime Minister Anker Jørgensen has said that the Queen takes a much more active part in the Council of State and in working with the government than her father (Jørgensen 1989: 196).[9] Apparently, she is very interested and

[5] According to Article 22 of the Constitution, a bill passed by Parliament shall become law if it receives the royal assent not later than thirty days after it was finally passed. Royal assent is given by the King's signature on the bill accompanied by the signature of a minister, article 14. See also Chapter 3.3. On article 22 in the Danish Constitution, see Blume (1989).

[6] There exists an instruction in the Ministry of State on meetings in the Council of State (*Vejledningomek-speditionafstatsrådssager*, 14 January 2002), and the instruction on quality in legislation has a few paragraphs on the Council of State (*Vejledning om lovkvalitet*, 3 June 2005, paragraph 5.9 and 5.10).

[7] In 2004–05, approximately 40 per cent of the governmental bills were introduced in Parliament without prior consideration in the Council of State; see Zahle (ed.) (2006:173).

[8] Despite the great importance of these meetings they are not regulated in the Constitution.

[9] See also Krag (1973: 115): 'The King is a nice man, well-liked and well-meaning, without political thoughts and without desire to spend more of his and our time than necessary. We have meetings in the Council of State, which last less than 20 minutes … A new Queen could be more difficult to cooperate with. Furthermore, she has political knowledge which is not necessarily an advantage'.

often asks the Prime Minister to elaborate on subjects, she comments on matters, and has her own opinions (Bjørn 2001: 258–59).

Informal Meetings with the Prime Minister and the Minister of Foreign Affairs

The Prime Minister and the Minister of Foreign Affairs keep the King updated on the political situation (see Larsen et al 2010: 187).[10] Since there are no minutes of these meetings, it seems possible for the monarch to comment on the political situation (Bjørn 2001: 93–94). Even though the monarch does not have much formal competence left there is still some room for influence (Sørensen 1973: 64). The former Danish Prime Minister Poul Schlüter stated that he valued the meetings with the Queen and that she had often given him good advice – she did not tell him what to do, but rather what she would do (Andersen 2011: 232). The weekly meetings probably form the most important direct informal competence for the monarch. They have no direct legal basis in the Constitution, but must probably be seen as part of the monarch's role as head of state.

Other Forms of Influence and Soft Power

The Queen visits foreign countries and she hosts foreign heads of state and heads of government. The Queen does not formally exercise foreign policy in these situations. Denmark benefits from the Queen representing Denmark, but these visits also strengthen the Queen's position as a player on the international scene. This gives her informal influence both internationally and internally in Denmark.

Greenland is part of the Danish realm, but it has gradually gained more and more self-determination. The Queen and her family regularly visit Greenland, where she is quite popular. Her close relationship with Greenland has probably had an impact on the relationship between Denmark and Greenland, influencing the speed of the process of self-determination. Though the Queen's interest in Greenland's culture and nature seems to be real, she has definitely played an important role for the political relations between Denmark and Greenland (Andersen 2011: 413–26). This strengthens the Queen's political importance in Denmark.

The Queen can bestow royal orders, medals, and titles. When a ministry recommends a person for an order, the Queen always follows this recommendation,[11] but she makes the final decision in every case (Larsen et al 2010: 177). This competence might not seem very important, but it has quite a strong symbolic importance and provides the Queen with informal power since it is still attractive for high ranking civil servants, judges, and others to receive orders. When the Queen has decorated foreign heads of state with orders, it has occasionally given rise to difficult situations. An example of this was when

---

[10] These meetings have no legal basis in the Constitution or in normal legislation.
[11] See statement from the Head of the Secretariat of the Royal Cabinet, in Fogt and Karker (2009).

the Danish Queen visited Bahrain in February 2011. She decorated King Khalifa with one of Denmark's most prestigious orders, and shortly after her visit a demonstration for democratic reforms in Bahrain was brutally handled by the police. This caused a public discussion on whether the Queen's award of medals was part of Denmark's foreign policy or whether it was part of the Queen's private actions. The conclusion was that the latter is the case.[12] However, when it comes to foreign policy, it seems quite difficult in practice to uphold such a distinction. The Queen is head of state and when she gives an order to another head of state or a Prime Minister, it seems unlikely that the receiver is always aware of the distinction and that they see it as a cultural exchange with the Queen rather than an action of the Danish state.

Another soft power with a strong symbolic effect is the fact that the Queen's picture is on Danish coins. This became clear when the Danes voted 'no' to European monetary union among other things because they feared that the Queen's picture would no longer be on the coins.

Finally, it is a tradition in Denmark that the King speaks to the Danish nation on New Year's Eve. Christian X's and Frederik IX's speeches concerned the events of the past year, the upcoming events of the new year and offered thanks to everybody who made a special effort in Danish society (Buttenschøn and Ries 2003: 69; Bjørn 2001: 259 ff).[13] Queen Margrethe II attaches a great deal of importance to her New Year speeches and they are a good example of the Queen's informal power, since they carry a lot of weight among the Danish people.[14] The content of the speeches are the Prime Minister's responsibility (article 13). Therefore, the Queen's speeches must be approved by the Prime Minister. A first draft – which the Queen then works on – is written by government officials. The Queen is known to make many alterations and give the speeches a very personal touch.

Conclusion

In an interview with the Queen in a Danish newspaper in 2010, the Queen stated: 'Even though one is not a co-player in political life – and one is not – I still believe that [the monarchy] plays a role, that one is an active participant in the country's constitutional life' (Bistrup 2010).

When reading this (and other statements) it is quite clear that the Queen takes her constitutional duties and competences very seriously and that she attaches substance and importance to the constitutional rules/conventions in which she plays a part. When the Queen insists on keeping her formal competences one must remember that if she loses those, then she may also lose important informal means of influence.

---

[12] See Letter from the Ombudsman to journalist David Tarp, 11 January 2012 and letter from the Ministry of Foreign Affairs to David Tarp, 1 March 2012.

[13] Since 1958 the new year's speeches have been televised live (and transmitted on the radio) from the King's/Queen's study at the Castle Amalienborg.

[14] The New Year speeches have no legal basis.

4.4. DAY-TO-DAY POLITICAL FUNCTIONS OF THE MONARCHY IN THE UK

Professor Robert Hazell, The Constitution Unit, University College London

This contribution describes the day-to-day political functions of the monarchy in Britain: working with the Prime Minister, other ministers, and senior officers of state; holding meetings of the Privy Council; giving audiences to incoming and outgoing ambassadors; and appointing senior officials.

Weekly Meetings with the Prime Minister

The Queen is kept informed of the business of government through daily boxes of papers to read, and to sign. She receives all the Cabinet papers and minutes, diplomatic telegrams and other government papers, especially about appointments. In addition, she hosts frequent lunches and dinners for politicians, and people from every corner of public life, which gives her a good understanding of current thinking, and the personalities involved. The 'golden triangle' of the Cabinet Secretary and the Private Secretaries in the Palace and No 10 are also in regular contact to ensure there is no grinding of gears between the monarch and the government. They seek to anticipate potential difficulties and deal with them before they get out of hand or cause reputational damage. These can range from major items like the planning of state visits or royal Jubilees to minor issues like trouble in one of the royal households.

When Parliament is sitting, the Queen has a weekly audience with the Prime Minister, held on Wednesday evenings, the day after the weekly meeting of Cabinet on Tuesday. The Private Secretaries in 10 Downing Street and the Palace liaise beforehand about the matters to be discussed, and the Number 10 Private Secretary accompanies the Prime Minister and talks to the Queen's Private Secretary during the audience. These are the occasions when the monarch can exercise Bagehot's famous trio of rights: the right to be consulted, to encourage and to warn (Bagehot 1867). No notes are taken and no record is published, so it is impossible to judge what influence the monarch has on government policy. Prime Ministers have always been discreet, saying only that they value the opportunity to talk things through with someone of such long experience. The nearest we can get to guessing what takes place is through drama, in Peter Morgan's play *The Audience* (2013), and his subsequent television series *The Crown* (2016).

The Queen also has audiences with senior officials from the military, the diplomatic and security services; and the judiciary, with the top 150 judges all being appointed personally by the Queen. She also has audiences with officials from other countries, in particular the 15 Commonwealth countries where she is also head of state (the Realms). And she receives in an audience newly appointed ambassadors and High Commissioners, and their families: with over 170 foreign missions in London, this is a frequent part of her weekly routine.

To give a sense of the Queen's official business, here is an analysis of her engagements for the month of November 2018, extracted from the Court Circular. The Queen had official engagements on 20 days that month. She met the President of Germany (who came for the Remembrance Day ceremony at the Cenotaph), and the King of Norway. She had three audiences with the Prime Minister. There were two meetings of the Privy

Council, at which five new members were sworn in, and two new Secretaries of State were appointed and received their seals of office. The Queen received 10 new ambassadors from foreign countries, and four British ambassadors before they went overseas; as well as the UK's new Permanent Representative to the EU, and to the UN. She also received the Governor-General of Australia, and of the Solomon Islands, and the Lieutenant-Governor of Newfoundland. There were five Investitures: two held by the Queen, one by the Prince of Wales, two by the Duke of Cambridge. And the Queen received a lot of military personnel: the new Chief of the General Staff, the new Chief of the Defence Staff, and 12 officers from different regiments of which she is Colonel-in-Chief.

In the same month the Prince of Wales went on a state visit to The Gambia, Ghana and Nigeria. This included visits to the British High Commission in each country, the British Council, Commonwealth war graves, and UK Border Force offices at Accra airport. When back in London, Prince Charles also met the President of Germany, and received visits from the Governor-General of Antigua, the President of Cuba and former President of Kosovo. He ended the month with a visit to a local police station, at King's Lynn.

State Opening of Parliament

Another regular fixture in the Queen's calendar is the State Opening of Parliament, when she delivers the Queen's speech setting out the government's legislative programme for the next annual session. The suggestion has been made that the Prime Minister should deliver the speech every year, since it is the government's legislative programme, and that the Queen should be involved only at the beginning of a new Parliament (Fabian Society 2003: 59). But the Queen continues to deliver the annual speech in the House of Lords, with peers arrayed in their full robes, and the Commons assembled at the bar of the House. In October 2019 there was criticism that the Queen's speech was a sham, since it was clear that the Prime Minister wanted an early election, not a new session of Parliament, and the Queen was being used to deliver a Conservative party broadcast (Hazell, 2019).

Meetings of the Privy Council

The Privy Council is the equivalent of the Council of State in other countries. It normally meets once a month, in Buckingham Palace. Its main business is to approve Orders in Council, a form of delegated legislation. The business is purely formal; the Orders will have been agreed beforehand by ministers, in consultation with any outside bodies as necessary. The Lord President of the Council (a government minister) reads out the title of each Order in Council, and the Queen says 'Approved'. Usually only three or four ministers attend; the meetings are brief; the Queen and the members remain standing. The dissolution, summoning and prorogation of parliament have been effected by royal proclamations in Council; as are the declaration of war, and its termination. Dissolution is now regulated by the Fixed Term Parliaments Act 2011. Prorogation has not normally caused controversy, but the five week prorogation advised by Prime Minister Boris Johnson in August 2019 was declared unlawful in *R (Miller) v the Prime Minister* [2019] UKSC 41, and the prorogation order to be null and void.

Informal Influence

It is hard to judge how much influence the Queen has on the business of government. Officials report that she is assiduous in reading all her government papers, and does not hesitate to query declining standards of record keeping, or submissions which are inadequate. So for the parts of Whitehall which have dealings with the Palace, from the planning of state visits, to recommendations for senior public or church appointments, to awards for gallantry or the grant of royal pardons, she helps to keep government up to the mark. As for politicians, successive Prime Ministers have commented on the value of their weekly audiences, and her unrivalled experience thanks to her very long reign. Being Prime Minister can be lonely as well as demanding, with Cabinet colleagues constantly jostling for position; it must be a relief to be able to confide in someone who is not a political rival. Typical are these reflections in their memoirs from Ted Heath, and Jim Callaghan:

> I looked forward to these for a variety of reasons. It was always a relief to be able to discuss everything with someone, knowing full well that there was not the slightest danger of any information leaking. I could confide in Her Majesty absolutely, not only about political matters, but also about the personal affairs of those involved, both at home and abroad (Heath 1998: 317).

> [There was] no doubt of the keenness with which she followed Commonwealth affairs and of her genuine concern for its well-being. Her very perceptive understanding comes not only from her many years spent reading Foreign Office documents, but also from numerous meetings with successive Commonwealth leaders and her regular overseas tours. These have given her a knowledge of Commonwealth politicians and politics unequalled by any member of the Diplomatic Service or any British politician (Callaghan 2006: 380).

But the Queen has been a model of political neutrality, and if she has had political influence, her ministers are too discreet to admit it. The main issue which we know has occasionally put her at odds with her ministers has been her devotion to the Commonwealth. This caused frequent tensions with Margaret Thatcher (Pimlott 1996: 466 ff, 503 ff), and before that with Ted Heath. After a bruising experience at his first Commonwealth Heads of Government (CHOGM) meeting in Singapore in 1971, Heath vowed not to attend again; but he was thwarted by nimble footwork by the Commonwealth Secretariat and the Palace, who persuaded the Canadian Prime Minister Pierre Trudeau to host the next CHOGM, and to invite the Queen to make a state visit. The invitation was accepted without reference to Downing Street: 'the Prime Minister was perturbed by the Queen's decision to accept, as The Queen of Canada' (Foreign Office memo quoted in Murphy 2013: 131). It is inevitable that occasionally the Queen's role as head of the Commonwealth, and head of state of 15 countries in the Commonwealth, will conflict with her duties as Queen of the United Kingdom: especially since her passionate interest in the Commonwealth has rarely been shared by her British ministers.

4.5. POLITICAL FUNCTIONS OF THE MONARCHY IN NORWAY

Eivind Smith, Professor of Public Law, University of Oslo

Chapter 3.7 presents the constitutional functions of the Norwegian monarchy in some detail. In order to facilitate the proper understanding of the system, that chapter pays particular attention to certain institutional aspects, namely the fact that it is for the King-in-Council, not for the King acting alone, to take any decision issued by 'the King' as head of state and of the executive (Smith 2017). Since a constitutional amendment adopted in 1911, the countersignature of the Prime Minister is not only required as a means for ensuring orderly decision making, but a condition for 'royal resolutions' to obtain legal effect. By consequence, the monarch alone never conducts formal decision making on behalf of the state. In other words, the several articles of the Constitution that vest both the executive power in general and a number of more specified powers in the King must be read in conjunction with articles 27 to 31 on the Council as the decisive state body. Within that supreme organ of the executive, the monarch's assent is required for any decision to be achieved, but insufficient if the countersignature is not provided.

During the 90 years' personal union between Sweden and Norway (November 1814 to June 1905), a number of conflicts between the Norwegian political institutions and the King of Norway unfolded. As King from 1818 to 1844, Karl III Johan (in Sweden: Karl XIV Johan), the former Marshal of France, eagerly vetoed legislation adopted by the Norwegian Parliament; in fact, this happened in 19 per cent of the bills adopted by Parliament between 1815 and 1837 (Jansen 1921). The last King of the Bernadotte dynasty (Oscar II, King of Norway 1872–1905) adopted a more modest attitude (for instance, he vetoed only 2 per cent of the bills between 1884 and 1905), and experienced a number of political defeats by the Parliament (*Stortinget*). His final legislative veto (1905) on a bill establishing separate consular services for Norway, replacing the existing services common to the two kingdoms, triggered the unilateral declaration that his reign had come to an end.

Since the arrival of King Oscar's successor in November 1905, none of the three kings have utilised their personal veto on legislation adopted by Parliament. This has not been accidental; we should understand the new equilibrium as the result of deliberate political efforts arising from three principal considerations. Firstly, although the monarchy has enjoyed strong popular support, leading politicians have regarded the choice to maintain a monarchical form of government as the result of political calculation in a rather unfriendly international environment dominated by monarchies rather than as one of conviction (similar to the origins of the Belgian monarchy: see Chapter 3.6). Admittedly, of course, many of the close to 80 per cent of the electorate who voted in favour of the new King in the referendum organised in November 1905 probably thought otherwise (Bjørklund 2005). Secondly, the initial collaboration between the government and the new King included instruction on how to behave as head of the modern Kingdom of Norway (Bomann-Larsen 2006). Third, the unhappy experiences during the last years of King Oscar's reign, a monarch that some would say behaved like a member of the Conservative Party (and – regarding Norway – as King of Sweden rather than of Norway), gave rise to desires to avoid similar experiences in the future.

Behind all three considerations, however, we can easily discern the growth of modern ideas about the proper role of an unelected monarch within the framework of an increasingly democratic system of government. In any case, King Haakon ended up by systematically demonstrating a strong commitment to the Constitution that he had sworn to maintain.

Since the constitutional amendment of 1911, imposing the monarch's personal veto on legislation adopted by Parliament without the Prime Minister's countersignature has, in fact, been formally impossible. The same goes for any other decision taken by the King-in-Council. Moreover, the three successive monarchs have gradually become less and less involved in the Council's deliberations. It is thus safe to affirm that, in reality, it is the Council's political element – the 'King's advisers' that we normally call 'the government' – that determines the substance of the decisions to be taken.

Outside this institutional framework, the monarch conducts a number of activities with obvious political connotations. As they meet at least once a week (except during holiday seasons) at the Council meetings, the number and frequency of formal meetings between the monarch and the Prime Minister, and between him and the Minister of Foreign Affairs, seems to be considerably lower than in some other countries. By contrast, the secretary general of the foreign ministry and the top military commanders appear in the Palace at regular intervals. The King also receives, for example, high-ranking foreign visitors and heads of state, to whom he offers his 'high protection'; prize-winning laureates; and those who have been bestowed with royal decorations.

Sometimes, both the list of visitors and the choice of places to visit reflect personal choices. A Palace reception followed by a seminar with religious leaders of all major faiths offers just one example of the first kind; while the royal couple's several visits to parts of Oslo with high numbers of immigrants during the Breivik trial (2011) illustrate the second. Moreover, personal influence of a more remote political kind flows, for example, from the royal family's speeches, presence at different kinds of public ceremonies, scenes of disaster and public mourning and the systematic travelling across the country of its members. The family's active involvement in the aftermath of the tragic killing of 77 people in July 2011, including landmark speeches by the King and the Crown Prince, is one powerful example. These activities are clearly not – and indeed could not be – devoid of any political connotations (on speeches, see also Chapter 7).

A number of examples where both King Olav and King Harald have been the first to pay public tribute to groups that, according to today's prevailing opinion, have been underestimated or even completely disregarded by the political authorities, deserve a particular mention. One telling example is a speech given by the latter during his very first years as King (1992) in North-Eastern Norway (Kiberg), which recognised the anti-Nazi actions and devotion of the Norwegian 'partisans' during the German occupation, actions which had been conducted in collaboration with Soviet authorities and therefore regarded with high suspicion during the cold war (Det Norske Kongehus Website: HM The King's Speech at the Partisan Building in Kiberg, August 3, 1992).

On the other hand, the choice of where to pay formal state visits or which heads of state to receive in Norway primarily belongs to the government or are, at least, subject to its informal consent. The royal couple's state visit to China in the autumn of 2018, symbolising the end of the Chinese diplomatic boycott of Norway in the aftermath of the 2010 Nobel Peace Prize to a Chinese dissident, provides a most eloquent recent example.

The formation of new governments are crucial moments in the life of any polity. As noted in Chapter 3.7, the King-in-Council appoints and dismisses both individual ministers and the entire government. Since the constitutional amendment of 1911, this has meant that no dismissal or appointment may take place without the consent of the politically responsible element in the Council; the government expresses itself by way of the Prime Minister's countersignature. Under ordinary circumstances, this effectively eliminates any kind of personal involvement by the monarch once the political processes have identified the identity, party affiliation and departmental responsibilities of new ministers. This implies, inter alia, that the outgoing government is responsible for appointing the next one, and for the dismissal of itself with effect from the moment the first meeting between the King and his new Council is scheduled.

The monarch's role during the search for the next Prime Minister and the formation of the new government is not clear-cut. The Constitution gives no explicit answer to this question. Since 1905, however, the practice is that the monarch consults, first, with the outgoing Prime Minister, next, with the political leader suggested to him by the outgoing Prime Minister and, if needed, with all the leaders of the political parties. Should the political situation still be unclear, it has even happened that the King has called upon the Speaker of the Parliament and asked him or her to conduct more thorough discussions.

Ordinarily in Norwegian politics, the identity of the new Prime Minister is obvious enough that the King can charge him or her with the appointment of the new government. On occasion, however, the King has been more intrusive. This happened most famously in 1928, when the still 'revolutionary' Labour Party came out of the general election as the biggest of the parties represented in Parliament, but with no majority to govern. At the same time, the centre-right 'bourgeois' political parties commanding the majority were unable to provide a more credible basis for forming the new government. In that situation, King Haakon – who, on one occasion, had declared himself as King even of the communists – insisted on appointing a Labour government.

Within a couple of weeks, Parliament passed a vote of no confidence and the Prime Minister applied for the Labour government's dismissal. In this sense, the experiment earned little immediate success. However, this example of direct royal involvement in the political life of the nation has since been generally regarded as an important contribution to the promotion of the Labour movement within Parliament, and thereby reducing any possible temptation to establish a 'proletarian dictatorship' that may have existed in the years following the establishment of the Soviet Union.

By far the most important example of the present dynasty's direct involvement in the strictly political sphere is provided by King Haakon's role during the German invasion in April-June 1940 and throughout the entire duration of World War II. There is no need, here, to tell the full story of the role of King Haakon and the royal family in Norway, London and the USA, but it is worthwhile recalling that it contributed substantially to strengthening the institution's legitimacy in post-war Norway (Bomann-Larsen 2011).

The single most important occurence ought also to be recounted: on 9 April 1940, the royal family, the government and members of Parliament managed to flee northwards from Oslo before the arrival of the German troops. The next day, the German ambassador, received on the ambassador's demand by the King in a small town North-East of Oslo, urged him to surrender and to appoint Vidkun Quisling, the leader of a Nazi-oriented micro-party, as the new Prime Minister. The King refused. At the same time, he declared that he – as a constitutional king – would not stand in the way should the government nevertheless accept the German ultimatum in order to avoid the destruction likely to follow. In that case, however, he would have no other option than to abdicate. This defiant attitude contributed substantially to the evaporation of any reservations on behalf of the government, now acting on behalf of the Parliament that had been abrogated – in principle temporarily – due to the ongoing invasion.

It would be perfectly legitimate to regard this historically decisive episode as an example of the monarch's use of a kind of deep reserve power in cases of crisis. In fact, discussions about whether to maintain a monarchical form of government regularly call upon this example as an argument in favour of monarchy: these discussions frequently refer to 'the King's No'. It seems less likely that a similar deep reserve power could credibly be exercised by a monarch who has lost all active constitutional functions (as in Sweden, discussed below).

4.6. POLITICAL FUNCTIONS OF THE MONARCHY IN SWEDEN

Henrik Wenander, Professor of Public Law, Lund University

The King and the Riksdag

The overarching principle of the 1974 Instrument of Government is that the King shall have no formal power. But he is not completely written out of the script. The King opens the Riksdag's yearly session on the request of the Speaker (chapter 3 article 6 of the 2014 *Riksdagsordning*, the Riksdag Act). The ceremony takes place in the Chamber of the Riksdagbuilding, and not – as under the old Constitution – in the Royal Palace (art 40 of the 1866 Riksdag Act). As Åse (2009: 11) has noted, the choice of venue symbolically indicates the changed constitutional roles.

The King is also the chairman of *Utrikesnämnden* (The Advisory Council on Foreign Affairs), a permanent constitutional body for discussions on foreign policy between the government and the opposition in the Riksdag (Nergelius 2015: 41). The Advisory Council does not make any formal decisions. The King may, however, decide on a duty of unconditional confidentiality for the Council's deliberations (chapter 10 article 11 and 12 of the 1974 Instrument of Government). Holmberg et al (2012: 510 ff) refer to this chairmanship as probably the most important political task of the King.

The King and the Government

Under the 1974 Instrument of Government, the King and the government constitute two separate constitutional bodies. The fundamental law requires that the Prime Minister keep the King informed of the affairs of the realm. The King, in turn, shall consult the Prime Minister before travelling abroad. The reason is that the King needs to be informed of current domestic and international developments in order to carry out his duties, especially when representing Sweden internationally. This is linked to the possibility of the government convening in *konselj* (Council of State) under the chairmanship of the King (chapter 5 article 3 of the 1974 Instrument of Government). This remnant of the old Council of State is a complement to the regular weekly government meetings (regulated in chapter 7 article 3), where the King does not take part. Such Council of State meetings generally take place around three times a year (Holmberg et al 2012: 277 ff).

Information can also be conveyed in other ways between the Prime Minister or the government offices and the King (Bull and Sterzel 2015: 144).

The King's public statements and other activities must not be in conflict with the government's policy. This could imply a certain legal scope for the Prime Minister to give instructions to the King (SOU 1972:15, 139). As Sterzel (2009: 157) notes, such directives would, however, not be legally binding. It is for the King to decide on what course to take.

Controversies have occasionally arisen concerning the King's international role. In 2004, the King made positive remarks on the political system of the Sultanate of Brunei after a state visit there. The parliamentary Committee on the Constitution examined the responsibility of the Prime Minister to advise the King before state visits. It concluded that the practices in the government offices for preparing state visits needed to be improved (Bet. 2004/05:KU20, 88 ff).

Under the current Constitution, the King does not have any formal decision making power over the military, which is organised under the government. Still, the King is considered the foremost representative of the Swedish defence forces. He is therefore bestowed with the highest military titles (Prop. 1973:90, 174; Strömberg 2001–02: 723).

Conclusions

The intention of the 1974 Instrument of Government was to remove all political functions of the monarch, and to leave the King with a purely symbolic and ceremonial role. But in practice the King has retained a limited political role. He still chairs meetings of the Council of State, around three times a year; and his role as the chairman of the Advisory Council on Foreign Affairs, including decisions on confidentiality, may be seen as the most far reaching example of 'hard' powers of the King. Still, this is only an advisory board, without formal decision making competence.

Equally important are the more 'soft' constitutional powers of the King, which flow from his continuing role as head of state, representing Sweden on state visits abroad, and receiving incoming heads of state and their ambassadors. This means that the King needs to be kept abreast of current domestic as well as international developments, and the fundamental law requires the Prime Minister to keep the King informed. The recurrent contacts with the Prime Minister may establish a certain scope for informal influence in domestic as well as international matters, which may not be much less than his counterparts with more formal powers.

4.7. POLITICAL FUNCTIONS OF THE MONARCHY IN BELGIUM

Quentin Pironnet, lecturer in public law, University of Liège

Introduction

'The King reigns, but does not rule'. Within a constitutional monarchy and a parliamentary regime like Belgium, the room for politics in the King's hands is small.

The political powers of the Belgian monarch are naturally limited. This can be explained by the conjunction of article 88 paragraph 1 of the Constitution, which provides that 'the person of the King is inviolable', and article 106 which provides for a ministerial counter-signature for all acts of the King. The King is, therefore, politically irresponsible for his actions and attitudes. There is no legal way to blame the King for the implications of a decision he has taken; he is not accountable to anyone. The place of the Belgian sovereign is therefore naturally in retreat and his government is in charge of the *res publica*.

However, this has not always been the case, as the first constitutional monarchs did not hesitate to take a more active part in the country's political life. Thus, Leopold I intervened considerably in the Kingdom's foreign policy (see Chapter 3.6), Leopold II was the main architect of the Belgian colonial era, and Baudouin clearly played a role in the Congo's independence in the 1960s. All these examples show the influential role that the King of the Belgians was (and still is) able to play. This role is sometimes implicit by the silence of the Constitution, as in the process of forming governments. Sometimes it takes a historian's work to discover the real influence of the sovereign in political relations, since all of this is clearly unofficial. In any case, the King retains, as Bagehot wrote, 'the right to be consulted, to encourage, to warn'.

Government formation Process

Article 96 of the Constitution entrusts the King with the task of appointing and dismissing his ministers. However, this constitutional provision does not say anything about how the negotiations and the formation of the government itself are conducted. It is therefore the custom of the Palace that has shaped this highly political exercise. The King's most important political power lies in the timeframe between the national election day and the installation of the new government. This power is that much greater in long periods of political crisis, as Belgium has regularly experienced (Belmessieri 2008: 810).

The formation of a government in Belgium has undergone three major stages in history. The first is that of unionism (political parties did not exist yet) and then the succession of homogeneous liberal and Catholic majorities. The King had wide room for manoeuvre to appoint his *chef de cabinet* (the word 'Prime Minister' would only appear after the First World War) and to veto certain personalities (Stengers 2008: 43–44). The second stage follows the creation of the Belgian Workers Party (predecessor of the Socialist Party) and paved the way for coalition governments, when Parliament became the main forum for discussion on the formation of governments, which reduced the King's power (Velaers 2019: 443–46). Finally, since the end of the Second World War, in Belgium, as in many other liberal democracies, the apparatus of political parties has become increasingly important, making the sovereign *a priori* almost useless since discussions are essentially led at the level of party leaders. However, as has been said, political crises can occasionally restore the influence of the sovereign's role.

In practice, the formation of a Belgian government takes place in several phases. The first is that of preliminary consultation by the King of leading politicians. These meetings take place at the discretion of the sovereign and are not public. Deciding which politicians to consult is inevitably political. Belgium has had moments of resurgence of extremist parties through its history. The King, who enjoys a wide margin of appreciation during these preliminary consultations, has therefore sometimes been faced with the dilemma of whether or not to receive a party of the extreme right (or left). Since 1936, when Leopold III received Léon Degrelle, head of the Nazi-related Rex Party, the Crown has usually refused to meet with extreme right-wing leaders. This rule was broken in the spring of 2019, after the elections of 26 May, which saw the Flemish nationalist party VlaamsBelang increase from three to 18 seats in the House of Representatives. King Philippe eventually agreed to receive the party's President in June 2019. The party in question remains, for the moment, unacceptable in the eyes of most other parties, and the King's undoubtedly political gesture was widely commented on in the press.

In the second phase, the King usually appoints an *'informateur'* (or two, since Philippe's reign) whose task will be to prepare the ground for the actual formation of the government. Most of the time, the *informateur* is not a member of the political party that is being considered for the post of Prime Minister. The *informateur* negotiates the important points of the future coalition agreement and secures the presence of a suffi-cient number of parties to represent a majority in the House. After hearing his report, the King then appoints a *'formateur'*, who will have the task of definitively setting up the government agreement and the list of ministers to be appointed. Even in the time of the first kings, a *formateur* was always used. It is, in a sense, an indirect way to avoid calling into question the neutrality of the monarch (Stengers 2008: 43).

When election results are more difficult to interpret and in the event of institutional crises, the King's role, which usually lasts only a few weeks, can be extended. The King may then have to use creativity to appoint personalities to resolve political tensions and reach a compromise, for example royal negotiators or groups of wise men. The long-est political crisis the country has experienced, in 2010–11, lasted for 541 days. Many authors have taken an interest in this episode and revealed the political intentions that marked Albert II's choices at the time (Samyn & Peeters 2011). Among these, it is said that the King, under the advice of his Chief of Staff, refused the Flemish nationalist leader a mediation mission, and that he held the President of the Flemish Liberal Party responsible for the institutional crisis.

Daily Relations with the Government

The King is kept informed by the federal government. To that end, the Prime Minister traditionally meets the King every week at the Palace, usually on Mondays. The King also receives in audience, but only once in a Parliament, the heads of the governments of the federated entities (the 'minister-presidents'), who take an oath before him after having taken it before their Parliament. All discussions between the King and members of the government are secret.

Indeed, the King's personal share in decisions taken under the guise of the ministers' countersignature cannot be known. As a result, the *colloquium singular* between the head of state and his ministers must remain secret. This is an old practice (Molitor 1994: 100), which has also been recalled by the Soenens Committee (see Chapter 3.6). However, it should be emphasised that compliance with this obligation is not always perfect and even tends, over time, to erode. If King Baudouin still had the luxury of having politicians who held the principle in high esteem, his successors did not have the same chance. Jan Velaers reports in particular a number of indiscretions reported on the political positions of King Albert II (Velaers 2019: 450).

The *colloquium singular* is a double-edged sword. On the one hand, it certainly protects the neutrality of the sovereign who, in any case, is inviolable. The prohibition of reporting the King's words is, in this sense, a prescriptive rule to confirm that 'the King can do no wrong'. On the other hand, it creates a certain screen behind which the King may be able to play politics.

The King consults on both sides of the political (and of course linguistic) spectrum, and is not obliged to speak only to members of the coalition parties of his current government (Molitor 1994: 50). However, the political power of the King should not be overestimated. Indeed, today the monarch is most often informed via the media of government decisions requiring his signature (Belmessieri 2008: 808).

Power of Influence

The King also has an undeniable representative function, which contains a political aspect. On the one hand, in carrying out representative functions within the country the King is the embodiment of national unity; this may run against separatist currents or help with the appeasement of institutional crises. This can be seen in the King's only two official speeches in a calendar year: 20 July (the day before Belgium's national day) and 24 December. Thus, King Albert II's speeches from 2006 onwards, although consensual (they had to be approved by the government, which takes responsibility for them), were an echo of the troubled times of the country's longest political crisis (Vuye & Wouters 2016a: 280–300).

On the other hand, at the international level, the numerous state visits and other royal economic missions often make the King the showcase of Belgium's economic policy: the King's presence increases the prestige of the delegation and the chances of attracting investment and contracts. The Palace's (and especially the chief of staff's) opaque role in this matter is crucial, since it negotiates the sovereign's agenda with the government (Vuye & Wouters 2016a: 135–47).

Finally, it should be noted that the King of the Belgians enters the *Palais de la Nation*, where the Parliament is located, in principle only once, during his swearing-in ceremony. There are no 'state of the Union' speeches or other official speeches to members of Parliament. His ministers are responsible for representing the executive branch in the Parliament, which can call on them to explain themselves, as well as ask for a vote of no confidence.

4.8. CONCLUSIONS

Professor Robert Hazell, The Constitution Unit, University College London

We have tried in this chapter to explain the day to-day political functions of the monarch. This is not easy, because on the whole they are less visible than the constitutional functions. The monarch is kept informed about the business of government through regular meetings with the Prime Minister, with other ministers, and with senior officers of state, and through receiving a regular flow of Cabinet and state papers. The monarch's consent or countersignature is given at meetings of the Council of State, but is also handled through exchanges of correspondence, reading official papers and signing documents of all kinds. It is hard grind, with a lot of paperwork: monarchs have to sign hundreds of documents every week. In the UK The Queen receives a box of official papers every working day, with a larger box at weekends, and for routine business turns round papers within a working day.

Formally the monarch has little or no discretion: little choice but to sign or approve every action or decision of the government. But through Bagehot's trio of rights, the right to be consulted, to encourage and to warn, monarchs can develop influence, even if they do not have a power of veto. The Dutch contributions show that a strong minded monarch can occasionally have influence: Queen Juliana in preventing the execution of war criminals, and withholding assent to legislation limiting the size of the royal family; Queen Beatrix in her close interest in the appointment of Queen's Commissioners, mayors or ambassadors. How much influence a monarch can have will vary from country to country: it is hard to conceive of a Danish monarch being as interventionist as these two Dutch Queens. It will also vary from monarch to monarch within the same country: Queen Margrethe of Denmark takes a much closer interest in politics than her father Frederik IX; and King Willem-Alexander appears to be less interventionist than his mother Queen Beatrix. And finally, how much influence a monarch can have will depend on the issue in question, the relationship between monarch and prime minister, and the willingness of each to give way.

We can never know the full extent of a monarch's influence, because our knowledge of their political role is based on anecdotal, indirect and incomplete information. But it is likely that interventions by the monarch are incidental, exceptional and at the margins. No one could claim that Queen Beatrix changed Dutch foreign policy through opening an embassy in Jordan, or having the ambassador to South Africa transferred. Nor has Queen Elizabeth changed British foreign policy through her own powerful attachment to the Commonwealth: her enthusiasm has not been shared by any of her governments, until Brexit led the present government to rediscover the Commonwealth, in search of trade deals.

A different kind of influence might be psychological rather than political: the potential for the monarch to provide encouragement and support to the prime minister through their weekly meetings. Being a modern prime minister is intensely demanding, emotionally and physically, and since their senior colleagues are potential political rivals there is often no one in whom they can easily confide. Many senior business and public sector leaders now have regular sessions with a mentor or coach, an independent figure with whom they can discuss their problems in complete confidence. It may not always be the case, but is it too fanciful to suggest that sometimes, when the chemistry is right, similar benefits can accrue to a prime minister from their weekly sessions with the monarch? How many European prime ministers might echo the words of Ted Heath, when he said 'I could confide in Her Majesty absolutely, not only about political matters, but also about the personal affairs of those involved'?

Monarchs who are too interventionist will encounter resistance and lose their reputation for neutrality. As Helle Krunke shows, the scope for the monarch to be a neutral actor is shrinking, as traditional areas for royal activity like humanitarian relief, sport or the arts have become increasingly politicised. This can make it harder for the royal family to demonstrate its utility while remaining politically neutral. In Denmark and in the Netherlands the monarch's Christmas speech has incurred criticism when advocating greater tolerance for refugees, immigrants and minority communities. But when it comes to organising the programme of visits within their own country monarchs still have considerable discretion, in terms of the causes they are seen to support, such as the visits made by the royal couple in Norway during the Breivik trial. And there is greater scope for the Crown Prince or Princess to support causes which might be deemed controversial or political, on the understanding that when they become monarch, their behaviour will need to become more restrained and strictly neutral. For examples of the different causes they support, see Chapter 8.5.

Finally, it is worth asking, not simply how much influence does the monarch have, but how much should they have? So far, no other country has followed the example of Sweden, and reduced the monarch to a purely ceremonial role. Luxembourg contemplated doing so: as Luc Heuschling explains (in Chapter 3.8), after the 2008 crisis the politicians initially planned a radical revision of the constitution, stripping the Grand Duke of all political functions, but have since opted for more modest reforms. The Netherlands have also taken a step towards the Swedish model, in removing the monarch's role in government formation since 2012.

The Swedish model seems a logical solution: it is hard to defend the retention of political power by a hereditary monarch in a modern parliamentary democracy. So why have the other countries resisted the Swedish example? There are three possible explanations. One is simply inertia, and a reluctance by politicians to challenge the powers of an institution which commands strong popular support (see Chapter 9). A second may be resistance by monarchs themselves, and a concern that if they lose their formal political role, they will also lose the means of informal influence. It must be unrewarding drudgery, signing hundreds of documents as a mere cypher, and it would be only human for monarchs to expect something in return. But a final explanation, developed more fully in Chapter 10, may be the value in a political system of a *pouvoir neutre*: someone above the political fray, with a legitimising role, whose legitimacy derives precisely from their complete neutrality.

5

Ceremonial Functions of Monarchy

Contents

5.1. INTRODUCTION

Dr Bob Morris, The Constitution Unit, University College London

THIS CHAPTER SURVEYS monarchs' ceremonial, including religious, roles. These are often high-visibility functions which reflect ideal constructions of constitutional arrangements where the monarch is presented as head of state and the ultimate source of political authority. In fact, and as described elsewhere in this book, the more modest the ceremony, the more likely it is to reflect workaday reality.

In the UK, the monarch, dressed regally and wearing a crown, attends Parliament to open annual sessions escorted by a cavalry detachment, is greeted by heralds, sat on a throne in a robed House of Lords to declaim the new programme of the monarch's government. The speech is written by ministers responsible to the Parliament rather than to the monarch, and the most important chamber is not where the speech takes place but the House of Commons. By contrast, in Belgium the monarch does not enter office immediately on the demise of the previous monarch until a constitutional oath is sworn before Parliament in a low-key ceremony.

Despite Europe nowadays having become one of the principal areas of secularisation, something more than the vestiges of confessional state churches remains with varying degrees of prominence. Scandinavian monarchs have to adhere to local Lutheran confessions and, whereas the state has withdrawn from active management of the former state churches in Norway and Sweden, Denmark retains a thoroughly Erastian model of state governance. In the UK, weak survival of national churches continues in England and Scotland only of the four nations of that union.

The questions that arise involve how far monarchical ceremonial contributes to the consolidation of support for the legitimacy of a country's political system. David Cannadine argues that the ceremonies are part of the answer to the 'elemental' question: 'how are people persuaded to acquiesce in a polity where the distribution of power is manifestly unequal and unjust, as it invariably is?' (Cannadine and Price: 19) Are monarchs more the prisoners of such systems than independent actors? On the other hand, is there a sense in which monarchs are not only heads of state but heads of the nation? How far is the compulsory association of monarchs with local religious confessions out of kilter with increasing secularisation, or does it have still some utility in assisting states to respond with readier accommodation to religious pluralisation in the greater presence of non-Christian religions?

5.2. MONARCHIES AND RELIGION IN EUROPE

Frank Cranmer, St Chad's College, Durham, and Centre for Law and Religion, Cardiff University

This section summarises the relationships between current European monarchies and religion.

Belgium

Under the Constitution, the monarch accedes to the throne after having sworn an oath before Parliament 'to observe the Constitution and the laws of the Belgian people, to preserve the country's national independence and its territorial integrity' (article 91). Belgium has no crown or regalia. The Venice Commission – more formally known as the European Commission for Democracy through Law– has described the Constitution of Belgium as 'the prototype of the constitutional monarchy' (Council of Europe 2002: CDL-AD(2002)032-e), citing article 105: 'The King has no powers other than those formally attributed to him by the Constitution and by specific laws passed by virtue of the Constitution itself'. To which might be added article 106: 'No act of the King can take effect without the countersignature of a minister, who, in doing so, assumes responsibility for it'.

The Constitution provide both freedom *of* and freedom *from* religion:

- 'Freedom of worship, public practice of the latter … are guaranteed' (article 19).
- 'No-one can be obliged to contribute in any way whatsoever to the acts and ceremonies of a religion, nor to observe the days of rest' (article 20)
- 'The State does not have the right to intervene either in the nomination or in the installation of ministers of any religion whatsoever' (article 21).

- Nevertheless: 'The State awards remuneration and pensions to religious leaders; those amounts required are included in the budget' (article 181).

The State recognises and finances certain religious groups and 'life stances': Roman Catholics (law of 8 April 1802), Protestants (law of 8 April 1802), Anglicans (law of 4 March 1870), Jews (law of 4 March 1870), Muslims (law of 19 July 1974), and Orthodox (law of 17 April 1985). Since 5 May 1993, non-confessional organisations have been given equal recognition. The provision authorises state funding [*traitement*] for the salaries and pensions of representatives of those organisations that are recognised by law, including those that offer moral services based on a non-confessional ideology. In addition, faith communities may appoint army and prison chaplains who are paid by the state (Torfs 2005: 9-34).

The degree to which the monarch's personal opinions and beliefs may be allowed to intrude on his or her duties is illustrated by the events of April 1990. Under article 93 of the Constitution, 'If the King finds himself unable to reign, the ministers, having had this inability stated, immediately convene the Houses. The Regent and Guardian are appointed by the joint Houses'. When King Baudouin concluded that he could not in good conscience as a Roman Catholic sign a new law permitting abortion the Cabinet declared him 'unable to govern', assumed his powers, promulgated and published the abortion law and recalled Parliament for a special session. The King resumed office on the following day.

The role of the monarch is, however, complicated by the fact that Belgium is a federal state with a very high degree of devolution and, though the president of each federate government takes the oath 'in the King's hands', 'there is no organic relationship between the King and the governments of the federate entities' (Belgian Federal Government 2019).

Denmark

Under the Constitution, 'legislative power shall be vested in the King and the *Folketing* conjointly. The executive power shall be vested in the King. The judicial power shall be vested in the courts of justice' (article 3). Article 4 provides that 'The Evangelical Lutheran Church shall be the Established Church of Denmark [*den danskefolkekirke*], and as such, it shall be supported by the State' and article 6 that 'The King shall be a member of the Evangelical Lutheran Church'. The Constitution further provides that the Constitution of the Established Church (article 66) and the rules of other religious bodies (article 68) 'shall be laid down by Statute'.

Historically, the monarch was crowned: however, the coronation was abolished with the adoption of the 1849 Constitution. Queen Margrethe II was not formally enthroned; instead, a public proclamation of her accession in 1972 was made from the balcony of Christiansborg Palace.

The Church of Denmark is probably subject to stricter state control than any other established church in Europe. It has no independent legislative body: instead, the monarch is the supreme authority in relation to such matters as organisation and liturgy, the Ministry of Ecclesiastical Affairs [*Kirkeministeriet*] is its supreme administrative authority, and church legislation is enacted by *Folketinget* and it is part of public law. So, when it was decided that the Church would ordain women, the decision was taken by *Folktinget* rather than by the Church itself. In an interview with *Der Spiegel* in 2016, Queen Margrethe described her position on religion and politics like this:

> Under the constitution, as the Danish Queen I am bound to the Lutheran faith, but that does not exclude people of other faiths. On the contrary, I believe that the fact that I am religious brings me closer to anyone with a different faith. Besides, I represent all people who are citizens of the Danish nation.

When asked what she would do if she wanted to take a political position on a particular matter, she replied:

> We have a wonderful tradition for that: the Queen's New Year's address. I prepare this address together with the office of the prime minister. It is not a harmless event, nor is it an announce-ment of trifling matters. It is about values, as well as positions. There are indeed ways for a Queen to say what she thinks (Ertel & Sandberg 2016).

There was speculation in the Danish press that after the death of her husband, Prince Henrik, in 2018 the Queen might abdicate: in the event, she did not.

Luxembourg

Under article 3 of the Constitution, the heirs to the Grand Duchy of Luxembourg are the House of Nassau 'in accordance with the pact of June 30, 1783, article 71 of the Treaty of Vienna of 9 June 1815 and article 1 of the Treaty of London of May 11, 1867'. Under article 3, the holder of the Grand Dukedom comes of age at 18. On accession to the throne, 'he shall, as soon as possible, in the presence of the Chamber of Deputies or a deputation appointed by it, take the following oath: "I swear to observe the Constitution and the laws of the Grand Duchy of Luxembourg, to maintain national independence and the integrity of the territory and public and individual liberties"'. In practice, the new Grand Duke or Duchess is enthroned at a ceremony held in Parliament at the beginning of his or her reign. The monarch takes an oath of loyalty to the Constitution, then attends Notre-Dame Cathedral. Luxembourg does not have a crown or other royal regalia.

In 2008, Grand Duke Henri's refusal on grounds of conscience to sign a bill to legalise euthanasia triggered a constitutional crisis; as a result, the Constitution was amended to remove the requirement for Grand Ducal approval.

There is no state religion and article 19 of the Constitution provides for its free exer-cise: article 106, however, provides for the salaries and pensions of clergy to be borne by the state and a wide range of religious groups that have signed agreements with the state receive financial support. A question to be included in the (advisory) constitutional refer-endum in June 2015 – '*Approuvez-vous l'idée que l'Etat n'ait plus l'obligation de prendre en charge les traitements et pensions des ministres des cultes reconnus?*' – was dropped after an agreement between the government and the religious groups: half those polled in a subsequent survey thought that the decision to remove it had been wrong (Luxemburger Wort 2014, 2015).

The government does not register religions or religious groups, but the vast majority of Luxembourgers are Roman Catholic. There is a single diocese founded in 1870; and under a law of 1873 the bishop must be a citizen of Luxembourg and the government must approve the Pope's nominee before appointment. There is a long tradition of religious education in state schools; and all private, religious, and non-sectarian schools are eligible for government subsidies.

The Netherlands

Separation of church and state in the Netherlands was established during the Batavian Revolution of 1795. Article 1 of the Constitution outlaws discrimination 'on the grounds of religion, belief, political opinion, race or sex or on any other grounds whatsoever' and article 6 §1 provides that everyone 'shall have the right to manifest freely his religion or belief, either individually or in community with others, without prejudice to his responsibility under the law'. The Constitution makes no provision as to the religious affiliation of the monarch – though, traditionally, the House of Orange-Nassau has been Calvinist.

The new sovereign is not crowned. Under article 32 of the Constitution, upon accession he or she

> shall be sworn in and inaugurated as soon as possible in the capital city, Amsterdam, at a public and joint session of the two Houses of the States General. The King shall swear or promise allegiance to the Constitution and that he will faithfully discharge his duties ....

The investiture takes place in the Nieuwe Kerk, with the crown, the orb, the sword of state and the sceptre on cushions, together with a copy of the Constitution. After the monarch has taken the oath, members of the States General take an oath of loyalty.

Traditionally, the population of the Netherlands was split into three roughly equal groups – one-third Protestant, one-third Roman Catholic and one-third secular – which operated their own institutions in a system traditionally described as *Verzuiling* or 'pillarisation'. Members of the three pillars maintained their own political parties, trades unions, newspapers, hospitals and other organisations. However, Dutch society has become increasingly secular and the Protestant denominations, in particular, have suffered a considerable decline in membership. A large-sample survey by Statistics Netherlands in 2015 revealed that half the population – 50.1 per cent – had no religion.

Norway

Article 3 of the Constitution vests executive power in the monarch, while article 4 provides that 'The King shall at all times profess the Evangelical-Lutheran religion'. As Robert Hazell notes, Norway is the only country apart from the UK that includes a religious element in its Royal Oath: 'I promise and swear that I will govern the Kingdom of Norway in accordance with its Constitution and Laws: so help me God, the Almighty and Omniscient' (article 9).

Historically, the Church of Norway was the state church. On 21 May 2012, however, the Norwegian Parliament passed a constitutional amendment removing the previous reference to an 'official religion of the state', granting the Church increased autonomy and loosening the historical ties between church and state. Article 16 of the amended Constitution declares that

> All inhabitants of the realm shall have the right to free exercise of their religion. The Church of Norway, an Evangelical-Lutheran church, will remain the Established Church of Norway and will as such be supported by the State. Detailed provisions as to its system will be laid down by law. All religious and belief communities should be supported on equal terms.

The separation came into effect on 1 January 2017: in practice, the change meant that the state relinquished any control over the Church, including in the appointments of clergy and bishops, though it continues to fund the Church.

The last King and Queen to be crowned were Haakon VII and Maud of Wales in 1906. The modern practice is consecration in Nidaros Cathedral, Trondheim, with the King's and Queen's Crowns placed on either side of the high altar. King Harald and Queen Sonja were consecrated on 23 June 1991, following the tradition introduced by King Olav in 1958. The Bishop of Nidaros placed his hand on the King's head and recited the conse-cration prayer, which included the words: 'Bless King Harald V, strengthen him and lead him in the exercise of his solemn responsibilities', then placed his hand on the head of the Queen and asked God to help her to use her abilities for the benefit of the country and the people. The King and Queen knelt at the high altar while the Royal Anthem was sung and were then conducted to the thrones (Det Norske Kongehus Website 2013).

Like Queen Margrethe of Denmark, King Harald's interventions have been apolitical, stressing the need for national unity. In a speech at a royal garden party in 2016 that went viral on social media, he said:

> Norwegians come from North Norway, Central Norway, Southern Norway – and all of the other regions. Norwegians have immigrated from Afghanistan, Pakistan and Poland, from Sweden, Somalia and Syria … Norwegians are enthusiastic young people and wise old people. Norwegians are single, divorced, families with children, and old married couples. Norwegians are girls who love girls, boys who love boys, and girls and boys who love each other. Norwegians believe in God, Allah, the Universe and nothing (Royal Norwegian Embassy in Cairo Website 2016).

Spain

Under article 51 of the Constitution:

> 'The King is the Head of State, the symbol of its unity and permanence. He arbitrates and moderates the regular working of the institutions, assumes the highest representation of the Spanish State in international relation, especially with those nations belonging to the same historic community, and performs the functions expressly conferred on him by the Constitution and the law.'

Juan Carlos I became King on 22 November 1975, two days after the death of General Franco, and began dismantling the Francoist inheritance, leading to the new Constitution in 1978 and the establishment of a constitutional monarchy. He played an active role in stalling the attempted coup in February 1981, when Lieutenant-Colonel Antonio Tejero led 200 armed Civil Guards into the Congress of Deputies during the vote to elect a prime minister and held the *Cortes* hostage for 18 hours – during which time Juan Carlos denounced the coup in a televised address. Subsequently, however, his popularity underwent a massive decline and he abdicated in favour of his son, now King Felipe VI (see chapters 6.5 and 9.3).

Article 6 of the Francoist Constitution stated that 'The profession and practice of the Catholic Religion, which is that of the Spanish State, will enjoy official protection ... No other ceremonies or external manifestations will be allowed than those of the Catholic Religion'. Article 16 of the Constitution of 1978 guarantees freedom and privacy of religion and belief and declares that no religion 'shall have a state character'. However, under article 16 § 3, 'The public authorities shall take into account the religious beliefs of Spanish society and shall consequently maintain appropriate cooperation relations with the Catholic Church and other confessions'.

In 1980, the Religious Freedom Act codified the law on freedom of thought and religion and defined the procedures under which the State might protect the individual and collective rights of religious minorities. It established an Advisory Commission on Religious Freedom, which, together with the Ministry of Justice, is responsible for ensuring religious freedom and implementing appropriate measures for its protection. Nevertheless, the Concordat Agreements of 1976 and 1979 gave the Roman Catholic Church a privileged position over the other religious traditions, regulating four areas: legal issues, economic affairs, educational and cultural matters and the military chaplaincy. In particular, the Concordats granted direct funding to the Church (Griera, Martínez-Ariño, García-Romeral 2014).

Sweden

Under the Constitution, the monarch is head of state (chapter 5 article 1). Succession to the throne is regulated by the Act of Succession. The head of state is to be kept informed about the affairs of the realm by the prime minister. The government convenes as Council of State under the chairmanship of the head of state when required (chapter 5 article 3). The monarch has no political power – the duties are representational and ceremonial – however, under chapter 3 article 6 of the Riksdag Act 2014 the monarch opens Parliament.

The Church of Sweden was the state church until 1 January 2000. Notwithstanding disestablishment, under the unaltered transitory provisions to the Instrument of Government 1974, the king must still belong to and profess the 'pure evangelical faith' as defined by the Augsburg Confession and the Uppsala Synod of 1593. According to article 4 of the Act of Succession 1810, this requirement also applies to those in the line of succession to the throne.

The last Swedish monarch to be crowned was Oscar II in 1873. The current monarch, Carl XVI Gustaf, simply made the then required Royal Declaration [*Konungaförsäkran*] at a meeting of the Cabinet and was subsequently enthroned at the Royal Palace in Stockholm on 19 September 1973 and made an accession speech. The requirement for the Royal Declaration was abolished in 1975. Also under the current constitutional provisions, it is expected that a new monarch makes a corresponding declaration of office [*Ämbetsförklaring*].

The United Kingdom

The monarchy of the United Kingdom differs from the others in several respects: the monarch is Supreme Governor of the Church of England, the heir apparent succeeds to the throne automatically on the death of his or her predecessor and the new monarch is crowned *and anointed* in Westminster Abbey. It shares some of these features with some of the other European monarchies – but the particular mix is unique.

The relationship between the Crown and religion is also unique. On accession, the new sovereign must make three statutory oaths: to uphold the Presbyterian form of government of the Church of Scotland; to be a true and faithful Protestant; and the Coronation Oath, which includes promising to uphold the rights and privileges of the Church of England. Though the monarch is Supreme Governor of the Church of England, he or she is regarded as a member of the Church of Scotland when north of the Border and there is a separate Ecclesiastical Household in Scotland. The Queen appoints a Lord High Commissioner to the annual General Assembly of the Church of Scotland 'to supply Our Presence and to hold Our Place' – and in 2002, Her Majesty attended in person.

Since the time of Henry VIII, the monarch has held the title – conferred on Henry by Pope Leo X – *Fidei Defensor*, which has traditionally been translated as 'Defender of the Faith'. On his 60th birthday, Prince Charles announced that, on his accession, he would prefer to be known as to be known 'the Defender of Faith' – which one of his courtiers described at the time as 'a subtle but hugely symbolic shift' (Pierce 2008). That said, since Latin has no definite or indefinite articles, *Fidei Defensor* can, of course, be translated either way.

Summary

Inevitably, both monarchical styles and monarchical powers vary across Europe, though all are 'constitutional monarchies'. Some of the main features can be tabulated as follows:

Table 5.1 Church/State relations in European monarchies

	Coronation	Religious test	Opens legislature	Speech at opening of legislature	Free to express own opinions	Christmas/ New Year Message or similar	State religion
Belgium	No Oath before joint sitting of parliament	No	No	No	No (unless under ministerial responsibility)	Christmas	No (six recognised religions)
Denmark	No	Yes Lutheran	No but is present at the opening in a gallery	No	Queen Margrethe has expressed strong views on the Church	New Year	Yes Church of Denmark

(continued)

Table 5.1 (*Continued*)

	Coronation	Religious test	Opens legislature	Speech at opening of legislature	Free to express own opinions	Christmas/ New Year Message or similar	State religion
Luxembourg	Enthronement followed by mass at the Cathedral [but Luxembourg does not have a Crown]	No (the first Grand Dukes were Calvinists – but, by implication, a non-Catholic is not going to attend mass)	No	N/A	N/A	Christmas	No
Netherlands	Investiture with crown present	No	Yes	Yes Constitution Art. 65	N/A	Christmas	No
Norway	'Consecration' in Nidaros Cathedral	Yes Lutheran	Yes	Yes Constitution Art. 74	N/A	New Year	Only in a very attenu- ated form
Spain	Investiture with crown present	No	Yes	Yes	Juan Carlos I prob- ably did so more than any other consti- tutional monarch; King Felipe VI is less inclined to do so	Christmas	No
Sweden	No	Yes Lutheran	Yes	Yes	No	Christmas	No
United Kingdom	Yes	Yes Anglican in England Presbyterian in Scotland	Yes	Yes	In principle, HM acts on the advice of ministers	Christmas Exception- ally during the coronavirus pandemic, the Queen also issued an Easter message.	Yes Church of England ?Church of Scotland

5.3. THE RELIGIOUS DIMENSION OF MONARCHY

Ian Bradley, Emeritus Professor of Cultural and Spiritual History at the University of St Andrews

In many ways Walter Bagehot's well-known aphorism about modern monarchy surviving and indeed thriving by appealing to the heart rather than the head rings even more true today than when he coined it just over 150 years ago. Although the exploits of certain presidents across the seas and the chaos swirling around UK politics have perhaps enhanced the British public's appreciation of a monarchical rather than a presidential system of government, it is almost certainly the ceremonial and also what might be termed the emotional and familial elements of royalty (not least as supplied by the royal weddings of its younger members) that primarily appeal to people and engage public interest today.

Bagehot's emphasis on the sacral and religious role of monarchy has also stood the test of time. For him, the two great features of monarchy are its intelligibility and the fact that 'it strengthens our government with the strength of religion' and constitutes 'the solitary transcendent element' in the state (Bagehot 1867: 41, 45). This religious and transcendent element is still very much in evidence, counter-cultural as it is in our increasingly secular society. At a very obvious level, it manifests itself in the fact that a very high proportion of the occasions when the sovereign and other members of the royal family are most visible and have their highest public profile are essentially religious in character: the annual Act of Remembrance at the Cenotaph, the Royal Maundy service, the Garter Service at Windsor, services of national thanksgiving and remembrance as well as royal weddings and funerals. The Queen is regularly photographed and shown on television either entering or leaving a church, often to join with local worshippers for regular worship, as when she attends Crathie Kirk during her annual stay at Balmoral, or Sandringham Parish Church at Christmas. The fact that she is so often portrayed in this church-going role, as well as leading the nation in prayer at much grander national occasions, reinforces, if only subliminally, the impression of the sovereign as a religious figure as much as if not more than a political figurehead (Bradley 2002: xii).

This perception has been much enhanced over recent years by the Queen's own deliberate choice to speak more openly about issues of faith and about her own faith in particular. This has been particularly the case with her Christmas broadcasts which changed markedly in tone from 2000 onwards, not least at the prompting of the Duke of Edinburgh, and have become noticeably more sermonic, increasingly being filmed in a church or chapel rather than in the drawing room setting that was long the norm, and ending with a prayer or quotation from the Bible. While being very explicit about her own deeply held Christian beliefs, the Queen has also gone out of her way to commend the teaching of other faiths. This has been paralleled by the Prince of Wales's notable contribution to the religious life of the country with his consistent call for more emphasis to be given to the spiritual and holistic dimension of life, his particular interest in Islam, interfaith dialogue and the persecution of Christians in the Middle East, his regular retreats to desert monasteries and his passionate championship of causes ranging from the Book of Common Prayer to sacred geometry in keeping with his self-proclaimed mission to act as 'Defender of Faith' (Dimbleby 1994: 528). These themes are discussed in David Lorimer's *Radical Prince* (2003) and brought together in *Harmony: A New Way of Looking at Our World* (2010) which the Prince co-authored with two of his advisers.

These very personal initiatives raise the question of the personal faith of the sovereign and the heir to the throne and the extent to which it, rather than official roles, such as Supreme Governor of the Church of England and Defender of the Faith, as traditionally understood and still proclaimed on certain coins of the realm, determine the spiritual and sacral character of monarchy. Younger members of the royal family, notably Prince William and Prince Harry, have not shown any interest in religion or followed their father in his spiritual interests, even if they have indicated their admiration for much of what he has stood for in this and other areas. It does seem highly likely that the strong spiritual commitment shown by both the Queen and Prince Charles will not be replicated by their heirs and will die out in the next twenty years or so.

Without this strong personal input from the faith and interest of the sovereign, will the religious role of the monarchy and its continuation as Bagehot's solitary transcendent element in the body politic substantially diminish? It is noticeable that among those writing about the future of the monarchy from a broadly sympathetic standpoint there is general agreement that it should be conceived and developed in more secular terms. Vernon Bogdanor has advocated 'a secularised monarchy ... more in tune with the spirit of the age' (Bogdanor 1995: 239). John Taylor has argued: 'let the crown be the British institution of secular culture' (Taylor 1996: 136). The secularisation of the monarchy through curtailing all its religious roles and links with churches was a major plank of the reforms proposed in the 1998 Demos pamphlet, *Modernizing the Monarchy*, as it was for the authors of *The Windsors: A Dynasty Revealed* who argued for a purely civil role for the monarch as defender of the Constitution 'rather than a religious one as defender of the faith' (Brendon & Whitehead 1994: 241).

Yet the fact remains that, even among the young royals, there remains a strong connection with church and established religion, even if it comes more out of custom and protocol rather than personal conviction. The Duke and Duchess of Sussex were in a distinct minority (less than 30 per cent) among modern British couples tying the nuptial knot in having a church wedding. The first modern royal marriage involving a divorced party to take place in the context of a Church of England service, their wedding was striking perhaps above all for the interest generated by the sermon delivered by the Presiding Bishop of the Episcopal Church of the United States of America, Michael Curry, an unexpected sign of the way in which royal occasions can still have significant spiritual impact.

There are other factors within the popular consciousness which suggest that the transcendent, magical and mystical dimension of royalty could still hold considerable public appeal. As I have argued elsewhere (Bradley 2012: xxvii-xxx) the impact of the *Lord of the Rings* films, the *Lion King* musical and the widespread post-Jungian cult of 'The King Within' and kingly archetypes in terms of modern understanding of masculinity, have reinforced the appeal of monarchy to the heart rather than the head. It seems to strike a chord with our post-modern culture where the emotional and experiential are valued as much as the rational, and the importance of symbol, ritual, mystery and that which belongs to the region of the imagination and not that of the intellect is being rediscovered and reaffirmed. One might also cite the impact of films like *The Queen* and *The King's Speech*, and not least the epic ongoing Netflix series *The Crown*, which have conveyed something of the loneliness and fragility of monarchy, if anything bolstering its emotional appeal while at the same time stripping away a little more of its magic.

It does seem to remain the case that for many people encounters with royalty often take on a character akin to a religious experience and that words like 'reverence' and 'blessing' are often used to describe them. This struck the American travel writer, Paul Theroux, on his journeys round Britain in the early 1980s. Arriving in the coastal town of Anstruther in Fife just after it had been visited by the Queen, he noted that 'it was as if the town had been refreshed by a blessing. In a way it had, for that atmosphere was the spirit left by the progress of the Royal Visit' (Theroux 1983: 257). Much more recent research by the sociologist Anne Rowbottom on the atmosphere engendered by royal visits has confirmed the use of religious language, at least among regular royal watchers and enthusiasts, to describe them (Rowbottom 1994, 1998). We may be somewhat removed from the national mood engendered by the coronation of 1953, as observed by the sociologists, Edward Shils and Michael Young, who described it as 'a great act of national communion' and berated their fellow academics for failing to acknowledge the continuing sacred aspects and appeal of monarchy (Shils and Young 1953: 64). However, it will surely be the case that the death of the Queen will trigger an expression of public mourning and social solidarity with a discernible spiritual element. It will also provide the occasion for a state funeral which will bring all the religious weight and import of these particular events which have recently been rightly described in an academic study as 'the grandest of all ceremonial occasions for which Britain is rightly famous' (Range 2016: 399).

There are several key questions hanging over the future religious direction and orientation of the United Kingdom monarchy which are likely to have to be decided in the next decade or so. Firstly, should the Church of England continue to have the sovereign as its Supreme Governor? This is, of course, bound up with the more general question of whether the Church of England should remain established with the various privileges that go with this status. Continuing declining congregations and membership mean that Anglicanism is now very much a minority faith in England and make it increasingly difficult to justify church establishment. A growing number of clergy within the Church of England are themselves keen on disestablishment and uneasy about having the monarch as their Supreme Head and Governor. However, there are still influential Anglican voices championing establishment and royal supremacy as a way of putting religion at the heart of national life and this is the position taken by many leaders of the minority faiths in Britain who, on the whole, are staunch champions of church establishment and more broadly of the religious and sacral character of the monarchy. Significantly, this is the position taken by two leading proponents of multiculturalism in Britain, Tariq Modood and Bhiku Parekh, both of whom have argued for the continuation of establishment of the Church of England as a way of keeping religion in the public sphere and in national life as a way of protecting religious and ethnic minorities (Bradley 2007: 204-7; Modood 1997; Parekh 2000).

Secondly, there is the vexed question of the royal succession and whether it should continue to be restricted to those of the Protestant faith. The anti-Catholicism implicit in this aspect of the British Constitution and the character of its monarchy has recently been somewhat tempered with the repeal in 2013 of the clause in the 1701 Act of Settlement banning anyone married to a Roman Catholic from succeeding to the throne. This followed a decision made in Perth, Australia, in 2011 by the leaders of the 16 Commonwealth countries that retain the British monarch as head of state. The ban only came into effect in 2015, finally ending the anomaly whereby the sovereign could be married to a Muslim, a Mormon, a Moonie or an atheist, but not to a Roman Catholic. The ban on the sovereign himself or herself being a Roman Catholic, however, remains in force. Understandably, there are periodic calls for it to be lifted on the grounds that it constitutes discrimination and a violation of human rights. The United Kingdom monarchy is not, in fact, exceptional or anomalous in this respect. Rules governing the religious affiliations of other traditional northern European Protestant monarchies are even more prescriptive. The Constitutions of Norway, Denmark and Sweden require their monarchs to be Lutherans and the king or queen of the Netherlands must effectively come from the Protestant House of Orange.

There are other aspects of the essentially and, indeed, defiantly Protestant character of the British monarchy which are also currently in contention. One is the title, already alluded to, of 'Defender of the Faith'. Ironically, this was first bestowed on Henry VIII by a grateful Pope in recognition of his defence of traditional Roman Catholic doctrine against the heresies of Luther and the early Reformers. However, it has come to be associated with the defence of the Protestant faith and specifically with the championship and support of the Church of England and the maintenance of the Presbyterian Church in Scotland. On accession, a new sovereign has to make three statutory oaths: the Scottish Oath, to uphold the Presbyterian system of church government in Scotland; the Accession Declaration Oath, to be a true and faithful Protestant; and the Coronation Oath, which includes a promise to uphold the rights and privileges of the Church of England in the broader context of maintaining in the United Kingdom 'the Protestant Reformed religion established by law'.

There is much debate and discussion about whether these oaths should be changed to end the privileging and prioritising of Protestantism, and whether, indeed, the monarch should be required to make a commitment to uphold and preserve any particular form of religion. Their continuation seems difficult to justify in the context of Britain's increasingly secular and religiously plural composition and character. If they are modified or, indeed, dispensed with (and it would not be the first time that the Accession oath has been altered to reflect embarrassment and unease over their anti-Catholic tone and sentiment), and the title 'Defender of the Faith' disappears or gives way to a more general 'Defender of Faith' appellation along the lines suggested by the Prince of Wales, not only will the distinctively Protestant character of the monarchy largely disappear but the last nail will also have been hammered into the coffin of Protestant Britain, an entity which was hugely important, indeed, normative in terms of national identity, from the late sixteenth to the early twentieth century but which has been slowly but surely dying for the last 70 years or so (Bradley 2018).

The final set of questions around the future religious complexion of the monarchy centre around the form and shape of the next coronation. More than any other feature of our national life or our constitution, the coronation service has symbolised and defined the sacred character of monarchy – in particular with the anointing of the sovereign carried out by the Archbishop of Canterbury behind a screen – and its link with Christianity and the established church. In the words of the liturgist, Edward Ratcliff, writing about the coronation of our present Queen in 1953, 'it reflects the persistent English intertwining of sacred and secular, of civil and ecclesiastical. It reflects particularly the historic English conception of the mutual relations of Sovereign, Church and People, and of all three to God. In a word, the English Coronation Service symbolises national continuity considered sub specie Christianitatis' (Ratcliff 1953: 23). Does this perspective still hold good in a country where less than half the population describe themselves as religious believers and only 10 per cent regularly attend church?

There has been much discussion at a high level about the appropriate venue for and structure of the next coronation. Should it take place in Westminster Abbey? Should the new sovereign be set apart and anointed as previous ones have been in direct imitation of what happened to the kings of Ancient Israel? Should it be stage managed and master-minded by the Church of England and located, as it has traditionally been, in the framework of an Anglican communion service? How much ecumenical and interfaith participation should there be?

Conversations continue. A consensus is emerging that the coronation service should definitely remain in Westminster Abbey. Much greater ecumenical participation than in 1953 is certain to be a feature of the next coronation, although the Church of England and Archbishop of Canterbury are likely to remain in overall charge. The anointing of the new monarch will probably also remain, although as Roy Strong has observed, its continuation, and indeed that of the coronation service as a whole, 'depends on the acceptance of the notion that one person can be set aside in this way and undergo such an initiatory rite, one which, in the medieval period, verged closely on a Christian sacrament' (Strong 2005: 500).

An idea gaining support is that in addition to the formal Christian coronation in Westminster Abbey, there should be another more secular ceremony, possibly in Westminster Hall, at which community leaders express their loyalty to the new sovereign. Wesley Carr, whilst Dean of Westminster Abbey, proposed that this ceremony should precede the Abbey service and allow 'the various religious groups and ethnic bodies that now constitute the nation to recognise their sovereign and offer a form of homage'. The new sovereign would 'then in the Abbey be able to present himself as carrying the unity of the nation as the basis on which the specifically Christian coronation would follow' (Carr 2002: p.15). Carr further suggested that following the coronation in the Abbey, the new sovereign would then process to St Margaret's Church, Westminster, to receive the homage of Members of Parliament and then return to the Palace of Westminster for an inaugural interfaith ceremony. Other leading churchmen have suggested similar 'rolling coronations' involving ceremonies at different locations (Bradley 2002, 231). The idea has also been floated of reviving the medieval practice of holding 'showings' of the new monarch around the country, with ceremonies taking place certainly in Edinburgh, Belfast and Cardiff and possibly in at least one northern English city.

The form of the coronation service is not rigid and immutable. Like the conception and the presentation of the sacred heart of monarchy, it is an evolving, organic process which is adapted and altered to conform to changing beliefs and mores. The exciting if demanding task now is to devise relevant and meaningful ways to represent the ceremonial and religious dimensions of the institution in a way which respects and builds on past tradition and yet speaks clearly to the present generation.

5.4. NORWAY: CEREMONIAL FUNCTIONS

Eivind Smith, Professor of Public Law, University of Oslo

Christian crowning ceremonies are (or, at least, are meant to be) powerful manifestations of royal dignity and power. The first crowning of a king of Norway took place in Bergen in 1163 (Magnus Erlingsson), conducted by a cardinal sent for the occasion; apparently, this was the first ceremony of its kind in Scandinavia. Later crowning ceremonies took place in Bergen, in Nidaros Cathedral (in present day Trondheim) or in Oslo, where the last one in Norway – before the start of the modern constitutional epoch marked by the 1814 Constitution – took place in 1514 (for a king of both Denmark and Norway).

According to the Constitution of 1814, a new king should be crowned and anointed in Nidaros Cathedral, Saint Olav's burial church. The first ceremony took place for Karl Johan (Bernadotte) who had become King Karl III of Norway (Karl XIII of Sweden) in 1818. He was followed by the three Bernadotte kings on the Throne of Norway throughout the nineteenth century.

The last crowning according to the relevant constitutional provisions took place in 1906, when the newly elected King Haakon VII and his wife, British princess Maud, appeared in Nidaros Cathedral accompanied by their small son, future Olav V. Shortly afterwards (in 1908), the obligation to be crowned and anointed in Nidaros was abolished by constitutional amendment. Politically, there was no longer a need for ensuring that the king of Norway did not adopt an attitude as king of Sweden only, and the political leadership – actually of a less monarchical mind than the bulk of the population – felt that similar pomp and circumstances had become less well in tune with Norwegian mentality.

However, the next King (Olav V) somewhat overruled the change by organising his own quite grandiose consecration or 'blessing' ceremony in Nidaros Cathedral on 22 June 1958, exactly 52 years after the coronation of his parents. The regalia were present in the church, but not used during the ceremony. The initiative was actively supported by the church, whereas the political, Labour-oriented leadership only joined in wholeheartedly much later.

In 1992, the present royal couple (Harald V and Sonja) reiterated the 'blessing ceremony' and developed it further under circumstances where any political resistance had disappeared.

With the formal end of the confessional state and the state church by constitutional amendments adopted in 2012, the continuation of the relevant practice by the next King (Haakon VIII) would certainly need some more reflection. On the other hand, the King's constitutional obligation to 'profess the Evangelical-Lutheran religion' (article 4) has remained (apparently at the explicit demand of the present King). In any case, it seems reasonable to guess that a third blessing ceremony will take place in due course, probably in the presence of leaders of other faith communities as well.

Among the monarch's other main ceremonial functions, the solemn opening of the new session of Parliament in October of each year (article 74) should be mentioned. If the throne speeches of the nineteenth century were the king's own, the monarch now reads out a text prepared by the government and ceremonially handed over to him by the prime minister in the chamber itself.

Also to be noted are events such as official state visits to and from Norway, the royal family's core functions during the huge and most popular 17 May celebrations commemorating the Constitution of 1814 including its declaration of independence (article 1), the king's speech on New Year's Eve widely disseminated by radio and TV, a series of royal visits (with speeches) recognising different regions or groups after (sometimes) years of public disregard, systematic visits to all parts of the country, often using the royal yacht ('*Norge*'), and the royal family's widely acknowledged, sometimes even striking role during national crises like the post-22 July 2011 period when 77 people were murdered by a right-wing fanatic. (For a more detailed breakdown see Table 6.4).

In itself, the mourning following king Olav V's death in 1991 provides a strong demonstration of national unity. Among many striking expressions, perhaps the spontaneous appearance of thousands of candles in front of the Royal Palace during the cold winter night was particularly moving.

Above all, the World War II experience, when King Haakon's attitude during the German invasion, his radio speeches from London and a lot of other events made him the undisputed national hero, stands out as more important than any other period of royal activity since 1905. In modern media culture, the popular movie *The King's No* to the requirement that he should secure peace with the German occupants by appointing Vidkun Quisling, the leader of a minor political party soon to become herostratically famous, as new Prime Minister, bears a striking testimony.

5.5. EUROPEAN ROYAL CEREMONIAL FUNCTIONS: SUMMARY

Dr Bob Morris, The Constitution Unit, University College London

'[N]o approach which defines power narrowly and ignores spectacle and pageantry can possibly claim to be comprehensive. Politics and ceremonial are not separate subjects, the one serious, the other superficial. Ritual is not the mark of force, but is itself a type of power.' (Cannadine and Price: 19)

Introduction

In all eight monarchies, the royal families are a focus of national sentiment but with differing degrees of intensity and in no case the kind of adulatory fanaticism encouraged in some less democratic societies. The nature of state-sponsored ceremonies reflects in each nation the relative salience of monarchical roles. The great expansion in recent decades of media capacity has been both intrusive and at the same time given greater opportunity for display by royal families to the extent of making it difficult always confidently to distinguish them from general celebritisation. On the other hand, display emphasising the passage of a family through life can reinforce a population's appreciation of social continuity and identification with the existing polity.

Scope

All constitutional monarchs are in practice required to follow the advice of the government of the day. Their programmes are ultimately subject to the approval of ministers and even the freedom of marriage for those closest to thrones is subject to political approval (see chapter 8.3). However, apart from the fixed points in their calendars, they have considerable leeway still in their ability to choose the charities they wish to support (see chapter 6) and the extent to which they develop distinct public personae for themselves. This contribution concentrates on ceremonies associated with the main features of monarchical duties common to the remaining European monarchies.

However, before embarking on those features, it should be noted that managing display is an important element of the presentation of monarchies.[1] Away from the heavier symbolism of crowns and coronations, orders of chivalry and the like, the way royal families dress for everyday purposes is a crucial part of their glamour. Furthermore, it has to be calibrated carefully for the occasion: ranging from full-on expensive stylish couture for the more serious public occasions on the one hand, to the 'we are just like you' winning little number from a chain store on the other. Less formal and more leisured occasions can accommodate not only twinset and pearls but, nowadays, well-cut jeans for the younger set.

Princesses are proverbially attractive and the female half of all populations pays special attention to their clothes and their patronage of designers. The younger royal women can have dynamic effects on the development of fashion and the promotion of national designers and fashion industries. It is not unknown for copies of royal women's dresses to appear almost immediately in clothing stores, or a dress from a store worn by a princess to result in its instant selling out. Popular newspapers publish patterns for women to make their own copies of favourite dresses. Even the older females are not without influence: Elizabeth II of the UK may be a nonagenarian but her dress sense and her use of bright colours still turns heads.

And dress is not just a flighty, passing thing but capable of delivering important messages. In a recent visit to Pakistan, the Duchess of Cambridge was careful both to wear a designer *salwar kameez* and to ensure that it was designed and made in Pakistan. Similarly, her husband at a formal dinner wore a male counterpart design to that of his wife. These were not trivial and accidental incidents but both deliberately planned compliments to their hosts and a reflection of royal acceptance and approval of customary dress styles used by an important section of the UK's now diverse population.

The Organisation of Ceremony

All royal courts have to organise their ceremonies and usually have an official – styled, say, the chamberlain or marshal – with that responsibility. Someone has to liaise with the military and the police in the planning of visits and travel. All royal families have police protection officers who will liaise with local forces. On the ground, municipal authorities will need to be informed and asked for advice. The degree of formality will vary with the engagement involved, and state ceremonies will, of course, require a greater investment in meticulous planning than visits, for example, to schools, enterprises or charities.

---

[1] Much of this and the next two paragraphs owes a great deal to conversations with Jean Seaton. See also her contribution to Chapter 9.

Conversely, the size of the royal family itself can be a limiting resource on ceremony outside the main national events. The smaller the royal family, the less service it can offer to the nation. Table 6.2 in the next chapter shows the extent of demand on the UK royal family defined as the monarch, the monarch's children and the monarch's own cousins. To help service demand for royal attention in a country of 66 million, every UK county has a local royal official, the Lord-Lieutenant, backed up with Vice and Deputy Lieutenants. Originating in Tudor times to organise part-time militia defence forces, the office nowadays represents the interests of the monarch in their areas, chairs the local committee that selects magistrates, liaises with the local military, sponsors local charitable effort and recognises local achievement. A member of the lieutenancy attends and helps to plan every local royal visit. Whereas Lord-Lieutenants were once invariably chosen from the local male aristocracy and better off 'gentry', in recent years the field of recruitment has widened considerably.

The organisation of state ceremony in England, Wales and Northern Ireland is in the hands of the Earl Marshal, an office hereditary in the Duke of Norfolk who superintends the heralds of the College of Arms, a royal corporation established in 1484. Wearing medieval tabards, the heralds can be seen, for example, at the annual opening of Parliament and, of course, at accessions and coronations. The counterpart of these functions in Scotland is Lyon King of Arms who is effectively both herald and marshal there.

The Cycle of Life Events

Demise and Mourning

Except for the UK, all other monarchies are structured around formal, written constitutions. Other than Belgium, where accession follows only on the new monarch's taking the constitutional oath in the Parliament, accession is automatic on the death of the monarch under the local dynastic regimen though reinforced by statutory oath-taking.

Practices of mourning following demise and celebration of accession vary. Generally, it seems that extravagant styles and lengthy periods of mourning have become replaced by more informal, though still solemn practices. These involve public procession and a funeral service in a principal church before private interment. In Denmark, a royal funeral is the only occasion on which the royal regalia is displayed: it is not at any time actually worn by the monarch. In the Netherlands, the deceased lies in state in a royal chapel to which the public have access to pay their respects. The funeral procession passes through a troop-lined route to the principal church of Delft where, after the service, there is a private interment.

The UK continues the practice from 1910 of the deceased monarch lying-in-state for up to three days in Westminster Hall where members of the public file past as a mark of respect. On the last occasion (in 1952) approximately 300,000 did so. Current plans for the next occasion envisage a similar practice though without the lengthy street procession after the lying-in-state formerly used as a prelude to travel to Windsor castle for funeral and interment. In his study of mourning in Victorian and Edwardian Britain, John Wolffe maintains that following the Prince Consort's death in 1861, the impact of royal deaths was a major factor in the resurgence of the monarchy as a pre-eminent focus for British national identity, through the cultivation of sympathy for the survivors and the expression of solidarity linked to idealised images of domesticity and public service (Wolffe 2000: 284).

The funerals of senior non-reigning members of royal families can also be occasions for significant display reinforcing a monarchy's place as a focus for national sentiment. A recent example is the 2014 funeral of Queen Fabiola, widow of King Baudouin of Belgium. On her death in December, the Belgian government decreed a week of public mourning. Her funeral service took place at the Brussels cathedral and was attended by European and some non-European royalty.

Similarly, the death of Prince Henrik, the Danish Prince Consort, in February 2018 had an important national resonance even though he had long expressed dissatisfaction with his role and the failure to award him the title of king. In a break with tradition, his funeral was a wholly private affair and, at his own wish, he declined the normal practice of burial ultimately beside his wife, Queen Margrethe II in the royal mausoleum. Nonetheless, the population – partly in sympathy no doubt for the widowed Queen – spontaneously responded by laying flowers at places with which the Prince was particularly associated, and large numbers filed past his coffin during the three days when it was displayed.

Mourning is not, of course, just about royal families: monarchs have to recognise and support the mourning of others. The then Spanish King and his heir visited the injured in hospital after the Madrid train bombings that killed 193 people and injured more than 2000 in 2004. The King of Sweden led his country's response to the Asian tsunami in 2014 which killed over 500 Swedes. In the UK in October 1966, a mining spoil heap collapsed onto a school in Aberfan, Wales, killing 116 children and 28 adults. Deeply affected and a young mother herself, the Queen visited and promised to return when the school was rebuilt, honouring the promise in 2012. Similarly, in 2017 and with her grandson the Duke of Cambridge, the Queen visited Grenfell Tower in London devastated by a fire that killed 72 residents. All monarchs find ways of responding to major calamities and thus channel public sympathy to alleviate tragedies of loss.

Inauguration and Investiture

Except for the UK, no other country marks accession with a coronation. Belgium, Luxembourg and the Netherlands have never held one; Denmark, Sweden and Norway discontinued coronations from respectively 1849, 1873 and 1908. (However, as explained in chapter 5.4 above, kings of Norway have since 1908 instituted cathedral blessing ceremonies possessing a proto-coronation form but without involving regalia).

From the dynastic unification of 1492, there have been no coronations in Spain. Current general practice centres on an investiture ceremony where the new monarch swears a constitutional oath in the Parliament. Whereas King Juan Carlos I held a blessing ceremony following the monarchy's restoration in 1975, his son (Felipe VI) did not follow suit in 2014. In 2013, the accession of the new King in the Netherlands took place in a ceremony immediately preceded by the abdication of his predecessor. The royal regalia are on display at the accession service in Amsterdam but have never been worn by the monarch. In Sweden the regalia were worn by the last crowned monarch, Oscar II, at the annual opening of the Riksdag. The practice was discontinued after his death in 1907 when the regalia were merely displayed at the formal openings which were themselves discontinued after 1974.

The last UK coronation – in 1953 – was a lavish affair of troop-lined processions to and from the coronation church, and a nearly three-hour Eucharistic religious service. In all 40,000 troops from the UK, Commonwealth countries and colonies took part. As Ian Bradley forecasts above, it is expected that the next coronation, although still Eucharistic, will be mounted more modestly and find ways to reflect the changed character of the UK's population and place in the world.

Royal Weddings

Now regarded as a permanent feature of the public landscape, it was not always so in the days before modern media. In the UK, for example, they were private affairs taking place usually at night and in the privacy of a royal chapel. Public interest grew from the time of Queen Victoria's wedding in 1840. Taking place in the afternoon at the small chapel in St James's Palace, the Queen made the short carriage journey from Buckingham Palace and was greeted by an enthusiastic crowd. But this was a wholly London phenomenon, as were the scenes in London when her son, the Prince of Wales, received his bride in 1863 before their marriage at Windsor. Influenced no doubt by those scenes, Bagehot in 1867 pointed out 'A princely marriage is the brilliant edition of a universal fact, and as such, it rivets mankind' (Bagehot 1867: 41).

What has changed, Julia Rowbottom argues, is the nature of the media available: The increase in opportunities of reportage that have characterised the modern nation state has encouraged a proliferation of such occasions across the lifetime of a monarch (Rowbotttom2016: 89). What was at first private and then local became national. Rowbottom dates the first example of the latter to the Pathé newsreel coverage of the wedding of the popular Princess Patricia of Connaught, a granddaughter of Queen Victoria, to Captain Ramsay RN at Westminster Abbey on 27 February 1919, the first royal wedding at the Abbey for nearly 600 years. She was also another example of the close relationship between the royal family and the military. When her father was Governor-General of Canada at the outbreak of the First World War, she was asked to give her name to a then newly raised (and still extant) regiment – Princess Patricia's Canadian Light Infantry. She remained its Honorary Colonel until her death in 1974.

Similar processes can be seen at work in all the other European monarchies. The marriage of the Dutch Crown Prince Willem-Alexander on 2 February 2002 was first solemnised at an Amsterdam civic ceremony and then celebrated at the city's main church. Crown Princess Victoria of Sweden's wedding on 19 June 2010 took place in Stockholm Cathedral where royal crowns were displayed. A carriage procession of nearly seven kilometres was seen by a crowd estimated at 500,000 strong; but almost 5 million Swedes watched the wedding on television – half the population of Sweden. Table 5.2 gives the viewing figures of six royal weddings over the last 20 years: in two cases (Prince Felipe in Spain, and Prince William of the UK) almost two thirds of the population watched the wedding on television.

Table 5.2 Royal weddings and their domestic television audience

Country	The Royal Couple	Total Number of Viewers *	Viewers as percentage of population
Norway (2001)	Crown Prince Haakon and Mette-Marit Tjessem Høiby	1.7 million	38%
Netherlands (2002)	Crown Prince Willem-Alexander and Máxima Zorreguieta	6.0 million	37%
Spain (2004)	Prince Felipe of Asturias and Letizia Ortiz	25.6 million	63%
Denmark (2004)	Crown Prince Frederik and Mary Donaldson	2.6 million	48%
Sweden (2010)	Crown Princess Victoria and Daniel Westling	4.7 million	50%
U.K. (2011)	Prince William and Catherine Middleton	38.7 million	64%

* Refers to total combined number of viewers – not to be confused with peak or average audience size.
Source:
UK: www.barb.co.uk/news/the-royal-wedding/
Spain: www.researchgate.net/publication/291861672_The_Spanish_royal_wedding_as_a_media_event_audiences_and_reception_strategies_in_the_broadcast_of_the_Spanish_Crown_prince's_wedding
Norway: www.nrk.no/nyheter/innenriks/kongehuset/kronprinsbryllupet/sendinger/1242958.html
Denmark: www.bt.dk/royale/26-mio.-saa-mary-og-frederik-sige-ja</a>
Netherlands: https://kijkonderzoek.nl/component/com_kijkcijfers/Itemid,133/file,j1-16-1-p

The most recent UK royal wedding – Prince Harry and the American actress Meghan Markle on 19 May 2018 – took place at St George's Chapel, Windsor, in bright sunshine and with a guest list weighted more to celebrities rather than the politicians who had attended his elder brother's 2011 nuptials in recognition of his status as the next heir presumptive. A carriage procession through troop-lined streets and enthusiastic spectators followed. While domestic viewing figures of 11.5 million were less than for his elder brother's marriage in 2011, the earlier wedding's US viewing figures were not surprisingly eclipsed by the estimated nearly 30 million US viewers in 2018. However, it does not follow that all royal weddings are greeted similarly. Thus, the same enthusiasm did not stretch to the Windsor marriage of the Princes' cousin, Eugenie, where some begrudged the display (including a carriage drive) for a person ninth in the line of succession and the fact that the (unannounced) costs of security fell to the public purse (Purves 2018).

Relations with the Military

Chapter 8 below explains the close relationship between all the monarchies and the military, and how all heirs obtain military experience as part of their preparation for succeeding to the throne. All monarchs are accorded high rank in their armed forces, and take care to demonstrate their interest in the forces. Most countries nowadays have some kind of Armed Forces Day which celebrates the importance of the military to the nation and which involve royal participation.

In the UK, the relationship is particularly close. Armistice Day – on or about 11 December every year, the date of the end of the First World War – is one of the most solemn of UK public ceremonies. It is preceded the day before by memorial events in each of the provincial capitals attended by a member of the royal family. At Remembrance Sunday – invariably attended by senior members of the royal family – the Queen herself is now an onlooker rather than a direct participant in the wreath-laying commemorating all those in the UK, the Commonwealth and other British territories who gave their lives in military conflicts since 1914.

Moreover, members of the royal family take a close interest in individual military units. Remembrance Sunday is preceded by a senior member of the family attending the Field of Remembrance in the grounds of Westminster Abbey where each military unit has a plot commemorating its own casualties. The Queen is Colonel in Chief or Royal Colonel of 16 regiments and corps, the Prince of Wales eight and other royals 17 between them. Royal programmes generally make sure that royal colonels visit their units at least once a year, usually on the unit's own regimental day. Audiences with retiring and incoming commanding officers are duly recorded in the Court Circular. Senior family members formally present new colours and guidons to their own and other units in ceremonies that see such emblems renewed every 25 years or so. Such activities reinforce the concept of the armed forces' apoliticality and their own notion that their first loyalty is to the head of state rather than to passing politicians (Beckett 2016: 131). Such ceremonies are not unique to the UK – Queen Letizia of Spain was pictured in *The Times* newspaper on 25 February 2019 presenting a new standard to a Spanish regiment.

Symbolising the Nation: National Days

The monarch is at the apex of events in countries which have a national day. Thus, monarchs in Belgium, Luxembourg, the Netherlands and Spain review military parades and attend thanksgiving religious services. For some years in the Netherlands the monarch has visited a particular city for the local celebrations. In Norway, apart from the 17 May National Day celebration, the focus is on local celebration and the opportunity to wear the local form of national dress. Events involve children in parades, including those in a sort of *rite de passage* about to graduate from secondary education. In Norway, one of the two surviving royal yachts, the *Norge*, facilitates the King's ability to visit what might otherwise be difficult to access coastal communities. The other royal yacht, the *Dannenbrog* of Denmark, is used for similar purposes in that domain and beyond.

The date of the national day usually reflects some specific constitutional or personal event: in Belgium the first oath of the first monarch on 21 July 1831; in Denmark the democratic Constitution of 5 June 1849 and its successor signed the same day in 1953; in Norway the Constitution of 17 May 1814. In Luxembourg and the Netherlands the date is the monarch's real or – to coincide with summer weather – 'official' birthday. The Spanish day has for long been 12 October, the date of Columbus's 1492 landfall in the 'New World'. Now deliberately distanced from its colonialist features, there is a grand parade in the capital and counterparts in regional centres.

The UK does not have a national day. The annual 'trooping the colour' – where monarchs review the household regiments in June on the monarch's 'official' birthday – is treated by UK embassies as a surrogate national day but is not in the UK itself the focus of any general celebration. Although the Stuart monarchs normally chose 23 April – the day of St George, the patron saint of England – for their coronations, that tradition did not develop into a national day nor was the practice followed by their dynastic successors. This absence of a national day derives most importantly from the fact that the UK is a union state. Each of the four parts has its own different saint's day, none of which is recognised as a UK-wide official holiday and which are marked only locally. With effect from 2007, the Scottish Parliament designated St Andrew's day (30 November) as a national day in Scotland though without quite the full effects of a UK Bank Holiday. Northern Ireland, on the other hand, celebrates St Patrick's day on 17 March as a bank holiday, a celebration shared with the Irish Republic. St David's Day – 1 March – is marked in Wales but is not an official bank holiday or the subject of any special designation.

An 'Empire Day' inaugurated in 1904 became rebadged as 'Commonwealth Day' following the dissolution of most of the colonial empire. It has enthusiastic support from a monarch who is also monarch of 15 independent Commonwealth countries – the Realms – with a lavish service in Westminster Abbey in March. A significant affirmation of the monarch's support for the Commonwealth, the event and Commonwealth Day itself passes almost wholly unmarked by the general population, though the inclusive character of the Abbey service has developed in ways which may influence the design of the next coronation service.

The quality of observance of national days varies. Luxembourg has a military review, a cathedral service and a big alfresco party in one of the main squares topped off with fireworks. The Netherlands has fireworks and anything orange. On the other hand, in Spain 12 October seems more an official venture than a popular one, and is actually contested by regions like Catalonia and the Basque territory. Similarly, the attempt to invent a Spanish Constitution Day from 1978 on 6 December has not ignited popular enthusiasm. To the contrary, it is thought that some of the dates in the Catholic religious calendar receive more popular support. In much the same way, the Swedish 6 June marking the end of the Union of Kalmar in 1523 and the beginning of a clearly separate Swedish state, as well as the adoption of the 1809 Instrument of Government, started up only in 1916 as Flag Day. Becoming an official public holiday from 2005 to replace Whitsun Monday, it has monarchical patronage but, unlike the Norwegian equivalent, only tepid general support. It is said that Swedes are much more likely to observe and celebrate Midsummer Day – and as only they know how.

Royal Visits

Table 6.2 enumerates the quantity of visits within the UK undertaken by the royal family. (UK Lord Lieutenants report that there are insatiable local demands for such visits.) The discussion above about National Days instances the nature of domestic visiting in other monarchies. State visits both to and from other countries are essentially tools of diplomacy and are discussed in more detail in Chapter 6.4 and 6.5 below. They follow fairly set patterns – often including a visit to a national memorial, elaborate formal state dinners and conferment of a national order. The UK custom is normally to receive one inward and to travel for one outward state visit each year. In addition, the UK monarch is not only the UK head of state but the head of the Commonwealth of 53 states and monarch also of 15 of them (the 'Realms'), facts which lead to calls for royal visits in support of Commonwealth diplomacy.

Local visits can not only give much pleasure to recipients but also reinforce local achievement and enterprise. They bring communities together, but there is a price because they require a judgement which balances the cost of monarchy against what it is reasonable to expect it to do. The smaller the royal family, the less it can do. While modern media can make spectators of people not actually present at events, it cannot increase the number of events themselves. If to be seen is to be believed, then the opposite must also be true. It could follow that reducing the size of a royal family too far could inadvertently, or deliberately, remove an important part of its rationale.

Monarchies and the Invention of Tradition

It has been observed that monarchies not only inherit and preserve tradition but also invent it. Tradition can also, of course, be disinvented. Thus, within a period of five years, the UK monarchy restored an annual formal state opening of Parliament from 1902 and the formal Swedish counterpart was discontinued from the death of Oscar II in 1907. While the Swedish King still opens each Riksdag session with a short speech, it is the Prime Minister who announces the government's programme. The UK restoration included – and continues – the lavish parliamentary ceremony described in the introduction to this chapter.

All current monarchies have chivalric orders and one way of investigating processes of invention is to analyse their origins. Only two orders are of any real antiquity – the originally Burgundian Order of the Golden Fleece (1430) and the UK's Order of the Garter (1348). The continuity of the Garter reflects the insular geopolitical stability of the UK. The Golden Fleece, on the other hand, has been migratory because of Hapsburg dynastic successions which saw Spanish and then Austrian control of the Low Countries leading to the Order developing exclusively Spanish and Austrian branches accordingly. Only the Danish Order of the *Dannebrog* (1671) dates from the seventeenth century and that kingdom's Order of the Elephant (1768), the Swedish Order of the Seraphim (1748) and the UK's Order of the Bath (1725) date from the century following. All the rest date from the nineteenth century and later.

Systems of chivalric orders of knighthood were developed which both looked outward to reinforce diplomatic reach and looked inwards to confer domestic recognition and associate honorands with the regime, if ranked in grades compatible with the prevailing social class structure. Further, their political significance was underlined by the fact that in most cases monarchs awarded honours only following ministerial advice. Modern monarchs seem to have retained control at least over household honours. The UK monarch has also regained control of the Garter and never lost that for the Victorian Order or the Order of Merit and Companions of Honour.

As the monarchies developed into parliamentary democracies, the numbers of orders increased as the circle of eligibility was widened. In the more populous monarchies, there was also a process of differentiation with orders targeted at different kinds of recipients. In the Netherlands, the new monarchy in 1815 established both the Military

William Order and the Order of the Netherlands Lion. In 1892, it set up the Order of Orange-Nassau. A separate series of royal house orders was inaugurated in 1858 and gained three new branches in 1969. In the UK, the Order of St Michael and St George was established in 1818 for diplomatic and colonial services, the Royal Victorian Order in 1896 to recognise personal service to the monarch, and the Order of the British Empire of 1917 for rewarding contributions to the arts and sciences, work with charitable and welfare organisations, and public service. The Order of the Bath (established in 1725) is used for senior civil servants. In addition, new honours were created with limited membership (as in the Garter) open to citizens of the UK and the Realms: the Order of Merit (1902) and Companions of Honour (1917). As in Belgium, orders specific to overseas territories of colonial empires – the Orders of the Star of India and the Indian Empire – were discontinued with the departure of such territories.

5.6. CONCLUSIONS

Dr Bob Morris, The Constitution Unit, University College London

As charted at 5.2 above, monarchy has historically had a very close, mutually support-ive relationship with religion. From Charlemagne's crowning in Rome by the Pope on Christmas Day 800, European monarchies developed coronation rituals that fused Old Testament legitimisation of Israelite kings with Christian theology and Byzantine prac-tice. Shakespeare has the English King Richard II, though later deposed, assert

> Not all the water in the rough rude sea
>
> Can wash the balm off from an anointed king;
>
> The breath of worldly men cannot depose
>
> The deputy elected by the Lord. (Richard II, Act III, Sc ii)

Exclusive Protestant establishment on the basis of state uniformity of religion in Scandinavia and the UK has – with the exception of Denmark – long since been watered down, in Sweden and Norway to the point of disestablishment. On the other hand, the vestiges of the confessional state linger in Scandinavia and the UK in so far as monarchs have to be members of the national Protestant churches. How far the religious aspects of monarchy can still play an active part in helping to induce acceptance and support for the UK state has, as Ian Bradley shows, a number of uncertainties in a country which has seen both the secularisation *and* the pluralisation of religion. It is doubtful whether the responses to the 1953 coronation claimed by Shils and Young – and contested at the time – are likely to feature at the next coronation, a ceremony nowadays confined to Britain alone of the European monarchies.

Even by 1904, Sidney Low in his Bagehot-style *The Governance of England* main-tained 'there is no doubt that Royalty has lost much of the semi-religious sanction, on which, in most ages it has rested. The divinity that hedges a throne is far less perceptible than it was ...' (Low 1904: 276-7).

With its much-diminished public presence the Church of England nonetheless main-tains a role for the whole of the UK as the orchestrator of what may be called 'civil religion', a practice originally identified as an unexpected outcome of the no establishment of religion clause in the US constitution and which has been defined as

> an inherently political phenomenon which, in the service of the state, attempts to comprehend, celebrate, sanctify and guide the state and its society within a framework that is compatible with popular opinion and the controlling interests of the state. (Bonney 2013: 97).

Ceremony is about marking out royal space and signing the more significant features of communal life. David Cannadine points out that, because of the loss of direct political functions

> modern monarchy is primarily about doing new things, finding new functions, and creating new rationales for its existence in societies no longer religious and hierarchical (where kings were charismatic and authoritarian leaders), but instead urban secular and democratic (where they are repositioned as heads of state) (Cannadine 2008: 41).

The rituals of birth, marriage and death common to us all are given greater salience and glamour by monarchy aided above all by the opportunities modern media – frequently now operating in real time – give to recording and distributing images where, amongst other things, female dress styles have great importance. The viewer can identify with the life pageant of monarchy not only because riveted by a wedding but also because the portrayal of a family over time facilitates an understanding of social continuity and personal identity. While royal lifestyles are distanced from the experience of the general population, royal family members can always be seen and appreciated as people different in many ways but not utterly remote. Their sponsorship of and support for liberal democracy helps to reinforce and legitimise the political system.

6

Service and Welfare; and International Functions

Contents

6.1. INTRODUCTION

Dr Bob Morris, Constitution Unit, UCL

IT HAS ALREADY been noted that monarchs' loss of direct political and constitutional power has seen a displacement of concentration on to 'softer' roles of welfare and service. Some of the range of resulting activities has been surveyed in the previous chapter's analysis of ceremonial functions. This chapter extends the analysis to sponsorship of charitable activities and royal visits, both domestically and overseas. It shows considerable variation in the number of royal engagements conducted in each country, which may in part reflect different traditions, but also reflect the limited capacity of some royal families because of their small size; the differences may also be influenced by different counting rules.

The chapter begins with an analysis of the British experience of royal charitable support, initiatives which can often combine welfarist and service attributes. Frank Prochaska shows how royal females played particularly significant roles in the development of these features at the same time as the political functions of the British monarchy were declining. The next section describes the main events in the royal calendar in each country, and then gives annual figures for less high profile activities, with tables showing how the load is spread between different members of each royal family.

In addition to the domestic dimensions, Philip Murphy and Charles Powell also look at how monarchs are deployed by their countries both to host incoming state visits and to lead similar visits abroad. Such visits can include leading delegations on more specific missions. Whatever the formal status of a visit, the promotion of trade nowadays frequently forms a part. The questions that arise include how far they have choice in these deployments and how far their reputations can be affected by missions that become controversial. The case of Spain has special interest and has separate treatment because a newly restored monarchy was early on used partly to restore the democratic credentials of a former dictatorship.

6.2. WELFARE: THE FEMINISATION OF THE BRITISH MONARCHY

Dr Frank Prochaska, Senior Research Fellow, Somerville College, Oxford

As the Victorian writer Walter Bagehot observed: 'A princely marriage is a brilliant edition of a universal fact, and as such, it rivets mankind' (Bagehot 1867: 41). The wedding of Prince Harry and Meghan Markle in 2018 was a reminder of his insight that hereditary monarchy creates a family on the throne, which brings down the pride of sovereignty to the level of common life. Every parent believes in the hereditary principle. Unlike the sovereignty of an abstract constitution or the vagaries of parliament, monarchy is theatrical and comprehensible to the mass of mankind. Against the background of today's troubled politics, a desire to escape into the beguiling theatre of monarchy is all the more understandable.

As the political importance of the crown declined over the centuries, the royal family filled the vacuum with social work. Indeed, the loss of political power purified the monarchy for civic and charitable purposes. By allying itself with respectable society and voluntary causes, the monarchy has reaffirmed its importance and heightened its popularity. What may be less well understood is that this shift of royal authority from political power to social influence has been largely propelled by the female members of the royal family (Olechnowicz 2007).

Queens are easier to love than sabre-rattling kings. And since the accession of Queen Victoria in 1837, Britain has had a reigning queen for 130 years. This has not been without impact on the life of the nation. So too the role of queen consorts and other female members of the royal family, who have largely driven the social agenda of the Crown. One thinks of the recklessly charitable Queen Alexandra, who pressed Edward VII into opening all those bazaars. Or Queen Mary, who steered her family's voluntary work after the First World War. Or Diana, Princess of Wales, whose name became synonymous with good works (Prochaska 1995). Every time a member of the royal family appears in public, reads a few prepared words and smiles upon a crowd of children, they chalk up another notch in the mystique of monarchy.

The commitment of the female members of the royal family to charity in the past is remarkable, but perhaps not surprising. Like other middle- and upper-class women without opportunities for employment, they found a niche in social work, particularly

causes related to women and children. This history of royal social work became notable in the eighteenth century with the work of the Hanoverian princesses, Caroline of
Ansbach, Augusta of Saxe-Gotha, and Charlotte of Mecklenburg-Strelitz, two of whom
became queen consorts. They took up various patronages associated with the growing
number of charitable institutions, from schools and hospitals to a society for decayed
musicians and a refuge for prostitutes (Marschner 2017: 4017-13).

A few figures on the expansion of royal patronage are worth noting. King George III
and Queen Charlotte had between them about 20 patronages. Queen Victoria and Prince
Albert between them had over 350. George V and Queen Mary roughly 600. The present
Queen now has about 600, which is down from a peak of 800 or so twenty years ago. The
extended royal family today serve as patrons and presidents to around 3000 institutions,
500 of them foreign and Commonwealth (Prochaska 1995). Between them, 15 members
of the royal family carried out 3793 engagements in 2018, most of them charitable: for
the details, see Table 6.2.

As these figures suggest, there has been a vast increase in the number of charitable institutions in the last two centuries, which was often driven by women volunteers
and subscribers. The charitable subscription lists, which often appear at the back of
annual reports, are very suggestive of the growing authority of women in philanthropy.
Typically, under 10 per cent of charitable subscribers were women in the 1790s. By
1830 it had risen to 30 per cent. By the end of the nineteenth century the figure was
over 60 per cent (Prochaska 1980). Intriguingly, this rise in female philanthropy coincided
with the growing role of *royal* women turning their attention to charitable campaigns.
Thus, the feminisation of philanthropy went hand in hand with the feminisation of the
monarchy.

The marked interest of royal women in charitable causes bears out a theme that
once suffused the literature about philanthropy, particularly the growing literature written for women. Countless books and pamphlets in the nineteenth century described a
world of separate spheres, of women being the more benevolent and compassionate sex,
whose lives centred on the affections, on neighbourly and family cares. The Victorian
campaigner and feminist Josephine Butler put it directly in 1869 when she wrote that the
system of personal ministration was essentially 'feminine' in character, while large legislative welfare systems were essentially 'masculine' (Harrison 1982: 258).

Clearly, the role of women contributed mightily to the ascendance of philanthropy in
the reign of Queen Victoria. In 1885, *The Times* announced that the charitable receipts
in London alone exceeded the budgets of several European states (*The Times* 1885: 9).
During the Queen's reign, the communion of interest between the middle classes and
the monarchy expanded. Increasingly, the public found the monarchy both an enabling
institution and a theatre of loyalty, which gave its disparate elements a sense of belonging,
unity and purpose.

The fact that Britain had such a long serving Queen as the focus of loyalty added
significantly to the allure of philanthropy, for not only were women thought to be
more prone to charitable conduct, but Victoria was well suited to represent and extend
the prevailing values of her subjects. Her cast of mind was moral and down-to-earth,
which was in keeping with practical philanthropic campaigns. There were moments
when her cult of benevolence drove her into maudlin flights of fancy. As she wrote to
Queen Augusta of Prussia in 1865: 'More than ever I long to lead a private life, tending

the poor & sick' (Fulford 1976: 51). Can one imagine a king making such a comment? The atavistic warrior tradition of kingship had collapsed into niceness.

Clearly, Queen Victoria's long reign provided a boost to the feminisation of the monarchy. But as the nation's pre-eminent model of female benevolence, she also boosted female philanthropy more generally. What we see developing in the reign of Queen Victoria is a dynamic alliance between the Crown and civil society. The monarchy's welfare work brought unprecedented vitality and success to a range of charitable enterprises. At the same time, it gave the monarchy a new moral authority in a period of waning political power.

In the nineteenth century, the royal family encouraged greater charity in all social classes, and they fully expected it to foster civic improvement, respectability, and deference to the Crown. Voluntary traditions, unlike the emerging social reforms of government, engendered loyalty to the monarchy. Increasingly, the court recognised the monarchy needed to be more sensitive to voluntary opinion as a hedge against oblivion in a burgeoning democracy.

If Edward VII was born with a silver spoon in his mouth, he also arrived with a pair of silver scissors in his hand, the better to cut all those ribbons. Whether at home or overseas, King Edward's willingness to comply with the wishes of charitable campaigners had much to do with the burden of his inheritance, and the pressure placed on him by the women in his life.

Much of the King's philanthropy was driven by the feather headed Queen Alexandra, who encouraged her husband's charitable leanings. Like other royal females she favoured the causes of women and children. But if one issue prevailed it was nursing, where her influence was considerable, if not always of certain benefit. At least six nursing bodies had her name affixed, many of them with military associations. As the historian of nursing Anne Summers remarked: 'It is not easy for the modern reader to appreciate the extent of royal influence in so vital a state interest' (Summers 1988: 241).

If the Queen pressed King Edward to step up his social work, so too did his mistresses, for even his adultery had benign effects. Certainly the time he spent with Frances Maynard, Countess of Warwick, was not all voluptuous immobility. The Countess was an eccentric example of aristocratic social conscience who persuaded Edward to join her on her charitable rounds. Whether he enjoyed visiting aged cottagers, signing workhouse visitors' books or sponsoring many of her pet projects we shall never know, but in order to be with her he did it. With regard to philanthropic activity the great womaniser was womanised. The same was happening to the monarchy generally.

One of the great dilemmas for monarchs in the early twentieth century was how to cope with disillusioned workers in a time of suffrage reform. At issue was whether monarchy itself was compatible with majority rule. The courtier Lord Esher asked whether the voluntary principle was compatible with democracy in the functions of a modern state. In 1910, he wrote that 'the great problem of the future for England and the English race, lies in the answer to the question whether or not ... the labouring classes, will develop an altruistic ideal'. Given the monarchy's limited room for manoeuvre, the strategy he advised was a greater commitment to the voluntary principle. Esher ventured to call it 'the "democratisation" of the monarchy' (Prochaska 2000: 149, 178).

In practice this meant that the royal family would open out across the social classes. The Crown would stay true to its allies in the aristocracy, the armed services, the City and leading charities, but it would shift more of its philanthropy to industrial workers, who were susceptible to royal entreaties to support popular causes. A democratised monarchy, visibly sensitive to the welfare of the poor, was a perfect complement to an imperial monarchy of spectacular display. With the years, it wove them into an ever more elaborate tradition of commemoration, particularly jubilees and coronations, where vast sums were raised for good causes at home and across the Empire.

Royal worries about the Crown's survival mounted dramatically towards the end of the First World War. Circumstances looked grim for the monarchy in 1918, for it now had to deal with the collapse of the European dynastic system, the Russian Revolution, a Labour Party with an explicitly socialist constitution, de-mobbed soldiers, high unemployment and the passage of universal suffrage. Against this background the Crown became ever more conscious of the reciprocal benefits of charitable attachments.

The result was the creation of a policy that George V's private secretary, Lord Stamfordham, elaborated in a series of letters, which illustrated the growing calculation of the Crown in its own defence. The thrust of the policy was to disarm republican threats through the cultivation of the working classes through good works and visits to industrial areas. In short, the Crown sought to convince the poor that it was, as Stamfordham put it: 'a living power for good, with receptive faculties welcoming information affecting the social well-being of all classes, and anxious to further their solutions' (Prochaska 2000: 174).

If any member of the royal family personified this policy, it was Queen Mary. Like her mother, the Duchess of Teck, she was a charitable bulldozer, clearing a path for hundreds of thousands of volunteers. During the war, she took the lead in a host of relief schemes. Countless projects occupied the Queen's diary during the conflict. Practical work was the priority, whether organising nursing services, ladling soup, or providing more effective artificial limbs for disabled soldiers. As Sir George Newman, the chief medical officer at the Ministry of Health wrote in 1921, the Queen's philanthropic work was invaluable and her social influence sound and statesmanlike. And he noted in passing that her beneficent efforts were 'enormously strengthening the influence of the Crown with the people' (Royal Archives, GV/CC 47/672.).

In the 1930s there was no reduction in the charitable efforts of the royal family. Queen Mary took the lead in marshalling her family to play an increasing part in voluntary work. Those famous visits by the Prince of Wales to distressed parts of the country, for example, were the result of pressure from Queen Mary. Along with its charitable work in the socialist heartlands, the monarchy's cultivation of Labour MPs and trade union officials took hold in the interwar years. It was enough to alarm the incorruptible Beatrice Webb, who lamented: 'This romancing about the royal family is, I fear, only a minor symptom of the softening of the brain of socialists' (MacKenzie 2000: 193).

The Second World War was in many respects a reprise of the First World War for the monarchy, but with a different royal cast in the leading roles. Princess Elizabeth moved effortlessly from the jollity of the Girl Guides to the rigours of the Auxiliary Territorial Service. She made her first public speech at the Queen Elizabeth Hospital for Children in Hackney in 1944, where, as President, she defended voluntary traditions. The Princess Royal travelled the country visiting welfare agencies and war canteens. Queen Mary moved to Badminton, where she visited evacuees, opened hospitals and salvaged scrap. Without ceremony or pretentiousness, but with due publicity, George VI and Queen Elizabeth turned Buckingham Palace into a royal war office, becoming symbols of national resistance. Queen Elizabeth, who had carved out a patronage role as Duchess of York, proved to be one of the greatest charitable campaigners the royal family ever produced. She had no constitutional duties as consort, and like Queen Mary before her, recognised that social service was at the heart of her work for the monarchy and the country (Shawcross 2009: 732-4). Over the years she became the patron of over 300 charities. As Harold Nicolson remarked after watching her performance at the opening of some new buildings at Morley College, she had an 'astonishing gift for being sincerely interested in dull people and dull occasions' (Nicolson 1971: 327).

With the stamina of a show business trouper, the Queen performed brilliantly at the bomb sites and feeding centres, in the shelters and the factories. Arguably, the tours during the blitz to the East End and the docks, Swansea and Plymouth, did more to impress on the public the caring and compassionate role of the Crown than her patronage work. She served as the monarchy's own best press agent. Her attention to journalists and cameramen set the standard for other members of the royal family. With a talent for imaginative gestures, she dispatched sixty suites of furniture from Windsor Castle to families who had lost their possessions through bombing and sent a message to each foster parent of an evacuee.

The death of the popular king in 1952 left the nation in grief and gratitude. With the reign of Elizabeth another woman was on the British throne. The dedication of this young, attractive and earnest Queen was not in doubt. She had inherited an exceptional sense of public service and a set of values that were traditional, indeed Victorian. With a built-in reverence for history and ancestral vocations, she subdued her individuality in the interest of the greater good. Like her father and mother, she would seek to provide a caring image that would give the country's disparate elements a sense of common purpose. In the post-war uncertainty, she was widely admired as a beacon of stability and continuity, a model constitutional monarch in keeping with a crowned republic.

Like every monarch since George III, Queen Elizabeth inherited the headship of philanthropy. Locked into its welfare role by custom and interest, the Crown remained well placed to make the most of its voluntary associations. As one of the more thoughtful royal commentators remarked in the 1950s, her granting of patronage was symbolic, suggesting that the entire community had an interest in the work of the organisations to which she extended her support. But more than that she stood for the idea that the ultimate reality at the heart of what often seems the soulless machinery of the modern state was not an abstraction but a human being with common cares like the rest of us (Morrah 1958: 43).

The female members of the royal family have made a notable difference to the nation in its transition to social democracy. It is fair to say that they have shown a decided preference for the personal over the corporate, in keeping with those traditional views about female character. In the process, they have feminised the crown, helping to create what I have called a welfare monarchy, which serves as a substitute for the Crown's loss of political power (Prochaska, 1995).

Against the background of the vast increase in the number of charitable societies, they cleverly fortified royal popularity by nurturing the belief that individuals and institutions, however humble, have a claim on royal services. The vast number of begging letters sent to members of the royal family over the centuries tells the story. As David Cannadine noted, in civic and charitable associations 'the royal culture of hierarchical condescension, and the popular culture of social aspiration ... completely and successfully merged' (Cannadine 1998: 30).

The gradual separation of the monarchy from governance is evident, but in the Crown's survival the exercise of its constitutional role should not be underestimated. But the constitutional and ceremonial roles of the monarchy have tended to obscure the social work that was taking place just below the political surface or behind the Palace window dressing. Yet the significance of the social side of the monarchy's national role through its promotion of welfare causes is largely lost on the Crown's defenders, who continue to dwell on those familiar nostrums of the Constitution and high politics. Do they neglect the welfare work of the monarchy because it has been largely driven by women?

Those hostile to the monarchy also dwell on high politics and the Constitution, while lingering over the royal costs and scandals. Whatever the merits of their case, they, like the monarchists, leave the royal family's welfare work out of the equation. Both royalists and republicans appear to be out of touch with public opinion. A survey in the 1960s showed that the public was more likely to see members of the royal family in a welfare setting than in any other (Harris 1966: 72-3). These days you can hardly turn on your television without seeing a prince or princess at a charitable event, smiling at an adoring crowd.

Bagehot famously made the distinction between the dignified and efficient parts of the Constitution. He celebrated the monarchy as the 'dignified' part, but he failed to notice that it was also becoming an 'efficient' part through its social work. And it is the monarchy's civic purpose, which underpins Britain's social democracy, that is likely to keep the royal family in business. Barring cataclysm or self-destruction, the monarchy is only likely to be in real danger when the begging letters cease to arrive at Buckingham Palace.

6.3. SERVICE: HOW MONARCHIES HAVE TO BE SEEN TO BE BELIEVED

Dr Bob Morris, Constitution Unit, UCL

Whereas the preceding chapter looked at the ceremonial functions of monarchies and the following two sections of this chapter look at the foreign roles of monarchies, this section concentrates on the domestic programmes of monarchies away from the more formal high state pageantry. The question it seeks to address is: what do members of royal families spend most of their public activities away from high ceremony actually doing? Wesley Carr, a former Dean of Westminster Abbey (religion central for the British monarchy), when discussing English church establishment, usefully distinguished between 'high' and 'earthed' establishment as a way of differentiating between august national church/ state interfaces and the local, quotidian manifestations of establishment on the ground. Similarly, there is clearly a range of domestic activities that deserve some more special examination than a mere nod to their existence.

Table 6.1 Royal calendars – annual sequence of major public duties

	Britain	Belgium	Denmark	Netherlands	Norway	Spain	Sweden
January		World Economic Forum (Davos) New Year receptions domestic and diplomatic including EU, NATO, SHAPE	Queen's New Year address to nation New Year's Day dinner for government and judiciary &c and receptions for other dignitaries			Reception for Armed Forces, Royal Palace (commemorates expulsion of British from Menorca in 1782) New Year Reception for foreign diplomats, Royal Palace	
February		Laeken Palace commemorative mass for deceased royals					
March	Commonwealth Day Service, Westminster Abbey						
April	Maundy Thursday ceremony – normally in a different cathedral every year.		Easter residence in Aarhus	King's birthday		Miguel de Cervantes literary prize (University of Alcalá de Henares)	King's birthday
May		Reception for Queen Elisabeth International Music Competition		National Remembrance Victims of Second World war II National Liberation Day	Liberation and National Days		Veterans Day

	Britain	Belgium	Denmark	Netherlands	Norway	Spain	Sweden
June	Queen's (official) birthday review of Household regiments, Horseguards, Whitehall Royal Ascot horseraces			Veterans Day	County visits[1] (King and Queen)		National Day Stenhammar Day[2] Summer residence at Solliden Palace, Öland, mid-June to mid-August
July		King's speech to nation in three languages on eve of National Day parades and Cathedral *Te Deum* on National Day	Residence in Gråsten Slot (Palace), South Jutland				Birthday of Crown Princess
August	Residence at Balmoral Castle, Scotland, into September					Residence at Marivent Palace, Mallorca; reception for local and regional authorities	

(continued)

[1] Norway has 18 counties.
[2] Event at Stenhammar estate focuses on agricultural issues.

Table 6.1 (*Continued*)

	Britain	Belgium	Denmark	Netherlands	Norway	Spain	Sweden
September	Attends Highland Games			Opening of Parliament speech	County visits (Crown prince and princess)	Inauguration of Judicial Year ceremony, Supreme Court Opening of Academic Year, with royal visit to different University every year	Opening of Parliament and speech to members
October	Opening of Parliament	Grand opening of Royal Military Academy year			Opening of Parliament with Speech from the Throne	National Day military parade followed by reception at Royal Palace. Princess of Asturias award ceremony, Oviedo	Opening of General Synod of Church of Sweden, Uppsala Cathedral
November	Remembrance Sunday ceremony at Cenotaph, Whitehall	First World War Armistice Commemoration Day Royal holiday and *Te Deum*			Remembrance Sunday, Oslo		
December	Christmas Day speech to nation and Commonwealth. Residence in Sandringham, Norfolk	Christmas Day speech to nation (in three languages).			Nobel Peace Prize Ceremony New Year's speech to nation	Christmas Eve speech to nation	Nobel Day, Stockholm Annual meeting of Swedish Academy King's Christmas Day speech to nation

Table 6.1 lists the principal fixed public engagements in the calendars of the seven main monarchies. The events occur fairly sparingly throughout the year and share some similar characteristics such as royal TV addresses to the nation (in Belgium in that country's three languages) at the year's end, and royal patronage of the armed forces. In the latter case, the precise nature of the events reflects whether countries participated in the two World Wars and celebrate national days. The Swedish and Dutch monarchies attend their Veterans' Day whereas the British monarchy concentrates its efforts of military recognition on Remembrance Sunday, established in 1919, and does not attend Armed Forces Day, an innovation from 2006 originally entitled Veterans' Day and organised on quite different principles.

The Tables that follow demonstrate in all the examples – Britain, Belgium, Norway, Spain and Sweden – how the formal annual fixed events are surpassed by a great range of other activities, some formal in character but many not very formal at all.[3]

Table 6.2 British royal family engagements 2018

	A	B	C	D	E
The Queen	66	30	187	283	-
Prince of Wales	156	83	159	398	109
Duchess of Cornwall	90	43	16	149	70
Duke of Cambridge	63	28	59	150	70
Duchess of Cambridge	42	10	12	64	23
Duke of Sussex	51	20	37	108	85
Duchess of Sussex	30	8	7	45	51
Duke of York	90	76	93	259	135
Earl of Wessex	94	88	81	263	200
Countess of Wessex	80	47	39	166	73
Princess Royal	229	130	88	447	71
Duke of Gloucester	118	33	42	193	50
Duchess of Gloucester	50	23	14	87	3
Duke of Kent	101	29	10	140	34
Princess Alexandra	48	11	8	67	-
Total	1,308	659	852	2,819	974
Total domestic	2,819				
Grand total	3,793				

A Official visits, opening ceremonies, sports, concerts and charity events.
B Receptions, lunches, dinners and banquets.
C Other engagements including investitures, meetings attended and audiences given.
D Total number of engagements in UK.
E Total number of engagements on official overseas tours.
Source: letter from Mr Tim O'Donovan, *The Times*, 31 December 2018.

[3] Because they are derived from different sources, the tables should be regarded as indicative rather than precise. Not all monarchies publish daily accounts of royal family activities like the British Court Circular

Table 6.3 Belgian royal family engagements 2018

	A	B	C
The King	107	51	80
The Queen	99	24	
The Crown Princess Elisabeth	5		
Prince Gabriel	5		
Prince Emmanuel	6		
Princess Eleonore	6		
King Albert II	7		
Queen Paola	6		
Princess Astrid	28		
Prince Laurent	22		
Princess Claire	9		
Prince Lorenz	13		
Totals	313	75	80
Grand Total	468		

A Official visits, opening ceremonies, sports, concerts and charity events
B Receptions, lunches, dinners and banquets
C Other engagements including investitures, meetings attended and audiences given
Source: www.monarchie.be/

Table 6.4 Norwegian royal family engagements 2018

	A	B	C	D	E
The King	34	41	93	26	155
The Queen			22	18	96
Crown Prince	25		41	22	239
Crown Princess			14	11	129

A State Council meetings
B Ambassadors
C Audiences for all purposes
D Receptions, lunches and dinners
E Official programme posts (published bulletins)

whose existence may tend to enumerate British royal activity more generously, for example where two or three separate events will occur in a single visit, than in other countries such as Belgium. Danish royal activities during 2018 may be found at http://kongehuset.dk/aarsrapport-2018/officielt-program. They show a range of activities similar to Sweden though with a larger 'constitutional' programme plus visits to dependencies in Greenland and the Faroes Islands.

Table 6.5 Swedish royal family engagements 2018

	A	B	C	D	E	F	G	H
The King	82	55	15	14	15	36	37	10
The Queen	4	36	6	36	15	31	23	10
Crown Princess	11	69	9	7	9	18	29	13
Duke of Västergötland	3	45	4	18	9	16	16	14
Duke of Värmland	3	22	8	5	6	17	5	4
Duchess of Värmland	3	13	1	7	6	10	4	4
Duchess of Hälsingland and Gästrikland		2		3	1	4		
Totals	106	242	43	90	61	132	114	55
Grand Total	843							

A Constitutional activities eg councils of state, opening of the Riksdag (and other ceremonies surrounding this), audiences with speaker of Riksdag, Prime Minister, foreign Heads of State and Government, foreign Speakers of Parliament, foreign ambassadors etc.
B Visits (eg municipal visits, company visits, seminars etc)
C Sports and cultural activities
D Foundations (eg meetings within royal foundations)
E Dinners and receptions
F Ceremonies, incl Royal State Ceremonies (christenings), medal presentations (royal and civil), award ceremonies, Formal Gatherings of Royal Academies etc.
G Meetings (eg representatives of government, government agencies, county governors and other international, national, and local representatives,
as well as representatives of various organisations)
H State and official visits

Table 6.6 Spanish royal family engagements 2018

	A	B	C	D	E	F	G	H	Totals
The King	31	23	30	7	17	44	27	7	186
The Queen	11	12	11	7	11	27	17	8	104
Totals	42	35	41	14	28	71	44	15	290

A Constitutional activities e.g. appointment of ministers, national anniversaries and national day, Christmas message
B Visits (eg municipal visits, company visits, seminars etc)
C Sports and cultural activities
D Foundations, e.g. Royal Institutes and Academies
E Lunch/dinners and receptions e.g. for visiting heads of state, diplomatic corps
F Ceremonies (eg presentation of awards, inauguration of national conferences, opening of major new enterprises)
G Meetings (eg participation in high level business and academic seminars, international congresses, working meetings of Spanish National Security Council
and with defence forces)
H State and Official inward and outward visits

The tables by themselves show much activity but do not, of course, itemise it. In the case of Norway, for example, they do not show that a small royal family where the King and Queen are in their early eighties managed to visit all eighteen of Norway's counties in 2018, on occasion assisted by the royal yacht *Norge* (for which see Philip Murphy below) to access remoter communities on that country's especially long coastline. In Britain, the Queen's husband finally withdrew in 2018 – and at the age of 96 – from public duties whereas the Queen herself – now 93 – persists save for undertaking state visits abroad. That and other functions are increasingly assumed by her heir, the Prince of Wales, assisted by other royal family members. British Lord Lieutenants (who represent the Queen in all UK counties) report that local demand for royal attention is insatiable and much careful planning tries to obtain reasonable equality of territorial attention and maximum good use of the visitors.

Although the quality of the data has to restrain generalisation, it seems that the British royal family spends more time than others on 'earthed', that is local, visiting whereas the smaller royal families seem more focused on 'high' functions at a national level. That difference is not caused by free choice but, rather, by limitation of capacity. Where, as in Spain, the royal family consists of only two adults, then the constitutional and national duties are bound to prevail and more 'earthed' activities have to take second place. Moreover, local invitations not only cannot be easily serviced but, because of limited capacity, also cannot be encouraged.Even if they wished to visit more widely, capacity restrains the ability to do so.

Table 6.7 Present size of publicly active royal families

	Britain	Belgium	Denmark	Netherlands	Norway	Spain	Sweden
Size of active family	15	12	6	3	4	3	7
Country population	67m	11.5m	5.7m	17m	5.4m	47m	10m

The issue of capacity is illustrated by Table 6.7. Although it appears that there is some rough relationship between population size and the number of active royals, the proportion in any particular case is vital because size is the essential delimiter of what monarchies can hope to achieve in their roles. Although they may have little or no choice about the fixed events listed in Table 6.1 and only limited influence over state visits as described by Philip Murphy and Charles Powell below, they have in principle more autonomy over optional events and charity sponsorship where they are responding to invitations. That said, all would have to be sure to respond as even-handedly as possible to local invitations to ensure no part of the country feels ignored. Charity sponsorship also has to be managed carefully. The Dutch monarchy relies principally on a single fund – the Orange Fund – to sponsor initiatives for social engagement in the Netherlands and the country's other territories abroad and conducts a limited number of provincial visits each year. Norwegian royal charities have effectively to requalify every five years to ensure that the sponsorship list is revivified continuously.

Relative size also influences individuals' ability to specialise, that is build up over time relationships with particular sectors of society. Some of the tables' data suggest that that happens in certain monarchies, and it is clear that the British monarchy has been arranging such sectoral concentration for some time. Local visits can not only give much pleasure to recipients but also reinforce local achievement and enterprise. They bring communities together, but there is at least implicitly a nice equation to be solved where the cost of monarchy has to be balanced against what it is reasonable to expect it to do. The smaller the royal family, the less it can achieve. While modern media can make spectators of people not actually present at events, it cannot increase the number of events themselves. If to be seen is to be believed, then the opposite must also be true. It could follow that reducing the size of a royal family too far could inadvertently, or deliberately, remove an important part of its modern rationale and whittle away at its legitimacy. This in turn raises the question whether the size of royal families should be more explicitly related both to population size and the level of public financial support. The Spanish monarchy seems particularly under-resourced in relation to Spain's large population, and is also under-resourced financially: see Table 7.1.

6.4. STATE VISITS MADE AND RECEIVED BY THE BRITISH AND OTHER EUROPEAN MONARCHICAL HEADS OF STATE

Professor Philip Murphy, University of London

Defining the State Visit

Terminology

As Erik Goldstein notes, 'state visits' generally have the following features:

(a) They are between heads of state (as opposed to merely heads of government);
(b) They are based in the capital city;
(c) They take place over a number of days;
(d) They involve a large ceremonial element;
(e) They are 'usually indicative of either warm relations or of an attempted rapprochement' (Goldstein 2008: 153-4).

To these we might add some additional characteristics which are, in large part, shared by the monarchical states of Europe:

(f) They are referred to as such by both the host and the visiting country, with terms such as 'informal' or 'official' visit being applied to other interactions;
(g) The invitation to an inward state visit is made by the monarch, acting on ministerial advice;
(h) Inward state visits are relatively rare occasions (there are generally no more than two or three per year), a fact that tends to enhance their status;
(i) The host government bears the costs of the visit.

To say that one of the distinguishing factors of a 'state visit' is that it is recognised as such by the host and visiting state might appear to be stating the obvious. There has certainly been a tendency in recent decades to standardise the terminology around visits by foreign heads of state. Although countries around the world may differ in the precise classification they apply, there is a broad consensus that a 'state visit' involves the elements mentioned above. The official website of the Norwegian royal family, for example, provides an excellent working definition of what are commonly held to be the standard features:

> The term 'state visit' refers to the official visit by one head of state to another. It is different from other official visits in that the programme has ceremonial elements such as arrival and departure ceremonies, a wreath-laying ceremony, banquets and meetings between the head of state and delegations. A state visit may also include bilateral political meetings, business conferences, activities promoting culture, trade and industry, and visits to social and cultural institutions (Royal House of Norway Website 2019: State visits).

Visits accorded a lesser importance tend to be designated by the title of 'official' and/ or 'working' (where the visiting head of state or government is due to have substantive talks with the host government). The British government currently uses the term 'guest of government' for cases in which the UK prime minister invites another head of government for talks in London. This, for example, was the designation given to the visits of the Israeli Prime Minister, Benjamin Netanyahu in February 2017 and the Indian Prime Minister, Narendra Modi, in April 2018 at the time of the Commonwealth Summit in London. The term 'private' visit is reserved for occasions where significant political business is not expected to be transacted. Belgium, for example, currently applies four distinct categories of visit: 'state', 'official', 'working' and 'private' (Kingdom of Belgium Foreign Affairs, Foreign Trade and Development Cooperation Website 2016: Visits of Foreign VIPs in Belgium). The term 'informal' is also sometimes applied to visits without a strong ceremonial element.

A significant factor behind this standardisation of terminology has been the imperative of preventing offence due to misunderstandings around the status of the visit. In the early 1970s, for example, a debate took place within Whitehall around the distinction that had previously been made between 'state' and 'official' visits. This was partly prompted by the decision by President Mobutu of Zaire to cancel a trip to London when he discovered that his scheduled 'official' visit did not have the same status in the UK as a 'state visit'. The decision was therefore made in July 1971 to drop the term 'official' entirely, and to distinguish instead between 'state' and 'private' visits (Brimelow to Hunt, 9 May 1974: FCO 57/636). A further consideration behind this was that the French Government used the term '*visite officielle*' to designate what the British would have termed a 'state visit' (something that might have contributed to the confusion in Francophone Zaire). Prime Minister Edward Heath, however, disliked the use of the term 'private visit as the guest of HMG' as it seemed to promise far less than what was often on offer, namely talks with ministers and entertainment at the Palace.

To address this, it was suggested that three different categories should be applied: 'state', 'semi-official', and 'private'. But some feared this would simply provide scope for further misunderstandings, and the Cabinet Office, with the support of the Palace, suggested yet another binary distinction, this time between a 'state' and a 'Government' visit (Hunt to Brimelow, 22 May 1974; Charteris to Brimelow, 28 May 1974: FCO 57/636). The dilemma was not so much resolved as side-stepped at a meeting of the Royal Visits Committee in June 1974, which decided that 'the best way of avoiding these difficulties might be to spell out fully in each case what was being offered to the visiting head of state and avoiding a precise term which might be misinterpreted' (Cabinet, Royal Visits, RV (74) 1st Meeting, 12 June 1974: FCO 57/636). As we shall see below, this 'creative ambiguity' was perhaps most clearly on display in US President Ronald Reagan's visit to the UK in 1982.

The Form of State Visits

The inward state visit tends to follow a standard format with certain key features which are always repeated and other discretionary elements agreed with the government of the visiting head of state. In the UK, it usually begins with the visiting head of state being met by the Queen on Horse Guards Parade, inspecting a guard of honour and then being driven down the Mall to the Palace in a horse-drawn carriage. Gun salutes are fired in Green Park and the Tower of London. In the evening, the Queen hosts a State Banquet in the Buckingham Palace Ballroom. The following day, there is generally a banquet given by the Lord Mayor and the City of London Corporation at the Guildhall. State visits also include meetings with the British prime minister, a visit to a particular place of interest, and usually a formal dinner hosted by the visiting leader at their country's embassy or at a London hotel. The formal part of the visit may be followed by a private stay by the head of state (Goldstein 2008: 156; Royal Household of the UK Website: State Visits). Perhaps surprisingly, given the increasing significance in recent years of the sacrifice in the World Wars as a focus of British national identity, the programme does not generally involve a wreath laying ceremony as happens, for example in the cases of Norway and the Netherlands.

A similar format is adopted in the case of state visits to Sweden with an arrival ceremony and evening banquet at the Royal Palace on the first day, a lunch hosted by the City of Stockholm at Stockholm City Hall on the second and a visit to another location in Sweden on the third (Swedish Royal Court Website: state visits). The Netherlands follows a similar pattern. On the first day, there is a welcome ceremony in Amsterdam, which includes the laying of a wreath at the National Monument in Dam Square, a visit to the mayor of Amsterdam and a banquet at the royal palace in the evening. The Dutch prime minister hosts a lunch on the second day, and on the third there is a visit to some other location in the Netherlands (Royal Household of the Netherlands Website: Incoming state visits). In Belgium a state visit 'usually comprises an official welcome ceremony and a gala dinner at the Castle of Laeken or the Royal Palace, hosted by Their Majesties the King and Queen. A visit to a Belgian province may be organised' (Kingdom of Belgium Foreign Affairs, Foreign Trade and Development Cooperation Website 2016: Visits of Foreign VIPs in Belgium).

While certain features of the state visit are standard, extensive consultations and negotiations clearly take place in advance to determine the precise shape of the programme. Ahead of the visit of President Chirac of France to London in 1996, for example, the Élysée Palace made clear that he wanted 'a minimum of pomp and ceremony'. British officials were therefore particularly worried about the formalities associated with the visit to the City of London, and one wondered whether it wouldn't be possible to 'keep the Lord Mayor and his flunkeys out of it?' (Rosenbaum 2008). On the other hand, Chirac was keen to have tea with the Queen Mother, an item not usually on the programme of state visits.

The Formal Invitation

The Belgian government defines a state visit as 'an official visit by a head of state to Belgium at the *invitation of His Majesty the King*' (emphasis added) (Kingdom of Belgium Foreign Affairs, Foreign Trade and Development Cooperation Website 2016: Visits of Foreign VIPs in Belgium). For the other European monarchies this is also a key element of any definition. Again, however, it provides scope for confusion, particularly when the foreign state places less importance than the host on matters of protocol. Although during her visit to Washington in January 2017 – shortly after the controversial new President's inauguration – Theresa May attracted criticism for inviting Donald Trump to undertake a state visit, she had been careful to make clear that she was doing so on behalf of the Queen (Walsh et al 2017). An earlier British Prime Minister had, however, risked breaching protocol in her eagerness to secure the visit of a new Republican US President. On Ronald Reagan's election in November 1980, Mrs Thatcher had sent him a message of congratulations, noting that 'he would always find a welcome in this country'. As Whitehall noticed, Reagan's press secretary, Ed Messe, interpreted this as an invitation for Reagan to visit despite there having been no formal notification from the Palace (Richards to Alexander, 21 January 1981: PREM 19/942).

The Frequency and Timing of State Visits

Another key feature of state visits is that they are special because they are rare. The Belgian government specifies that there be no more than two per year (Kingdom of Belgium Foreign Affairs, Foreign Trade and Development Cooperation Website 2016: Visits of Foreign VIPs in Belgium). In the case of the Netherlands, between 1980 and 2013, Queen Beatrix only twice hosted more than two state visits in a single year (in 2000 and 2012, when three took place) (Royal Household of the Netherlands Website: State visits). The Danish royal family have hosted no more two a year since 1974 (Royal House of Denmark Website 2019: State visits). Norway, meanwhile, specifies that 'Between two and four state visits are usually made each year: one or two visits by The King and Queen to a foreign head of state and one or two visits by another head of state to Norway' (Royal House of Norway 2019 Website: State visits).

In the UK, the Queen has never hosted more than three state visits in a single year. Given, however, the understandable tendency to try to fit a number of different visits into each of the British monarch's overseas trips, the Palace has been reluctant to be unduly prescriptive about how many of these she undertakes. In June 1974, her private secretary, Martin Charteris, told the Foreign and Commonwealth Office (FCO), 'there has never been any policy enunciated in respect of the number of outward state visits the Queen should pay in any one year. The policy is that when possible, there should be three inward State (or Commonwealth) Visits, but that this number depends on how much time The Queen spends abroad in that year' (Charteris to Brearley, 17 June 1974: FCO 57/637).

In the case of the UK, the timing of inward state visits is restricted not merely by sometimes considerable periods of travel overseas by the monarch (necessitated in part by the demands of the other Commonwealth Realms), but also by set fixtures in the royal diary. These include not only prolonged visits to Balmoral over the summer and Sandringham at Christmas, but also some key points in the sporting calendar. In 1974, responding to formal advice about forthcoming engagements, Charteris reminded Downing Street that as well as the Queen's Official Birthday in the middle of the month, the first week of June was 'complicated by the Derby and the Oaks' (Charteris to Armstrong, 21 January 1974: FCO 57/636). Royal Ascot also rendered part of the second half of June off-limits for royal engagements (Note by Collins, 15 February 1974: FCO 57/636).

The Costs of the Visit

It is conventional practice that the host government covers the costs of the visiting delegation during state visits. It does so, however, only for the duration of the official programme, and the cost of international air fares is borne by the visiting government. In the UK context, in relation to the Sovereign Grant, introduced in 2012, the funding of state visits raises an important point. The Sovereign Grant replaces the Civil List, which was previously the main source of income of the royal household (along with a number of smaller grants covering things like royal travel and the maintenance of royal build-ings). It now funds most overseas trips by members of the royal family, including visits to Commonwealth countries.

Yet as the FCO recently made clear in a reply to a Freedom of Information Request about the Chinese state visit in 2015:

> For a State Visit, Principals are invited to the UK as a guest of Her Majesty The Queen. The Foreign and Commonwealth Office (FCO) covers the costs of a State Visit, which includes accommodation, transport, food and incidentals (to a set limit) in the UK. Costs towards food and incidentals are grouped under entertainment and FCO will pay these costs for the Official Delegation (Principal plus 10 ministers or senior officials) during the official programme only. In addition, the FCO will cover entertainment costs for one advance recon-naissance programme for the official members of that delegation (Foreign and Commonwealth Office 2016).

These entertainment cost, the reply noted, included those of the State Banquet at Buckingham Palace. As it has been for many decades, the funding is administered by the Protocol Directorate of the FCO.

The Planning of the State Visit and the Role of Ministerial Advice

In the UK, a Royal Visits Committee, serviced by the Cabinet Office plays a key role in coordinating inward and outward state visits and other major overseas visits by members of the various royal households. The Cabinet committee on 'Royal Visits Overseas and Visits by Foreign Heads of State' met for the first time in July 1959, and included repre-sentatives from the Foreign Office, the Colonial Office, the Commonwealth Relations Office, the Treasury and the Palace (Cabinet Committee on Royal Visits Overseas and Visits by Foreign Heads of State, GEN 693/1, 20 July 1959: CAB 21/3899). The idea of convening such a meeting was raised by Prime Minister Harold Macmillan, and enthusiastically endorsed by the Queen's private secretary, Michael Adeane. Adeane was, however, keen to underline a constitutional principle that remains central to the function-ing of the committee: that the prime ministers of the Commonwealth Realms had the right of direct access to the Queen, and the British Prime Minister was not competent to advise her on visits to her Realms (Adeane to Brook, 15 June 1959: CAB 21/3899).

The Cabinet Office is responsible for passing the recommendations of the Royal Visits Committee to the minister responsible for offering formal advice to the Queen. This was initially the Foreign Secretary, on the basis that overseas royal visits outside the Realms were essentially acts of British foreign policy. From the early 1970s, however, it has been the prime minister who has advised the Queen on her overseas trips (Du Boulay to Goodall, 5 January 1976: FCO 57/680). Despite this change, the convention has been retained that on her outward state visits (including visits to Commonwealth republics) the Queen should be accompanied by the British Foreign Secretary or, when that was not possible, by another FCO minister (Du Boulay to Goodall, 5 January 1976: FCO 57/680). Norway also specifies that when its King and Queen are travelling abroad on state visits they are accompanied by the country's foreign minister (Royal House of Norway Website 2019: State visits).

Given the large element of contingency in the planning of state visits the decisions of the Royal Visits Committee were always hedged around with qualifications and had something of the quality of the manipulation of a Rubic's Cube. The following extract from the minutes of the Committee's meeting in May 1981 gives a strong flavour of this:

> If it proved impossible to arrange for Sultan Qaboos to visit Britain in November this year, he should be the first inward state visitor for 1982. The two priorities for 1982 should be President Karamanlis of Greece and King Juan Carlos of Spain. The visit of President Karamanlis, given his age, could best take place in June. A visit by King Juan Carlos was dependent upon developments over Gibraltar. The King would also be a good candidate for a June visit if President Karamanlis was not available. There were three reserves for 1982: The Shaik of Kuwait, Queen Beatrix and President Marcos. If the visit by Sultan Qaboos could not take place until March 1982, it would probably be undesirable for the Shaikh of Kuwait to pay a State Visit that year. If, however, a visit by Sultan Qaboos took place in November 1981, the Shaikh of Kuwait would be a very good reserve candidate for 1982. Queen Beatrix would be a good choice for a visit to Windsor in the late spring or early summer (Royal Visits Committee, Extracts of the Minutes of a Meeting held in the Cabinet Office, 18 May 1981: FCO 57/975).

In turn, the formal ministerial 'advice' which issued from these meetings was often similarly tentative, offering the Palace considerable discretion and room for manoeuvre.

The UK Royal Visits Committee is currently chaired by the permanent under-secretary at the FCO. The private secretaries to the Queen, the Prince of Wales and the Duke of Cambridge all attend, as does the prime minister, the keeper of the privy purse, the chief executive of UK Trade and Investment (UKTI), the national security adviser and the director of protocol at the FCO (Sovereign Grant Annual Report 2019: 16).

Like the UK, the Netherlands has a committee to coordinate state and royal visits which includes representatives of the court, the Prime Minister's office and the Foreign Office.[4] Meanwhile, according to the official website of the Royal Court, the decision-making process in Sweden works in the following way:

> The Ministry for Foreign Affairs draws up a list of possible countries, and the list is then approved by the Prime Minister's Office. The Minister for Foreign Affairs visits The King and

---

[4] I am grateful to Bart van Poelgeest for this information.

Queen a couple of times a year, and one or two main proposals are presented. Of course, The King assents to the Government's wishes. After a country has been decided on, we hold further discussions on timings and the exact date of the visit, and The King and Queen then send an official invitation (Swedish Royal Court Website 2011: A State Visit: how it works).

State Visits and Trade Promotion

In describing the format of its inward state visits, Sweden is quite explicit in highlighting their role in trade promotion: the second day of the Visit 'tends to be more business-oriented, with a focus on issues of economic cooperation. For example, the programme for this visit includes visits to the Swedish Trade Council and the electricity supplier Svenska Kraftnät' (Swedish Royal Court 2011 Website: A State Visit: how it works). The Trade Council invites business representatives from the guest country and devises its own, parallel programme for them. Likewise, on outward state visits by the Swedish monarch, the Council will normally organise its own parallel visit and programme.[5]

Whether or not the other European monarchies are as transparent as the Swedish in this respect, it is clear that they share this appreciation of the role of state visits in promoting national economic interests. In the wake of the Chinese state visit to the UK in October 2015, the British government was keen to announce that up to £40 billion worth of deals had been agreed between the two countries over its course, including a £6 billion Chinese investment to build two new nuclear reactors at Hinkley Point C in Somerset (UK Trade and Investment 2015).

Trade has sometimes proved the imperative for potentially controversial and politically embarrassing state visits. Ahead of the visit to the UK in 1981 of King Khalid of Saudi Arabia, the British Ambassador, James Craig, reminded the British Foreign Secretary of the extent of the economic interests that could be affected by the success or failure of the visit, noting 'we have vast commercial interests in Saudi Arabia which the visit should do much to promote. She has just launched the third of her five-year plans, on which the sum of $235 billion is to be spent and there are splendid opportunities for contracts and sales' (Craig to Carrington, 18 May 1981: PREM 19/901). An earlier visit, scheduled for the previous year, had been cancelled in extremely embarrassing circumstances after the British television channel ITV had broadcast a documentary about the execution for adultery in 1977 of a Saudi princess.

Commercial imperatives also played a role in probably the most inglorious chapter in the history of inward state visits to London, that of the Romanian dictator, Nicolai Ceausescu, in 1978. Although idea of a visit had originally been raised earlier in the decade under the Conservative government of Edward Heath, the Labour administration of James Callaghan faced strong economic pressure to honour the invitation, despite reports of the appalling behaviour of Ceausescu and his retinue on earlier foreign trips. In particular there was the prospect of him signing a deal for British Aircraft Corporation passenger jets worth £200 million and Rolls Royce engines worth another £100 million, a much-needed boost to the UK's aircraft industry (Hardman 2018: 90).

---

[5] See, for example, Business Sweden 2015: State Visit to Lithuania 7-9 October 2015.

Factors Complicating UK State Visits: Imperial Legacies, Religion and the Special Relationship.

The Commonwealth

The British royal family is unique in terms of the range and regularity of its outward visits to its country's former colonies. In other European monarchies visits have been far less frequent. Queen Juliana of the Netherlands made her first to Indonesia in 1971, 22 years after the country's independence (Sterba 1971). King Baudouin waited 10 years after his controversial visit at the time of the country's independence celebrations before visiting Zaire again in 1970 as the guest of President Mobutu. Thereafter, visits to the country by members of the Belgian royal family have been rare, and Prince Laurent, the younger brother of the current King, earned a reprimand by making an unauthorised trip in 2011.

The institution which serves to bind the UK monarchy to the former territories of the British Empire is the Commonwealth. All Commonwealth countries recognise the Queen as the organisation's 'Head', and in 15 outside the UK (the 'Commonwealth Realms') she is the sovereign. In constitutional terms, although all Commonwealth Member States tend to attract more visits from the UK royal family than their size and significance might otherwise warrant, it is the Commonwealth Realms that pose specific problems.

The first of these relates to the very term 'head of state'. The Queen is represented in the non-UK Realms by a Governor-General, generally a national of the country concerned appointed on the advice of its prime minister. Governors-General have increasingly been accorded the status of heads of state on official visits overseas, and when the Queen makes state visits it is generally recognised that she does so in her capacity as sovereign of the UK (or occasionally, in the case of some Commonwealth republics, as head of the Commonwealth) and not as sovereign of her other Realms.

This is a point on which the Palace has arguably tried to 'have it both ways'. A significant argument by some monarchists in the Realms is that they already have a local 'head of state' in the form of the Governor-General and that, as such, the move to republican status would add nothing of substance in terms of the 'patriation' of their constitutions. During the course of the 1999 referendum in Australia on the introduction of a republic, the Palace appeared to buttress the arguments of the monarchist camp by removing the term 'head of state' from its description of the Queen's relationship to the Commonwealth Realms, and using the term 'sovereign' instead (Boyce 2008: 216; Murphy 2013: 184; Twomey 2018: 737).

Yet although the 1926 Imperial Conference, which recognised what were then referred to as 'the Dominions' as having complete control over their own external policy, also empowered Governors-General to represent the sovereign in meetings with other foreign heads of state, it did not give them equal status. As a consequence, the practice of Governors-General making state visits was relatively slow to develop. The Canadian Governor-General did not make a state visit to Europe until 1971 and to Asia until 1987. And the issue of status posed particular problems in some countries which had retained a monarchy, with Japan proving unwilling to invite Australian Governors-General to make state visits (Goldstein 2008: 157).

Indeed, as the constitutional historian Anne Twomey has recently suggested, both logic and general practice suggest that Governors-General are not heads of state. Perhaps the most telling example comes from Australia. Here, the constitutional role of the Governor-General operates only at a national level and not at the level of the states, where the Queen is represented by the state Governors (Twomey 2018: 734-9) The constitutions of some Commonwealth Realms, like Papua New Guinea and Tuvalu, specifically identify the Queen as their head of state. In Canada, although a recent Governor-General attempted to stake a constitutional claim to the title 'head of state', there was subsequently push-back from the government of Stephen Harper, and by 2017 the Governor-General's website explicitly stated that the Queen was head of state of Canada and the Governor-General merely her representative (Twomey 2018: 741).

The constitutional link provided by the Crown means there has never been a 'state visit' by a representative of one of the Realms to the UK. By contrast, from 1963 when President Sarvipalli Radhakrishnan of India visited London, state visits by the heads of Commonwealth republics and indigenous monarchies have been fairly regular events (Hardman 2018: 542). Over the next couple of decades, India was followed by Pakistan (President Ayup Khan) in 1966, Nigeria (the head of the military government, General Gowon) in 1973, Malaysia (the Yang di-Pertuan Agong and the Raja Permaisuri Agong) in 1974, Tanzania (Julius Nyerere) in 1975, Kenya (Daniel ArapMoi) in 1979, Nigeria (President Shehu Shangari) in 1981, and Malawi (Hastings Banda) in 1985.

State Visits by the Queen to Commonwealth Republics began in 1961, with tours of India, Pakistan and Ghana. Thereafter, it is notable how these visits have been arranged to coincide with her attendance at the (roughly) biennial Commonwealth Heads of Government Meetings (CHOGMs) which from 1971 onwards have generally been scheduled outside the UK. Although the Queen was only given a formal ceremonial role at these gatherings in 1997, she has made a point of being present when the meetings took place and giving a banquet for heads. The only exceptions before 2020 have been the 1971 CHOGM in Singapore (when Heath formally advised her not to go, fearing that she might become embroiled in a row over British arms sales to South Africa) and the controversial meeting in Sri Lanka in 2013 (when the Palace offered the plausible but not necessarily convincing explanation that she was cutting down on her long-haul travel). Clearly, however, the *expectation* that she would visit Singapore in 1971 had led to arrangements being initiated for state visits to Singapore itself as well as Malaysia, Brunei and Kenya, and when she was obliged to cancel her attendance at the CHOGM, these were simply postponed to the following year. The CHOGM in Lusaka in 1979 provided the opportunity for state visits to Zambia, Tanzania, Botswana and Malawi. The Delhi CHOGM in 1983 provided the focal point for state Visits to India, Bangladesh and Kenya, the Kuala Lumpur CHOGM in 1989 led to state visits to Malaysia and Singapore, and the Harare CHOGM of 1991 to state visits to Zimbabwe and Namibia. The Durban CHOGM of 1999 saw the Queen paying state visits to South Africa, Ghana and Mozambique, and she made individual state visits to coincide with the CHOGMs in Nigeria (2003), Malta (2005), Uganda (2007), Trinidad and Tobago (2009), and Malta (2015).

Given the significance of CHOGMs in determining the timing and destination of the Queen's Commonwealth visits, a perennial problem for the Royal Visit Committee was that the precise date and location of these meetings was sometimes only fixed at a relatively late stage. In January 1974, for example, the Cabinet Office noted that there remained some uncertainty about whether the next CHOGM, due to take place in Jamaica, would meet in late 1975 or early 1976. An official from the department approached one of their counterparts in the FCO asking whether, 'since we do not want to create an impossible burden for the Queen in 1975', enquiries could be made about this (Webster to Curle, 28 January 1974: FCO 57/636). Yet at this stage, liaison between the Palace and the Commonwealth Secretariat (which took a leading role agreeing the schedule for CHOGMs) seems to have been quite rudimentary. In March 1974, the FCO noted that the Secretariat was

> aware of the Queen's personal interest in the arrangements for the next [C]H[O]GM and Her wish to be present when the Heads of Government meet. There is, however, no indication that [Commonwealth Secretary General] Mr Arnold Smith intends to sound [sic] the Palace before proposing a Heads of Government Meeting in May next year (Note by Storar, 5 March 1974: FCO 57/636).

When the Royal Visits Committee met in May 1978, it was decided that there should be a working assumption that the next CHOGM would take place in Lusaka in Zambia in in August 1979. Yet it also noted that the Queen had still not been officially advised to make a visit to Zambia (Wall to 'Nick', 4 August 1978: FCO 45/2569). Indeed, given that the guerrilla war in neighbouring Rhodesia periodically spilled over into Zambian territory, security fears were such that, following her election in May 1979, Mrs Thatcher seriously contemplated advising the Queen not to make the trip.

Rather as in colonial times, the British officials often saw Commonwealth countries in terms of their position within regional groupings. They were particularly conscious that a country's leader might be offended if the Queen did not visit it during a tour of the region. In 1978, for example, Britain's High Commissioner in Lilongwe warned that President Hastings Banda would feel 'personally slighted' if the Queen visited neighbouring Zambia for the 1979 CHOHM without also visiting Malawi (Scott to Mansfield, 30 June 1978: FCO 45/2569). Likewise, in 1974, officials at the FCO noted that it would cause offence if the Queen visited Lesotho without also paying a visit to the other former 'high commission territories' Botswana and Swaziland. If, however, she visited all three without paying a visit to South Africa (which was considered to be out of the question on political grounds), this might appear as a calculated snub (Note by Central and Southern Africa Department, 3 June 1974: FCO 57/636).

Ireland and the Holy See

Two additional and related features of British history – its embrace of Protestantism and creation of a national church with the monarch as its 'Supreme Governor' in the sixteenth century, and its quasi-imperial relationship with Ireland – have until very recently precluded the exchange of state visits with the Republic of Ireland and Vatican. Until the 1990s, strained relations between the UK and Eire (which had become a republic in 1949), exacerbated by the outbreak of violence in Northern Ireland, meant that no President of Ireland had visited London in an official capacity during their tenure in office. One of the problems was terminology: their designation as 'President of Ireland' implied a claim to Northern Ireland that the British government could not accept (Goldstein 2008: 173). President Mary Robinson made the first such visit in 1991 to receive an honorary degree from Cambridge University (conferred by its Chancellor, the Duke of Edinburgh). She met the Queen in London in 1993 and again in 1995, and the following year she made a further visit, at the invitation of the British Prime Minister, John Major, during which she had lunch with the Queen and inspected a guard of honour in the grounds of Buckingham Palace (Robinson 2014). Yet even this occasion was designated as an official rather than as a state visit. It was therefore of major political significance when the Queen made the first state visit to the Irish Republic in 2011, hosted by President Mary McAleese, and when, another three years later in 2014, the Irish President, Michael D Higgins, paid a return state visit to London.

The first state visit to Britain by a Pope (in their capacity of head of state of the Holy See) only came in 2010 when Pope Benedict XVI visited London. This was not the first papal visit to the UK since the Reformation. That came in 1982. But John Paul II's tour of the UK was treated as a 'pastoral' visit by the UK (British Embassy Holy See 2015).

The 'Special Relationship' with the United States

Given the importance successive British governments have placed on the 'special relationship' with the US, it is striking how infrequent inward state visits to London by American presidents have been and how recently the first took place. The first occasion that was mutually recognised as such only came in 2003 with George W Bush's state visit. This has been followed by two further state visits: Obama's in 2011 and Trump's in 2019. Presidential State Visits to other European countries took place well before 2003. Bill Clinton, for example, paid a State Visit to Norway in 1997.

Theresa May faced criticism for seeking a state visit so early in President Trump's time in office. The former permanent under-secretary at the FCO, Lord Ricketts, for example, complained in a letter to *The Times* that there was 'no precedent for a US president paying a state visit to this country in their first year' (Lord Ricketts 2017). Yet given that only two US state visits to London had taken place by that stage, and, as we shall see, Mrs Thatcher had been keen for a state visit by Ronald Reagan early in his term in office, it would be difficult to argue that a strong precedent actually existed.

Their infrequency has been due in part to specific features both of the American presidency and the state visit programme in London. The relatively brief tenure in office of US presidents has tended to limit their capacity to fulfil a significant number of state visits, and the use of the state visit as a vehicle of US diplomacy only really got going under Nixon (who undertook 12 of them, compared with Johnson's 4, Kennedy's 3, and Truman and Eisenhower who both undertook only two each) (Goldstein 2008: 160). It was simply more efficient for US presidents to undertake brief visits to overseas policymakers focusing on business rather than ceremony. Indeed, the notion of a state visit, either inward or outward, was not officially recognised by the US government until 1947 when Harry Truman visited Mexico City (Goldstein 2008: 156). The first inward state visit recognised as such by the US was not until 1954, when South Korean president Syngman Rhee visited Washington.

Although presidents Kennedy and Nixon made highly publicised visits to the UK, neither of these were state visits. Kennedys' visit in June 1961, on his way back from Paris, was billed as a private stop-over to attend the christening of the daughter of Jackie

Kennedy's sister, Lee Radziwill (Smith 2012: 157). The Queen gave a dinner for them at Buckingham Palace the day after the christening. By contrast, Kennedy paid what was generally recognised as a 'state visit' to the Republic of Ireland in 1963. When Nixon came in October 1970, it was part of a working visit at the invitation of Prime Minister Edward Heath. The Queen was still in Balmoral. The Palace expressed concern that it would appear discourteous if the Queen did not meet Nixon, but was also worried that it might be difficult to entertain such a large party at Windsor or Buckingham Palace. The Queen therefore accepted Heath's invitation to fly down and meet Nixon for lunch at Chequers (Smith 2012: 244-5).

In the case of the UK, the tradition of guests of state visits being driven down the Mall seems to have had a direct bearing on the frequency of state visits by American Presidents. In effect, following Kennedy's assassination in Texas in 1963, the notion of the US president being driven in an open, horse-drawn carriage was just too risky for American security officials to contemplate.[6] As the FCO told Downing Street in January 1981, 'For logistic and security reasons Presidents of the United States do not usually pay state visits to Britain' (Richards to Alexander, 21 January 1981: PREM 19/942). Keen that the new US President should be suitably honoured, Mrs Thatcher asked whether it would be possible to offer President Reagan a state visit, even if this had to omit the Open Carriage Ride (Alexander to Richards, 22 January 1981: PREM 19/942). What was eventually agreed was a unique amalgam of different elements, nicely illustrating the 'creative ambiguity' referred to above. Reagan received a specific invitation from the Queen to stay with her at Windsor Castle in June 1982 in between a European Economic Summit and a NATO meeting, both of which were already in the President's diary. Yet despite having some of the elements usually associated with the 'state visit', including a banquet hosted by the Queen, it was not referred to as such by the British government.

The horse-drawn procession down the Mall was omitted from the official programme of the state visits of Bush, Obama and most recently (in 2019) of Trump. The state banquet for Trump was boycotted by the leader of the Opposition, Jeremy Corbyn. This was an unusual but not unprecedented gesture. The then Labour leader, Harold Wilson, boycotted the state banquet for King Paul and Queen Frederika of Greece during their highly controversial state visit to London in 1963, the first in the current Queen's reign to attract significant public protests (Bradford 1996: 301-2).

More broadly, it is possible to detect deeper cultural differences between the UK and its US ally when it comes to ritual and ceremony. Although Britain has prided itself in its ability to choreograph major ceremonial events involving the royal family, as we have already seen in the case of Chirac's state visit in 1996, not all nations placed the same emphasis on public display. Like France, the United States was proud of its unostentatiously sober, republican political formation. By extension, US administrations sometimes appeared somewhat impatient with the British distinction between the head of state and head of government, especially when the latter was a particularly valued ally. For Mrs Thatcher's visit to Washington in November 1988, the British embassy reported that

---

[6] As Goldstein notes (Goldstein 2008: 161), a rare occasion after 1963 when a US President rode in an open-topped vehicle was Nixon's visit to Cairo in 1974. By that stage, however, Nixon might have decided that he had nothing to lose.

'American officials had repeatedly pointed out to us in the run-up to the visit that it was a state visit in all but name' (Telegram from British Embassy, Washington, to FCO, 18 November 1988, Thatcher Mss: uncatalogued, Churchill Archive Centre).

Indeed, British officials feared that what they perceived as the Americans' lack of aptitude for ceremonial occasions might embarrass the Queen. Four years ahead of the US bicentennial celebrations in 1976, the British Ambassador in Washington, Lord Cromer, warned London against the Queen taking part. 'As you know', he suggested,

> these affairs are often organised here in a slip-shod and informal way while at the same time involving a high degree of publicity. I think that there would be a very real chance not only of embarrassment to Her Majesty, but of impairment to the dignity of the monarchy (Cromer to Greenhill, 18 October 1972: FCO 57/636).

By May 1974, the FCO noted that preparations for the bicentennial celebrations had 'got off to a very bad start', and that the situation had been complicated further by the Watergate controversy (Note by Gordon Lennox, 28 May 1974: FCO 57/636). It saw no reason to overturn Cromer's advice that Prince Charles should go in the Queen's place. In February 1982, the UK's ambassador to the US, Nicholas Henderson, complained of 'the degree of casual incompetence displayed by Washington' in the arrangements ahead of Reagan's stay as a guest of the Queen (Henderson 1994: 435).

Diplomatic Assets: 'Junior' Royals and Royal Yachts

The 'Junior' Royals

Britain's extended royal family gives the UK a unique degree of 'coverage' when it comes to ceremonial occasions. According to the most recent annual report by the Sovereign Grant Fund, in recent years members of the royal family have, between them, undertaken around 3200 annual public engagements at home and overseas (Sovereign Grant Annual Report 2019: 6). Their visits overseas help to maintain the public profile of the UK and its monarchy in other parts of the world. Other family members also ensure that when the Queen herself is overseas a large number of royal engagements can continue to be carried out in Britain. Although the Royal Family of Sweden is less extensive, its members are still able, between them, to attend a far wider range of events than would be possible for a single ceremonial president. In 2018, for example, while King Carl XVI Gustaf was able to participate in 217 official engagements (including domestic and overseas visits, state functions and meetings) and Queen Silvia 128, their two eldest children and their spouses participated in an additional 319: for details, see Table 6.5.

As monarchs age, their ability and inclination to take on arduous overseas travel naturally decrease, and more junior royals step in to take their place. As the Queen has reduced her long-haul travel commitments in recent years, other members of the British royal family have taken on prominent overseas commitments. In the case of Norway, Crown Prince Haakon has undertaken a series of major overseas tours in recent years. Nevertheless, his father King Harald, although 82, was prepared to undertake a state visit to Chile in March 2019, having carried out visits to Argentina and China the previous year.

An important and sometimes overlooked benefit of junior royals is the way in which they could be deployed on overseas engagements which were considered too controversial, unsuitable or premature for the Queen to undertake. Prince Charles, for example, made a private visit to the Expo 70 in Japan in 1970 and had dinner with Emperor Hirohito and the Imperial family (Hardman 2018: 474). This served to prepare the ground for the controversial state visit to London the following year by the Emperor, when veterans of the Second World War conflict against Japan staged a silent protest during his ride down the Mall. Prince Bernhard of the Netherlands also attended Expo 70 ahead of an even more controversial Dutch state visit by Hirohito in October 1971. Despite the thaw in relations with the West after Mikhail Gorbachev's rise to power in the USSR, the Foreign and Commonwealth Office remained cautious about the appropriateness of the Queen making a state visit to Moscow. It was therefore left to Princess Anne to 'break the ice' with a visit in May 1990. The record of a meeting with Mrs Thatcher the following month produced by Charles Powell noted, 'Gorbachev commented that the Princess Royal's recent visit had been very successful. He had liked her very much. Her visit drew a line under the old conflict about the Romanov dynasty' (Note by Charles Powell, 'Prime Minister's Meeting with President Gorbachev in the Kremlin on Friday 8 June': PREM 19/3176).

Members of the British royal family also played a significant role in representing the Queen at the ceremonies marking the independence of Britain's colonies (Murphy 2008: 667-76). As the Colonial Office noted in May 1966, it had by that stage become 'a well-established Palace rule' that neither the Queen nor the Queen Mother presided over independence celebrations (Minute by Poynton, 18 May 1966: CO 1032/496). King Baudoiun of Belgium notoriously attended the Congo's independence celebration on 30 June 1960, and gave a highly provocative speech in front of the national assembly in Kinshasa, praising his country's record in the territory and presenting the day as the culmination of Belgium's 'civilising mission'. In reply, the Congo's new Prime Minister, Patrice Lumumba, denounced Belgium's colonial record in a very public rebuke to the King. There was clearly a desire to avoid the symbolic affront to national dignity that would be entailed by the Queen herself or her mother (the wife of the final Emperor of India) witnessing the lowering of the Union Flag. But perhaps more importantly, there was a sense that it would not be appropriate, constitutionally, for the Queen, who remained Head of the Commonwealth and in some cases sovereign of the countries concerned, to be present at an 'independence' ceremony.

The link between inward and outward royal visits and trade promotion has helped to encourage 'junior' royals to take on business-related roles. In 2016, for example, the Dutch Government appointed Prince Constantijn Special Envoy of StartupDelta, a public-private venture which aims to promote new businesses in the Netherlands (StartupDelta Website: Constantijn-van-oranje). Nevertheless, the connection has not always been a happy one. In 2001, the Blair government gave Prince Andrew, the Queen's second son, the formal designation of 'special representative' for Trade and Investment. He was, however, forced to step down from that role in 2011 after his private life and foreign contacts attracted controversy (BBC News 2011). Prince Laurent, the controversial younger brother of King Philippe of Belgium, became embroiled in an ongoing dispute over his business dealings with Colonel Gaddafi's Libya (Marks 2019). Perhaps the greatest post-war scandal to hit the Dutch royal family came in 1976 when it emerged that the US Lockheed aircraft manufacturers had made a secret payment of $1.1 million to Prince Bernhard, the consort of the Queen (Madden 1976). Bernhard had become a pivotal figure in the public life of the Netherlands, combining a series of directorships with the specially created role of Inspector General of the Dutch Armed forces.

The Royal Yacht Britannia

An unusual but not unique element in some visits by the UK royal family was the Royal Yacht Britannia. The final such vessel with that name in a tradition dating back to the seventeenth century, it came into service in 1954 and was finally decommissioned in 1997. It was, in effect, a floating palace, enabling the royal family both to be accommodated and to host major dinners and receptions when overseas without having to rely on local venues and providers of hospitality. As the British Minister of Defence noted in 1974, this enabled the Queen 'to visit many poor countries, whether Commonwealth or foreign, without putting her hosts to expenses and trouble which might embarrass them' (Mason to Wilson, 19 November 1974: PREM 16/267). Large enough to travel across the world, it called at around 600 ports in 135 countries in its 44 years of service (Royal Yacht Britannia Website: History). Its value was sometimes as much symbolic as practical. As we have seen, the Queen made a point of attending Commonwealth heads of government meetings; but the FCO felt that it would be inappropriate to frame her trip to the Cyprus CHOGM in 1993 as a state visit, given the continuing disputes around the status of the divided island (Gozney to Wall, 1 February 1993: PREM 19/4035). In this context, the yacht provided a convenient means of distancing the royal couple from any controversy associated with the territory. Although the Queen and the Duke of Edinburgh travelled there by plane and were the guests at a lunch given by Cypriot President Clerides, they based themselves on the Britannia, and used the yacht as the venue for the Queen's traditional banquet for Commonwealth heads.

Such advantages proved insufficient, however, to save the royal yacht. Under pressure from the Treasury, in 1994, the government of John Major announced that the Britannia would be decommissioned and launched a review within Whitehall about the feasibility of proving a replacement. In a rare piece of evidence showing the Palace actively lobbying on an issue of resourcing, the National Archives recently released a letter written in May 1995 by the Queen's Deputy Private Secretary, Kenneth Scott, who wrote to the Cabinet Office, to update it on her views. He noted that he had deliberately taken 'a back seat' in the discussions since the matter was 'very much one for the Government and since the last thing I should like to see is a newspaper headline saying "Queen Demands a New Yacht"'. He continued, however:

> At the same time, I hope it is clear to all concerned that this reticence on the part of the Palace in no way implies that Her Majesty is not deeply interested in the subject; on the contrary, The Queen would very much welcome it if a way could be found of making available for the nation in the 21st Century the kind of service which Britannia has provided for the last 43 years (Scott to Williams, 5 May 1995: BD 41/457).

Despite this intervention, calls for fiscal discipline initially prevailed (Scott to Williams, 5 May 1995: BD 41/457). Yet with a general election on the horizon and the Conservatives trailing in the polls, in January 1997, Major and senior Cabinet colleagues overruled the objections of Chancellor of the Exchequer, Ken Clarke, and agreed that the political and commercial advantages of the new royal yacht justified the government spending £60m on commissioning one (Seldon 1997: 698). The decision did not, however, survive the election of a Labour Government in May 1997, and the idea of replacing Britannia was abandoned.

With the decommissioning of Britannia in 1997, there remained only two royal yachts in the world: those of Denmark and Norway. Constructed in 1931-2, the Danish Royal Yacht, *Dannebrog*, serves as the official residence of the Danish royal family on some overseas engagements, while acting as a working sea-rescue vessel for other parts of the year (Royal House of Denmark Website 2019: The Royal Yacht *Dannebrog*). In the case of Norway, the provision of a royal yacht was one of the inducements offered to Prince Carl of Denmark when he was offered the Norwegian Crown in 1905. Yet financial exigencies meant that Carl, who was crowned as King Haakon, did not actually receive his yacht until 1948. Originally built in England in 1937 for the British aircraft manufacturer, Thomas Sopwith, the ship, then called the *Philante*, was used by the Royal Navy as an escort vessel in World War II. It was bought for King Haakon with the help of a public appeal for his 75th birthday, and renamed the *Norge* (Royal House of Norway: The Royal Yacht: History). Although the *Norge* has a similar range to the Britannia, at 1,628 tonnes it is considerably smaller than its former (5,769 tonne) British counterpart.

6.5. STATE VISITS MADE AND RECEIVED BY KING JUAN CARLOS I AND KING FELIPE VI OF SPAIN

Charles Powell, Director of the Elcano Royal Institute, Madrid

Preliminary Observations

The Spanish case is somewhat unusual due to the political circumstances surrounding the restoration of the monarchy in November 1975, after almost 40 years of right-wing authoritarianism under General Franco (1939-75). Due to both the help he received from Nazi Germany and Fascist Italy during the Civil War (1936-39), and the assistance he later provided them during the Second World War (1939-45), Franco was very much a pariah in the early post-war years. Indeed during his almost 40 years in office, he only travelled abroad on official business on three occasions: to meet Hitler at Hendaye in southern France in 1940; to see Mussolini at Bordighera and, on his way back to Spain, Pétain at Montpellier in 1941; and for talks with the Portuguese dictator Salazar in Lisbon in 1949. With the outbreak of the Cold War, Franco gained some respectability in the eyes of the West, particularly the United States, which enabled Spain to gradually overcome this post-war isolation. As a result, three US presidents went to Madrid on state visits: Eisenhower (1959); Nixon (1970) and Ford (1975). Nevertheless, his regime was never fully accepted by the major democracies, and not a single European head of state visited Spain officially while Franco was in office (though he did host De Gaulle in 1970, after his retirement). Unsurprisingly, most of the state visits hosted by Franco thus involved Latin American, African, Asian and Arab leaders who were unconcerned by his political history. Consequently, in addition to spearheading the transition to democracy, King Juan Carlos's most important task after his proclamation in November 1975 was the normalisation of Spain's standing abroad.

Another anomaly that needs to be taken into account is that, during the first few years of his reign – until a new democratic constitution came into force in January 1979 – Juan Carlos retained many of the powers he had inherited from Franco, and was therefore largely responsible for defining and implementing Spain's foreign policy. As a result, the state visits made and received by the King during the years 1976-78, which were very frequent, largely reflect his political priorities as head of state. Once he became a more conventional parliamentary monarch, foreign policy was largely left to the democratically elected governments of the day. Nevertheless, because of both his role as the founding father of the new political system and his standing and prestige abroad, Juan Carlos initially continued to play a significant role in Spain's foreign policy, which was quite unlike that of other European monarchs. For example, elected officials implicitly understood that the King should be allowed to establish a personal relationship with US and French presidents as soon as they took office, and over the years it was assumed that he should meet them before his prime minister did. In sum, Juan Carlos performed a political role which led him to travel abroad far more frequently (and extensively) than was generally true of other European parliamentary monarchs. Though undoubtedly important, state visits were thus only a relatively small part of the story of Juan Carlos's involvement in Spanish foreign policy.

Another unique feature worth mentioning is the role the Spanish Constitution defines for the King, who is described as 'the highest representative of the Spanish State in international relations, especially with those nations belonging to the same historic community' (article 56). It should be noted that the expression 'historic community' is somewhat vague, and although it is generally thought to refer to Spain's former Latin American colonies, it could be interpreted to include the United States (since much of its current territory was once ruled by Spain), or non-Spanish speaking former colonies such as the Philippines, which was under Spanish rule for more than 300 years. Whatever the case, the Spanish monarch had a constitutional mandate to pay special attention to this 'community', which Juan Carlos put into practice by encouraging the institutionalisation of an Ibero-American Community of Nations in 1991, to which 22 states (including Portugal and Brazil) currently belong (the US enjoys observer status). This organisation, which is not unlike the British Commonwealth in some respects, provided the monarch with a chance to meet the heads of state of these countries at least once every two years.

Juan Carlos used to take pride in the fact that, unlike the Queen of England at Commonwealth summits, his role was virtually identical to that of other heads of state, which allowed him to sit in on important political debates. However, although he was always accompanied by the Prime Minister, this did not always provide the necessary political protection: at the 2007 Ibero-American summit, the Venezuelan President branded former Prime Minister José María Aznar a 'fascist' for having allegedly supported a coup against him in 2002, and when Prime Minister José Luis Rodríguez Zapatero rose in his defence, Chávez interrupted him repeatedly, prompting a visibly angry Juan Carlos to exclaim: 'Why don't you shut up?' This unseemly outburst went down very well with the President's many critics in Venezuela, but also revealed the risks involved in exposing a hereditary head of state to highly charged political debates, in which he should theoretically always defer to his democratically elected Prime Minister.

Juan Carlos was also different from other European monarchs in that he was able to establish exceptionally close relations with most Arab hereditary heads of state, particularly those of Morocco, Jordan and the Gulf states, who publicly referred to him as their 'brother'. Some of them were often reluctant to deal directly with Spain's democratically elected senior officials, including the Prime Minister, and demanded that Juan Carlos be personally involved in any serious negotiations. This sometimes proved extremely valuable, allowing the monarch to explain Spain's decision to recognise the State of Israel in 1986, solve fishing disputes with Morocco, close highly favourable oil deals with several Gulf states, or lobby successfully for Spanish companies competing for public contracts, such as the Mecca-Medina high-speed train in Saudi Arabia, inaugurated in 2018. Far from trying to resist being used to promote trade and investment, Juan Carlos often went out of his way to demonstrate his skills in this arena, largely as a way of justifying the monarchy's *raison d'être*. Paradoxically, it was one of his former Prime Ministers, Aznar, who took most exception to Juan Carlos's personal ties with certain Arab rulers, on the grounds that 'a democratic king cannot negotiate with a non-democratic king'; in his view, it was preferable for such relations to be conducted 'between the executive powers of one country and the executive powers of the other'. Moreover, he had always harboured doubts about the wisdom of allowing the monarch to act as the 'head of a trade mission', even going so far as to state that 'in the event of his wanting to lead such a mission, he should be prevented from doing so' (Ónega 2015: 232-3). Almost by definition, in order to be effective, the monarch's mediation in these negotiations often had to take place in private, in the absence of Spanish elected officials or diplomats who might supervise the transaction in question. Inevitably, this led to questions being raised (in parliament and the media) as to the precise nature of his involvement and the widespread belief that kickbacks were often involved, which gradually undermined his reputation and popularity at home.

Finally, Juan Carlos also enjoyed a special relationship with the Holy See. His first state visit to the Vatican, hosted by Pope Paul VI in February 1977, was only the second ever undertaken by a reigning Spanish monarch (King Alfonso XIII and Victoria Eugenia had visited Pope Pius XI in 1923). Strictly speaking, Spain was still a confessional state then, and this was the first and last time that Juan Carlos would proclaim that he stood in the Pope's presence as the 'head of a state which, throughout the centuries, has taken pride in calling itself Catholic'. Although Spain ceased to be a confessional state with the adoption of the 1978 Constitution, the latter still acknowledged that 'the authorities shall take the religious beliefs of Spanish society into account and shall in consequence maintain appropriate co-operation with the Catholic Church and the other confessions' (article 16.3). Furthermore, the King thought of himself as a devout Catholic, and attached considerable importance to Spain's Catholic identity. During his reign, he thus hosted (or took part in) a total of eight papal visits: five by John Paul II (in 1982, 1984, 1989, 1993 and 2003), and a further three by Benedict XVI (in 2006, 2010 and 2011). In addition to the 1977 state visit mentioned above, the King also visited the Vatican to attend the coronations of John Paul I and John Paul II (1978), as well as the latter's state funeral (2005) and canonisation (2014).

Spanish State Visits: Achievements (and Some Controversies)

For the reasons outlined above, some of King Juan Carlos's early outbound state visits were unusually significant. His first state visit, in May 1976, was to the Dominican Republic, making him the first Spanish monarch to set foot on territory that had been claimed on behalf of the Spanish crown five centuries earlier. From there he embarked on his first state visit to the United States, where he was hosted by President Ford in the context of the Bicentennial celebrations. In Washington, Juan Carlos addressed a joint session of Congress, where he announced that the monarchy would ensure 'the orderly access to power of distinct political alternatives, in accordance with the freely-expressed will of the people', which is remembered as his first unequivocal public commitment to democratisation.

The King then turned his attention to Spain's partners in Europe, embarking on state visits to France (1976), Germany (1977), Belgium (1977), and Portugal (1978). The adoption of a democratic constitution later paved the way for state visits to countries which had been particularly hostile to the Franco regime, such as Sweden (1979), Denmark (1980), the Netherlands (1980), Luxembourg (1980), Italy (1981) and Norway (1982). Due to the Gibraltar dispute, Queen Elizabeth did not host a state visit for Juan Carlos until 1986, which she returned in 1988. Although Madrid invited President Karamanlis for a State Visit in 1984, the royal couple did not reciprocate until 1998 on account of the difficult relations between Athens and former King Constantine, who was Queen Sofia's younger brother.

Several outward state visits stand out for their symbolic importance, or for the controversies they gave rise to. In November 1978, Juan Carlos took part in his first state visit to Mexico, whose authorities had never recognised the Franco regime and had only reestablished diplomatic relations with Spain in March 1977. Mexico had given asylum to thousands of Spaniards who fled the country after the Civil War, and during the visit the King visited the elderly widow of a former president of the Second Republic, Manuel Azaña. The visit thus symbolised not only a reconciliation between two states that had parted company in 1939, but also between Spaniards who had opposed each other implacably during the Civil War and beyond.

In November 1978 Juan Carlos and Sofia also embarked on a state visit to Argentina, which was then governed by a military Junta led by General Videla. Although this took place before the new democratic Constitution had been adopted, the parliamentary opposition questioned the wisdom of legitimising a military dictatorship in this manner but were somewhat appeased when Juan Carlos secured the release of several political prisoners who held Spanish passports.

Like Mexico, Israel had also refused to recognise Franco's Spain (largely due to its association with Nazi Germany), and diplomatic relations were not established until January 1986. This not only facilitated the normalisation of relations, but also Spain's long-overdue reconciliation with the Spanish (and international) Jewish community. In keeping with this spirit, the royal couple played a very active role in the numerous activities organised for the Sefarad '92 commemoration, which sought to mark the 500th anniversary of the expulsion of the Jews by fostering awareness of their contribution to Spanish culture. The most solemn of these was probably the ceremony held at the Beth Yaacov Synagogue in Madrid during the state visit by Israeli President Chaim Herzog in March 1992, exactly five hundred years after Ferdinand and Isabella signed the edict ordering Spain's 200,000 Jews to either convert to Catholicism or leave their kingdoms. This rapprochement allowed Juan Carlos to pay a state visit to Israel in 1993, during which he became the first European monarch to address the Israeli Knesset.

Outward State Visits

As is true of other countries, the Spanish authorities distinguish between state and official visits, though the distinction is not always clearly made, and the royal household website does not provide a complete list of either.

During the course of his reign, Juan Carlos undertook a total of 120 outbound state visits, which is almost double the number of those carried out by Queen Elizabeth (61) or Carl XVI Gustav of Sweden (66) during the same period (1976-2014). In particularly busy years, such as 1980, he embarked on as many as 10 outbound state visits to different regions of the world (Europe, Asia, Latin America, Africa and the Middle East), nearly always accompanied by Queen Sofia. This may partly be attributed to the King's unique role in the normalisation of Spanish foreign policy during the early years of his reign, which entailed the (re)establishment of diplomatic relations with countries that had shunned (or been shunned by) the Franco regime in the past: when the dictator died in 1975, Spain had diplomatic relations with 85 states, but by the time of Juan Carlos's abdication in 2014, that figure had increased to 191. If official visits are added to this list, the king travelled to a total of 103 countries on 241 occasions (averaging more than six per year, and a record 13 in 2009).

Unsurprisingly, the King's destinations reflected Spain's international priorities: there were a total of 80 (state and official) visits to Latin America (with an emphasis on Mexico, Argentina, Colombia, Chile, Brazil, and Venezuela), slightly under 80 to more than 30 European countries (the most frequently visited being Portugal, Germany, Italy, France and the Holy See), 15 to the United States (the country he visited most often), another 40 or so to the Maghreb and the Middle East (Morocco and the Gulf monarchies in particular), and a not insignificant number of journeys to more distant locations, in the Asia-Pacific region and Sub-Saharan Africa. Additionally, Juan Carlos also made official visits to a number of regional and international organisations such as the European Union, the Council of Europe, NATO, and the United Nations and its many agencies.

The Reign of Felipe VI

During his first five years on the throne (2014-19), King Felipe VI has undertaken eight outward state visits and has hosted another seven. This level of activity is very modest compared to that registered during the early years of his father's reign, which is largely attributable to the instability which has characterised Spanish politics in recent years, resulting in an unprecedented four general elections being held in the years 2015-19. More generally, due to both his relative youth and inexperience and the fact that his personal prestige is not yet comparable to that of his father at the height of his popularity, King Felipe enjoys less autonomy than his predecessor in his dealings with senior elected officials. It is inconceivable, therefore, that he should refuse to carry out a visit to a state with a politically questionable regime if the Spanish government requests him to do so. This was confirmed when he was sent to Saudi Arabia in January 2017 by the Rajoy government to expedite the sale of five corvettes – valued at €2 billion – to the Saudi Navy, at a time when Riyadh's involvement in the civil war in Yemen was generating considerable criticism in Spain. As he had feared, it was not long before this was held against him: while attending a vigil after the jihadist terrorist attacks carried out in Barcelona in August of that year, demonstrators displayed photos of him being greeted by the Saudi authorities, which they held responsible for condoning these acts. Conversely, the King was not always allowed to accept some of the invitations he received: in 2018, Prime Minister Modi, who had been very taken with Felipe after meeting him in Madrid, invited him to be the keynote speaker at the following year's Raisina Conference, India's most prestigious international conference. However, the Prime Minister's office turned down the invitation on the grounds that Pedro Sánchez had not yet been invited to Delhi himself; in the end, Spain was represented at the Raisina event by Foreign Minister Borrell.

Inward State Visits

State visits to Spain normally last two days. During the first couple of years of Juan Carlos's reign, foreign heads of state were housed at the Royal Palace of Aranjuez, but given that this is some distance from Madrid, since 1983 they have stayed at the Royal Palace of El Pardo (Franco's residence until 1975), which is on the outskirts of the capital and very close to La Zarzuela Palace, the king's residence. State visits generally begin at El Pardo, where foreign heads of state are greeted by the Spanish monarch and his consort, and later review the assembled troops while their respective national anthems are played. On the first evening of the visit, the King normally hosts a state dinner for his foreign guests at the Royal Palace in central Madrid, which was the residence of the Spanish monarch until 1931, which is also attended by the prime minister and senior government officials. On the second day, visiting heads of state normally host a return dinner for the monarch at the Royal Palace of El Pardo. Spanish state visits are planned and organised by the prime minister's office, in consultation with the foreign ministry and the royal household, and their cost is defrayed by *Patrimonio Nacional*, the public organisation responsible for Crown-owned property that was formally donated to the Spanish state under the 1982 Law on National Heritage.

The Role of 'Junior' Royals

Since 1975, the Spanish royal family has operated as a nuclear family, consisting of King Juan Carlos, Queen Sofia, the Prince of Asturias (Felipe), and the two *infantas* (Elena and Cristina). Other members of the family have never been expected to perform any official role, nor do they receive any emoluments from the state or the royal household. Consequently, during Juan Carlos's reign, only the heir to the throne, Prince Felipe, was expected to perform a public role abroad. In particular, from 1996 onwards, Juan Carlos entrusted him with the task of attending the inauguration of Latin American heads of state on his behalf, with the result that by the time his father abdicated in 2014, the future monarch had taken part in 69 of these ceremonies, thereby acquiring an intimate knowledge and understanding of the region and its political leaders. Paradoxically, in the wake of his abdication, Juan Carlos performed this role on his son's behalf on several occasions, until he formally withdrew from public life in 2019. Presumably, the Princess of Asturias, Leonor, will begin to carry out this task when she comes of age.

Royal yacht

Spain does not have a royal yacht, but Juan Carlos was always passionate about sailing, and normally spent his summer holidays at the Royal Palace of Marivent, in Palma de Majorca, where he often invited visiting heads of state. In 1979 King Fahd of Saudi Arabia gave him the luxury motorboat 'Fortuna' as a present, which became a very visible (and somewhat controversial) symbol of Juan Carlos's special relationship with the Gulf monarchies. The boat, which hosted Prince Charles and Lady Diana (1990) and Bill and Hillary Clinton (1997), amongst others, suffered frequent breakdowns, and was finally replaced with a more reliable (and luxurious) 136ft model in 2000, which was paid for by a consortium of businessmen from the Balearic Islands, on the grounds that the presence of the royal family there was good for the tourist industry. However, following the scandal caused by his elephant shooting expedition to Botswana in 2012, the King returned the boat to his sponsors, who changed its name and put it up for sale.

6.6. CONCLUSIONS

Dr Bob Morris, Constitution Unit, UCL

This chapter has sought to chart how European monarchies, having been removed from almost all primary executive functions, have developed suites of active secondary roles for themselves still political but non-partisan. As Frank Prochaska has shown, charitable endeavour has been an early exemplar of beneficent social concern signposting how social elites might help address social change. Aligned with very gradual changes in gender roles, charitable endeavour made early august female-led activism uncontroversial and acceptable. Simultaneously, more urbanised societies created demands for royal attention at times when older royal political roles were becoming attenuated and new forms of legitimation became both acceptable and increasingly sought. Established by Elizabeth I to lick county militias into shape, British Lord Lieutenants became agents for visiting royalty as a result. The ceaseless peripateticism of the old monarchies has been remade in new forms of royal attention.

Modern state visits, though part of that transformation, are in a class of their own. Even incoming visits are by no means wholly domestic affairs. All visits have the monarch and the monarchical family representing their nation in a nation-to-nation event. As Philip Murphy has shown, visits play an important part in reinforcing royal legitimacy and, in the British case, have helped to normalise relations with former colonies of all kinds even where Queen Elizabeth II's imperial crown has not been translated into a local indigenous crown – as remains the case in fifteen of the fifty-three Commonwealth states.

As Charles Powell shows, the Spanish monarchy has been a special case. Following its restoration, the new crown symbolised the extent of regime change, and an energetic programme of state visits helped Spain, once a pariah to liberal democracy, to relegitimise itself in the comity of respectable regimes. On the other hand, as both writers point out, state visits are not risk free to monarchies and monarchs. Moreover, the Spanish experience suggests that they cannot by themselves compensate for a lack of domestic depth. As this and other chapters have shown, the Spanish monarchy is not only the least well-resourced of the European monarchies, it is also the most potentially fragile. This situation makes it particularly vulnerable to royal misbehaviours. Whereas it used to be maintained that the royal institution could always survive the personal bad behaviour of its occupants, even in Britain that is no longer true or, indeed, anywhere else. On top of it all, the Spanish monarchy is not allowed the depth of support available to more continuous monarchies whose reach has allowed them to renew their legitimacy through works more credibly addressing all the parts of their nations.

Part III

Regulating Monarchy

7

Regulation of the Monarchy: Regulating the Size of the Royal Family, the Line of Succession, and Royal Finances

Contents

7.1. INTRODUCTION

Dr Bob Morris, The Constitution Unit, UCL

WHEREAS PART I of this volume considered the functions of the monarchies, this Chapter looks at the management of the royal families themselves. The principle of hereditary succession defines the unique character of monarchy but how it is expressed in practice has to be a matter of law. In all but the UK, the law is contained in distinct written constitutional provisions usually with a special status distinguishing them from ordinary statutes. In the UK, the law governing these matters is indistinguishable from ordinary statute.

The questions that arise include: what are the purposes and means of regulation? How is financial support set? And what is the relationship between that support and policies of controlling the 'active' size of royal families? Table 7.1 at the end of this chapter summarises the financial support currently made available to the eight monarchies and the authorising legal regime in each case.

7.2. DEFINING A ROYAL HOUSE: CONTINENTAL MONARCHY AND THE NETHERLANDS

Dr Bart van Poelgeest, Civil Servant, Prime Minister's Office, The Hague (writing in a personal capacity)

Continental monarchy

In the context of the monarchies in Western Europe in the twenty-first century it is legitimate, as Sieyès once did for the Third Estate, to raise the question of what a royal house actually is and who defines this. In practice the popular press often uses the general phrase 'royal family' for all close and distant relatives, by blood or marriage, of the monarch. This designation may be useful for communication and publicity but is inadequate when it comes to a precise definition of the term, membership and the constitutional, financial and legal implications concerned.

A closer look at the definition and meaning of the terms 'royal house' and 'royal family' is meaningful because all hereditary monarchies in Europe by nature and constitutionally not only consist of a monarch, but also of a specific group of relatives of the monarch, always including the heir. This paper will first present an overview, mainly based on the texts of constitutions and specific legal documents, of general similarities and differences in the constitutional and legal situation in the hereditary continental monarchies with a parliamentary democracy and a written constitution, and then will focus in more detail upon the situation in the Netherlands.

Problems of Definition

There is no common legal approach or vocabulary in the continental monarchies of Europe to define the group consisting of the monarch's relevant relatives. Differences involve the legal status of relevant documents, the terms used therein and their legal consequences. In legal terms the term and its definition may be part of the constitution, a law of constitutional status, a specific law, a family pact or combinations of these.

The legal consequences of membership of a royal dynasty, house or family may vary, also depending on the legal nature of the documents involved, with regard to the succession; regency; finances; and all different sorts of subjects such as titles; styles; names; nobility; decorations; taxes; membership of state organs and legal procedures. The monarch is usually both a member of and head of the house or family. The legal consequences of the constitutional capacities and position of the monarch as such belong to another chapter.

Despite these differences in defining a royal dynasty, house or family there are also some basic common features. One of them is the shared historical origin of the *Hausgesetz* (house law or family pact) developed during the ancien régime, mainly in the Holy Roman

Empire. These documents, emanating from a ruling prince or from a common agreement between members or branches of a princely family, define a princely house, its religion, organisation, succession, membership and consequences of its membership for marriage, residence, titles, finances and inheritance. They served, sometimes together with the use of a *Fideikommiss* (fee tail) for family goods and property, as instruments for the head of a princely house to maintain or elevate the rank, dignity and order of the house. This could include sanctions against morganatic marriages, marriages of members with persons of a status considered below the rank of the house, such as the loss of rights to the succession, hereditary titles, property and inheritance.

With the French Revolution, the establishment of its principles in continental constitutions and the development of constitutional monarchies, ministerial responsibility and parliamentary democracy, the traditional *Hausgesetze* gradually lost much of their meaning. They continued to play a role in the nineteenth and early twentieth century as part of negotiations for marriage settlements of members of royal families marrying members of families with a *Hausgesetz*.

In legal terms a *Hausgesetz* still operates in two continental monarchies. The principality of Liechtenstein is the most obvious example. The Liechtenstein Constitution (article 3) refers the order of succession and the regency to a *Hausgesetz* of the princely house of Liechtenstein. The most recent version of this *Hausgesetz* was officially published in 1993 (Marxer 2003). In the Grand Duchy of Luxembourg, the Constitution (article 3) indirectly refers the hereditary succession of the Crown to the 1783 *Erbverein*, a family pact, of the house of Nassau. This document was changed several times after 1890 – the year the personal union between the Netherlands and Luxembourg ended – by Grand Dukes of Luxembourg, including a fundamental change in 1907, then approved by Cabinet and Parliament, to ensure the succession of women. The 1907 revision also included changes in the *Hausgesetz* (*Familienstatut die Hausverfassungbetreffend von 5 Mai 1907*).

In other European monarchies the function and contents of the *Hausgesetz* have reappeared, partially and modernised, in provisions of public law. This is only a logical consequence of the process of constitutionalising monarchies as, for instance, the necessary regulation of matters concerning the succession or allowances, once matters of private family law, have become essentially public matters in a modern parliamentary democracy.

Controlling Succession

The order of succession is an important element in the definition of a royal house or royal family. A common development in the United Kingdom and all continental hereditary monarchies, apart from Spain and Liechtenstein, was the revision of the order of succession, introducing equal treatment of the sexes as a consequence of treaty obligations and modern developments in law and society (see also 7.6 below). This meant that age became the new main criterion and the elder child, irrespective of sex, got precedence in the order of succession over younger children.

For the group of the monarch's relevant relatives the constitutional documents for Denmark (article 11) and Sweden (articles 4, 5 and 7) and the Constitution of the

Netherlands (articles 39 and 40) use the term 'royal house' while the Constitutions of Spain (article 65), Belgium (article 98) and Norway (article 75) use the term 'royal family'. The Luxembourg Constitution uses both terms (articles 3 and 43) while the Nassau house law of 2012 clearly distinguishes between the two (paragraph 2).

The constitutional documents of all monarchies, with the exception of Sweden and Belgium, use the term 'royal house' or 'royal family' in relation to the budget (see Table 7.1). In practice, there is a wide variety with respect to what sums are part of the budget for the monarchy, what sums are relevant for the monarchy and part of other budgets, and who is entitled to what allowances, either directly or indirectly. There is also a wide variety in the composition and total sum of the budgets involved. In the Netherlands, Belgium and Denmark the adult heirs are legally entitled to an allowance of their own. Limited forms of tax freedom for some members of the royal house or family may be part of the constitution (Netherlands) or legislation on specific subjects.[1]

The Netherlands

The challenge to define a royal house as such in public law was taken up in the Netherlands. Over time the Netherlands developed a system of three different legal circles of royalty for, respectively, the succession (rights to the throne), the budget (right to an allowance) and the house (several rights of a different nature), indirectly excluding the term royal family as a legally relevant circle. Only the adult heir of the monarch is part of all three legal circles.

The order of succession in the Dutch Constitution was amended several times since the first constitution of a Dutch monarchy was adopted in 1814. That Constitution even made it possible that descendants of the sister of *stadtholder* Willem V (signatory to the 1783 Nassau *Erbverein*), basically the ancestors of the later grand dukes of Luxembourg, would succeed to the Dutch throne; and the revised Constitution of 1887 brought other distant German relatives of Princess Juliana, single surviving grandchild of King Willem III, into a similar position.[2]

From 1922 onwards the Constitution narrowed such possibilities considerably by restricting the succession to descendants of Queen Wilhelmina. The general revision of the Constitution in 1983 limited the right of succession further to relatives of the monarch in the third degree of consanguinity born of marriages with consent of Parliament given by law. In 1983 the preference of males over women in the succession was abolished while the preference of the elder child over a younger child was maintained. This had no practical consequences then because Crown Princess Beatrix and Princess Margriet, her only younger sister remaining in the order of succession, both only had sons from their parliamentary approved marriages. At the moment, there are eight persons with a constitutional right of succession.

---

[1] For instance, in Denmark. The situation in other monarchies requires further research: see Matthijs 2013: 143–53.

[2] About the end of the personal union between The Netherlands and Luxembourg in 1890, see Tamse 1991: 84–102. About the order of succession before the birth of Princess Juliana in 1909, see Fasseur 1998: 298–302.

In the Netherlands, all constitutions since 1806 only used the term 'house' to describe the group of relevant royal relatives of the monarch. In the first half of the nineteenth century King Willem I had to give up his plan to establish a traditional *Hausgesetz* because his ministers did not accept the exceptions to general civil and criminal law which this extended to his relatives. The term 'royal house' acquired a new legal dimension after a change in the Constitution in 1972, establishing ministerial responsibility as its constitutional basis.

This was the result of a specific event. In 1964 Princess Irene, second daughter of Queen Juliana, became a Roman Catholic and engaged to Prince Carlos Hugo de Bourbon de Parme, heir to a branch of the Bourbon family claiming the then vacant Spanish throne and member of the Carlist movement that cooperated with the Franco regime. The Dutch Cabinet decided not to ask for parliamentary consent for the marriage. The Pope married the couple in Rome and the absence of parliamentary consent for the marriage constitutionally excluded Princess Irene and all her descendants from the succession. The Cabinet got constitutional advice from two senior Ministers of State on the matter of ministerial responsibility for relatives of the monarch. This advice was not only a consequence of the marriage in Rome but also of the fact that the number of relatives of the monarch was about to increase. Between 1884 and 1957 the royal house had basically consisted of no more than two to four adult members, including the monarch and heir, as both Queen Wilhelmina and her daughter Queen Juliana had no brothers or sisters and there were no longer any Dutch princes. The fact that Juliana was a mother of four children, all daughters, between 1938 and 1948, opened therefore, for the first time in decades, the perspective of a significantly larger royal house for generations to come.

The advice made it clear that there is full ministerial responsibility for the monarch; but also a limited ministerial responsibility for members of the royal house with a right to the succession (and their spouses) in cases involving the public interest, becoming more limited the further down they are in the order of succession. The advice also concluded that membership of the royal family as such did not imply any specific ministerial responsibility. So, ministers were no longer deemed to be responsible for ex-successors like Princess Irene, their spouses and descendants. A consequence of the reaction to the advice was an amendment to the Constitution in 1972, meaning that the definition and membership of the royal house should be established by law.

For a number of years government and Parliament could not agree upon the definition of membership of the royal house. Parliament wanted to limit the membership of the house only to some of the successors, while the government insisted upon a broader definition. Finally, after the abdication of Queen Juliana, a compromise was reached in 1985 with the new law on the membership of the royal house. Membership of the house was limited to the monarch, the predecessor(s) of the monarch and those of the monarch's relatives with the constitutional right to succeed, their spouses and widows or widowers (until remarriage or changes in the order of succession) (Poelgeest 1993: 41–45; Visser 2008: 161–81). The law of 1985 explicitly made the monarch the head of the royal house but did not provide him with special powers in this respect, apart from the possibility, under ministerial responsibility, of a royal decree to appoint or dismiss members. The constitutional amendment of 1972 had also made it possible to introduce a separate law to reorganise, modernise and limit the variety of different legal documents regulating specific subjects for members of the royal house. This law came into force in 1981.

In 2002 the law on the membership of the royal house of 1985 was revised. The membership was narrowed to a smaller group of relatives of the monarch with the right of succession in the second degree of consanguinity, limiting the house to brothers and sisters, children and grandchildren of the monarch while excluding children of brothers, sisters, aunts and uncles and great grandchildren of the monarch (retaining their constitutional rights to the succession). Furthermore, the law now regulates the distribution of titles and names, reserving the title 'Prince (or Princess) of Orange' for the heir and the title 'Prince (or Princess) of the Netherlands' for (some) members only. Upon the loss of membership, a royal decree may be necessary to establish a surname. This royal decree may then also confer the ex-member with the title 'Prince (or Princess) of Orange-Nassau' as a non-hereditary title. It is also possible on this occasion to give ex-members a hereditary noble title by royal decree.[3]

The new system, partially giving the impression of the reappearance of the *Hausgesetz* in modern times, entered into force in May 2002, some months before the first grandchild of Queen Beatrix was born. When she abdicated, and was succeeded by her eldest son and heir in 2013, the constitutional order of succession changed accordingly. The children of Princess Margriet, her younger sister, then lost both their rights of succession to the throne and their membership of the royal house, while the children of Prince Constantijn, younger brother of King Willem-Alexander, lost their membership of the royal house but retained their places in the order of succession. Princess Margriet and Prince Constantijn remained members of the royal house and successors. The royal house now has 10 members.

The system is effective in practice in the sense that ministers are not held responsible for ex-successors, ex-members and non-members of the house, or indeed any other relatives of the monarch; these persons remain free from ministerial interference (though not completely free from attention by the media). In some cases, ministers nevertheless became involved in matters of royal relatives because of some of their links with the monarch, the heir or members of the royal house, for instance in matters of security checks and taxation. On the whole, however, the system works effectively according to its general purposes.

Regulating Financial Support

The constitutional amendments of 1972 to the Dutch Constitution also included a new regulation of the budget of members of the royal house. In 1972 a new law, the financial

---

[3] King Willem I and Queen Juliana were the only members of their dynasty who lived to see a great grandchild born as heir presumptive. The only person who lost his membership of the royal house under the law of 2002, Prince Friso, by royal decree of 19 March 2004 got the personal title 'Prince of Orange-Nassau' with the style of 'Royal Highness', the hereditary title 'graaf van Oranje-Nassau' and the surname 'Van Oranje-Nassau van Amsberg'. By another, earlier royal decree of 11 May 2001 the hereditary title 'graaf van Oranje-Nassau' and the surname 'Van Oranje-Nassau van Amsberg' had already been given to the children from the marriage of 'Prince Constantijn' before the first of them was born in 2002.

statute for the royal house, laid down the general structure of the annual royal budget, including the definition of the members of the royal house entitled to an allowance of their own, the amount of these allowances and its annual indexation. Although at the time there was no law on the membership of the royal house, it was beyond any doubt that the monarch, his heir and their spouses were entitled to these allowances. This also continued existing practice (see van Baalen, Bovend'Eert et al 1972). Any amendment of this law constitutionally requires a two-thirds majority in both Houses of Parliament. After the abdication of Queen Juliana in 1980 the law was amended to continue the allowances for her and her husband. The allowances in general include some expenses and a salary free from income taxes. The royal budget also covers all other, different sorts of expenses of the monarchy, including the royal household since 2008.

In 2008 the law was modernised to increase transparency. The circle of those members of the royal house entitled to allowances was extended to include the predecessor of the monarch and his spouse and, as long as they are members of the royal house, the widow or widower of the monarch, his predecessor and his heir. The modernisation also included a partial redistribution of expenses for the monarchy from several departmental budgets to the royal budget. The expenses for palaces, state visits and security have remained part of the departmental budgets concerned but the sum of all expenses (apart from security) is now visible in the royal budget to provide an overview.[4] At the moment three members of the royal house (the King, his wife and his predecessor) get an allowance of their own.

Whereas the developments in the order of the succession and transparency of the budget in the Netherlands are similar to those in other continental monarchies, the legal development of the royal house as a separate legal entity in public law is a special phenomenon. This partial and modernised reappearance of the *Hausgesetz* in a constitutional and democratic framework has contributed to the transparency and stability of the Dutch monarchy.

7.3. NORWAY

Eivind Smith, Professor of Public Law, Oslo University

The story of the constitutional monarchy in Norway starts with the adoption of the Constitution of 1814, a core achievement of which was the end of the absolute form of monarchy that Denmark-Norway had known since the 1660s (and that subsisted in Denmark until that country's Constitution was adopted – indeed, formally *octroyée* – in 1849).

---

[4] Het koninklijkhuis website 2019: FinanciënKoninklijk Huis provides the actual information about the 2020 budget. The total (in millions euro) of the 2019 budget for the monarchy (royal budget 44.4m) and other budgets (18.0m) together, excluding security) is 63.4m euros. The royal budget for the 2020 allowances is 8.4m (king: 5.9m (including salary of 0.9m), his wife 1m (including salary of 0.4m) and his predecessor 1.6m euros (including salary of 0.5m). The 2020 royal budget for the royal household is 18.5m, the 2020 departmental budget for the palaces is 15.9m euros.

As amended in 1990, article 6 tightly regulates the line of succession. With one exception, the point of departure is traditional:

> The order of succession is lineal, so that only a child born in lawful wedlock of the Queen or King, or of one who is herself or himself entitled to the succession, may succeed, and so that the nearest line shall take precedence over the more remote and the elder in the line over the younger.

The succession line is explicitly delimited by article 6 paragraph 3:

> The right of succession shall not, however, belong to any person who is not born in the direct line of descent from the last reigning Queen or King or a sister or brother thereof, or is not herself or himself a sister or brother thereof.

It is also important to note that the 1990 amendment established equal access to the throne for men and women (see even article 3 on the word 'king' meaning 'queen' in case the monarch is a female). However, the change was not given immediate effect because the younger child of the then Crown Prince Harald kept his position as the next in the line even if his sister was older. The conservation of the young Prince's status resulted from the rather intricate formula in the last paragraph of article 6:

> For those born before the year 1971, article 6 of the Constitution as it was passed on 18 November 1905 shall, however, apply. For those born before the year 1990 it shall nevertheless be the case that a male shall take precedence over a female.

At the time of the amendment, the Prince (born in 1973) had already spent an important part of his life as heir directly following his father, whereas his sister had always known that she would never become reigning Queen. Crown Prince Haakon Magnus' (now approaching his 50s) oldest child (Princess Ingrid) is a girl.

Contrary to the initial (1814) text, the Constitution no longer prescribes the monarch's own title. Other royal titles are decided by the King by virtue of article 34, stating that the King 'shall make provisions concerning titles for those who are entitled to succeed to the Crown'; in practice, the power has been used regarding a few individuals with no succession rights as well, like the two Queens and the Crown Princesses since 1905. In general, the three monarchs since 1905 have made use of this power in a way that many would regard as wise in a society like Norway, systematically keeping the official 'royal family' small. Children not entitled to the throne (only females so far) who have married, have lost their quality as royal highness, and the monarchs have never bestowed their husbands and children with royal titles. In this way, Norway is far away from the inflation of more or less remote royalty found in some of the other European monarchies.

Under article 75(e) of the Constitution, it is for Parliament [*Stortinget*] 'to decide how much shall be paid annually to the King for the royal household, and to determine the royal family's appanage, which may not, however, consist of real property'. The financial regime (from time to time negotiated between the Palace and the executive) is framed in correspondence: For the time being, only the members of the two top families (the royal couple, the Crown Prince and Princess) receive public funds. By virtue of an ordinary statute, they are also the only members of the extended family enjoying complete exemption from taxation.

Of course the calculation of the total amount of money spent on the institution cannot be made on the sole ground of the annual budgetary measures adopted under the chapter devoted to the monarchy. What is the value, for instance, of the executive's maintenance of public property left at the disposal of the royal family, the royal police squadron, the staffing of the royal yacht (the '*Norge*') by the Royal Navy and so on? Unsurprisingly, thus, public interest is sometimes devoted to similar issues.

The power to accept royal marriages belongs to the King by virtue of article 36:

> A Prince or Princess entitled to succeed to the Crown of Norway may not marry without the consent of the King.

The power to consent has been kept as a personal prerogative for the monarch. It has reportedly been made known, however, that all three Kings of the present dynasty have sought advice from the government via the Prime Minister before consenting. For Haakon VII, the key question was about the choice of a Swedish (Bernadotte) Princess in the aftermath of the 1905 breaking up of the personal union between Norway and Sweden; for Olav V and Harald V, the key question was about the choice of non-royals as the future queens. For the present Crown Prince, however, a step further was taken by his wish to marry a woman with a child born out of wedlock. All three marriages turned out to be successful.

7.4. SWEDEN

Axel Calissendorff, Solicitor to the King of Sweden

Regulating the Size of the Royal House

From the birth of the King's grandchildren, the House of Bernadotte – the 'royal house' (*Kungl.Huset*) – has increased considerably in recent years. It consists of 15 persons, of which 10 are included in the order of succession. In the next generation, one can expect additional persons who are entitled to right of succession. If all were to act as official representatives of Sweden, they would constitute a relatively large group of people who would carry out activities funded by Parliament's allocations to the royal court (see SvenskaDagbladet 2018).

In the spring of 2018, representatives of the Committee on the Constitution (*Konstitutionsutskottet*) announced that a parliamentary inquiry would – *inter alia* – analyse the commitments of the royal court. The background was that the royal court's legitimacy and trust were deemed to be at risk of being undermined if an increasing number of members were to act as official representatives of Sweden. Therefore, the purpose of the parliamentary inquiry is to consider how the structure of Parliament's allocations to the royal court may contribute to the royal family's official commitments primarily being carried out by a limited number of its members and drawing up principles for the same. The parliamentary inquiry is supposed to consult with the royal court during the process.

In October 2019, the King decided to limit the group of persons within the Royal House that perform official duties to Their Majesties and the Crown Princess and her husband. (The same people already undertook most of the representative duties). To foster confidence and trust in the representative monarchy, it seems a sound development that the representative duties become entrusted to only a few members of the Royal House. The change does not affect the rights set out in the Order of Succession on the rights to inherit the throne.

The Royal Finances

The funding allocations for the operations of the head of state are allocated by Parliament. The royal finances are divided into the royal court (*Hovstat*) and the Palace administration (*Slottsstat*). The first receives an estimated SEK 69 million (€6,614,142.79) in funding each year, while the latter receives SEK 66,3 million (€6,355,328.51) as of 2016. In addition to these allocations, the Palace administration derives revenues from tourism and retail at the palaces. The department is responsible for the administration and supervision of the 11 royal palaces with their buildings, parks and gardens. In accordance with an agreement made with the government, the Swedish National Audit Office audits the financial statements of the Palace administration on a yearly basis (Swedish Royal Court Website: Ekonomi).

The allocation for the royal court – the appanage – shall cover the cost of the King's official duties. These include travel and expenditure by the Office of the Marshal of the Realm and its staff, the Information and Press Department, and the Office of the Marshal of the Court (which organises the activities and households of the King, the Queen and the Crown Princess) (Swedish Royal Court Website: Ekonomi). As regards to the distribution of the appanage, the King prioritises himself, the Queen, the Crown Princess and her family. The specific amounts are not released as public information.

7.5. THE UK

Dr Bob Morris, The Constitution Unit, University College London

Table 7.1 on European monarchies' financing includes a summary of current funding arrangements in Britain. What follows investigates how royal family recipients of state support are defined; outlines the sources of royal funding provision from 1698 to the present day; and offers some concluding reflections.

Defining the Royal Family

British law has not used defining membership of the royal family as the route to determining eligibility for public funding. Indeed, there are no statutes specifically designed to define which persons are to be regarded as royal family members and no tradition of *Hausgesetz*. The closest analogous provisions are contained mostly in *Letters Patent*, a form of royal ordinance issued with ministerial approval and which, although they include the rules for conferring the title of 'His/Her Royal Highness' on the closest members of the sovereign's family, are vehicles also for subsidiary legal regulation for a great range of public bodies, such as universities and professional medical bodies. This is because the UK has not experienced the processes of 'constitutionalisation' of family definition described particularly at 7.2 above. Thus, even conferment of the title 'Royal Highness' (a title which may also be forfeited if the marriage occasioning conferment ends), implies no entitlement to public financial support.

In modern times, determining the right of succession has been controlled by Parliament, the relevant statute still being the 1701 Act of Settlement. Even the statutes aimed at controlling royal marriages, which might be expected also to function if only incidentally to define Royal Family membership, do not. Both the Royal Marriages Act 1772 requiring all descendants of George II to seek permission to marry from the current sovereign and the Succession to the Crown Act 2013 which limited that requirement to the six nearest to the throne are not wholly adequate vehicles. This is because the 1772 Act included too many to be regarded as members and the 2013 Act because it included too few.

As so often in Britain, the issue is decided in practice informally in a number of ways. One visible means, for example, is as to those who may be included – a reduced number in recent years – in the 'balcony party'. These are those closer relatives of the sovereign who appear regularly on the balcony of Buckingham Palace at the conclusion of special national ceremonies. The royal website itself defines this core group: 'Those who undertake official duties are members of The Queen's close family: her children, grandchildren and their spouses, and The Queen's cousins (the children of King George VI's brothers) and their spouses (Royal Household of the UK Website: The role of the Royal Family). The Sovereign Grant Annual Report emphasises the significant role of the extended royal family:

> The activities of the wider Royal Family are vital in bringing the institution of Monarchy into direct and personal contact with all sections of society, including the disadvantaged and the marginalised. The different generations of the Royal Family help to make the work of the Monarchy relevant or accessible to people at every stage of life' (Sovereign Grant Annual Report 2019: 6).

Royal Finances

1688–1760

Until the late seventeenth century there was no clear distinction between the Crown's resources for the purposes of executive rule and those at the personal disposal of the monarch. From the 'Glorious Revolution' of 1688 a form of limited monarchy was established where the monarch's ministers were answerable to Parliament and Parliament controlled the public finances available to the Crown in both its executive and personal capacities.

This financial settlement following the 'Glorious Revolution' of 1688 'marks an important stage in constitutional transition from a convention of financial deference to a sovereign ruling by divine right towards a much more pragmatic treatment of a reigning monarch as a tenured executive, a public servant ...' (Roseveare 1991: 32) From 1698

Parliament devised the mechanism of a Civil List for asserting control by including all the sources of royal finance within the curtilage of an annually available sum set at the beginning, and for the duration, of a reign. Originally, these sums were not paid from public funds at large but derived from assigned revenues which principally included those from hereditary crown land holdings which attached to the institution of the monarchy – and which from 1702 could not be alienated – rather than to the person of any particular sovereign. There was no question of annual estimates or annual account to the House of Commons, 'and what the Crown did with it thereafter was its own responsibility' (Roseveare 1969: 101). Similarly, the sovereign and heir had access to the revenues of the Duchies of Lancaster (held in the 'Privy Purse') and Cornwall.

The yield was designed to cover both the expenses of the royal household and all the expenses of civil government. Irregularities in yield and unforeseeable additional demands led to deficiencies which Parliament was forced to address on several occasions up to 1760 when the succession of a new king, George III, gave an opportunity to review the system.

1760–1952

The settlement for George III aimed to eradicate the existing system's faults by converting the revenue-based annual sum into a guaranteed fixed total received directly from the Treasury and the King, reciprocally, surrendering hereditary Crown land revenues.[5]

The changes did not attack the independence of the crown. As the then Prime Minister, the Duke of Newcastle, told the King: 'It is Your Majesty's own money. You can do with it what you like' (Roseveare 1969: 88–9). The new system did not, however, produce a wholly or lastingly stabilised regime and Parliament still found itself obliged both to make up deficiencies and relieve pressures on the Civil List by permitting the government to take on certain spending responsibilities directly.

The Civil List system settled on a process of fixing the annual sum for new reigns within six months of the death of a previous sovereign and, from the 1780s, in a political environment where Parliament was setting no limits on its ability to investigate any civil expenditure. From 1830 the executive took over the costs of civil government so that the Civil List became confined to funding the monarchy's public duties and supporting the 'honour and dignity' of the Crown. From 1830 changes also included – for the Crown – a politically awkward parliamentary process involving the appointment of a Select Committee to consider and recommend what the reign-length sum should be.

Civil List audit arrived only with the Civil List Audit Act 1816. However, except when expenditure exceeded a statutory level, there was no requirement for accounts to be laid before Parliament, and it became the practice to appoint the Treasury Permanent Secretary as Auditor in what was effectively a closed, non-transparent system.

Victoria's long reign (1837–1901) and having to provide support for her nine children saw the system stressed in the late 1880s (Cox 1873). On the other hand, a long period of price stability followed by price deflation permitted avoidance of a system reset. Nonetheless, Queen Victoria is thought to have – lawfully – transferred

---

[5] From 1961 management of the latter was consolidated into a single, arms-length autonomous statutory entity, the Crown Estate, whose profits are fed into the Exchequer for the general state revenues.

about £800,000 Civil List savings to her Privy Purse, quantities of which were spent on acquiring, rebuilding and expanding her private Osborne and Balmoral estates (Kuhn 1993: 656–57).

More important in the longer run were unstated changes during Victoria's reign. The brief phenomenon of elite republicanism from 1870 was partly a response not only to Victoria's wilful seclusion for the decade following her husband's death in 1861 but also to the fact that the seclusion meant that the patterns of royal public philanthropy established by the Prince Consort fell into abeyance. Though republicanism quickly wilted, it was clear there had been a step change which had led to 'a general expectation that ... the royal family was to be visibly active in public-spirited endeavour' (Kuhn 1993: 660). This lesson was taken very much on board by three of her four successors who further developed what has been called the welfare monarchy – Edward VII (1901–10), George V (1910–36) and George VI (1937–52) (Prochaska 1995). The fact that Edward VIII (1936–7) did not demonstrate the same acceptance of that role was almost certainly one of the factors silently in play during the negotiations that led to his abdication.

1952 to 2010

Following Elizabeth II's accession in 1952 at the age of 25, the Select Committee on the Civil List – aware that there was a prospect of a long reign – recommended that a reserve should be established from Civil List surplus years and royal trustees – the Prime Minister, the Chancellor of the Exchequer and the Keeper of the Privy Purse (the royal household's financial controller) – appointed to superintend the List's operation. Certain annuities were fixed for the most senior members of the royal family and some burdens which otherwise would have fallen on the List were removed. As on all occasions when costs were treated as grants-in-aid on government departmental budgets – for example, the Queen's flight, the royal yacht *Britannia*, the royal train – the effect was that such expenditure had to be the responsibility of a minister answerable to Parliament and subject to audit by the Comptroller and Auditor General, an official with wide investigative powers reporting directly to Parliament. But it followed too that expenditure otherwise remained free from public audit.

The hope of establishing a reign-lasting system was defeated by inflation in the 1960s. Various expedients, including annual increases, were adopted to maintain the real value of financial support, though the Civil List Act 1972 had rejected the most radical proposal of indexation and transforming the royal household into a government department. Instead, the Act specified the new Civil List total, and itemised the annuities for the monarch's most senior relatives with special allowance for those members of the royal family not otherwise provided for. When inflation returned to more regular levels, in 1990 the government decided, in the interests of encouraging more stable and responsible management, to go back to the system of fixing provision for a term of years at a level allowing the accumulation of reserves. In practice, the Treasury had always preferred to rely on a system that forced economy by requiring the royal household to live within means granted to it for a period rather than annually. For that reason, it disliked an annual Civil List system because it 'would remove the inbuilt incentive of the present system to economy'. Should the system become annual, then the Treasury would have to take more control of the expenditure (Minute of 24 April 1970: BA 6/96).

There was controversy over royal taxation in the early 1990s when it became apparent that, although the monarch had paid income tax voluntarily since its reintroduction in 1842, an unannounced concession by the then Chancellor of the Exchequer (Lloyd George) on the accession of George V in 1910 had removed the burden. Moreover, it emerged that not only did the Queen pay no income tax as alone entitled but the Treasury had made orders relieving three other senior members of the royal family of their entire tax liability and some others to lesser extents all on the grounds that their annuities were more or less consumed by the cost of their public duties.

When the Queen (and the Prince of Wales) volunteered to end the exemptions from personal tax both enjoyed, the Prime Minister moved swiftly to announce new arrangements in late 1992. This was partly in an effort to defuse parallel public concern over the cost of refurbishing Windsor Castle following a severe fire in a year of royal domestic calamities that the Queen dubbed her *annus horribilis*.

As a result, from 1 April 1993 the Queen has paid tax on her personal, private income and that part of the Privy Purse income she uses for personal purposes but not on Civil List funding because that was designed to meet official expenses. She also agreed to refund not only the three parliamentary annuities she then already covered from the Privy Purse but also a further five of those remaining, leaving only those for the Queen Mother and the Duke of Edinburgh. The Prince of Wales, already subject to income tax except on his Duchy of Cornwall income where he had formerly voluntarily paid 25 per cent, would pay income tax instead on the portion not devoted to public duties. Both already paid indirect taxes and local rates.

In addition, the Queen pays tax on any realised gains on her private investments and on the private proportion of assets in the Privy Purse. However, because 'the Monarchy as an institution needs sufficient private resources to enable it to continue to perform its traditional role in national life, and to have a degree of financial independence from the Government of the day' (HM Treasury 2013: 2), it followed that the monarch was to become liable to inheritance tax on all bequests and gifts but not on transfers of assets from one sovereign to a successor. The royal collection of paintings and works of art held but not personally owned by the Queen and passed to her successors would become the responsibility of a new charitable trust – the Royal Collection Trust – funded by admission charges and other sources.

Sovereign Grant Act 2011

This broke entirely from the previous reign-specific systems and aimed to produce a funding mechanism that would settle the monarchy's financial support for the future. It did so by consolidating all previous Civil List payments, including those made via grants-in-aid from government departments, and adopting a proxy form of indexation where future grants would be based on a percentage of the net profits of the Crown Estate. To begin with, the percentage was set at 15 per cent under a statutory formula with the royal trustees now obliged to report on the new system's operation every five years rather than the former ten and with power to alter the percentage through a debateable statutory instrument. Moreover, the whole of the sovereign grant and a reserve fund were made subject to audit by the Comptroller and Auditor General and all financial reports to be laid before Parliament. With the exception of the parliamentary annuity for the Duke of Edinburgh, all other annuities ceased and the Queen (who had been refunding annuity costs to the Treasury since 1993) undertook to meet the costs of other royal family members who performed official duties on her behalf.

The working outcome is a clearer and more transparent regime consistent with modern financial and accounting practices, answerable to Parliament but with a significant degree of operational independence under the general superintendence of the royal trustees.

Conclusions

The British Parliament's gradually increased control over royal finances has been in lagged step with the decline of the sovereign's constitutional powers and political authority during increasingly democratic, and occasionally inflationary, times. Struggles about the principles of funding as opposed to amount reflect in the end arguments about the degree of independence to be allowed to the monarchy as one of the principal players in the British Constitution. Although the monarch's former powers over the dissolution of Parliament and selection of Prime Minister are now in other hands, the monarch remains both head of state not bound by the advice of UK ministers when present in the 15 other Commonwealth Realms, and it is thought retains ultimately a deep reserve – or latent – power to act at times of constitutional crisis.

The royal household has always argued that sovereigns require a capacity to think and act independently of government and rely on staff whose first loyalty is to them alone. It has maintained that any form of control that implied politicisation of the monarchy would imperil the monarchy's essential constitutional independence. When a minority of the 1971 Select Committee argued for financial annuality and making Palace staff civil servants under a Permanent Secretary (Houghton 1971: 88–90), a household official was unambiguous:

> The Queen has confirmed her views to me in no uncertain terms. Her Majesty would see great objection, both on grounds of management efficiency and on grounds of wider principle, to transfer the control of her Household staff out of the hands of herself and her officers. (Lord Chamberlain to Treasury 30 June 1971: T 326/1321).

In what appears to be a Palace assisted book, the Prince of Wales is quoted as taking the same position in an unattributed quote said to have been uttered in 1992:

> I think it of absolute importance that the Monarch should have a degree of financial independence from the State. I am not prepared to take on the position of sovereign of this country on any other basis. I must have independence and you can only have that through financial independence (Longford 1993: 167).

The government rejected the Houghton 1971 proposals because, although couched in terms of achieving greater economy, they would in practice ensure 'that the Royal Household would be an entirely different institution'. Moreover, it 'would intrude a piece of United Kingdom machinery ... between the Queen and Commonwealth countries' (Commons Hansard, 14 December 1971: §§288–90). They have nonetheless continued to find favour in some quarters distinguishing between the sovereign's private and public activities (Richards 1996: 17; Fabian Society 2003: 141–43; and at least one historian, Cannadine 1998: 18).

It remains too early to judge whether the 2011 regime will succeed in finding a truly lasting settlement across future reigns. There is no doubt that the royal household has been alive to how it is regarded and done a great deal to respond. Heroic efforts – some not before time – have led to reductions in real costs. The Queen herself has not been slow to shoulder more of the costs directly, for example taking on former Parliamentary annuities and devoting more sums from the Privy Purse to defray the cost of public duties.[6] Perversely, the Queen's assumption of responsibility for all former royal family parliamentary annuities (save for her husband's) has led to a diminution of public knowledge of what family members receive because the Privy Purse accounts are not published.

However, as a former civil service head of the Treasury and Cabinet Secretary pointed out in the Lords debate on the 2011 Bill (Turnbull, Lords Hansard, 3 October 2011: §§ 996–97), tying financial support to the value of the Crown Estate would be vulnerable to changes in the property cycle (then at a low ebb) and make the link unsustainable. What was presented as indexation should be seen for what it was – a direct charge on the Consolidated Fund – and the implied notion of entitlement in the link to the Crown Estate bogus.

David McClure in a wide-ranging review of royal finances from Queen Victoria to the present reign has also counselled caution about the effects of the 2011 Act:

> To its critics, the key weakness of the new settlement is the absence of any clear connection between the level of funding and the actual requirements of the palace. Just as the revenues from the Duchies of Lancaster and Cornwall are in no way directly linked to the needs of the Queen and the Prince of Wales, so the revenues of the Crown Estate seem to be divorced from the requirements of the Royal Household. To some, this amounts to an invitation to inefficiency (McClure 2014: 425).

It is true that the 2011 Act is inconsistent with former Treasury objections to indexation on the grounds that it would relax the financial disciplines inherent in fixed annual allocations. Similarly, the Act overrode earlier royal adviser apprehensions that a link with Crown Estate revenues would call into question whether the Duchies of Lancaster and Cornwall revenues should remain wholly at their beneficiaries' disposal and not be taken into account in the funding settlement as a whole. To the extent that the Queen has conceded bearing (save for the Prince of Wales's costs and Prince Philip's parliamentary annuity) royal family personal costs from the Privy Purse, then the sharpness of previous adviser concerns may have been blunted.

All that said, there can be no doubt that the current regime is light years away from the position in 1952 which was difficult to understand and sometimes presented with a lack of entire candour where explanation was offered at all. In the longer view, the embarrassing tax episode of the 1990s – which may have contributed to a climate where a new government in 1997 declined to replace the royal yacht *Britannia* despite Palace

---

[6] The Privy Purse is principally funded from the net annual surplus – £21 million in 2018–19 – of the Duchy of Lancaster. The latter estate was not included with the Crown Estate when that hereditary revenue source was surrendered in 1760 in return for parliamentary annuities.

lobbying (Low 2018) – reflected less discredit on the monarchy perhaps than on the pusillanimous and foxy behaviour of successive governments. This is because governments, accepting that the monarchy required adequate funding, had failed always to be entirely frank about detailed arrangements, particularly on the balance between direct and indirect funding.

The present regime promises at least greater frankness and accountability. In the end, such principles must prove the best way of judging the means of supporting the monarchy for as long as it remains preferred as the apex of Britain's Constitution.

7.6. GENDER EQUALITY AND THE LINE OF SUCCESSION

Olivia Hepsworth, the Constitution Unit, 2430 words

This examines the change from male primogeniture to absolute primogeniture in Belgium, Denmark, the Netherlands, Norway, Sweden, Luxembourg and the United Kingdom. It aims to illuminate what, or who, facilitated this change and the contemporary support or opposition to its introduction. Also discussed is the continuation of male primogeniture in Spain, and why the Spanish monarchy has not followed the trajectory of their Western European counterparts. Gender discrimination could be seen as outdated in an age where gender equality is expected to be met in all facets of society. Nevertheless, is this the primary reason for the monarchy's movement to absolute primogeniture? Was this change driven by our contemporary conception of the importance of gender equality or perhaps changes in human rights law?

The UN Universal Declaration of Human Rights (1948) 'guarantees equality of dignity and rights, equality of race, colour, sex, language, religion, political or other opinion, national or social origin, property, birth or other status'. The European Convention on Human Rights (1950) also provides that 'The enjoyment of the rights and freedoms set forth in this Convention shall be secured without discrimination on any ground such as sex, race, colour, language, religion, … birth or other status'. In 2000 this was widened by Protocol 12 to provide

> the enjoyment of any right set forth by law shall be secured without discrimination on any ground such as sex, race, colour, language, religion, political or other opinion, national or social origin, association with a national minority, property, birth or other status.

In this modern era, gender equality has come to be expected in all aspects of society, notably in the workplace. Since the 1970s, the EU has implemented thirteen pieces of legislation that have been adopted with the aim of eliminating gender discrimination in the workplace. All countries studied are members of the EU and subject to EU law with the exception of Norway, that is nevertheless (with few exceptions) a fully-fledged part of the internal market through the European Economic Space mechanisms, and possibly soon also the UK. The role of a monarch cannot easily be likened to any other job that is regulated by EU laws and the ECHR; nevertheless, the existence of these laws demonstrates a societal consensus against exclusion from any role based on gender. Undeniably, these changing attitudes have had knock on effects on how these monarchies dictate their rules of succession.

The 1980s and 1990s

Given that the movement to absolute primogeniture occurred within years of each other in Sweden, the Netherlands, Norway and Belgium, this paper begins by examining the introduction of absolute primogeniture in these countries and whether the events were connected in a domino effect.

In Sweden, the 1810 Act of Succession was altered in 1980 from male preference primogeniture to absolute primogeniture.[7] In 1979, the Riksdag decided that female heirs would now have equal rights to inherit the throne. This change promoted Princess Victoria (born 1977) to heir apparent displacing her brother, Prince Carl Philip, still in his infancy. Because the Swedish Act of Succession was submitted to and passed through Parliament, it was presented as an act of the public will (Corcos 2012: 1624).

In 1983, the Netherlands implemented the same change, and introduced another means to determine the heir: proximity of blood. However, given the absence of any living male heir of William III, the Netherlands had already by 1884 abolished Salic law (a law excluding females from dynastic succession). His daughter Wilhelmina then became Queen in 1898 (after her mother Queen Emma acted as Queen Regent) and her daughter, Juliana, inherited the throne from her in 1948, as her daughter Beatrix did in 1980. Although gender equality was only introduced in 1983, a precedent had already been set for the legitimacy of female monarchs by four queens in a row.

Norway had also previously implemented Salic law. Gender equality was introduced in 1990 by constitutional amendment but in a way that preserved the position of the adult Crown Prince by not coming into force until the next generation. Article 6 of the Norwegian Constitution now states:

> The order of succession is lineal, so that only a child born in lawful wedlock of the Queen or King, or of one who is herself or himself entitled to the succession, may succeed, and so that the nearest line shall take precedence over the more remote and the elder in the line over the younger (Constitution of Norway, 1990).

Until 1991, Salic law had excluded Belgian female monarchs from ruling. The 1991 Act of Succession abolished this exclusion. Title IX of article 85 of the Belgian Constitution contained a transitional clause to remove the barring of women from inheriting the throne. The process by which the Belgian Constitution and its articles are changed is called 'coordination'. This has occurred only once, in 1993, when a new consolidated version of the Belgian Constitution was proposed to the Federal Parliament by the government, adopted in 1994. This amended Constitution cemented women's place as future monarchs.

In Norway and Belgium, this change to the line of succession was not retrospective. The elder female siblings of the current monarch do not become eligible; but the female children of the current monarch will be. For example, the sisters of the then King of Norway, King Harald V, remained excluded from the line of succession, his daughter

---

[7] The political manoeuvres behind the change were seen by the Swedish right as strengthening the monarchy – see Åse 2013: 176–78.

Princess Märtha Louise however did become eligible to inherit the throne, though behind her younger brother in the line.

It is difficult to speculate as to what specifically drove all these nations to abolish gender exclusionary laws from their constitutions within just over a decade, in what could be argued to look like a domino effect. The birth of a daughter to King Carl XVI Gustaf of Sweden, Princess Victoria, was closely aligned with the introduction to the amendment of the 1810 Act of Succession. The rebirth of second wave feminism in the 1970s and 1980s also coincided with the changes to the line of succession. No doubt feminism and calls for gender equality held a much greater influence and platform. Gender equality and conceptions of modernity were becoming interlinked.

The Danish Referendum

Denmark alone addressed the question of absolute primogeniture through a referendum. The 2009 referendum on changing the Danish Act of Succession was held in Denmark, the Faroe Islands and Greenland. The referendum was held alongside the European Parliament elections. The law (requiring 40 per cent to be passed) was passed with 85.4 per cent of the popular vote. Any constitutional amendment must pass both Parliaments before and after an election, and be supported in a popular referendum. There was opposition to the proposed change to the content of the 1953 Constitution from both the left and the right. Calls by the left to have the Universal Declaration of Human Rights and other rights enshrined in the Constitution was rejected by the Conservative-Liberal cabinet of Anders Fogh Rasmussen. However, all parties in Parliament, with the exception of Enhedslisten, did ultimately give their support to the change. Enhedslisten was a far left party whose abstention was based upon two objections. They opposed the continued barring of children born out of wedlock from the throne, and the requirement that any heir to the throne must have their marriage approved by the ruling monarch.

The government at a cost of five million Danish Kroner (just short of €700,000) launched the campaign in favour of the referendum. Opposition emerged from parts of the Social Liberal Youth, Enhedslisten and republican circles in favour of a blank vote. The Conservative Youth of Denmark wanted a no vote, desiring to protect royal tradition. The referendum had a 58.3% turnout, with a high number of blank or no votes, notably in Copenhagen. Upon the passing of the referendum Prime Minister Lars Løkke Rasmussen stated that the referendum 'was important for gender equality' and 'a strong signal that shows that we want to be a society where men and women have the same opportunities, whether it is for ordinary people or princes and princesses' (Deutsche Welle 2009).

This referendum aimed to build upon the 1953 constitutional amendment to the line of succession that had allowed Princess Margrethe to take the throne instead of her uncle (Corcos 2012: 1629). Whilst the previous constitutional amendment was arguably born out of necessity, the 2009 referendum was clearly framed, in the words of the Prime Minister himself, as a clear statement of Danish commitment to gender equality in all facets of society.

The 2010s

In 2010, the Grand Duke of Luxembourg, Henri II, introduced a decree to institute gender equality in the line of succession. On the signing of the UN Convention on the Elimination of all Forms of Discrimination Against Women in 1979, the government of Luxembourg had made a reservation with respect to article 3 of its Constitution because of the rules of succession. This reservation was removed in 2008 (Corcos 2012: 1631). This marked the first indication of the decision to move towards absolute primogeniture. As of 2011 article 3 of the Constitution now dictates age and birth shall determine the heir, not gender. Being a founding member of the European Union and a member of the United Nations, many argued this change was long overdue, being contrary to the principles of gender equality promulgated by these bodies (Corcos 2012: 1631). Additionally, the Luxembourg Constitution also provides that citizens of the Duchy are equal before the law (Corcos 2012: 1631). The Grand Duke's Marshal issued an addendum to the decree explaining why this change occurred in response to the United Nations' 1979 call for nations to eliminate all forms of discrimination against women. It is evident through their own words that the monarchy felt the gender discrimination in their line of succession was incompatible with contemporary values.

In October 2011, the UK Prime Minister David Cameron spoke of his desire to abolish gender discrimination, and religious discrimination from the British line of succession at the Commonwealth Heads of Government meeting. Cameron argued these rules were 'outdated' and

> the idea that a younger son should become Monarch instead of an elder daughter, simply because he is a man just isn't acceptable anymore. Nor does it make any sense that a potential Monarch can marry someone of any faith other than Catholic … the thinking behind these ideas is wrong (Bloxham and Kirkup 2011).

Gordon Brown, a previous Prime Minister, had been supportive of the change; nevertheless, for this change to be introduced required all 16 Realms to approve – a huge undertaking. Perhaps this can account for the significant delay in introducing gender equality in contrast to previous countries examined in this chapter. The 2013 Succession to the Crown Act altered the laws of succession following on from the 2011 Perth Agreement, coming into effect in March 2015. This push to abolish male primogeniture also coincided with the first pregnancy of the Duchess of Cambridge, but as it happened her eldest child was a boy (Prince George, born in 2013). Had the child been a girl and the law unchanged, the Princess could have been displaced by a later male sibling.

Spain

Spain is the only European monarchy to retain male primogeniture. Under article 57 of the Spanish Constitution the crown passes first to the male heirs and then to any female heirs of the sovereign from older to younger, in the direct line (Corcos 2012: 1635). As King Felipe VI has had two daughters, the heir apparent, Princess Leonor, will become queen; nevertheless, she could lose the throne if he were to go on to have a son. Critics have noted that the preference for male heirs expressed in article 57 seems contrary to the expressions of human rights and human dignity in article 10 and principles of equality in article 14. Article 10 reads:

> The dignity of the person, the inviolable rights which are inherent, the free development of the personality, respect for the law and the rights of others, are the foundation of political order and social peace. The norms relative to basic rights and liberties which are recognised by the Constitution shall be interpreted in conformity with the Universal Declaration of Human Rights and the international treaties and agreements on those matters ratified by Spain (Corcos 2012: 1636).

However, such instruments do not have direct effect, nor is it clear how a case for change could be based on the European Convention on Human Rights. In practice, King Juan Carlos designated his son as Duke of Asturias and heir at a very early stage of his reign when it was thought desirable to take steps to consolidate the monarchy. There are also two practical considerations: changing the Spanish Constitution is a very difficult project; and the fact that the present King has daughters only does not make the gender question pressing.

In the 1990s, female aristocrats launched a legal challenge against male primogeniture laws. The Spanish judiciary, and ultimately its highest court, ruled against them, as did the European Court of Human Rights in 1998 (Corcos 2012: 1640). However, in 2006 the Spanish Parliament passed a retroactive ruling abolishing gender discrimination in the succession to aristocratic titles. Instead, the eldest child would inherit titles. The Spanish Nobles Association a conservative faction of nobility heavily opposed this change. The passage of the 2006 statute was aligning Spanish law with CEDAW, the Convention on the Elimination of All Forms of Discrimination Against Women, and in response to an adverse ruling from the Spanish Constitutional Court dating from 1997:

> Nevertheless, the rules which regulate the inheritance of aristocratic titles come from the historical period in which the titled nobility was consolidated as a privileged social class, and contained rules such as the principle of masculinity or primogeniture without doubt adapted to the values of the Old Regime, but incompatible with contemporary society in which women participate fully in political, economic, cultural, and social life. This full equality of men and women in all legal and social spheres is recognised in the Convention on the Elimination of All Forms of Discrimination Against Women, adopted in New York on 18 December, 1979, and ratified by Spain in 1984 (Corcos 2012: 1639).

The abolition of gender discrimination in aristocratic inheritance has set a precedent. It seems a natural consequence that the question of gender equality and the succession to the throne will too have to be questioned. This inevitably leads one to consider to what extent are the monarchy part of the aristocratic class, and thus also subject to changes in aristocratic inheritance? The view so far taken in the UK is that there is no necessary connection.

Conclusion

The movement to absolute primogeniture has been a staggered process across Western Europe. Sweden, the Netherlands, Norway and Belgium all introduced cognatic succession within a number of years of each other. Though Luxembourg and the UK took decades to follow suit, they both cited a modern belief in gender equality as the driving factor. Discrimination based on gender has become incompatible with twenty-first century beliefs and values.

7.7. COMPARATIVE SUMMARY AND CONCLUSIONS

Dr Bob Morris, The Constitution Unit, University College London

Although the hereditary principle suggests stability and longevity, in practice some of the monarchies are relatively new in historical perspective. The Dutch, Belgian, Luxembourg and Norwegian monarchies in their present form date respectively from 1814, 1831, 1890 and 1905, although the Norwegian Constitution remains that (amended) of 1814. Moreover, new dynasties have been introduced as in the Bernadotte in Sweden from 1818 and the Saxe-Coburg-Gotha in the UK from 1837 succeeding a Hanoverian dynasty itself installed only in 1714. Indeed, from 1837 the UK monarchy ceased to be also rulers of Hanover because the Salic law there forbade the succession of females.

This relative modernity seems also related to the extent to which monarchies have become, in Bart van Poelgeest's phrase, 'constitutionalised' – that is, defined in written constitutions, including prescribing how membership of the royal family is to be defined. This characteristic has been relatively absent in the UK whose Constitution is less formally organised than elsewhere.[8] Membership of the royal family is not defined directly in law and no definition of the family is behind the UK monarchy's funding. The upshot in Britain is that the monarchy enjoys a degree of financial independence which, although far from absolute, nonetheless allows it to maintain a good degree of autonomous operational distance from executive government itself.

Comparative Levels of State Support

Table 7.1 below attempts to summarise available data about the arrangements for public financial support for each of the European monarchies save for Luxembourg. Per capita costs for each monarchy show a majority lying in a band of between €1.04 and €2.14 with outliers at €0.17 for Spain and €5.46 for Norway. The figures are best regarded as indicating orders of magnitude rather than precision and, as Table 7.1 explains, the Norwegian figure may well overstate the position. The Spanish figure, on the other hand, represents the newest of the monarchies and a determination to avoid excessive expenditure. Neither of the monarchs since 1976 have, for example, actually occupied the royal palace, and King Felipe reduced his civil list payment by twenty per cent on his accession in 2014. (Keeley 2016.) Because Duchy of Lancaster figures are not public revenues, the UK figure does not include the annual surplus paid into the UK Queen's Privy Purse and which amounted to €21 million for 2018–19.

---

[8] Indeed, standing regency legislation – which specifies which royal relatives can act in the monarch's minority or absence abroad – dates only from 1937.

Table 7.1 Financing the European Monarchies 2019

This Table summarises from publicly available sources current funding arrangements for the monarchies of Britain, Belgium, Denmark, Norway, The Netherlands, Spain and Sweden. While there are some broad similarities – financial control by national parliaments and, with the possible exception of Spain and Norway, not dissimilar levels of support expenditure – there are detailed differences deriving from distinct national histories. A more detailed examination of the material is to be found in the Chapter Summary and Conclusions above.

	Britain	Belgium	Denmark	Netherlands	Norway	Spain	Sweden
Total Amount Received from State/ Civil List	Sovereign Grant= €84.6m, as of 2017–2018[9] *Additional expenses such as security are not covered in the Sovereign Grant and are not released as public information.	Civil List = €11.8m, as of October 2017. *Additional funds required from government departments reached €22.8million for 2018.[10]	Civil List= Queen receives €11m, as of October 2018.[11]	King's budget = €40.1m, as of 2015.[12] *Costs relating to the security of members of the royal house, state visits, and the maintenance and upkeep of the royal palaces continue to be funded by government ministries and not included in the royal budget.[13]	€26.4m (for the royal house, to be distributed between the royal family) + €1.2m (grant for the King and Queen to cover personal expenses) + €1,001,348.51 (for the Crown Prince and Princess.) = €28.7m in 2017.[14]	€7.8m, as of 2018.[15]	€6.3 million for Court Administration + €6.1m for Palace Administration = €12.4m, as of 2015.[16]
Population-Year/Cost per Capita	66,573,504–2018/ €1.27	11,350,000–2017/ €1.04	5,754,356–2018/ €1.92	16,900,000–2015/ €2.14	5,258,000–2017/ €5.46	46,397,452–2018/ €0.17	9,747,000–2015/ €1.27

(continued)

[9] The Sovereign Grant and Sovereign Grant Reserve Annual Report and Accounts 2017–18. Available at: https://assets.publishing.service.gov.uk/government/uploads/system/uploads/attachment_data/file/719582/SovereignGrant2017-18_Final.pdf.
[10] All information in above text not available at: www.brusselstimes.com/brussels/9431/budget-of-belgian-monarchy-will-exceed-36-million-in-2018.
[11] Available at: http://kongehuset.dk/en/organisation-and-contact/state-civil-list-annuity.
[12] Available at: www.royal-house.nl/topics/finances-of-the-royal-house/the-king%E2%80%99s-budget.
[13] Available at: https://en.wikipedia.org/wiki/Monarchy_of_the_Netherlands#Royal finances.
[14] Available at: www.businessinsider.com/richest-royals-what-europes-royal-families-get-from-their-taxpayers-2017-7?r=UK&IR=T#king-harald-v-norway-258m-11.
[15] Available at: www.casareal.es/ES/Transparencia/informacioneconomica/Paginas/organizacion-y-presupuesto_presupuestos.aspx.
[16] Available at: www.kungahuset.se/royalcourt/monarchytheroyalcourt/royalfinances.4.3961605115842572180005637.html.

Table 7.1 (*Continued*)

	Britain	Belgium	Denmark	Netherlands	Norway	Spain	Sweden
How the amount is determined	The core Sovereign Grant is based on 15% of the net surplus income of the Crown Estate[17] for the financial year two years previous. From 2017–18, the Sovereign Grant will be raised to 25%, with the additional 10% to be used to fund the Re-servicing of Buckingham Palace over the next ten years.[18]	Article 2 of the Act of 2013 sets the basic amount of the Civil List at €11.5m.[19]	The annual parliamentary allowance to the queen is laid down in the Civil List Act, as last amended in 2001. It is adjusted in line with the pay index for state sector employees.[20]	The Royal House Finances Act of 1972 as amended in 2008 sets allowances for the king and other royal family members. The allowances have two components: income A & B. Annual increases or decreases are provided for: the A component is linked to changes in the annual salary of the Vice-President of the Council of State; the B-component is linked to changes in civil service pay and the cost of living.[21]	The sum is determined by the Parliament and appears in the state annual accounts. It is also contained in the monarchy's published annual reports.	Under Articles 65 and 134 of the Constitution, following a government initiative the Cortes Generales approves each year the Law on General State Budgets, which establishes a global amount for each year. The purpose is to ensure that the Head of State has a sufficient budget to carry out his work with the independence inherent in his constitutional functions.[22]	Determined annually by the government. Website states: 'The Court Administration and the Palace Administration receive funding allocations from the State, which are reported together with government funding allocations in the annual budget proposition under the heading Governance of the Realm.'[23]

[17] Owned by the monarch during their reign, but is not the private property of the monarch, managed by an independent institution the Crown Estate Commissioners.
[18] The Sovereign Grant and Sovereign Grant Reserve Annual Report and Accounts 2017–18. Available at: https://assets.publishing.service.gov.uk/government/uploads/system/uploads/attachment_data/file/711982/SovereignGrant2017-18_Final.pdf.
[19] Available at: www.monarchie.be/en/monarchy/civil-list/financial-resources.
[20] Available at: http://kongehuset.dk/en/annual-report-2016/economy.
[21] Available at: https://en.wikipedia.org/wiki/Monarchy_of_the_Netherlands#Royal_finances.
[22] Available at: www.casareal.es/EN/Transparencia/informacioneconomica/Paginas/organizacion-y-presupuesto_presupuestos.aspx.
[23] Available at: www.kungahuset.se/royalcourt/monarchytheroyalcourt/royalfinances.4.39616051158425 7f218000 5637.html.

	Britain	Belgium	Denmark	Netherlands	Norway	Spain	Sweden
Where does the money go?	To carry out official duties. These include: travel for official engagements in the UK and overseas; the maintenance of royal residencies used for formal entertaining and ceremonial events; and salaries for those household employees who support[24] the work of the Queen as Head of State.[25]	All the expenditure directly incurred by the king in the exercise of the royal office in the broadest sense of the term: staff under contract, equipment, daily operating costs for the king and the queen, including activities, receptions, etc., maintenance of the interior of the royal palace in Brussels and the Castle of Laeken, the cost of utilities, the fleet of vehicles and fuel, administration, insurance etc[26]	The government allowance covers the expenses of the queen relating to staff, operation of the royal household, administration and properties as well as the queen's expenses of a more private nature. In addition to the government allowance for the queen, the Civil List Act provides an allowance of €226,616.53 a month for the crown prince, and crown princess[27]	The king's budget sets out the projected expenditure associated with the performance of his official duties. This finances: 1. Allowances paid under the Royal House Finances Act. 2. Expenses incurred in the performance of official duties. 3. Other expenses relating to the management of the royal house. As of 1 January 2014, the king's budget no longer covers private flights. This will save a total of nearly €300,000 on a structural basis.[28]	The sums cover the cost of the king and his families' official expenditure; the cost of staff members; royal travel etc. Lately, the sums have been increased to cover major refurbishment costs of official residences – see below and also the current levels of provision in Britain for similar purposes.	The annual budget pays for senior management staff, management staff and career civil servants, other minor staffing positions, and for general office expenses. The head of household, Secretary General, and other management staff salaries must be comparable to civil service staff, though in no way do they form part of the government or administration. Additionally, the annual budget pays for the maintenance and expenses of senior members of the royal family who undertake royal duties.[29]	The Court Administration has to cover the cost of the king's official duties, including travel and expenditure by the Office of the Marshal of the Realm and its staff departments – personnel, finance, information and press, the office of the marshal of the court and the households of HM The Queen and the Crown Princess Lilian, as well as the royal mews.[30]

(continued)

[24] Pensions of palace staff were taken over by the government under the 1952 Civil List Act.
[25] Available at: www.royal.uk/royal-finances-0.
[26] Available at: www.monarchie.be/en/monarchy/civil-list/financial-resources.
[27] Available at: http://kongehuset.dk/en/organisation-and-contact/state-civil-list-annuity.
[28] Available at: www.royal-house.nl/topics/finances-of-the-royal-house/flights.
[29] Available at: https://en.wikipedia.org/wiki/Monarchy_of_Spain#cite_note-Royal_Household-112.
[30] Available at: www.kungahuset.se/royalcourt/monarchytheroyalcourt/royalfinances.4.396160511584257f2180005637.html.

Table 7.1 *(Continued)*

	Britain	Belgium	Denmark	Netherlands	Norway	Spain	Sweden
Personal Income /Savings	Income from the Duchy of Lancaster forms part of the queen's privy purse[31] income. Duchy of Cornwall Income funds the private and official expenditure of the Prince of Wales and the Duchess of Cornwall and is taxed to the extent it relates to wholly private expenditure. It also covers the expenditure of the Duke and Duchess of Cambridge and the Duke and Duchess of Sussex.[32] There is much speculation about the queen's private wealth but no authoritative public evidence.	With royal residences being state owned, aside from the income received from the state Information on personal wealth/ savings is not publicly available.	No public information about extent of personal wealth.	There has been speculation about the wealth of former Queen Beatrix who abdicated in 2013 but there is no authoritative public account.[33]	The Norwegian King purportedly has a personal fortune consisting of real estate, investments, and a stake in Shell Oil.[34] His personal wealth has been a contentious issue in the Norwegian press with circulation of stories that the king has a personal wealth much greater than previously known, reports which the palace denied. (Apparently, the bulk of the inherited wealth originates from Queen Maud's heritage as a member of the British royal family.)	With royal residences being state owned, and aside from the income received from the state, there is no public information on personal wealth/savings. Although there has been speculation about the extent of private wealth, it is likely that Juan Carlos's father's long, penurious exile could not have been conducive to capital accumulation.	Most personal income/savings appears to come from investment. The chief financial officer at the court is responsible for the investments. In 2016, the Princess Madeline earned almost €230,000 capital surplus on her investments. Her Royal Highness paid €70,865 in taxes.[35]

[31] The Privy Purse is an historical term used to describe the queen's private income and it is largely used to meet official expenditure incurred by Her Majesty and other members of the royal family which is not met by the Sovereign Grant and is taxed to the extent that the income is not used for official purposes.

[32] Available at: www.royal.uk/sites/default/files/media/sovereign_grant_2017-18_summary_final.pdf.

[33] Available at: https://en.wikipedia.org/wiki/List_of_royalty_by_net_worth.

[34] Available at: www.businessinsider.com/royal-family-net-worth-europe-ranked-2018-5?r=US&IR=T#5-queen-beatrix-netherlands-6.

[35] Available at: http://royalcentral.co.uk/europe/sweden/swedish-royal-finances-and-taxes-revealed-88061.

	Britain	Belgium	Denmark	Netherlands	Norway	Spain	Sweden
Royal properties	10 crown-owned properties including primary residence of Buckingham Palace. Additionally, 7 privately owned properties; 3 crown estate owned and 3 Duchy of Cornwall owned. The royal yacht was discontinued from 1997.	6 state-owned properties in the Royal Trust including primary residence of Belvédère Castle.[36] 2 privately owned properties.	7 state-owned properties that belong to the 'Kingdom of Denmark' and a yacht. In addition, there are 3 privately owned properties.	The Royal Palaces include 3 state-owned properties of which the king's residence since January 2019 is Huis ten Bosch in The Hague.[37] Of former Palaces, Het Loo is now a public museum and Soestdijk is privately owned – not by a member of the royal family.	The Royal Palace in Oslo is the king's main residence. There are 4 royal residences in other parts of the country. All five belong to the state Together, the king and the crown prince own 6 private properties, including the official residence of the latter (outside Oslo), a yacht and some smaller vessels.[38] The yacht belongs to the king but is crewed by the Norwegian Navy	The royal sites are a set of palaces, monasteries, and convents built for and under the patronage of the Spanish monarchy. The principal palace is the Royal Palace of Madrid, alongside 7 other properties and a yacht.	13 crown properties are state owned, with the exception of the privately owned Solliden Palace.

(continued)

36 Available at: www.monarchie.be/en/monarchy/civil-list/financial-resources.
37 Available at: www.royal-house.nl/topics.
38 Available at: www.royalcourt.no/seksjon.html?tid=27681.

Table 7.1 *(Continued)*

	Britain	Belgium	Denmark	Netherlands	Norway	Spain	Sweden
Reporting/ Transparency Agreements	Accounts are subject to C&AG inspection[39] from the National Audit Office rather than, as in the past, subject only to unpublished Treasury audit. Accounts for the Duchies of Lancaster and of Cornwall are presented to both Houses of Parliament annually.[40]	Since the start of the current reign and for the sake of transparency all budget lines for this [Civil List] purpose have been grouped in a common budget programme in the General Expenditure Budget of the Federal State.[41]	The financial statements of the Civil List and the Parliamentary Annuity paid to the crown prince are presented in accordance with the provisions regarding class A enterprises under theDanishFinancial Statements Act.[42]	In 2009, the government decided that the annual State Budget of the Netherlands should show in a transparent way all the costs of the royal house, some of which had previously been borne by various government ministries. Three sets of costs are now separately allocated in the annual budget for the royal house (Budget I of the annual State Budget).[43]	The monarchy's budget is recorded in the Norwegian state budget and appears in the monarchy's annual reports[44]	According to the sixth additional provision of Law 19/2013, of December 9, on Transparency, Access to Public Information and Good Governance, the General Secretariat of the Government's Presidency will be the competent body to process the procedure by which it is requested Access to information held by the House of His Majesty the King.[45]	The accounts of the Court Administration are audited by external auditors. By agreement with the government, theactivities of the Palace Administration Offices are audited by the Parliamentary Auditors.[46]

[39] Office of Comptroller and Auditor General, an officer of the House of Commons.

[40] Available at: www.royal.uk/sites/default/files/media/sovereign_grant_2017-18_summary_final.pdf.

[41] Available at: www.monarchie.be/en/monarchy/civil-list/financial-resources.

[42] Available at: http://kongehuset.dk/en/annual-report-2016/economy.

[43] Available at: https://en.wikipedia.org/wiki/Monarchy_of_the_Netherlands#Royal_finances.

[44] Available at: www.royalcourt.no/binfil/download2.php?tid=168770.

[45] Available at: www.casareal.es/EN/Transparencia/informacioneconomica/Paginas/subhome.aspx.

[46] Available at: www.kungahuset.se/royalcourt/monarchytheroyalcourt/royalfinances.4.396160511584257f2180005637.html.

	Britain	Belgium	Denmark	Netherlands	Norway	Spain	Sweden
Taxation	In 1992, the queen volunteered to pay income tax and capital gains tax, and since 1993 her personal income has been taxable as for any other taxpayer. The queen has always been subject to Value Added Tax and pays local rates on a voluntary basis. Other members of the royal family are fully liable to tax in the normal way.[47]	Since a finance reform in 2013, the Belgian monarchy is subject to taxation.	Exempt from income tax. The queen, the crown prince, the crown princess, Prince Joachim, Princess Marie and Princess Benedikte are subject to the standard regulations concerning payment of death duties, inheritance tax and real property tax.[48]	Royal house members receiving a stipend are exempt from income tax over that stipend. The monarch and the heir-apparent are exempt from inheritance tax on inheritances received from members of the royal house.[49]	The royal couple and the crown prince's family are exempt from taxation. The exemption does not cover other members of the family (including Princess Märtha Louise, the Crown prince's elder sister).	All members of the royal family are subject to taxation.	All members of the Royal Family follow the same tax rules as other citizens in Sweden. However, part of the income of the King and his children is regarded as appanage which means that it is not taxed.[50]

(continued)

47 Available at: www.gov.uk/government/publications/sovereign-grant-act-2011-guidance/sovereign-grant-act-2011-guidance.
48 Available at: http://kongehuset.dk/en/organisation-and-contact/state-civil-list-annuity.
49 Available at: https://en.wikipedia.org/wiki/Monarchy_of_the_Netherlands.
50 Available at: http://royalcentral.co.uk/europe/sweden/swedish-royal-finances-and-taxes-revealed-88061.

Table 7.1 (*Continued*)

	Britain	Belgium	Denmark	Netherlands	Norway	Spain	Sweden
Additional costs (palace refurbishments)	The funding requirement for the programme to re-service Buckingham Palace in the 10 years to 2026–27 is €418 million including VAT.[51] The additional Sovereign Grant for re-servicing for 2017–18 is €34.5 million.[52]	No apparent large-scale current renovation works.	In 2010, Amalienborg Palace was renovated. It cost the taxpayer €29.4m.[53] No significant current renovation works.	The renovation of the royal palace Huis ten Bosch will be completed in 2019. The costs are estimated at €63.1 million.[54]	€51m was in the late 1990s allocated to the extensive refurbishments of the Oslo Palace and other royal residences, namely those of notable historic value, that have been taking place and are still underway. The restoration of the Royal Palace in Oslo went far beyond the original budget,[55] but the overruns seem mainly to have been a consequence of a step-to-step attitude by the relevant state agency instead of thorough initial planning	Not included in the annual budget is the maintenance and upkeep of Spanish royal sites, which are owned by the state and made available to the king as the head-of-state, but administered by Patrimonio Nacional.[56] The Royal Palace of Madrid, along with other residences, began to be adjusted in 2014 to improve disabled accessibility.[57]	Stockholm Palace, the official residence of the monarchy, is currently undergoing extensive renovation over the next 22 years. This will cost €19.4million.[58]

[51] Royal Household Framework Agreement Relating to the Sovereign Grant. Available at: www.royal.uk/sites/default/files/media-packs/sovereign_grant_framework_agreement_-_2018_final.pdf.

[52] The Sovereign Grant and Sovereign Grant Reserve Annual Report and Accounts 2017–18. Available at: https://assets.publishing.service.gov.uk/government/uploads/system/uploads/attachment_data/file/719582/SovereignGrant2017-18_Final.pdf.

[53] Available at: www.dailymail.co.uk/femail/article-2931259/Beige-walls-crystal-chandeliers-quirky-murals-galore-Inside-Danish-royal-palace-left-Duchess-Cambridge-green-envy.html.

[54] Available at: www.dutchnews.nl/news/2019/07/fit-for-a-king-willem-alexander-shows-off-e63-million-palace-renovation/.

[55] Available at: https://en.wikipedia.org/wiki/Monarchy_of_Norway#Finances.

[56] Available at: https://en.wikipedia.org/wiki/Monarchy_of_Spain#Annual_budget_and_taxation.

[57] Available at: www.ibtimes.co.uk/spanish-queen-letizia-examines-renovations-18th-century-royal-palace-madrid-1543186.

[58] Available at: www.svd.se/stockholms-slott-renoveras-i-22-ar.

	Britain	Belgium	Denmark	Netherlands	Norway	Spain	Sweden
Controversies	Receiving apparently higher sums than their counterparts, the British monarchy is often criticised in the British media for the large amount spent on their behalf.	In 2013, the Belgian monarchy became taxed as a result of financial reforms, in an effort to increase financial transparency			There has been controversy over the extent of the king's own personal fortune and alleged discrepancies between the amounts given to the monarchy, as stated in the state budget and the supposed real figure. Efforts have been made, involving also the relevant Parliamentary standing committee, to secure a better public understanding of the spending streams which extend to those originating from the budgets of several ministries (eg police and defence).	Former King Juan Carlos has been accused of money laundering and tax evasion of over €80 million from a contract with Saudi Arabia for a high-speed railway. As of 2018, Princess Corinna zu Sayn-Wittgenstein released recordings allegedly implicating King Juan Carlos in further financial misconduct.[59]	

[59] Available at: www.forbes.com/sites/ceciliarodriguez/2018/08/12/royal-family-in-trouble-spanish-monarchy-mired-in-new-ugly-scandal/#53b490d0480a.

The gross figures tell a rather different story and reflect both the comparative sizes of the countries and, less obviously and calculable, indicate the scale of royal families' activities because they will be limited by the resources available to them. It should be noted, however, that the figures are not calculated on an entirely common basis because of the extent to which monarchies are supported by expenditure falling on government departments, as opposed to the monarchies directly. In no case are security costs itemised because to do so would reveal the extent and probable deployment of protection operations. Although there is now greater general transparency, the gross figures are substantial and continue to draw criticism though without apparently threatening the institution itself. No attempt has been made here to compare the costs of a monarch as against a president head of state: more than money would need to be put in the balance and such an inherently subjective approach would require some heroic financial estimation.

Further, as Axel Calissendorff has pointed out, the purpose of defining official royal family membership is not confined to determining which members should receive public funding. It also serves to specify those who may represent the nation abroad. While King Juan Carlos of Spain's notably energetic programme of foreign visits following regime change in 1976 was exceptional, it seems that this function is given a special salience in some monarchies as against UK practice which is less concentrated on the foreign as opposed to the Commonwealth role.

Gender Issues

To republicans the persistence of hereditary monarchy in some of the most advanced democracies in the world might seem a mystery. While as Olivia Hepsworth has indicated it is difficult to point to immediate, specific causes for the move to absolute primogeniture in particular cases, there can be no real doubt that, in principle, it reflects the enormous changes in the last half of the twentieth century in the social, educational and occupational status of women. These will have been felt in different ways in different countries and, although Spain is the outlier, there are for the present understandable political and dynastic explanations. So far, it is only titles of nobility in Spain rather than royalty that have felt the effects of the changes.

What Regulation does

In the end, regulation may be best seen as a series of devices which both control and preserve monarchy. Rules approved by popular legislatures confer legitimacy on descent and draw the boundaries for public financial support. In Norway there has been a conscious policy of limiting full royal status to the monarch, his heir and their spouses.

Similarly, in the UK successive proclamations have tightened royal status rules and the non-royal spouses of royal daughters seem likely in future not to accept earldoms – and therefore arranging hereditary titles for their children – as was once the case. Royal great grandchildren, nephews and nieces increasingly merge into private life and independent careers, and their relative remoteness from succession signalled by the recent decision in the Succession to the Crown Act 2013 to confine the requirement for marriage consent to the first six in the line of succession.

In Sweden only very recently the King has reduced the numbers of his descendants who are eligible for state support by withdrawing the titles of His/Her Royal Highness from the five of his grandchildren not in the direct line of descent. The move has been interpreted as designed to forestall an impending report from a parliamentary inquiry into the costs of the monarchy (Stickings 2019)

This Swedish decision to downsize illustrates some of the difficulties involved in determining the ideal size of the royal family. On the one hand it needs to be large enough to address national service and welfare functions, which will require a bigger royal family in countries with large populations like the UK. But a bigger royal family increases the likelihood of public criticism about its cost, and it increases the risk that one of its members may go off the rails and bring the monarchy into disrepute.

There is another, less noticed cost, which is the personal cost to the individuals concerned: they have no real prospect of succeeding to the Crown, but they are subject to the same restrictions which apply to direct heirs, discussed more fully in Chapter 8. It can be difficult to provide satisfying roles for minor royals, who as junior members of the team carry out a lesser range of public duties, and have little prospect of forging independent lives and careers of their own. One possible example of the frustrations this can engender might be Prince Andrew in the UK, forced to withdraw from public life (Low 2019); another might be Prince Laurent, brother of King Philippe of the Belgians, said to be 'the black sheep of the Belgian royals with a life dogged by financial irregularities and gaffes' (Waterfield 2019).

Choices are made and renewed for successive generations about which of the monarch's kin are to carry out public functions and receive public subsidy. In Britain nowadays it is more a case of expenses of public duties being defrayed and other support at the discretion of the monarch from the Privy Purse or the Prince of Wales's Duchy of Cornwall estate than publicly declared parliamentary annuities for individuals.

At the same time, however, the choices also determine the capacity of the monarchies independently to develop new public roles of the kind reviewed in Chapter 5 above. The limited scope for delegation and development is clearly demonstrated in the Norwegian and Spanish instances. All the monarchies are in one way or another controlled by their governments, and the history of gender descent rules emphasises how monarchies must also adapt to their times if they are to remain relevant and therefore acceptable to their societies.

8

Constraints on the Monarchy

Contents

8.1. INTRODUCTION

Robert Hazell, The Constitution Unit, University College London

THE PREVIOUS CHAPTER was about regulating the monarchy as an institution: regulating the line of succession, the size of the royal family and the royal finances. This chapter is about regulating the individual behaviour of the monarch and other members of the royal family. They are severely constrained in terms of life choices: they lack freedom of speech, freedom to travel, freedom to marry whom they want, freedom of religion (in Scandinavia and the UK), free choice of career, and the right to privacy and family life which ordinary citizens take for granted.

In the first part of the chapter, Robert Hazell develops these points, suggesting that these constraints amount to a denial of basic human rights. The only escape for royals who find the life too restrictive is to opt out, leaving behind the royal title and their place in the line of succession. The next two sections, by Axel Calissendorff and Eivind Smith, discuss in more detail the constraints on the monarchy in Sweden, and in Norway. The final section by Olivia Hepsworth is about the education, training and career choices of the heir apparent in all eight countries; their education and training follows a common pattern, and their career choices are very limited.

8.2. THE ROYAL FAMILY'S LACK OF HUMAN RIGHTS

Robert Hazell, The Constitution Unit, University College London

Constraints in the Constitution; in the Law; and in Conventions

Royal families enjoy very privileged lives, living in large palaces with lots of staff. But their lives are also very restricted: they live in a gilded cage, denied basic freedoms which the rest of us take for granted. This contribution will discuss the restrictions on their freedom of speech, freedom to travel, freedom to marry, freedom of religion, and free choice of career.

Some constraints on the monarch and the royal family are written in the constitution: with controls on marriage, religion, and travel. But the more important constraints are not legal or constitutional, but matters of custom, practice and convention. The greatest constraint of all, their lack of privacy, is a product of the modern media, including social media. The demands of the media for news and photos of the royals are insatiable; as we shall see in Chapter 9, that gives them coverage and popularity ratings which politicians would die for. But it also risks trivialising the monarchy, making it part of celebrity culture; and it leaves the royals very exposed and vulnerable when things go wrong.

Freedom to Marry

This is restricted in all eight monarchies, as part of the constitution. As we saw in Chapter 2, all the constitutions impose tight controls on royal marriages. Typical is this requirement in article 28 of the Dutch Constitution:

> 28.1 The King shall be deemed to have abdicated if he contracts a marriage without having obtained consent by Act of Parliament
> 28.2 Anyone in line of succession to the Throne who contracts such a marriage shall be excluded from the hereditary succession, together with any children born of the marriage and their issue.

This is not just a formality: there are several examples in recent Dutch history of members of the royal family who have been excluded from the line of succession on this ground. This happened to one of the sons of Queen Beatrix, to one of her sisters, and two of her nephews. Prince Friso was her second son, and initially second in line to the throne. In 2003, Prince Friso announced he was to marry Mabel Wisse Smit, who worked for Soros' Open Society Foundation. But the Prime Minister later announced the couple had not been entirely frank about her past, in particular her relationship with a Dutch drugs baron. As a result, the government did not seek permission from Parliament for the marriage: Prince Friso was excluded from the line of succession, but kept the title HRH Prince of Orange-Nassau.

Christina, the youngest sister of Queen Beatrix, chose to marry a Cuban exile, and decided not to ask permission from the government and Parliament. On her marriage in 1975, she lost her place in the line of succession, but also kept her royal title. Likewise with Pieter Christiaan, and Floris, the two youngest sons of Princess Margriet, the younger sister of Queen Beatrix. They were in the line of succession, but both chose not to ask permission from the government and Parliament when they married. They both married in 2005. They lost their place in the line of succession, and membership of the royal house, but kept the title HRH, Prince of Orange-Nassau.

There was also a case in the nineteenth century, this time involving the Crown Prince, Willem Alexander, the son of King Willem III. He failed to gain the consent of his father for the woman he wanted to marry. He left the country, and died in exile in Paris. And there are cases in other countries: most famously in the UK, where King Edward VIII was forced to abdicate in 1936 because the government would not agree to his marrying an American woman, Wallis Simpson, who had been twice divorced. They were also forced into exile and died in Paris. A generation later, Queen Elizabeth II had to tell her sister Princess Margaret that the government could not approve her proposed marriage to Peter Townsend, a divorced man with two children. Despite a proposal that she could renounce her right to succession but retain her royal titles and Civil List allowance, in 1955 Princess Margaret issued a statement that she would not marry Peter Townsend, 'mindful of the Church's teachings that Christian marriage is indissoluble, and conscious of my duty to the Commonwealth'.

There have also been difficulties in the Scandinavian countries, particularly in Sweden. The original Swedish Act of Succession of 1810 required Swedish Princes to marry people of equal rank, and during the twentieth century four Swedish Princes were excluded from the line of succession due to their choice of spouse. The Swedish Prince Lennart and Prince Sigvard were removed from the line of succession and stripped of their royal titles when they married commoners in the 1930s; as were Prince Carl in 1937, and Prince Carl Johan in 1946. Lennart and Sigvard both considered themselves cruelly treated, and after 30 years of argument and controversy, Sigvard took a case to the European Court of Human Rights in an effort to have the government of Sweden acknowledge his princely title; but in 2004, after his death, the ECtHR declared the application inadmissible (*Bernadotte v Sweden (dec) no 69688/01*). Prince Bertil of Sweden adopted a different approach, when he fell in love with a commoner (Lilian Craig from Wales) in 1943. They lived together, but in order to enable him to act as Regent if required, and hence secure the monarchy into the next generation, they did not marry for 30 years, until finally they were allowed to marry in 1976.

In recent times, there has been greater acceptance of royals marrying commoners, and also of divorce. So Prince Charles felt able to marry Camilla Parker-Bowles in 2005; and in 2018 his son Prince Harry married a divorced woman in Meghan Markle. Perhaps the strongest sign of changing public attitudes has been the acceptance in Norway of Crown Prince Haakon's marriage in 2001 to Mette-Marit. There had been initial hesitation because she was a single mother with an illegitimate child and a rebellious past, but the Norwegians have since taken her to their hearts (see Chapter 9). There were also initial doubts in the Netherlands over Crown Prince Willem-Alexander's choice of Máxima, because her father was an Argentinian Cabinet minister during the military dictatorship; but she too gained acceptance, the Dutch Parliament approved their engagement, and in 2011 the Parliament went a step further and confirmed that upon her husband's accession she would become Queen.

Freedom of Religion

There are constraints on the monarch's freedom of religion in half of the monarchies considered in this book: in the three Scandinavian constitutions, and the UK. In the UK, the monarch upon accession must swear to be a faithful Protestant, and to uphold the laws which secure the Protestant succession to the throne. Under section 3 of the Act of Settlement 1700 the monarch must also be in communion with the Church of England; and the Coronation Oath Act 1688 requires the monarch at his coronation to swear to maintain the settlement of the Church of England, and its doctrine, rights and privileges (Hazell and Morris 2018).

The restrictions in the Scandinavian countries are no less strict, and in Sweden they extend to the Princes and Princesses of the royal house. The relevant provisions from their constitutional documents are as follows:

Denmark, article 5   The King shall be a member of the Evangelical Lutheran Church.

Norway, article 4   The King shall at all times profess the Evangelical-Lutheran religion.

Sweden, article 4   In accordance with the express provision of Article 2 of the Instrument of Government of 1809 that The King shall always profess the pure evangelical faith, as adopted and explained in the unaltered Confession of Augsburg and in the Resolution of the Uppsala Meeting of the year 1593, princes and princesses of the Royal House shall be brought up in that same faith and within the realm. Any member of the Royal Family not professing this faith shall be excluded from all rights of succession.

A monarch who failed to meet the religious requirements would have to renounce the throne. And in Sweden, other members of the royal family would lose their rights of succession. There are no cases in recent times where the monarch has been disqualified on religious grounds; but in the UK, the Queen's cousin Prince Michael of Kent, who was once eighth in line to the throne, lost his place when he married a Catholic in 1978. That particular ban was ended by the Succession to the Crown Act 2013, which removed the bar on those in line of succession from marrying Catholics; but the requirement that the monarch must be a true and faithful Protestant remains in place.

There can also be constraints of tradition and conventional expectation rather than strict constitutional requirements. In 1963, the second daughter of Queen Juliana of the Netherlands, Princess Christina, converted to Catholicism in order to marry Prince Carlos Hugo of Bourbon-Parma. Public outrage was not simply against her choice of religion, but also of a Spaniard, when the Low Countries had fought an 80 year war of independence against Spain, and no member of the royal family attended the wedding a year later.

Freedom to Travel

Restrictions on foreign travel apply to the monarch, and in some cases the heir, such as these provisions in Sweden:

Instrument of Government, chapter 5, article 2   The Head of State shall consult the Prime Minister before undertaking travel abroad

Act of Succession, article 7   The heir to the throne may not undertake travel abroad without the knowledge and consent of the King.

Sweden is the only country where travel is restricted under the Constitution. But in the other countries it is restricted by convention: the monarch and members of the royal family generally require consent to travel abroad. Consent may be withheld for security reasons (the risk of terrorism, or kidnapping), or for diplomatic reasons, or simply out of spite: after de Gaulle refused Britain's application to join the European Community in 1961, Princess Margaret was required by the British Prime Minister Harold Macmillan to cancel a visit to Paris.

In addition to not being able to travel where they like, royals can be required to go on state visits or trade missions abroad in order to promote trade deals. This can lead to the monarchy being criticised for being too close to undesirable regimes. The monarchy in Spain has got into trouble for its close links with the royal family in Saudi Arabia: links which helped Spain win big infrastructure contracts and arms deals (see Chapter 6.5). The Spanish King Juan Carlos played an important role in Spain winning a €7 billion contract for a high speed train link in 2011, and in 2017 his son King Felipe was sent to Saudi Arabia to help Spain bid for the sale of five warships. Juan Carlos was a willing trade envoy, King Felipe much less so, with criticism from left-wing parties and human rights groups (Keeley 2018). In Sweden, the King was similarly criticised after praising the Sultan of Brunei on a state visit there in 2004; and in Denmark the Queen incurred criticism for bestowing a medal on King Khalifa during her state visit to Bahrain in 2011 (see Chapter 4.3).

The obverse of trade missions or state visits abroad is receiving incoming visits from heads of state at home. Here too monarchs have little choice but to offer a warm welcome to visitors who may be deeply unwelcome: Queen Elizabeth's guests on state visits at Buckingham Palace have included Presidents Mugabe of Zimbabwe, Ceausescu of Romania, Assad from Syria, Mobutu of Zaire, Vladimir Putin from Russia, and in 2019 President Trump from the US.

Freedom of Speech

The monarch and close members of the royal family have very little freedom of speech. Like freedom to travel, this has two dimensions. Almost all their public speeches are scripted by the government, or require clearance from the government. The speech which caused the King of Sweden such trouble during his visit to Brunei in 2004 was provided by the Foreign Ministry; a subsequent parliamentary inquiry was critical of the government, but in the public mind the blame stuck to the King, and his popularity slumped (see Chapter 9).

How much freedom of speech the monarch enjoys varies from country to country: in Norway, the King and Crown Prince are more outspoken than their counterparts elsewhere (see the examples in 8.4 below). The one exception in all countries, where the monarch has greater freedom, is the annual Christmas or New Year speech, broadcast to the nation. In all countries (save Norway) the speech is shown in draft to the government (in Denmark, the first draft is supplied by the government), but the final version always has the monarch's personal touch. In the public mind, it is the monarch's speech, and not the government's.

It is a speech in which the monarch addresses people as head of the nation, not head of state, and can be more open about their values. Queen Elizabeth has been more open about her religious faith (see Chapter 5.3). In her New Year speech in 1984, Queen Margrethe urged the Danes to be more tolerant towards asylum seekers, refugees, and immigrants. This created a stir, which surprised her.

It shouldn't have done: as an experienced monarch she must have known the strict limitations on royals' freedom of speech. Because of the relentless scrutiny from the media, one misjudged phrase, one stray remark can land them in trouble. Sometimes that can be anticipated: Prince Charles must know that some of his interventions, like his 'monstrous carbuncle' speech about modern architecture in 1984, are bound to cause trouble (Glancey 2004; Weir 2013). But more often royals have no such intent, or expectation. In 2007, Crown Princess Máxima inadvertently caused massive criticism when in a speech to the Scientific Council for Government Policy she said that in the seven years that she had been in the Netherlands, she had been unable to find the Dutch identity. The text seemed innocuous; the reaction disproportionate. But it was a reminder how careful royals need to be in all their public utterances; phrases can be taken out of context, twisted and turned against them – they have very little freedom of speech. Indeed their speech is so tightly controlled that in the Netherlands royal communications are managed not by the Palace, but by the Office of the Prime Minister.

Freedom to Choose a Career

The limited career choices open to the heir apparent are described by Olivia Hepsworth, at 8.5 below. There are no legal restrictions; but in practice the heir and others close in the line of succession cannot choose a profession or pursue a business career, lest they be accused of exploiting their position for commercial gain. All the heirs apparent do military training, most gain further experience of diplomatic or other public service, and they then support charitable activities, including the work of their own royal foundations. Minor royals are less constrained, and some do pursue a business career; but there is a grey area about what is acceptable and what is not. Princess Märtha Louise of Norway and Prince Edward in the UK have been accused of using their royal connections for commercial gain, as have several spouses of minor royals. In the Netherlands, members of the royal family and their spouses cannot take a job without first seeking government approval.

To escape these restrictions in order to pursue a wider career, they would need to step out of the line of succession and shed their royal connections to do so. We discuss below the feasibility of opting out; in practice, very few royals have done so.

Privacy and Family Life

The most exceptional cases of media intrusion into the private lives of the royal family come from the UK, where the intense competition in the tabloid press has led to extraordinary invasions of their privacy. These range from 'Camillagate', when a tabloid newspaper *The People* published a transcript of a late night phone conversation between Prince Charles and Camilla Parker-Bowles (The People 1993) to the illegal hacking of the phones of staff to Prince William and Prince Harry, to paparazzi using dangerous tactics to get photos of the two-year old Prince George (Addley and Booth 2016).

Harassment of the royals in pursuit of photos or stories about their private lives is not confined to the UK. In the Netherlands, gossip magazines have published unauthorised photos of Princess Amalia, nine-year old daughter of the Crown Prince, in a breakdown of a media code intended to allow the young royals to lead as normal lives as possible. The Government Information Service began legal action, describing the photos as 'an unacceptable invasion of privacy'. But the editor of *Story* magazine retorted with a very different moral code, saying: 'Willem-Alexander earns a personal income of €825,000 a year in taxpayers' money apart from his private wealth, and can give up his job any time. Would you not give up some of your privacy for that money?' (Cluskey 2013).

Nor is harassment confined to the media: it is also rife on social media. If an eligible Crown Prince does not have a girlfriend it is assumed he must be gay. That is the social media speculation about Hereditary Grand Duke Guillaume in Luxembourg. And it was the speculation amongst the gay community about Prince Friso in the Netherlands: speculation which, when it spread to the mainstream media, led the Government Information Service in 2001 to issue the extraordinary one line statement 'Johan Friso is not homosexual, but heterosexual'. Sweden saw a similar surge of interest in the youthful indiscretions of King Carl XVI Gustav following the publication in 2010 of an unauthorised biography, *The Reluctant Monarch* (Alexander and Oscarssen 2010).

Despite court cases in several countries, it has proved impossible to protect the royals from constant intrusion by the press. Princess Caroline von Hannover has even taken cases to the European Court of Human Rights, which ruled that 'photos appearing in the tabloid press are often taken in a climate of continual harassment which induces in the person concerned a very strong sense of intrusion into their private life or even of persecution' (*von Hannover v Germany 2004*). Even if the press in one country are restrained, other countries may not follow suit: in 2012 topless photos of the Duchess of Cambridge which were turned down by British papers were published in France, Denmark and Sweden. And even if legal action is successful, it takes years to obtain a judgement: the topless photos were judged an invasion of privacy by the French courts, but it took five years for the Duchess to obtain a judgement and damages (Willsher 2017).

The Right to Vote

This may not be deemed a very important right, compared with the others discussed above; and where royal families have the right to vote, in practice they choose not to exercise it. Only in Denmark and the UK do royal families lack the right to vote; as does the monarch in Belgium and Luxembourg. By contrast, in Spain, Sweden, the Netherlands, and Norway the monarch and royal family can vote; as can the royal family in Belgium and Luxembourg. But by convention the royals choose not to exercise this right; save in Belgium and Luxembourg, where they must because voting is compulsory (but the monarch is exempt).

There is one other exception, in Spain, where the King and Queen are expected to vote in referendums, and have done so four times; but they do not vote in elections. The reason is historic: when democracy in Spain was fragile and in its infancy, and supporters of Franco were boycotting the new institutions, King Juan Carlos felt it important to show his active support by participating in the 1976 and 1978 referendums on the new Constitution.

Abdication: The Right to Opt Out

This is one area where the monarch does have autonomy: no European government would require the monarch to remain on the throne against his or her will. Some constitutions (Netherlands article 27, Spain article 57.5, Denmark Act of Succession article 6) recognise the monarch's right to abdicate; but most remain silent. In the Benelux countries and Spain there is a tradition of abdication; in the Scandinavian countries and the UK much less so. For the current Scandinavian and British monarchs, who are all elderly, abdication would be regarded as a breach of their oath of office and their public duty.

The country which has seen abdication most frequently is the Netherlands, starting with King Willem I in 1840. The last three Queens, Wilhemina, Juliana and Beatrix have all abdicated on reaching the age of around 70: Queen Beatrix abdicated in 2013 at the age of 76. There is a similar tradition in Belgium: King Albert II abdicated in 2013, following the example of his father Leopold III who abdicated in 1951. And Luxembourg has seen the abdication of two Grand Duchesses, Marie-Adélaïde in 1919 and Charlotte in 1964, and of Grand Duke Jean in 2000. Spain also witnessed several abdications in the nineteenth century, and a recent one when King Juan Carlos abdicated in 2014.

By contrast abdication is not normally practised in the Scandinavian monarchies, or the UK. In Britain Edward VIII was forced to abdicate in 1936, but his bad example makes abdication unthinkable for his niece Queen Elizabeth II, whose sense of public duty is reinforced by her Coronation Oath. Likewise for Queen Margrethe II of Denmark, who has said 'I will remain on the throne until I fall off'; and for King Harald V of Norway, who when interviewed for his 80th birthday, said 'I took an oath on the Norwegian Constitution. For me, this oath applies to my entire life' (RoyalCentral 2017). There is a similar tradition in Sweden, where no Bernadotte monarch has ever abdicated.

Most abdications have been voluntary, but some have been forced. Grand Duchess Marie-Adélaïde was forced to abdicate in Luxembourg in 1919, because of her conduct during the First World War; as was King Leopold III of Belgium after the Second World War. The abdication of King Juan Carlos of Spain in 2014 came after a series of scandals which greatly reduced his popularity, and opinion polls showing almost two thirds of Spaniards thought he should abdicate (see Chapter 9).

For those in the line of succession who have opted out, a similar distinction can be drawn between voluntary opting out and forced exclusion. There have been plenty of examples of royals who have not gained approval for their marriage, and who have therefore been excluded from the line of succession; these are recorded above in the section on freedom to marry. There have also been examples of royals who have reluctantly opted in, such as Prince Bertil of Sweden or Princess Margaret in the UK, who placed their sense of public duty above the pull of their hearts. But there have been almost no cases of royals who have deliberately opted out of the royal family and line of succession in order to pursue their own career or to gain more of a private life. That changed in January 2020 when the Duke and Duchess of Sussex announced that they were leaving the British royal family to pursue their own careers. Although they had hoped to perform some royal duties while leading more independent lives, the Palace concluded that the contradictions and conflicts of interest were too great to make it possible. In so far as the Sussexes' preferences become shared by other junior royals, then their automatic availability to support monarchs may no longer be taken for granted.

Conclusions

Marrying, or being born into a royal family involves big sacrifices. They lack fundamental freedoms which ordinary citizens take for granted. In the next two sections we explain in greater detail the constraints on the monarch and royal family in Sweden and Norway. Then in the final section we illustrate this by exploring the limited educational and career choices open to the heir apparent. Although the constitution imposes no formal restrictions (save in Norway: see 8.4 below), in practice royal heirs all tend to follow the same narrow career path, of military and public service, and support for voluntary and charitable activities.

8.3. CONSTRAINTS ON THE MONARCHY AND ROYAL FAMILY IN SWEDEN

Axel Calissendorff, Solicitor to the King of Sweden

Marriage

The Act of Succession contains the following on the right of succession:

> A prince or princess of the Royal House may not marry unless the Government has given its consent thereto upon an application from The King. Should a prince or princess marry without such consent, that prince or princess forfeits the right of succession for himself, his children and their descendants (section 5).

> A prince or princess of the Swedish Royal House may not become the sovereign ruler of a foreign state whether by election, succession, or marriage without the consent of The King and the Riksdag. Should this occur, neither he nor she nor their descendants shall be entitled to succeed to the throne of Sweden (section 8).

The above provisions on the retention and deprivation of the right to succession do not clarify the uncertainty over the right to retain a birth title [*bördstitel*] such as 'Prince' or 'Princess', or the loss of such title (Bramstång 1990: 54). Loss of right of succession is one matter, while the deprivation of birth title is considered a completely different one (Bramstång 1994: 293-294).

Deprivation of a birth title is a question for the King. The King regulates the title 'Royal Highness', and can limit the circle of those who should be granted this right. For instance, one may lose the title if one commits a crime. Birth titles, association with a royal house [*hustillhörighet*] and use of the title 'Royal Highness' fall within the King's discretion and are not regulated in the Swedish Constitution (Bramstång 1994: 294).

Religion

The Act of Succession states that the monarch shall profess the pure Evangelical faith, as adopted and explained in the unaltered Confession of Augsburg. Furthermore, Princes and Princesses of the royal house shall be brought up in that same faith. Section 4 of the Act of Succession states any member of the royal family not professing this faith will be excluded from all rights of succession. A Prince or Princess may marry a person that is not of this faith. However, the children must be Protestants in order to be entitled to the throne.

Citizenship, and Foreign Travel

According to Chapter 5 section 2 of the Instrument of Government, the head of state must be a Swedish citizen. Since a person with the right to succession may be appointed as temporary regent [*riksföreståndare*] such a person must also hold Swedish citizenship; as was outlined in the government bill proposed in 1977. Furthermore, section 4 of the Act of Succession prescribes that Princes and Princesses must be brought up within the realm. If a person with a right to succession is raised abroad, he or she as well as his or her descendants, loses the right of succession following on from the 1977 government bill. However, the limits are not entirely clear. It is assumed that an heir to the throne must attend school in Sweden, but a year or possibly two at school in a foreign country may not disqualify them.

Like other Swedes, the King and the royal family are entitled to vote, though by tradition this right is never exercised (Swedish Royal Court Website: Duties of the Monarch).

Moreover, section 7 of the Act of Succession states that the heir to the throne cannot undertake travel abroad without the knowledge and consent of the King.

Career

The heirs to the throne shall, in turn, be prepared to take the King's place as head of state when the King is temporarily prevented from carrying out his duties, which is why the choice of career of the members of the royal family is subject to certain restrictions.

Anyone who intermittently carries out the role as interim head of state or who may permanently take over the role must live in a way that meets the demands and expectations on someone who will represent the Swedish people. Those in line to the throne may not be involved with employments or assignments that could damage the public's trust in their independence. That is why they receive government funding. There exists a mutual commitment between Parliament and the royal house. The royal house prepares successors to ascend the throne, while Parliament bears the living expenses of those entitled to succession (Eliasson 2013: 308-309).

Abdication

Sweden has no recent experience in the matter of abdication.

8.4 CONSTRAINTS ON THE MONARCHY AND ROYAL FAMILY IN NORWAY

Eivind Smith, Professor of Public Law, University of Oslo

The requirement that 'The Royal Princes and Princesses must not hold senior civil offices' in article 21 of the Norwegian Constitution provides the only constitutional limit to the right to work for members of the royal family. In other words, they may even pursue military careers and are free to accept more junior positions in the governmental services or to accept paid work elsewhere in the labour market. In reality, King Haakon VII was a Danish naval officer before becoming King of Norway. King Olav V, King Harald V and the future King Haakon VIII have all completed higher military education. But even though none of them has subsequently pursued a military career, they have been promoted to higher ranks in more or less the same way as their contemporaries at military school, ending up as top ranking generals and admirals. This also reflects, of course, the King's position as the supreme commander of the armed forces (article 25 of the Constitution).

The Constitution says nothing about the monarch's freedom of speech. It is understood, however, that present day political conditions require them to strike a proper balance between saying something in public that it is worth listening to, but without exposing themselves to criticism for engaging in partisan politics. Traditionally, the freedom of expression of Norwegian royals seems comparatively high and they make use of it in ways that are not always uncontroversial. For instance, the present King and Crown Prince have long supported efforts in favour of the integration of immigrants, religious tolerance and acceptance of differences (like homosexuality; among other things, the Crown Prince and Princess visited the Oslo Pride festival). They have sometimes recalled that in a sense, the first two Kings of the present dynasty were both immigrants (the immensely popular Haakon VII spoke Danish all his life), and that the present King is the son of two immigrants, with a Swedish mother and Danish father. The King's speech at a party in the Oslo Palace gardens in 2016 provides a number of prominent examples, for example:

> Norwegians are also immigrants from Afghanistan, Pakistan, Poland, Sweden, Somalia and Syria. It is not always easy to say where we come from, to which nationality we belong … Norwegians believe in God, in Allah, in the universe – and in nothing.

The speech was given at a time when anti-immigration rhetoric was mounting in Norway, with an estimated 30,000 asylum seekers arriving the previous year (2015), and when there was a centre-right coalition in government which had been criticised for its efforts to deport asylum seekers. It went viral and rapidly spread on Facebook and other social media as well.

Traditionally, the Crown Prince undertakes a number of activities that would probably not be acceptable for the monarch himself. However, that tradition supposes that he (or she) adopts a more restrained attitude once the succession takes place.

The Constitution is silent about the right to vote for members of the royal family. In principle, they have the same rights in this respect as any other citizen of the realm. In practice, however, close members of the family never vote, although the possibility of doing so remains in a future where surmounting some kind of crisis might benefit from them showing a good example.

According to article 36 of the Constitution, 'A Prince or Princess entitled to succeed to the Crown of Norway may not marry without the consent of the King'. The power to consent is regarded as a personal prerogative for the monarch. It has been made known, however, that the three Kings of the present dynasty have sought advice from the Prime Minister before consenting. For Haakon VII this consent regarded his son's marriage to a Swedish princess in 1929, relatively soon after Norway's unilateral break-up of the personal union with Sweden, which had brought an end to the Bernadotte dynasty's possession of the Norwegian throne (1905). For Olav V and Harald V, it was about their sons' marriage to commoners (in the case of current Crown Prince Haakon, with a woman with an illegitimate child). All three marriages turned out to be successful.

Article 4 of the Constitution, as framed after the abolition of the confessional state in 2012, constrains the monarch himself to professing the Evangelical-Lutheran religion. In this respect, it is interesting to note that before 2012, the King appeared in uniform as head of state at the enthronement of new bishops. After 2012, he still appears at such events, but now clothed in an ordinary dark suit.

Formally, this obligation – a condition for being the monarch – does not apply to the Crown Prince and other members of the family. So far, this has not given rise to practical questions; the Crown Prince married in church, their children are baptised, and in 2019, the current heir Princess Ingrid celebrated her religious confirmation in the Royal chapel in Oslo. On the other hand, an heir openly deviating from the line would create some tension, but in the twenty-first century, probably no crisis. When the constitutional clauses on the confessional state and the state church were abolished in 2012, the provision on the monarch's obligation to be an Evangelical-Lutheran was kept at the King's own request as communicated through the government. There is nothing to prevent it from finally being abolished should the next monarch so wish, or for other reasons.

Some would argue that this situation entails a violation of the monarch's freedom of religion, and to a lesser degree, of that of other close members of the family. The legal answer would probably be that renouncing the position as King or heir to the throne would suffice for the full enjoyment of that particular freedom. In practice of course, the situation is somewhat more complex.

The Constitution says nothing about retirement or abdication. Whether a right to abdicate even exists has been open to doubt; by the end of his life, King Haakon VII actually asked advice on this question from the then Professor of Constitutional Law at the University of Oslo, Frede Castberg. In practice, however, the question has never become acute. During the personal union with Sweden (1814-1905), none of the Kings stepped down before their death. The Kings of the present dynasty have maintained the tradition, and nothing indicates that this will change. King Harald V (born in 1937) has several times reiterated his firm conviction that the oath on the Constitution which he took before Parliament following his father's death was a promise of service for the rest of his life (cf article 9 of the Constitution).

The price to pay, however, is the possibility that the Crown Prince serves as Regent if the King becomes ill or otherwise unfit for service (article 41), which actually happened towards the end of the lives of both King Haakon VII and Olav V. Their duties involved presiding at Council meetings as well as accomplishing any other tasks required of the King as head of state.

8.5. EDUCATION, TRAINING AND CAREER CHOICES OF HEIRS APPARENT

Olivia Hepsworth, The Constitution Unit, UCL

A constitutional sovereign must in the common course of government be a man of but common ability ... Theory and experience both teach that the education of a prince can be but a poor education, and that a royal family will generally have less ability than other families (Bagehot 1867: 61).

Introduction

The constitutions of the countries under review are all largely silent on the heir apparent. There is a clear prescription on how to identify the heir, but very little on what they can and cannot do. However, all heirs apparent tend to follow a similar career path – school and university education, military training, charitable involvement, diplomatic experience; but this has developed through custom, practice and convention rather than through constitutional prescription. Brazier's article on the constitutional position of the Prince of Wales concludes: 'The daily job of a Prince of Wales is largely what he chooses to make it. There is now, however, a sizeable body of convention and law which gives a constitutional setting to the Prince's position' (Brazier 1995: 7).

Heirs apparent have little autonomy over their education, which is chosen for them by their parents. It is hard to tell how much choice they have over their subsequent careers, for example in choosing between military or diplomatic service. It is mainly in their selection of charitable causes that we can determine an element of personal choice, especially if these are different from traditional royal causes. And occasionally we can detect preference in the causes they choose to support through patronage, through visits, or through speeches. The Prince of Wales has incurred criticism for his interventions over architectural design, town planning, the environment and other aspects of government policy. In 1991, the Prince gave a speech, that failed to be pre-approved, that attacked the teaching of English in schools and by implication the government's educational policy (Brazier 1995: 3). In 2015, he attracted further criticism for his numerous letters to government ministers offering his own policy suggestions, 'black spider' memos ordered to be released following a series of freedom of information requests by the *Guardian* newspaper (Booth and Taylor 2015; Guardian 2015).

It is a difficult line to tread for any heir apparent who takes a serious interest in public policy. It may be particularly difficult for Prince Charles, who cares passionately about the causes he supports. It may also be easier, because he is less dependent than other heirs on government funding, having a secure source of income in the £20 million annual revenues from the Duchy of Cornwall (see Chapter 7.1). But the Crown Prince in Norway traditionally has more latitude than the monarch (see 8.4 above); and it may be that other countries have a similar tradition.

Demographics

Four of the current heirs are female: the Crown Princess of Sweden, Princess Victoria (born 1977); the Princess of Asturias, Princess Leonor (Spain) (born 2005); the Princess of Orange, Princess Catharina-Amalia (Netherlands) (born 2003) and the Princess of Belgium, Princess Elisabeth (born 2001). The remaining four heirs apparent are male: the Prince of Wales, Prince Charles (born 1948); the Crown Prince of Denmark, Crown Prince Frederik (born 1968); the Crown Prince of Norway, Crown Prince Haakon (born 1973) and the Hereditary Grand Duke of Luxembourg, Prince Guillaume (born 1981). The ages of the male heirs range from 38 to 70 years old; while the ages of the female heirs run from 14 to 42, with two still being under 18. The Crown Princess of Sweden is the only female heir who currently performs official duties. All heirs apparent have to wait to begin their role as monarch and for a large amount of their lives perform as the understudy, demonstrated most dramatically by the 70-year-old Prince of Wales. King Felipe of Spain, King Willem-Alexander of the Netherlands and King Philippe of Belgium all waited for over 25 years of their adult lives before ascending the throne, being aged 46, 44 and 52 respectively when they became King, having been eligible to rule from age 18.

Education

The typical career path for heirs apparent has involved graduate study, service or training in the armed forces and charitable work. All current heirs apparent who are over the age of 18 have completed undergraduate studies. Aside from Prince Charles who attended Cambridge University in 1967, the current king of the Netherlands (King Willem-Alexander) and the Hereditary Grand Duke of Luxembourg who also studied in the UK, all other heirs apparent have gone on to complete further postgraduate studies, mainly in the United States. Two monarchs who recently succeeded to the throne (King Felipe VI of Spain and King Philippe of Belgium) also both studied in the US. Furthermore, the current heirs in Sweden, Norway and Denmark and the new Kings in Spain and Belgium have completed postgraduate studies. King Felipe VI of Spain, after his postgraduate studies at Georgetown University, is now the most highly educated monarch in Spanish history. Higher education at demanding and prestigious institutions is a common experience held by all the heirs apparent, with the UK being unusual in that neither Prince Charles nor Prince William went on to do a postgraduate degree, nor did they study at a university abroad.

Military Training

Another shared experience is service with the armed forces. The heirs apparent of both Sweden and Denmark focused their military training on defence studies. In 2004 the Crown Princess of Sweden studied at the Swedish National Defence College in Stockholm where her courses included political science, international relations and conflict resolution. The Crown Prince of Denmark became a senior lecturer at the Royal Danish Defence College. In 2010, the Crown Prince was appointed a commander in the navy and a colonel in the army and air force. Prince Charles qualified as a helicopter pilot in 1974 before joining the 845 Naval Air Squadron. He then took command of the coastal minehunter HMS Bronington for the final nine months of his navy service. The Crown Prince of Norway has had an extensive naval career, and is an admiral in the Royal Norwegian Navy. The Hereditary Grand Duke of Luxembourg completed an officer training course at the Royal Military Academy at Sandhurst (2001-02), and currently holds the rank of major in the Luxembourg army. Those monarchs who have recently succeeded to the throne have all also served in the military. Both King Felipe VI of Spain and King Willem-Alexander of the Netherlands served in the navy, while King Philippe of Belgium joined the air force and later qualified as a fighter pilot.

Further Experience

Some heirs have completed further programmes within their own governments, demonstrated most notably by the extensive record of the Crown Princess of Sweden. Her earliest involvement was a programme to provide her with insight into the Riksdag (the Swedish Parliament) and the Swedish government. She has undertaken numerous study programmes. For example, with the Swedish International Development Cooperation Agency (SIDA) that included visits to countries such as Uganda and Ethiopia in 2002. As Prince of Orange, King Willem-Alexander completed an intensive programme to familiarise himself with Dutch society. He studied the constitutional and legal systems of the Netherlands and learned how central government and other authorities function through visiting European institutions, Dutch ministries and the High Councils of State.

In particular, the heirs apparent of the Scandinavian countries have completed diplomatic programmes, interning with embassies or intergovernmental organisations. The Crown Prince of Denmark served at the Danish UN mission in New York and was subsequently posted as first secretary to the Royal Danish Embassy in Paris. The Crown Prince of Norway was a member of Norway's third delegation to the UN General Assembly in 2000. In 2001, he then completed the Foreign Ministry's trainee programme for diplomats. The Crown Princess of Sweden has undertaken an extensive number of internships: at the UN, the Swedish Embassy in Washington DC and the Swedish Trade Council in Berlin and Paris, as well as completing the Ministry for Foreign Affairs' Diplomat Programme.

Reflecting the commercial interests of the royal family of Luxembourg, the Hereditary Grand Duke has pursued commercial experience, completing internships at the Belgian Chemical Union (2003); at Deutsche Bank London (2004) and the Spanish branch of

Arcelor-Mittal Steel Group (2005). Several heirs apparent have also been prominent in the sporting world. As Crown Prince of Norway Harald represented his country in sailing at the 1964, 1968 and 1972 Olympic Games, and later became patron of the governing body of the sport, World Sailing. Similarly, before he succeeded to the throne King Felipe of Spain sailed for the Spanish Olympic sailing team at the 1992 Olympics held in Barcelona.

Official Duties

Most heirs apparent in Western Europe have assumed royal and official functions at the age of 18, and become members of the Council of State. On his 18th birthday, the current King of the Netherlands, Willem-Alexander, became a member of the Council of State and entitled to attend its weekly meetings. Similarly, upon his 18th birthday the Crown Prince of Norway became entitled to take a seat in the Council of State. Upon turning 18, the Prince of Wales was appointed as a counsellor of state, a position that is provided for under the 1937 Regency Act. Acting together with another counsellor of state, the Prince can act on behalf of the Queen if she is temporarily unable to undertake her official duties, such as attending Privy Council meetings.

Upon turning 18, the Crown Princess of Sweden had a ceremony for the declaration of her majority in the Hall of State in the Royal Palace of Stockholm. This entitled Princess Victoria to become eligible to act as head of state when the King is not in the country. It also marked her first public speech and the commencement of her attendance at the Advisory Council on Foreign Affairs and the information councils with government ministers that are presided over by the King (see Chapter 4.6).

A particular emphasis is placed on heirs representing the monarchy overseas. This helps to spread the load, and increases their international experience. As heir apparent King Philippe's main area of involvement included his international visits to promote the Belgian economy and Belgium's image abroad. The Prince of Wales regularly represents the Queen at overseas events, particularly state funerals, and undertakes more such duties as the Queen gets older.

Charitable Involvement

Alongside their official duties, all heirs are involved with numerous charitable organisations and as patrons of organisations. Many of the charities are ones which they started themselves, to help an area of society they feel particularly passionately about.

As the Prince of Asturias, King Felipe supported numerous organisations including the Prince of Asturias Foundation, which seeks to promote cultural and moral values, and the Hesperia Foundation that supports projects involving youth, notably those from disadvantaged backgrounds. When he was the heir, King Willem-Alexander chaired the House of Orange-Nassau Historic Collections Trust, and represented the royal family on the management board of the royal domains. During his tenure as heir apparent King Philippe of Belgium's main focus was on sustainable development. From 1993 to 2013, he was honorary chairman of the Federal Council for Sustainable Development, and he was also active in supporting dialogue between Belgium's three language communities of French, Dutch and German speakers, setting up the Prince Philippe Fund to help promote this cause.

The Crown Princess of Sweden is particularly involved in issues concerning children and young adults. The Crown Princess Victoria and Prince Daniel Foundation supports children and young people, with a focus on promoting good health. Her separate fund set up in 1997 aims to provide support for leisure and recreational activities for children and young people with functional disabilities or chronic illnesses. The Hereditary Grand Duke of Luxembourg is one of the four directors of the Foundation of the Grand Duke and Grand Duchess, which works to help integrate the more vulnerable members of society, and to help disadvantaged individuals around the world. Similar to his counterparts he is also a patron of various charitable organisations such as Young Entrepreneurs Luxembourg – one of his special interests.

The Prince of Wales's charities are an umbrella for a group of non-profit organisations: the Prince's Trust Group (which provides help to disadvantaged and vulnerable young people and support for environmental projects), the Prince's Foundation (which focuses on the built environment, heritage, community education projects and promoting culture across the UK), and the Prince of Wales's Charitable Foundation (a grant making body that supports a wide range of causes).

The Crown Prince of Denmark's Foundation provides financial assistance to students of social policy and sciences for one year's study at Harvard; financial support for scientific expeditions (particularly to Greenland and the Faroe Islands) and financial support for sports. The Crown Prince of Norway has established a humanitarian foundation that supports projects for disadvantaged youths. Crown Prince Haakon also serves as a goodwill ambassador for the UN Development Programme, participating in the World Economic Forum, and is the founder of Global Dignity Initiative. His particular passion for environmental issues is clear in his charitable involvement, notably his activism to help tackle ocean pollution.

Further Responsibilities

Another important role is to help promote and protect national traditions, both within their own nation and abroad. As heir apparent, King Felipe made a series of official visits to Spain's autonomous communities, holding meetings with constitutional bodies and with the main institutions of Spain's central administration. The Crown Princess of Sweden and the Crown Prince of Norway similarly try to engage with the wider national community. Every year the Crown Prince and Crown Princess of Norway pay a visit to a Norwegian county and carry out a wide variety of official engagements with the public during this trip. The Prince of Wales places a special focus on highlighting less publicised issues such as the need to support Britain's rural communities and to encourage sustainable farming.

The international aspect to the role of heir apparent is especially the case for the Prince of Wales given the vast size of the Commonwealth. In the past four decades, he has visited 44 out of the 53 Commonwealth nations. The Hereditary Grand Duke of Luxembourg is honorary president of the Board of Economic Development, taking him on missions to Europe, Asia, America and Africa. As Prince of Asturias, King Felipe carried out many activities abroad, with a particular focus on promoting knowledge of Spanish language and culture through support for the network of Instituto Cervantes centres. He made official visits annually to Ibero-American countries, EU states, and countries in the Middle and Far East where Spain held strategic interests. When heir apparent, Prince Philippe of Belgium held the role of honorary president of the Belgian Foreign Trade Agency, and led five economic missions abroad over a twenty-year period. The international visits undertaken by the Crown Princess of Sweden have taken a particular focus on issues relating to crisis and conflict management, aid work and international peacekeeping activities. The Crown Princes of Norway and Denmark hold similar international responsibilities representing their nation abroad.

Conclusion

Clear patterns emerge from this brief comparative study. All heirs apparent complete at the minimum an undergraduate degree, with many also holding postgraduate degrees. Military service is another crucial aspect to their training. Though their military careers vary in their nature and duration, involvement with the armed forces is universal. There is more variety in the other formative experiences undertaken by heirs apparent. Some have focused on sports (King Felipe of Spain), whilst others have gained commercial insights (the Hereditary Grand Duke of Luxembourg). The Scandinavian countries place a particular emphasis on the heirs completing a diplomatic programme. The training offered to the British heir is notably thin by comparison, lacking any element of postgraduate study, of studying at an overseas university, or induction in the public services or diplomacy.

The heirs apparent have followed very similar paths in terms of their education and training, and subsequent careers. These paths have been designed to:

- Develop their understanding of politics, international affairs and international relations;
- Develop their understanding of military matters, and through military service and training gain the respect of the armed forces;
- Increase their understanding of government and the public services;
- Support charities and the work of non-profit organisations;
- Familiarise themselves with different parts of the country, and different language and minority communities;
- Undertake state visits, and represent their country abroad;
- Deputise for the sovereign when required.

Their training and subsequent activities are restricted to the public and voluntary sectors: with the exception of Luxembourg, none of the heirs are encouraged to gain experience of business and the private sector. And their charitable work, though extensive, tends to be focused on a limited range of safe subjects: children and young people; heritage and culture; sustainable development and environmental issues; and sport.

This suggests a strong self-denying ordinance not to get involved with causes which are deemed risky or controversial. The monarch must remain strictly neutral, and as the understudy, the heir apparent must prepare for that neutral role. The constitutions outline no clear role for the heir apparent, and yet it is clear that there is a set framework which they all follow. In recent years there has been less emphasis on military service and more on diplomacy, sustainable development, international aid work and peacekeeping: the Crown Princess of Sweden may provide the role model for the future.

8.6. CONCLUSIONS

Professor Robert Hazell, The Constitution Unit, University College London

This chapter has been about the formal and informal constraints on the behaviour of the monarch and other members of the royal family. They are severely constrained in terms of life choices, with restrictions on their freedom of speech, freedom to travel, freedom to marry whom they want, freedom of religion (in Scandinavia and the UK), free choice of career, and their right to privacy and family life. For the heir apparent, and those close in the line of succession, their career choices are limited to public and voluntary service, because they risk threatening the independence and neutrality of the monarchy if they engage in any kind of commercial activity.

Marrying, or being born into a royal family thus involves big sacrifices. They lack fundamental freedoms which ordinary citizens take for granted. It is true that in this they are not alone: diplomats, civil servants, judges are also restricted in their behaviour. But there are two crucial differences. First, public officials will have chosen their career, knowing the limitations; whereas royals have no choice. Second, the loss of freedom is far greater for royals, particularly in terms of the loss of privacy; no senior officials receive anything like the intense media scrutiny and speculation which is inflicted every day on royals, old and young. Nor is the loss of the other freedoms to be minimised; indeed it is so great, that one government felt the need to prepare a defence to demonstrate that the restrictions on the royal family did not breach the international conventions on modern slavery and forced labour.

The only way members of the royal family can escape is by opting out, leaving the line of succession and the royal title, and themselves becoming ordinary citizens. So far few royals have done so. This may be due to a lack of imagination, but more likely is due to a strong sense of public service. This is ingrained in them from an early age, and lasts a lifetime: exemplified in the four elderly monarchs in the Scandinavian countries and the UK, determined to serve as long as they shall live.

9

The Monarchy, Public Opinion and the Media

Contents

9.1. INTRODUCTION

Professor Robert Hazell, Constitution Unit, University College London

THIS CHAPTER IS about the legitimacy of the monarchy as an institution, about public attitudes and support for the monarchy, and about the role of the media in reporting on the monarchy and helping to set the agenda about the monarchy's performance and its future.

As Helle Krunke says in her opening contribution, it might seem difficult to legitimise a non-elected head of state as part of the government in a modern democracy. Formal legitimisation in Denmark lies in the Danish Constitution, and in the 1953 referendum which approved the Constitution and changed the line of succession: it can thus be said that in Denmark the constitutional monarchy was legitimised by popular will. But that is no longer deemed sufficient. New legitimisation arguments have been developed: for example, that the monarch is a scrupulously neutral protector and guardian of democracy. Continuity is another argument: prime ministers come and go, but a monarch can reign for decades, accumulating wisdom from long experience. The monarchy is also defended for its contribution to society, through royal visits and patronage; and to the economy, as a tourist attraction.

To demonstrate its contribution to society, the monarchy is heavily dependent on the media, who have the power to strengthen the image of the royal family, but also to harm it. The press help to hold the monarchy to account, and they can frame perceptions of the monarchy through commissioning opinion polls. Roger Mortimore's analysis of the polling data shows that support for retaining the monarchy is highest in Denmark, the Netherlands, Norway and the UK, where it ranges between 70 and 80 per cent. It is a little lower in Belgium, Spain and Sweden, at around 60 to 65 per cent. But opinion polls do more than simply measure public opinion; they also help to frame the terms of debate about the monarchy and its future. This is especially the case with polls commissioned by the media, who want to create a headline from the poll's findings. So the polls ask questions like, should the monarch abdicate? Are the royal family paid too much? Are you satisfied with their performance?

Lennart Nilsson takes this a stage further, exploring the differences in attitudes towards the monarchy between journalists, parliamentarians and the public. Swedish journalists are to the left of the public politically, and much more republican, which may explain some of the critical reporting. But parliamentarians are also more republican than the public, especially those on the left. Public confidence in the Swedish monarchy has steadily declined over the last 20 years; but so long as the monarchy retains broad public support, the left wing parties in parliament seem unlikely to implement their wish for Sweden to become a republic.

Jean Seaton offers an equally detailed analysis of media reporting about the monarchy in Britain. This can involve serious invasions of privacy, and in the case of Princess Diana, a hunt which led to her death. Royal stories always make good copy, and sensationalist reporting was driven by big changes in the media's business model, desperate to retain falling circulation as the readership went online. The new social media can be even more vicious, with even less regard for the truth. The Palace has become more adept at its handling of the press, but with trust collapsing in all political institutions, the monarchy cannot expect to be immune from cynical and reckless reporting.

9.2. MODERN FORMS OF LEGITIMISATION OF THE MONARCHY

Helle Krunke, Professor of Law, University of Copenhagen

The formal legitimisation of the monarchy is to be found in article 2 of the Danish Constitution, according to which the form of government shall be that of a constitutional monarchy; and men and women can inherit the throne, in accordance with the provisions of the Act of Succession to the Throne of 27 March 1953. Thus, the Danish constitutional monarchy has its legal basis in the Constitution, which was last amended in 1953. As the Danish voters approved the Constitution by referendum in 1953, the constitutional monarchy is legitimised by popular will. The special procedure for amending the Constitution is to be found in article 88 of the 1953 Constitution.[1]

---

[1] Art 88: 'Should the *Folketing* pass a Bill for the purposes of a new constitutional provision, and the Government wish to proceed with the matter, writs shall be issued for the election of members of a new *Folketing*. If the Bill is passed unamended by the *Folketing* assembling after the election, the Bill shall, within

As is evident from article 88, it is extremely difficult to change the Danish Constitution. Therefore, one might argue that even though the voters – it was back in 1953 – have accepted the Constitution, most of the present voters have actually not accepted the Constitution. This means that the popular will argument is not as strong as it is often considered. Furthermore, Denmark has a different monarch today from that in 1953, when the voters approved the Constitution. As demonstrated below, this argument will have greater weight in the future because each monarch to some extent will have to legitimise their own position. One might put forward, that since the purpose of the amendment of the Act of Succession to the Throne in 1953 was to make it possible for the current Queen, Margrethe II, to inherit the throne, and the electors voted in favour of this amendment, Margrethe II has a special kind of popular legitimacy, which subsequent Kings and Queens will not have.

As a starting point, it might seem difficult to legitimise a non-elected head of state as part of the state government in a modern democracy. Nonetheless, most interestingly a new legitimisation argument for the constitutional monarchy precisely based on democratic aspects seems to have developed during the era when the monarch has lost formal political influence. Following this argument the monarch is seen as a protector and guardian of democracy because they have a position that is politically neutral. The Danish Prime Minister for instance expressed this view in January 2012. According to her, the appointment process of new governments, in which the monarch plays a role (referred to as the *Dronningerunde*: see Chapter 3.3), 'secures that everything is carried out the right way and that we have an unassailable setting of democracy' (Thorning 2012). In the Danish context, the following example is often brought forward: the Queen played an active role in 1993 when the Prime Minister no longer had sufficient support in Parliament because of a political scandal, which eventually led to an infringement case against ministers of his government. The Prime Minister realised that he could no longer continue acting as Prime Minister but he did not want to call for an election. He simply wanted to replace himself with a new Prime Minister from the current government. Since the government did not have sufficient support in Parliament this was not possible within the constitutional setting. The Queen and her administrative staff cleverly handled the situation and the Prime Minister ended up calling an election. After the election a new government building on a different political coalition was formed (see Larsen et al 2010: 190–91).

What does this example show? Well, the monarch definitely acted in the proper manner in this particular situation, supporting the democratic process in the best way possible. Still, one might ask whether the situation would have been solved anyway and whether a different actor could have carried out this role. The parliamentary Speaker is often mentioned as an alternative actor in the process of forming a new government: as happens in Sweden (see Chapter 3.4). However, the Speaker of course comes from a political party and thus is not politically neutral. Actually, 53.9 per cent of the Danes want to abolish the *Dronningerunde* and let the Speaker perform the role currently carried out

---

six months after its final passage, be submitted to the electors for approval or rejection by direct voting. Rules for this voting shall be laid down by statute. If a majority of the persons taking part in the voting, and at least 40 per cent of the electorate, have voted in favour of the Bill as passed by the *Folketing*, and if the Bill receives the Royal Assent, it shall form an integral part of the Constitutional Act'.

by the Queen when a new government is created.[2] Furthermore, the strength that lies in the monarch's role as a neutral factor in the state government depends on each monarch's way of administering it.

It is questionable, however, whether the monarch is actually 100 per cent neutral, or indeed whether it is possible to be 100 per cent neutral. The Queen is normally very careful about not expressing political views, both as head of state and as a private person. Nonetheless, she sometimes does express views that may be regarded as political views, even though the distinction between political and non-political is often difficult to draw. In a radio interview from 1973 the Queen expressed some statements on equal rights for women in general and in relation to the Act of Succession from 1953 (see Holm 2008: 92–93). Equal rights for women were certainly a political topic in the 1970s, supported by the left-wing parties. Female accession to the throne is also a political subject. In the Queen's New Year's speech in 1984, she talked about immigration and urged the Danes to be more tolerant towards refugees and immigrants. This must be seen as a political subject, even back in the 1980s. Still, the Prime Minister always approves the Queen's New Year speeches beforehand. A few years later in an interview in 1988, the Queen was asked whether or not immigration was a political question. The Queen responded that it had to do with human rights and, as head of state, she had signed Denmark's accession to the UN Human Rights Charter. If the head of state could not discuss human rights, her signature was pointless (see Andersen 2011: 214). It is interesting that she makes a connection between her signature as head of state and her right to discuss human rights. As aforementioned, in 2005 and 2010, the Queen came up with interesting statements on whether the King should play a constitutional role in a prospective new constitution. This seems to be a political statement and one on her own constitutional position. Another example is that the Queen in 2005 expressed approval for European cooperation in the EC/EU (see Bistrup 2005: 118–19). In a recent interview in 2020, the Queen said she was not convinced that climate change is wholly caused by humans. Her statement was much debated and criticised by some political parties: climate change had been one of the biggest issues in the 2019 election (Corfixen and Thygesen 2020). In general, it seems that it has become more difficult for the monarch not to express political views when even areas such as culture become politicised in political battles over identity and values. The monarch must try to make the distinction between political actions and non-political actions and doing this is in itself a political choice.

Neutral or not, even though the Danish monarch is not allowed to express political views or act in a political way without the consent of a minister, the monarch is still an actor on the political scene both formally and informally. For instance, the monarch discusses political matters with the Prime Minister once a week; he plays a (potentially important) role in the appointment of a new government; he travels to foreign countries and meets with heads of state, prime ministers and ambassadors. Thus, the argument that the monarch is the guardian of democracy might be based on an assumption of neutrality, which might not be entirely present.

The legitimisation rhetoric based on the monarch's neutrality and thus the monarch as a protector and guardian of democracy is not the only modern argument put forward in defence of the constitutional monarchy. Continuity also appears in the debate in support

---

[2] See the results of an exit poll carried out by Rambøll Analyse and cited in Cordsen 2010: 1.

of the constitutional monarchy (Larsen et al 2010: 61). Prime ministers, ministers, and other politicians come and go but a monarch can be head of state for decades. This will of course provide a monarch with much experience, insight into political history and a good overview. One may argue that this strengthens the monarch's informal political position, for instance when giving the prime minister advice once a week. Furthermore, the argument can be made, that continuity is and should be represented in the ministries and the administration and not with the monarch. Finally, the quality of the monarch as a representative of continuity very much depends on the personal skill and diplomacy of each monarch.

These arguments are definitely the strongest legal and semi-legal arguments in favour of a constitutional monarchy. However, as shown they are based on at least two assumptions. First, the argument is dependent on the skills and personal qualities of the monarch and they might change from monarch to monarch. Second, the argument is based on the monarch avoiding political expressions and acts, which in practice might prove to be extremely difficult. The new legitimisation arguments depend very much on the individual skills of the monarch. They only secure the legitimacy of the constitutional monarchy for one monarch at a time – or maybe even just from situation to situation for a current monarch; it must be remembered that the monarch is now highly exposed in the media so there is less room for mistakes.

Additionally, the arguments in favour of constitutional monarchy can be flipped. The paradox is that if one wants to argue in favour of the monarch having an important enough role in the state government to legitimise the monarch remaining part of it, this at the same time exposes the fact that the monarch actually still has a position and influence in government and the political system. If used in the proper way this could contribute something valuable to the state, but used in the wrong way it may damage the state. The monarch in other words still has the potential to be an active player with the ability to manoeuvre policy, which, even if the ability is very limited nowadays could potentially be misused. Of course, in countries like Denmark where monarchs have generally known when to relinquish power at the right times in history thus avoiding revolutions, the monarch has a stronger case in situations like this because it is not expected that he/she would misuse their powers. The challenge lies not in showing that one is still an important actor in the state government, but a neutral and objective one.

Leaving the legal and quasi-legal arguments for a constitutional monarchy, we turn to other legitimisation arguments. In today's world, every institution must demonstrate that it contributes to society. This goes for universities as well as the royal houses. This implies, firstly, that the royal houses must contribute to society and, secondly, that such contributions must be communicated to society. A good example of an argument based on 'contribution to society' is the commercial value of the royal house. This argument should not be underestimated. First of all the royal house is a tourist attraction. Being one of the world's oldest kingdoms fits very well with many tourists' picture of Denmark as a little fairy tale country, similar to that portrayed in Hans Christian Andersen's fairy tales. Second, the royal family is very engaged in representing Danish products and the Danish business community when they travel around the world. It is frequently pointed out that the royal house is of a much greater economic value to Denmark than the amount spent on supporting the royal family (for example by Janting and Tolstrup 1999: 184; Redder and Palshøj 2008: 247–257). In addition, the members of the royal house travel around

Denmark taking part in the opening of museums and so on. The weakness of the contribution argument is that the royal family would still be able to contribute in this way to Danish society if the monarch had no formal competences in the state governance. It is interesting that once again we see an argument based on the skills and behaviour of the present monarch, and not an everlasting argument for constitutional monarchy as a state form.

This brings us to the 'popular' argument. In today's society, the strongest source of legitimacy for a monarch is found in the royal houses' popularity among their citizens. The Danish royal house is very popular among a majority of the Danes including citizens with a different ethnic background.[3] In a poll from June 2009 77.8 per cent of Danes supported the monarchy, while 15.3 per cent preferred a republic. In a poll from 1997, 89 per cent of the Danes believed that the Danish monarchy would survive in the end. 71 per cent did not support the idea that the constitutional duties (signing bills etc) should be taken away from the monarch if the Constitution were changed. Around 66 per cent of the Danes supported the monarchy even if the monarch came from another family than the present royal family (Bjørn 2001: 272–73). The referendum on an amendment of the Act of Succession to the Throne in 2009 might have played a part in the drop in popularity from 1997 to 2009. Even though the theme for the referendum was gender equality in succession to the throne, the referendum caused a general debate on whether Denmark should be a monarchy or a republic.[4] The popularity of the Queen's heir is high. In a survey from 2018, 75 per cent replied that they believe that Crown Prince Frederik will be a good King and he is the most popular member of the royal family (Karker 2018).

Most of the political parties represented in Parliament are in favour of the constitutional monarchy.[5] Only a few parties represented in Parliament are critical of the constitutional position of the monarch. Enhedslisten is the only party which actually wants to abolish the monarchy.

Even though the royal family is popular among a majority of the Danes,[6] the royal house constantly has to be aware of its image. Times have changed dramatically and the press and media have become very powerful actors. The press has the power to strengthen the image of the royal house, but also to harm it. One might say that the royal house and the press are dependent on each other. The royal house must show itself to be useful to Danish society,[7] and maintain its image in order to keep its competences and privileges.[8] Journalism on the royal family is 'good' news and sells newspapers and magazines. There has also been media criticism. When a 'scandal' in the royal family occurs, the future of the monarchy is discussed in the media. Discussions on the future of the monarchy

---

[3] However, as we shall see, the popularity of the royal house has dropped in the past 10 years.

[4] Interestingly, the Crown Prince's oldest child is a boy, so the referendum on gender equality was one of principle rather than practical.

[5] For a thorough description of republican advocates in Denmark since 1849, see Bjørn 2001: 29–45. For statements from the different political parties on the monarchy, see Bjørn 2001: 273–76.

[6] For instance, the Crown Prince has several times been nominated as 'Dane of the year'.

[7] According to Bjørn 2001: 298–99, the monarchy's future depends on whether the Danish citizens feel the *need* to have a monarchy.

[8] The Queen has been very much aware of this and she has carried out her role as monarch so well that even critics of the monarchy praise her efforts and competences as a monarch.

seem to appear when members of the royal family speak or act *too* politically.[9] Another example is when they abuse their special status and immunity. For instance, this was the case when the Crown Prince drove too fast in his car and when his younger brother, Prince Joachim, was accused of buying things VAT-free for his friends. Yet another example of behaviour that causes public discussion on the future of the monarchy is when their personal lives become too 'ordinary' or too 'messy'. Prince Joachim's divorce in 2004, followed by his former wife's marriage to a photographer 14 years her junior who had worked on several broadcasts on the royal family since 1999, and Prince Joachim's second marriage in 2008, are further examples.

Moreover, in 2002 when the Queen's husband Prince Henrik gave an interview to the Danish press and expressed dissatisfaction with his role as prince consort, especially with ranking under his own son the Crown Prince, the future of the monarchy was discussed. Prince Henrik's statements might also be seen as political. In 2017, he said that he did not want to be buried next to Queen Margrethe, which caused another scandal. Similarly to politicians, the royal family can be seen as role models for the Danish population. Therefore, they are expected to be perfect, which is of course not possible. This may have caused less concern before the media became so powerful and intrusive. Mistakes by the royal family are now increasingly difficult to hide. Maybe for these reasons, the royal house has a communications section which currently employs six staff members.

Other events besides 'scandals' can trigger public debate. Each year, books are written on the royal family and the royal house. Most of these books are very positive and they often build on interviews with the royal family. On the other hand, a few critical books on the royal house have been published (Høigaard 2002; Villemann 2007). Villemann raises questions like: Is the appanage of the royal family too high? Do certain members of the royal family take enough part in public appearances? Høigaard recommends a modernisation of the Danish monarchy, and proposes that the Danish monarch, like the Swedish monarch, should be without constitutional duties such as giving assent to legislation.

One might ask how the monarch and the royal house can be so popular in a modern democracy. The royal house seems to be a symbol of national unity, stability, and identity in a constantly changing and globalised world. One might say that the monarchy has become a *'psychologischen Staatsform'* (Häusler 1995: 505; Petersen 2001: 293). It might have lost competence, but it still has influence. The weakness of this argument is of course that it is possible to have a royal family without formal competences in the state government. In the public debate, however, this distinction is often not made. Their popularity is used as an argument for having a constitutional monarchy. It is interesting that the present Danish monarch insists on keeping her formal competences (chairing the Council of State, signing legislation, and appointing new governments). She expressed this view during her recent 40 year jubilee and in 2005 (Bistrup 2005: 259–60; Bistrup 2010). She seems to contribute to a political discussion when commenting on her own position and competences. Different political parties have different opinions on this matter and therefore the Queen's expressions become party political, which is the delimitation she claims

---

[9] Eg the Queen's New Year's speech in 1984 and Prince Joachim's statements on the EU's agriculture politics in 2004.

to use when she decides what she can express views on. The Queen seems to use her 'political' platform when she expresses these views in the media. The 'popular' power of a monarch can be strong in the sense that a government (especially if it has weak support among the electorate) can be forced to support the monarch's constitutional position as long as the monarch is popular. It can be dangerous for politicians to try to make the distinction between formal competences and having a royal house, because the electorate might see it as an attack on the royal family. Again, this is a legitimisation argument that is short sighted; it depends on each monarch in every situation keeping their popularity among the citizens.

The combination of the popularity of the Danish royal house and the fact that it is extremely difficult to change the Danish Constitution seems to protect the constitutional monarchy in Denmark quite effectively against changes. However, most of the legitimacy of a monarch in a modern democracy depends upon each monarch's skills and popularity, and the monarch is constantly evaluated by the public and political opinion and closely followed by the press. This goes for the monarch's work life as well as for their private life. This is not easy to master. In some cases it may be impossible. It can be extremely difficult to appear politically neutral while at the same time having to appear useful to society and the state.

9.3. POLLS AND PUBLIC OPINION

Professor Roger Mortimore, King's College London and Ipsos MORI

In Western Europe today, the principle of popular consent is generally accepted as the basis of the legitimacy of all the institutions of the state. A monarchy, even if not explicitly a democratic institution, is ultimately subordinate to public opinion. Its ability to perform its functions and perhaps its role within the state may depend upon its popularity, its funding is liable to be controlled to some degree by an elected government attentive to the demands of voters and, ultimately, its very existence could probably be ended by an adverse vote in a referendum.

Polls are regularly conducted in nearly all the European monarchies to measure public opinion. The information that they give helps the news media in reporting royal issues, and can at the same time help the monarch and his or her advisers to stay in touch with the way in which the people are thinking. But opinion polls are more than just measuring instruments. It was one of the explicit aims of George Gallup when he first introduced polling in the USA that it should strengthen the democratic process by empowering public opinion, giving it an audible voice which would force the powerful to be more responsive to the will of the majority (Gallup & Rae 1940). The change that this has wrought worldwide has affected the position of monarchies as well as elected institutions, not least in that public opinion may now change the terms of debate rather than merely reaching a verdict on its outcome. By informing citizens of what other members of the public think, polls become events of importance in themselves, contributing to the debate and perhaps changing minds; and by the terms in which they measure public opinion, they can also set the agenda. They need to be studied, therefore, not merely as evidence of the state of public opinion, but as a possible influence upon its development.

This contribution attempts an overview of recent polling on the monarchies of Europe. It compares their popularity and identifies some common patterns in public opinion, an exercise which has not apparently been previously conducted in recent years; but it also notes some features in the practice of polling on royal issues which might have implications for the direction of public debate.

In most respects, there is no shortage of material (although polls and market surveys of all kinds are much less frequent in Luxembourg than in larger countries, and we have failed to find any polls of opinion in Liechtenstein or Monaco). It has not been practical to attempt a fully comprehensive survey of all research that has been published in the countries covered, let alone of all research that has been conducted, even over the last few years; and the detailed study of longer-term trends must wait for another day. Nevertheless, by concentrating on those reports of recent polling most readily available through online news sources and the websites of some individual polling agencies,[10] it has been possible to outline the shape of public opinion today in the seven European states with a king or queen. Further, if this media coverage is representative of the sources of information on which the public in those countries relies, which seems likely, we can gain a clear picture of what the public themselves in those countries are being told about public opinion.

Popular Support for the European Monarchies

A monarchy is subject to public opinion in many different ways. In the extreme case, of course, any proposal to abolish the monarchy would almost certainly need at some stage to be approved in a referendum: many European countries, indeed, have held referendums on whether to abolish or reinstate their monarchies (see Table 10.1).[11] A modern monarchy needs to command sufficient public support not merely to win any such referendum but, ideally, to ensure that it will not be called in the first place.

But public opinion also has leverage in less drastic ways than referendums. The powers and functions of the monarchy, the rules by which it operates and the funding upon which it depends to carry out its role, are all matters on which the people may have views and involve decisions in which they may participate through elections or through the influence of their opinions on elected politicians. Moreover, the ability of the monarch and royal family to carry out their functions successfully (certainly the ceremonial public facing ones, if not necessarily any practical constitutional or religious ones) may depend upon whether the people like or trust members of the royal family or value the monarchy's symbolic or ceremonial aspects. The strength of a modern monarchy is fortified by its popularity, and on its being seen to be popular.

---

[10] The author is grateful for the invaluable assistance of Sarah Kennedy-Good in tracking down online coverage of recent polling on the monarchies across Europe, and also for the help of Ipsos colleagues in several countries, notably Sjoerd van Heck (Netherlands) and Nicklas Källebring (Sweden).

[11] As recently as 1997, Albania voted on whether its form of government should be a monarchy, although it chose by a two-to-one margin to retain its republic (Hill & White 2014: 36).

There is no general agreement across or even within countries on the best way of measuring the popularity of the monarchy, but opinion polls which pose a simple binary choice of retaining the monarchy or abolishing it, while allowing the 'don't knows' to offer no opinion, have the advantage that they have been conducted recently in all seven countries which have any regular polling and in most cases are fielded with reasonable regularity by more than one polling agency. For the sake of making preliminary comparisons, therefore, Table 9.1 shows the result of a recent straight-choice public opinion poll in each country which is broadly in line with the majority of other recently published polls there.[12] There is some variation in question wordings used (some polls talk simply of abolishing the monarchy, others of replacing it with a republic or an elected president), and – as discussed below – in some countries a minority of polls show significantly different findings which cannot necessarily be dismissed as inaccurate; the table should therefore be read in conjunction with the more detailed discussion of each country which follows.

Table 9.1 Support for retaining or abolishing the monarchy – recent polls by country

Country	Date	Agency	Retain monarchy	Abolish monarchy	Don't know
Belgium	September 2017	iVOX	58%	25%	16%
Britain	February 2016	Ipsos MORI	76%	17%	7%
Denmark	February 2018	Voxmeter	77%	15%	9%
Netherlands	April 2018	Ipsos	68%	15%	c. 17%
Norway	February 2017	Norstat	81%	15%	4%
Spain	January 2019	NC Report	58%	28%	14%
Sweden	April 2016	SIFO	65%	24%	c. 11%

Table 9.1 suggests substantial differences in the level of public support for Europe's various monarchies. Nevertheless, there are a number of common features that seem to be true of all, or almost all, of the monarchies. The first is that, except probably in Spain, there has been very little recent volatility in the level of support for abolishing the monarchy. Over the last couple of decades, there does seem to have been a slow and steady movement of opinion in Sweden and two small but perceptible step changes in Britain, but there are none of the dramatic swings or fluctuations in support that often characterise political opinion polls. Most people seem to know whether they want a republic or not, and their opinions are not easily changed.

Sir Robert Worcester, founder of MORI, has described attitudes towards the monarchy in Britain as 'the most stable measure in British polling' (McAllister 2006).

---

[12] Selecting a single poll as representative of each country is a subjective exercise, but was preferred to attempting a systematic 'poll-of-polls', which would also necessarily be subjective in defining the criteria for inclusion of polls with widely differing questions and other methodological details, and which would show differences between countries more reflective of the extent of methodological unanimity among pollsters than of the level of popular support for the monarchy.

He has reasoned that this is probably because support for the monarchy or for a republic is a 'value' rather than an 'opinion' or an 'attitude', learned early, well established and deep seated in the mind (Mortimore 2016: 147–48), and such values may not be easily swayed by current events or the opinions of one's fellows, or even be very susceptible to persuasion by rational argument. The same explanation may apply elsewhere.

This stability might possibly be obscured in popular impressions of the polls' findings because in several countries occasional polls have been reported which are well out of line with the majority. However, these seem clearly to be 'house effects' – systematically different findings between different companies' polls – probably for methodological reasons (which might include differences in question wording that mean that in fact the different polls are measuring different things). Polls which seem far apart can sometimes therefore be published within a short period of each other, yet without any dramatic movements within any single poll series; they are not evidence of fluctuations in public opinion.

A second feature, which might also give the impression of volatility, is that in several countries there has been more variation in the measured levels of support for retaining the monarchy than in support for a republic, with swings to and from the 'don't know' category accounting for the difference. In the Netherlands, for example, support for a republic has not significantly risen over the last decade but support for the monarchy has fallen: in the 2008 Synovate survey, 80 per cent said they thought keeping the monarchy was best; in 2018, the figure was 68 per cent (van Heck 2018). This probably indicates that supporting the monarchy is the default option for those with no strong feelings. This will be liable to happen when the general public mood is enthusiastically supportive, so that neutrals feel discouraged from expressing their ambivalence, an example of social desirability bias.[13] It will inflate the strength of support for the monarchy measured by the polls; but it also means that any subtle changes in the public mood, such as a weakening of the supportive atmosphere, will have a heightened impact on the polls as the unenthusiastic feel freer to admit to their indifference even if few minds have been actually changed. For the same reason, the 'monarchy' figure will tend to be more sensitive to differences in survey methodology or question wording than the 'republic' figure. In Britain, for example, Ipsos MORI's telephone polls using one question wording find similar support for a republic to YouGov's online polls with a different question, but consistently and significantly higher support for retaining the monarchy (Ipsos MORI 2016: Monarchy v Republic 1993–2016; YouGov2018: Survey Results).

We might also note what seems to be the outstanding common demographic characteristic of support for the monarchy: that the youngest citizens are least enthusiastic for it, although differences are usually relatively small so that there is in most cases a pro-monarchy majority even in the least-supportive age group. This pattern has

---

[13] Social desirability bias is the tendency of some respondents in interviews to give responses they believe will be more acceptable to the interviewer. In a country where support for the monarchy is well known to be the view of the overwhelming majority, it may well operate to persuade some people to express the same view, and so increase the level of support found in the polls. It has been surmised that self-completion polls, including online polls, may reduce the risk of social desirability bias.

been found in Britain (Ipsos MORI 2016: Queen's 90th Birthday celebrations), in Sweden (Giertz 2017) and in Spain (Lucas-Torres 2019; Ipsos 2018; Martínez-Fornés 2018). But in Norway, support for the monarchy is high across the board, with no significant differences between age groups in the most recent poll studied (Brekke & Skrede 2017). Nor, it seems, is there much difference by age in support for the monarchy in Belgium, although the young are a little more likely to believe that it costs too much (Weber 2017).

As might be expected, it is also the case that republicanism generally tends to be higher among supporters of the parties of the left than of those of the right. But again, with some exceptions, monarchists are in the majority even among those who vote for less conservative mainstream parties, and this indeed probably acts as a restraint upon parties whose ideologies might otherwise dictate that they should actively campaign for a republic.

As helpful as Table 9.1 may be in establishing an overall picture, it is potentially misleading in its simplicity and, while offering a static snapshot, says nothing about the dynamics of opinion. We should, therefore, take a more detailed look at each country.

Denmark

In Denmark, the majority of recent polls by different companies, using various question wordings, have put support for a republic well below one in five. For example: 15 per cent by Voxmeter in 2018, 10 per cent by Norstat in 2017, 15 per cent by Epinion in 2016 and 13 per cent by TNS Gallup in 2013 (*Jyllands-Posten* 2018; Kvalvik 2017; Ingvorsen 2016; TNS Gallup2013: 4). This suggests a stable state of public opinion, all of these figures being within the normal 'margin of error' of each other.

Other polls, however, put the figure much higher. In 1963, Gallup devised a methodology intended to distinguish between support for the monarchy as an institution and for the monarch personally. This involved including a hypothetical question about attitudes if the throne were to be occupied by a king who was not a member of the present royal family. They concluded that support for abolition of the monarchy was about 8 per cent (Gallup 1963), and later polls put that number at 15 per cent in 1992 and 22 per cent in 1997. Apparently following this methodology, Analyse Danmark reported support for a republic to be 34 per cent in 2009, and YouGov found 31 per cent in 2013 (although that was an online poll excluding anybody aged 75 or over).

Norway

The contrast in findings between competing pollsters is also striking in Norway. Norstat in 2017 found 81 per cent preferring the monarchy and 15 per cent a republic (Brekke & Skrede 2017), and InFact found a 75 per cent to 15 per cent margin in 2012, although a narrower 65 per cent to 19 per cent margin in 2014 (Norsk Telegrambyrå 2014). While support for a republic varies only across a narrow span in these polls, the differences in support for the monarchy are wider, corresponding to variations in the number of 'don't knows'. The highest number recorded was 82 per cent support in May 2014, by Norstat for NRK (Kalajdzic 2014) (higher than the 79 per cent of Norwegians who voted in favour of a monarchy in the referendum which originally established it in 1905).

Yet in contrast to these figures, which show a margin of five-to-one or more in the most extreme cases, TNS Gallup (whose figures were reported only after the exclusion of 'don't knows') found a margin of almost exactly two-to-one in 2016 (Norsk Telegrambyrå 2016); and Gallup is in line with a 2005 poll by Opinion AS for *Aftenposten* and NRK, which found 63 per cent for the monarchy, 30 per cent for a republic (Sarpsborg Arbeiderblad 2005). However, media reports carried no details of the question used or detailed methodology.

The Netherlands

In the Netherlands, most of the polls show recent opinion as stable and with support for a republic between 10 per cent and 15 per cent, although ground has been lost since the 1990s, when the figure was consistently below 10 per cent. The long-running TNS/NIPO series has been joined since 2008 by annual Synovate (now Ipsos) polls for the public service broadcaster NOS (van Heck 2018); as Figure 9.1 shows, their results have been very similar (as have less frequent polls from other agencies such as Motivaction and EénVandaag, not included in the graph). But one pollster, Maurice de Hond (polling for *Hart van Nederland*, a news and current affairs programme), disagrees: despite asking an apparently-similar question, de Hond has consistently found different results, with support for a republic in the 20 per cent to 30 per cent bracket, and bigger poll-on-poll movements.

Figure 9.1 Support for abolition of the monarchy in the Netherlands, 1995–2018 (per cent)

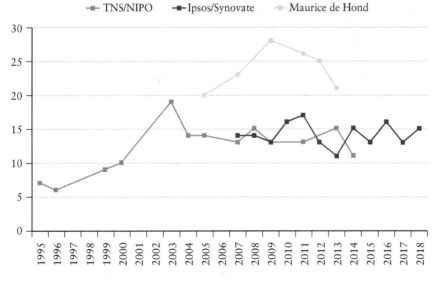

Britain

In Britain,[14] only two poll series – those by MORI (later Ipsos MORI) and by YouGov – have tracked responses to a straight-choice question in recent years, and they have found similar results on support for a republic (Figure 9.2). Opinion has moved little over the 25-year span of the MORI polls, and it is notable that support for a republic was apparently marginally lower in the late 1990s, when the monarchy was seen as being under pressure, and when other indicators were very much poorer, than in the first years of the twenty-first century when it seemed less vulnerable. Different question formulations, however, have found different results. Polls by ICM have asked whether Britain would be better off or worse off without a royal family, and found higher levels thinking it would be better off, peaking at 38 per cent; but the academic British Social Attitudes Survey, which asks how important it is that Britain should continue to have a monarchy, or whether it should be abolished, generally finds support for abolition in single figures (Mortimore 2016: 143).

Figure 9.2 Support for abolition of the monarchy in the UK, 1993–2017 (per cent)

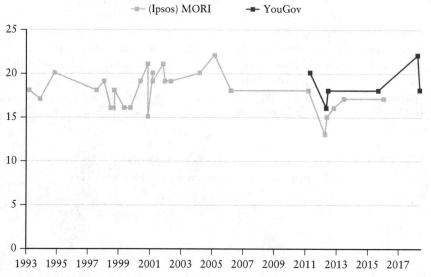

Source: The National SOM Survey.

---

[14] These polls, like most commercial opinion polls in Britain, do not cover the whole UK: they exclude Northern Ireland, which when it is polled at all is usually polled separately. This is not a peculiarity of polls about the monarchy, and applies to most market research and social research on all topics. Northern Ireland makes up only 2.5% of the UK population, so its exclusion can have only minimal impact on the overall figures.

Sweden

In Sweden, too, there have been some significant differences between the results reported by different agencies, but a graph showing the trend of results from the four most prolific sources – telephone polls by SIFO (now Kantar SIFO) and by Synovate/ Temo (now Ipsos), online polls by Novus Opinion, and self-completion surveys with random sampling by the SOM Institute at the University of Gothenburg – is revealing (Figure 9.3). This shows that there is little evidence of fluctuation in opinions but a very clear agreement between SIFO, Synovate and SOM in showing a slight but clear and consistent deterioration in the situation since the start of the twenty-first century.

Figure 9.3 Support for retaining monarchy in Sweden, 2000–16 (per cent)

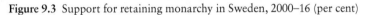
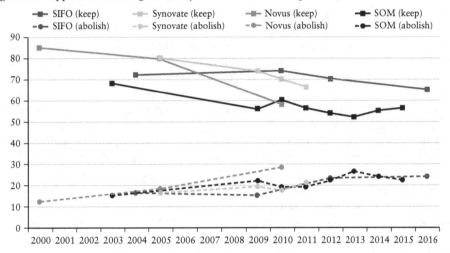

SOM's surveys using the straight-choice question have found a broadly similar level of support for a republic but consistently lower opposition to it (and a correspondingly higher number of 'don't knows') than SIFO and Synovate, yet a direction of movement and slope fully in line with the others.[15]

However, polls by Novus Opinion for the Republican Association asked questions on whether the head of state should be elected democratically or should inherit the position and whether the monarchy, where the head of state inherited the title, was compatible with a modern democracy, before the straight-choice monarchy-or-republic question. These polls found a bigger movement in opinions (Broshammar 2010). It is well established that poll results can be distorted by the content of previously asked questions, and the Novus trend cannot be considered comparable with the other polls, but the very fact that such distortions are possible suggests a greater degree of uncertainty in Swedish opinion than the results of the other polls might imply.

---

[15] SOM has experimented with several different forms of question to measure support for a republic (Nilsson 2017); only those surveys using a straight-choice question which are directly comparable with those of the other pollsters are included in the chart.

Belgium

Opinion polls including a direct monarchy-or-republic straight-choice question have been less frequently published in Belgium than in the other kingdoms, and the one included in Table 9.1 (by iVOX for the RTL programme *Place Royale*) is the only recent one which has been located. As with other polls on different aspects of the Belgian monarchy, it showed a very substantial difference between Flemish speakers and French speakers, the former splitting only 54 per cent to 30 per cent in favour, the latter more emphatically supporting it by 65 per cent to 19 per cent (Belga 2017).

Spain

In Spain, also, where the preferred measurement of support for the monarchy has usually been a score out of 10 for the institution's performance rather than a percentage backing its retention, there have been only a few polls using a straight-choice question comparable to those used elsewhere. The state sociological and population research agency, CIS, measured attitudes towards the monarchy on a performance score basis for many years, a method which enabled direct comparisons to parallel measurements for other institutions; but the King personally, and other members of the royal family, can also be (and have been) rated in the same way.

Nevertheless, some commercial agencies have recently published polls offering respondents the direct choice between retaining the monarchy and abolishing it. These suggest that support for the Spanish monarchy in recent years has been weaker than in the other countries studied, although not quite so low as to make a republic the more popular option. They also suggest that attitudes are relatively volatile, with much bigger short-term movements in support than other countries. Sigma Dos conducted four polls for the newspaper *El Mundo* between December 2012 and June 2015, a period spanning the abdication of King Juan Carlos in June 2014: when the margin was at its narrowest, in December 2013, 50 per cent said they supported the monarchy and 43 per cent that they did not. But by June 2015, support had climbed to 61 per cent and opposition fallen to 34 per cent (Sigma Dos 2015). The June 2014 poll, immediately after the announcement of the abdication, put opposition at 36 per cent. Moreover, a separate Metroscopia poll for *El País* conducted at the same time, asking respondents to choose between a monarchy led by the future king, Felipe VI, and a republic with a president as the head of state, also found 36 per cent preferring a republic (Toharia 2014).

It is evident, then, from all the countries studied, that the exact level of popular support for the monarchy depends on the way in which it is measured. It would be unsafe to assume that the most frequently used methodologies are necessarily the most accurate. In any case, however, the notion of accuracy may not be a helpful one – what is being measured may well be unformed tendencies or vague sentiments, rather than a fixed commitment for or against the monarchy. In most of these countries today a referendum on the future of the monarchy is entirely hypothetical, rather than a real and imminent event against which voting intentions expressed in a poll could be theoretically tested, as in a general election. Nevertheless, the apparent fragility of any findings suggests that there may be a good deal of uncertainty in public opinion, which might be unlocked in certain circumstances; but what those circumstances are remains unclear.

The Potential Impact of Polls

Polls try to measure the shape of public opinion towards the monarchies, but that shape may also be affected by them. How would this operate?

One effect would be in relation to the media's agenda setting role.[16] Because the news media is the chief instigator of polling in most countries, the choice of what polling is conducted is largely driven by the news agenda (and although other polls may be independently commissioned, they can expect little exposure unless they are judged sufficiently newsworthy for the media to report them). Most polls that are published, therefore, ask about issues that journalists think are important.

Further, the very framing of questions about the monarchy or the assumptions that underlie them may shape the way in which those opinions are understood, even by the members of the public themselves who hold them. In particular, by asking questions about the monarchy which parallel those asked about other political institutions that are expressly answerable to the public, they may seem to assume that the monarchy is also such an institution and perhaps, ultimately, cause that assumption to be more widely held (Glencross, Rowbotham & Kandiah 2016: 19–20). Moreover, the modern news media tend to see part of their role as helping to hold those in power to account on the public's behalf. So, when the polls show that the political issues which the media are raising are ones of public concern, this is taken as justifying their decision to cover those issues, acting in the public's interest. By approaching royal affairs in the same way, taking polls that show the public's interest in a given issue as legitimising coverage of that issue, the media put the triangular relationship between the media, the monarchy and the public on the same footing as applies to other political institutions.

It is accepted that the perceived trustworthiness and competence of elected politicians, their past performance in office and their anticipated future performance are all issues for which the voters may hold them to account, and that it is for the voters to choose the criteria by which they will judge their fitness to be elected or re-elected. Polling on the monarchy tends to be framed in similar terms: approval may be measured in terms of how well the monarch is 'doing his (or her) job'; support for the monarchy is related to tangible benefits for the country from its existence, and it may be explicitly rated in terms of 'value for money', or the amount which is spent on it questioned so as to implicitly draw on such considerations.

The public are assumed to be both entitled and qualified to answer the questions. Their judgments may be based on a very imperfect understanding of what the king or queen actually does or is meant to do, and may well depend much more on vague impressions or emotional responses than upon detailed knowledge and deliberative

---

[16] For a general discussion of agenda setting by the media, see for example McCombs & Shaw 1972.

reasoning. This criticism might be held also to apply to political polling and to the electoral decisions to which it is related, but that situation is inherent in a democratic structure which gives power to the people; it is not equally inherent, it might be argued, in a monarchy.

Moreover, suggestions of radical changes to the way in which the monarchy operates may be proposed to a public with little understanding of their implications, and their reactions then reported as if they were a considered judgment rather than a tallying of top-of-the-head reactions to a complex and previously unconsidered question. Polls can (and do) measure support for abdication of an ageing monarch in a monarchy with no tradition of retirement, for relaxing traditions that require the monarch to be politically neutral in public, and for altering the succession to the throne in favour of a (perhaps temporarily) more popular member of the royal family. Such issues are thereby elevated to a place in the news agenda and in public debate, not because there is necessarily evidence of any existing demand but because the decision has been taken to look for it.

Opinion polls, therefore, must be understood not merely as passive observers but as potentially affecting the form and content of debate about the future of the European monarchies. They are of interest not only because of their findings, but because their very existence may be significant.

The Breadth of the Agenda in Monarchy Polls

The range of subjects covered by polling on royal issues is considerable in every country studied, and a comprehensive survey is far beyond the scope of this paper. However, it is possible to highlight some topics which are covered frequently in many countries.

An obvious and frequent tactic is to personalise the issue by asking the public whether they are satisfied with the performance of the monarch, much as political polls measure approval of presidents or prime ministers. These measurements often rate the monarch considerably higher than parallel surveys on the institution (and generally at much higher levels than are achieved by any elected politician). Recent polls have found 93 per cent thinking that the King was doing a good job for Norway (Norsk Telegrambyrå 2012), 86 per cent satisfaction with the Queen in Britain (Ipsos MORI 2016: High satisfaction levels with Royal Family as the Queen turns 90), and 73 per cent satisfied with the way the King had been governing the Netherlands (van Heck 2018). Those approving the individual monarch's performance frequently include a substantial proportion of those who say they would prefer to abolish the monarchy.

Ratings of other members of the royal family can similarly be collected. This might be in terms of satisfaction with performance, whether they 'provide a good return on taxpayer investment', general favourability towards the individual or simply as a ranking of who is 'most liked'; such polls are familiar in one form or another in all seven countries studied. Yet often they include members of the royal family who have no constitutional role or perform no public duties (Romero 2017; Norsk Telegrambyrå 2012; JessRulz 2017). Whereas polls about the monarch or the institution of monarchy can perhaps be considered an instrument of accountability to the public, the justification of these polls is sometimes less clear, and critics could argue that they treat members of the royal family more like celebrities from television or sport, and encourage the public to think of them in this way.

Popularity polling of this sort may naturally be wounding to the individuals who score least well, and might conceivably stoke up real or imagined rivalries between different members of the royal family, to be reported in the popular press. Perhaps, these are simply the hazards of public life today; however, when the relative popularity of different royal figures is used to discuss issues such as abdication or succession, with the apparent implication that public opinion has a legitimate role to play in contributing to such decisions, this may be less easily reconciled with the traditions of the monarchy or its independence.

In Denmark, Queen Margrethe has repeatedly indicated that she intends to remain on the throne until she dies; nevertheless, polls regularly ask whether she should retire, and find that many of the public say that she should. In 2010, at the time of her 70th birthday, Rambøll Management/Analyse Danmark polling found that 46 per cent thought that she should abdicate, split evenly between those who believed she should retire immediately and those who thought she should wait another ten years (Jyllands-Posten 2010). In 2018, 30 per cent thought that she should abdicate within the coming year, according to Voxmeter (Jyllands-Posten 2018). There seems to be no suggestion that any denigration of the popular Queen is implied by these opinions, and support for her retirement may be permissive as much as anything else; nevertheless, they may be fostered by the popularity of the Crown Prince Frederik and his wife, and the poll questions usually mention that if the Queen were to relinquish the throne then the Crown Prince would take over.

In Sweden, the tone of calls for King Carl Gustaf to abdicate has sometimes been different. In 2011, *Aftonbladet* reported its SIFO poll under the headline '*Lämna Tronen*' ('Leave the Throne'), and led its story with the statement that a majority wanted the Crown Princess Victoria to take over, although closer inspection revealed that while 56 per cent had said that the King should step aside within 10 years, only 17 per cent thought that he should do so immediately. Such polls were published more frequently in the 2010–12 period than more recently, but they continue to find backing for the King's abdication: in 2017, a Demoskop poll pointed out that King Carl Gustaf would be 71 on 30 April, and asked whether he should then renounce the throne and leave it to Crown Princess Victoria; 43 per cent thought that he should. As in Denmark, it is surely a factor that the Crown Princess is very popular, regularly topping polls to find the most respected or liked member of the royal family (Victorzon 2011; Giertz 2017).

In Spain, King Juan Carlos had fallen in the public's favour by the early years of the present decade, whereas Crown Prince Felipe had apparently not, and this contributed to the pressure for a change of monarch. A poll immediately after King Juan Carlos abdicated in June 2014 found that 76 per cent of Spaniards felt that he had been right to do so. Moreover, the abdication precipitated an immediate if perhaps short-term increase in positive perceptions of his record: 65 per cent said they believed that the former King's reign had been 'good' or 'very good', whereas only 41 per cent had thought the same in the previous poll in January, when he was still on the throne (Sigma Dos 2014).

In Belgium, by contrast, the majority seem to have been against the abdication of King Albert II in July 2013: in May, when rumours of a forthcoming abdication were circulating, polls were reported showing that 54 per cent of Belgians in one case, and

60 per cent in another, wanted King Albert to remain on the throne. Other answers suggested that this reflected misgivings as to whether his heir, Prince Philippe, was yet ready to take over (Belga 2013).

In Britain, occasional polls have suggested that many of the public would support the Queen if she chose to retire, but a much more frequently posed question has been whether Prince Charles should succeed at the end of his mother's reign or whether the Crown should 'skip a generation' and pass to his son, Prince William. Prince Charles is less popular with the public than either his mother or his two sons (Ipsos MORI 2012), and frequent polls are published to show that many of the public would prefer Prince William rather than Prince Charles to be the next monarch, although the most recent polls suggest this is now a minority view (YouGov 2018: Did you commemorate Remembrance Day? Plus, dementia, and the monarchy results). Similarly, polls have frequently asked whether Prince Charles's wife, the Duchess of Cornwall, should 'become Queen', or should be allowed to take the title of Queen, when he succeeds to the throne, and have often found majorities of the public saying that she should not (Winchester 2015; Ipsos MORI 2006). Such findings offer the press the chance of hostile coverage that perhaps reinforces the negative feelings that some of their readers hold towards particular members of the royal family; whether they also create or strengthen a belief that the public is entitled to a say in such decisions is unknown, but it seems possible.

Another frequent topic for polling is whether the role of the monarchy should be altered, either proposing specific curtailment of powers or suggesting that it should become 'entirely ceremonial' (although what this would mean in practice is not normally spelled out). Even where the monarchy and the monarch are popular, these suggestions can find majority support. In Denmark, a 2010 poll by Rambøll Management/ Analyse Danmark for *Jyllands-Posten* found that 54 per cent thought that the President of the Folketing rather than the Queen should appoint the Prime Minister when a new government is formed, and that 50 per cent would choose to end the requirement of formal royal assent before laws can come into force (Cordsen 2010). In Britain in 2012, more people (51 per cent) said the Queen should not have any real power than said that she should (44 per cent) (YouGov 2012). The margin is wider among Flemish speakers in Belgium, who split two-to-one (61 per cent to 30 per cent) in favour of a ceremonial monarch rather than one with power in a 2017 poll (Belga 2017). Even there, however, the proposal seems likely to be being kept alive by being raised in opinion polls rather than having much active political momentum behind it.

When a controversy has already made an issue one of public debate, however, support for change can be stronger. In Luxembourg, after the Grand Duke refused his assent to a law permitting euthanasia and assisted suicide in 2009, the procedure was abolished with a unanimous parliamentary vote in favour (see chapter 3.8), and a poll showed that 70 per cent of the public backed the new law (Frieden 2009; Associated Press 2008).

In fact, the idea of a purely ceremonial monarch sometimes also attracts those who would normally consider themselves republicans. In the Netherlands, Ipsos found in 2017 that, if offered the third alternative of a ceremonial monarchy rather than a republic, just eight per cent would choose to abolish the monarchy outright; 19 per cent would prefer a ceremonial monarchy and 54 per cent the status quo (NOS Nieuws 2017).

In Britain, a more frequently tested suggestion for 'reforming' or 'modernising' the monarchy has been that it should be 'slimmed down', with the size of the formally recognised royal family reduced or the scale of ceremonial activities restricted. These polls, however, should probably be seen as one instance of a wider tendency to question the cost of the monarchy, which has been a theme in the published polling in several countries. Far more of the public seem prepared to criticise the amount of money being spent than would support the establishment of a republic. Such concerns are not restricted to royal issues – polls can find disquiet expressed at many other aspects of public spending – and may well be based on little or no understanding of the sums involved and how they compare with other sources of expenditure and revenue. Nevertheless, they tap into real emotions in the public which might be damaging to the monarchy – however ill-informed – and might offer a focus for discontent when other factors are more in the monarchy's favour.

Polls revealing unease about the cost of the monarchy are regularly published even in those countries where the monarchy is most strongly supported. In a 2013 Gallup poll in Denmark, 43 per cent 'agreed' or 'partly agreed' that the country spent too much on the royal family (TNS Gallup 2013: 7); in 2016 in Norway, an Ipsos MMI poll (which seems to have been commissioned as part of a concerted *Dagbladet* campaign on the level of spending on the monarchy) found that 40 per cent thought too much was being spent (Lindblad 2016); in the Netherlands, a 2017 survey found 57 per cent thinking that the King's annual income of €800,000 was too high (JessRulz 2017). In Britain, similar findings date back many years, and 48 per cent agreed that 'The Royal Family should not receive as much money as it does' as long ago as 1972. The figure was as high as 76 per cent in May 1992, when the monarchy was coming under pressure on various grounds; and a more recent poll, in 2012, found it still at 52 per cent (Mortimore 2016: 152). In Belgium, where opposition to the monarchy is more widespread, doubts about cost are correspondingly higher: in 2017, 64 per cent said they believed that the €35 million annual cost was too high, while only 29 per cent thought it about right (Weber 2017).

Spending on special occasions provides a natural prompt to ask such questions. In 2015, an Ipsos poll commissioned by NOS in the Netherlands pointed out that €2 million of public money had been earmarked for the celebration of the bicentenary of the monarchy: 52 per cent said they thought this was too much (NOS Nieuws 2015). In 2018 in Britain, YouGov polled for the anti-monarchy pressure group Republic on the cost of Prince Harry's wedding. Respondents were told that 'For the Royal Wedding, it is said that the royal family are currently paying for the ceremony and reception, whilst the government are paying for policing and security'. 57 per cent then gave their opinion that the royal family should pay for the entire wedding, while only 36 per cent were content that the royal family should only pay for the ceremony and reception and the government should pay for the policing and security. The follow-up question then proposed was 'Imagine you had the choice of whether your taxes contributed to paying for the Royal Wedding'; predictably, the vast majority (76 per cent) said they would choose not to pay towards the wedding (YouGov 2018: Republic survey results). But even the present Queen's wedding, in 1947 when she was heir to the throne, was judged to be too elaborate by 29 per cent of the public. This was the first poll inviting criticism of the royal family that Gallup ever published in Britain (Gallup 1976: 165).

Perhaps a more usefully revealing measure than any of the foregoing, and one which is very sensitive to changes in the public mood, is the level of confidence that the monarchy will survive in the long term. In the UK, more than two-thirds of the public,

69 per cent, said in January 1990 that they thought that Britain would still have a monarchy in fifty years' time. After the vicissitudes of the next decade, however, this had fallen to just 29 per cent by November 1999, while 45 per cent thought that it would not. At this nadir, more of those predicting that the monarchy would not survive were themselves supporters of retaining the monarchy than were advocates of establishing a republic. But by 2012 confidence had recovered, and 60 per cent thought that the monarchy would last at least another fifty years (Mortimore 2016: 149). A similar question asked in Denmark in 2015 found that 64 per cent thought there would still be a monarchy there in fifty years' time (Ingvorsen 2016), and in Norway, three-quarters of those who had an opinion in 2016 thought that Princess Ingrid Alexandra (born in 2004, granddaughter of the current King) would one day be Queen, which is a not dissimilar measure (Norsk Telegrambyrå 2016).

This may be an important indicator because the belief that one's views are, or are not, shared by other people seems to be a powerful influence on one's attachment to them. The impact of the perceived public mood on individuals' opinions is exemplified by a phenomenon called the 'Spiral of Silence' (Noelle-Neumann 1984): those who believe their opinions are unpopular become less likely to express them; this strengthens the impression that these are indeed minority opinions and, eventually, some of the apparent minority will change their minds. A supporter's confidence that the monarchy will survive, reflecting a belief that the support of others for it is strong and stable, is probably therefore evidence of the stability and resilience of one's own support; the same expectation in one who would prefer a republic suggests defeatism and perhaps less effectiveness in advocating that cause.

Conclusion

There is nothing new about the importance of public opinion to the functioning and even the survival of a monarchy: most of the European monarchies that have ceased to exist in the last 250 years owed their demise, at least in part, to mismanagement of their relationship with the people. The advent of opinion polls in the latter half of the twentieth century has offered both insiders and outsiders the opportunity to monitor this relationship more closely than was previously possible, and should allow the monarch and his or her advisers to ensure that they do not get out of touch with the public mood.

However, the expression of public opinion through the publication of polls can be an influential event in itself, with the power to affect what is being measured. Most polls are reported by the media to their audiences, who are often those self-same citizens whose opinions are being assessed, and there is good reason to suppose that their opinions may be affected by the knowledge of what other citizens are thinking. Politicians, too, read the opinion polls, and may be influenced by the implications for their own support that they read there. But most polls are also commissioned by the news media, in line with the current news agenda, which they may help to reinforce by enriching the reporting and legitimising its focus. Less obviously, perhaps, but no less importantly, they may also help to frame the debate through the terms in which their questions are asked and the context in which their findings are put. The polling of public opinion may therefore be an important consideration as well as the state of opinion when it is polled.

This situation is not necessarily fixed for the future. The traditional news media may not retain their near monopoly on commissioning polling, nor can they expect to retain a monopoly on interpreting and disseminating its findings now that online sources and social media are challenging their dominance as information providers; but these two considerations do characterise the situation as it has existed for many years, and define the current role of the polls. Defenders of the monarchies may find more opportunities to intervene, highlighting positives and steering the terms of debate towards an understanding more compatible with the traditional role and functions of the Crown, if the market in information about public opinion becomes freer; on the other hand, these opportunities will be open to their opponents as well. But it seems certain that, however the role of polls and the reporting of them in shaping public opinion may change, the importance of public opinion itself to the future of the monarchies will remain undiminished.

9.4. THE LEGITIMACY OF THE SWEDISH MONARCHY: THE DIFFERENT PERCEPTIONS OF PARLIAMENTARIANS, JOURNALISTS AND THE PEOPLE

Lennart Nilsson, Professor Emeritus, University of Gothenburg

The monarchy represents a deviation from the democratic principle that otherwise prevails in Sweden. The principal argument for preserving the monarchy is the importance of their being representatives of the nation as a whole, who are neutral in relation to current political issues, and that the monarchy embodies the continuous development of Swedish society (Strömholm 2006).

The monarchy is associated with history, tradition and cultural heritage. The head of state and the royal house are to serve as Swedish symbols that strengthen national solidarity and identity. In today's parliamentary democracy, the head of state, according to the 1974 Instrument of Government [*Regeringsformen*], is deprived of all formal powers, with only representative and ceremonial duties remaining (see Chapter 3.4). Nevertheless, there is a tension between the democratic principle, which is based on equality and differences of opinion, and the national principle, which stresses hierarchy and unity. The current situation gives rise to a number of paradoxes: the hereditary succession of the post of head of state; the formally powerless monarch still holding the highest office; and the contrast between royal elevation and normality (Åse 2009). The principles upon which hereditary monarchy is based are anachronistic in a democracy based on all human beings' equal value and on government of the people, for the people and by the people. The monarchy, however, is firmly established in democratic practice in the sense that, in modern times, decisions concerning the Instrument of Government and the Order of Succession have been made by the Parliament following official inquiries (Berg Eriksen 1999).

Sweden became a monarchy in the Middle Ages and is one of the oldest monarchies in the world. For centuries, the King or Queen who ruled Sweden was also the head of state of other Nordic countries. In 1818 the French marshal Jean Baptiste Bernadotte became

King of Sweden and, since that time, the Bernadotte family has been the royal house of Sweden. Until 1905, the Swedish King was also the King of Norway.

The King and the royal house are constantly the objects of media attention, particularly in connection with anniversaries and other special events. On the occasion of Carl XVI Gustaf's accession to the throne in 1973, the King's wedding to Queen Silvia on 19 June 1976, ceremonial days and other special events, the media have produced many news stories and reports. However, Crown Princess Victoria's wedding on 19 June 2010 attracted reporting on unprecedented levels.[17] Few people have any personal contact with the royal house. Rather, information on the King, Queen and other royals has always been conveyed through the media and other channels (see Jönsson and Lundell 2009).

Media coverage of the royal house long lacked any critical scrutiny, although there have always been, among the great number of articles, occasional editorials and cultural pieces arguing for a republican form of government, based on reasons of principle. This situation meant that the question of monarchy-versus-republic was long irrelevant in the Swedish public debate. In recent years, however, the theme has emerged in articles and been the subject of more critical analyses.

Apart from constituting an important avenue of communication between citizens and those in power, the media serve other purposes:

> The media are more than a link between government and politics, and the citizens. They play dual roles: together with other actors, sources and audiences, they create media content; secondly, their output influences both sources and audiences – and the media themselves (Asp 2007).

This analysis is highly applicable to the media's coverage of the Swedish monarchy and the royal house. In this connection, two related questions arise: what views do journalists hold? What is the influence of journalists' opinions on media content and, ultimately, on people's image of the head of state and the monarchy?

Studies of the Swedish People, Journalists, Members of Parliament and the Monarchy

Research on the status of the monarchy was for a long time exclusively a question of constitutional law, reserved for professors of law, history and political science. Current research is broader in scope, including contributions from scholars in many additional disciplines, such as ethnology, sociology, film studies, business administration as well as media and communication. A 2009 anthology focusing on media and the monarchy, entitled *Media and Monarchy in Sweden*, contained contributions from researchers from seven different disciplines (Jönsson and Lundell 2009).

In a democracy, it is crucial that the position of the monarchy and the head of state be examined. How is it possible to combine the idea of democratic rule and general elections

---

[17] Nearly half of the Swedish people followed media reports on the wedding to a great or relatively great extent. Only one in five did not follow the event at all.

with a royal house based on heredity? When studying the legitimacy of the Swedish monarchy, two primary dimensions are involved: the choice between the principles of monarchy and republic; and the perceptions of how the royal house functions.

In the absence of general elections and a referendum in Sweden, we must rely on scientific investigations to establish the legitimacy of the monarchy and to understand support for it.[18] Since 1995, questions related to this area have been included in the annual public opinion and media surveys carried out in Sweden by the SOM Institute, a research organisation at the University of Gothenburg. The response rate has declined from 65 per cent in 1995 to 54 per cent in 2014 (Vernersdotter 2015). However, results of the surveys are very similar to the official election results.[19] This is very important, as party sympathy is a strategic variable in this study. The population includes both Swedish citizens and citizens of other countries living in Sweden.

The choice between the principles of monarchy and republic has been measured using two different questions: whether to 'preserve or abolish the monarchy'; and whether to 'establish a republic in Sweden', with or without the specification with an elected 'president'.

The functioning of the monarchy has been analysed based on questions concerning respondents' confidence in how well the royal house carries out its duties compared to other institutions and groups in Sweden. This analysis compares the popularity of the Swedish King and Crown Princess to other heads of state, international leaders and the political party leaders in Sweden.

These analyses of the Swedish people are based on the SOM Institute's national surveys since 1995. The exact wording of the respective questions and response alternatives are provided below. In 1995 two novel questions on the position of the monarchy were included; the question concerning confidence in how well social institutions or groups (such as the royal house) carry out their duties has subsequently been part of the survey each year. The second question concerned the possible introduction of a republic with an elected president and this question has been included in the national SOM surveys in 1995, 1999–2001, 2003 and 2005–14. The 2003 and 2009–14 surveys have also included a question concerning whether to preserve or abolish the monarchy.

Beginning in 1989, the Department of Journalism, Media and Communication at the University of Gothenburg has carried out six surveys aimed at Swedish journalists (Asp 2012a). In 1999, 2005 and 2011, these surveys included the same question on

---

[18] In Norway, a referendum on the monarchy was carried out in connection with the dissolution of the union between Norway and Sweden in 1905. On the day of the signing of the Karlstad Treaty on 26 October 1905, King Oscar II had renounced his and any of his descendants' claims to the Norwegian Crown. On 18 November of the same year, a popular vote was held in which the Norwegian people were requested to take a stand on asking Prince Carl of Denmark to allow himself to be elected King of Norway. The result was very clear: 79% of the votes were in favour of the proposal, and 21% were against it. The voter turnout amounted to 75%. The referendum is considered to have given the monarchy strong legitimacy in Norway (Jonsrud 1996; Listhaug 1993). In Denmark, moreover, a referendum was held on female succession to the throne in connection with the European Parliament elections in June 2009. With a turnout of almost 60 per cent, a clear majority of 85 per cent voted in favour of this change.

[19] Although in 2014 survey respondents having voted for the Sweden Democrats are under-represented.

confidence in institutions posed in the SOM surveys, albeit in relation to fewer institutions. The question on establishing a republican form of government in Sweden was included in the two most recent surveys. The response rate has been 59–60 per cent (Andersson 2012).

Since 1969, the Department of Political Science at the University of Gothenburg has conducted 10 surveys aimed at the elected members of the Swedish Parliament. In the studies of 2002, 2006 and 2014, the surveys have included questions on confidence in the royal house and, in 2014, on the establishment of a republic in Sweden. The response rate in 2014 was 88 per cent, compared to 94 per cent eight years earlier.

These surveys allow us to make comparisons between the Swedish people, Swedish journalists and members of Parliament regarding the principle of establishing a republican form of government in Sweden and respondents' confidence in the way the royal house carries out its duties compared to other institutions, as well as how these attitudes and evaluations have changed over a twenty-year period.[20] The results will be presented in the following sections:

- The Swedish people and the monarchy;
- Establishing a republican form of government;
- Confidence in the way the royal house carries out its duties;
- Members of the Swedish royal house in a comparative perspective; and
- Confidence in the royal house and support for the monarchy.

In the second and third sections a comparison is made between the Swedish people, the journalists and the parliamentarians.

The Swedish People and the Monarchy

When the Government Commission on Constitutional Matters presented its proposal for a new Instrument of Government in 1963, an intense debate on the position of the King followed. Paragraph 4 of the 1809 Instrument of Government stated that the King was the absolute ruler of the realm. However, according to the political reforms of 1905–17, the parliamentary principle was to be applied, and this practice came to be considered law. The King was to appoint Cabinet ministers based on the parliamentary representation of the political parties. Yet, in practice, the government settled all governmental matters (Holmberg and Stjernquist 1980).

Following a political compromise reached in 1971 by the then four major political parties – the so-called Torekov Compromise, named after the summer resort where it took place – the republic-versus-monarchy question was removed from the political agenda for a long time. Once the head of state had been stripped of his powers, only representative and ceremonial duties remained. The Torekov Compromise, which was reached while the constitutional committee was at work, enabled broad political consensus on the decision concerning the head of state. Not even the introduction of female succession

---

[20] The present contribution is based on earlier articles in Swedish by the author on the same topic, most recently 'The Swedish people, the journalists and the monarchy' (Nilsson 2013).

to the throne in 1979 gave rise to any far-reaching constitutional debate. According to Stjernquist, the decision on female succession had rather strengthened the position of the monarchy (Stjernquist 1971; Holmberg and Stjernquist 1980).

When, for the first time, the 2003 National SOM Survey raised the question of preserving or abolishing the monarchy, the result was unequivocal: the Swedish people did not wish to change their form of government. Two thirds opted for preserving the monarchy, 15 per cent were in favour of its abolition and 17 per cent did not voice an opinion. Just as confidence in the royal family has changed after 2003, support for the monarchy has also been affected. Thus, when the same question was posed in 2009, considerable changes in opinion had occurred. The proportion of respondents in favour of preserving the monarchy had decreased by 12 per cent, whereas there was an increase in the proportion of those who wished to abolish the monarchy and those who lacked an opinion. In 2014, over half of the survey respondents were still in favour of preserving the monarchy, one quarter wanted to abolish it, whereas approximately one fifth did not voice an opinion.

Figure 9.4 The Swedish people's opinions on preserving or abolishing the monarchy, 2003 and 2009–14 (per cent)

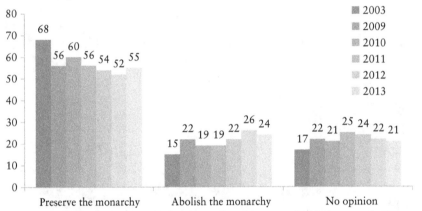

The question was: Are you of the opinion that Sweden ought to preserve or abolish the monarchy? The response alternatives are shown in the figure.

Source: The National SOM Survey.

The main result is very clear. Respondents have favoured preserving the monarchy: young and old; women and men; those with only an elementary education as well as academics; people living in rural as well as urban areas; entrepreneurs; civil servants and blue-collar workers; Swedish and foreign citizens alike. Despite the strong support for the monarchy within various groups, however, there have been differences. Support for the monarchy has been strongest among older people, although the age differences were relatively small. Women were somewhat more likely to be royalists than men were. Looking at different occupational groups, the royalists were most strongly represented among employers; otherwise, the differences were minor. Non-Swedish citizens were less likely to favour the monarchy, but a greater proportion of respondents in this group than of Swedish citizens lacked an opinion. In all groups except for foreign citizens, support for the monarchy was lower in 2014 than in 2003.

Figure 9.5 The Swedish people's attitudes toward preserving the monarchy by sex, age and citizenship, in 2003, 2010 and 2014 (per cent)

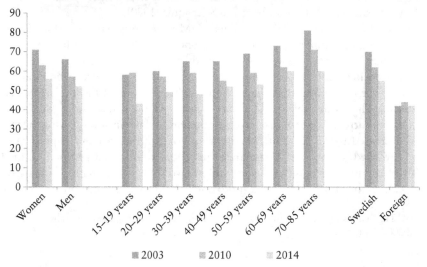

Figure 9.6 The Swedish people's attitudes toward preserving the monarchy by occupational group and political party preference, for 2003, 2010 and 2014 (per cent)

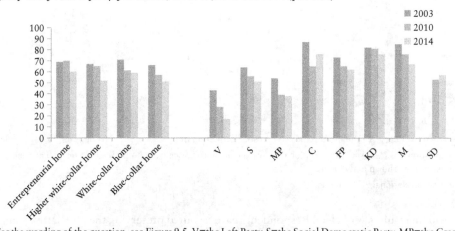

For the wording of the question, see Figure 9.5. V=the Left Party, S=the Social Democratic Party, MP=the Green Party, C=the Centre Party, FP=the Liberal Party, KD=the Christian Democratic Party, M=the Moderate Party, SD=the Sweden Democrats.

Source: The National SOM Survey.

In 2014, there were clear differences between supporters of the various political parties in terms of preserving the monarchy. This is an ideological issue. Followers of the Centre Party (C) and the Christian Democrats (KD) were most likely to be royalists (about three quarters of them), followed by supporters of the Moderate Party (M) (about two thirds of them) and the Sweden Democrats (SD) and the Liberal People's Party (FP) (about 60 per cent). Royalist preferences within the other parties amounted to 50 per cent for the Social Democratic Party (S) and 40 per cent for the Green Party (MP) and less than 20 per cent for the Left Party (VP). Within all parties support for the monarchy was lower in 2014 than in 2003.

Support for Establishing a Republican Form of Government in Sweden

A survey carried out in 1976, in conjunction with the first election held after implementation of the new Instrument of Government and the same year as the King's wedding, showed that a proposal to establish a republican form of government in Sweden had very limited support and that the monarchy was deeply rooted in the consciousness of the Swedish people. Only nine per cent supported the proposal, and nearly 70 per cent were against it (Petersson 1978). However, the response alternatives were associated with the importance of carrying through the proposal: they emphasised the degree of urgency of the matter, not just the principle (see Figure 9.7). This may be assumed to have limited support for the republican proposal to hardcore anti-royalists, who considered it justified in principle as well as a politically pressing issue.

In the national SOM surveys of 2003, 2005 and 2010–13, respondents were asked to respond to the same question posed in the 1976 Election Survey. In the 2003 SOM Survey, the question concerned the proposal to establish a republican form of government in Sweden. It did not, however, mention the urgency of the issue, as had been done in the 1976 Election Survey. In the 2003 survey, support for a republic increased by a few percentage points, amounting to 14 per cent. The proportion of responses against the proposal decreased to just over 60 per cent. In 2011, the proportion of respondents who considered the republican alternative a bad proposal had decreased to about 50 per cent, the uncertain responses had increased to nearly 30 per cent, and the proportion of those in favour had also increased to 20 per cent. During subsequent years, however, the proportion of negative responses has increased once again.

Figure 9.7 The Swedish people's attitudes toward the proposal to establish a republican form of government in Sweden, in 1976, 2003, 2005 and 2010–13 (per cent)

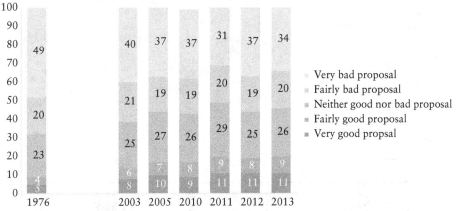

The wording of the question was: 'Below are a number of proposals that have appeared in the political debate. What is your opinion of each of them.' Among them, 'Establishing a republic in Sweden'. The response alternatives are given in the figure. The percentages refer to those who responded to the question. The data for 1976 are from the election survey, whereas those for the other years are from the SOM survey. The response alternatives used in the 1976 election survey were somewhat different from those used in the SOM survey.

Source: The 2003, 2005 and 2010–13 National SOM Survey and the 1976 Election Survey.

The desire to abolish the monarchy says nothing about what the alternative should be. It has been argued that the question of choosing between the monarchy and a republic is essentially meaningless, as republican forms of government may vary from systems with strong presidential power (such as those in the US and France) to systems with a purely representative head of state (such as in Switzerland and Germany). As long as no alternative to the present system has been specified, it is difficult to take sides (Herlitz 1966). The question in the SOM surveys assumes that the choice concerns the method of appointing a head of state with the same constitutionally defined functions as those of the present head of state. However, the question of who is to select the holder of this office was not stated. We cannot rule out that the much-noted presidential elections in other countries, particularly those in the US, have affected opinions on the question of shifting from a monarchy to a republic. From a democratic perspective, following the development over time and within various groups is of great interest.

In the SOM surveys of 1995, 1999–2001, 2003 and 2005–14 the question has concerned establishing a republic with an elected president. The response alternatives, presented on a five-point scale, have ranged from 'a very good proposal' to 'a very bad proposal'. As we see in Figure 9.8, at the beginning of the period, approximately 10 per cent of respondents supported the proposal, whereas almost 70 per cent were against it. The proportion of uncertain responses was 20 per cent; these individuals found the proposal neither 'good nor bad'. At the end of the period, the proportion of respondents who felt that establishing a republic with an elected president was a bad proposal had decreased to 60 per cent, while the proportion of positive responses had increased to 16 per cent. The more recent years have witnessed only minor changes in that response pattern.

Figure 9.8 The Swedish people's attitude toward establishing a republic with an elected president, 1995–2014 (per cent)

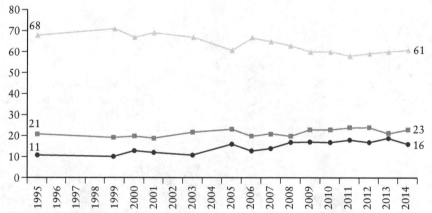

The question was: 'Below are a number of proposals that have appeared in the political debate. What is your opinion of each of them?' 'Establish a republic with an elected president.' The response alternatives were: 'very good proposal', 'fairly good proposal', 'neither a good nor a bad proposal', 'fairly bad proposal' and 'very bad proposal'. In the figure, the categories 'very good' and 'fairly good' as well as the categories 'very bad' and 'fairly bad' have been added. The percentages are based on those who responded to the item.

Source: The National SOM Survey 1995–2014.

According to these surveys, a majority of the Swedish people did not wish to change the form of government and thus rejected the proposal to establish a republic. In all socio-economic groups, a clear majority was against the proposal. This applies to the young and the old, women and men, entrepreneurs, civil servants and blue-collar workers as well as supporters of all of the political parties except the Left Party. This was also true irrespective of education level or rural-versus-urban place of residence. In almost all of the groups, however, support for establishing a republic had increased somewhat since 2003.

In a more detailed analysis, we have studied and controlled for the effects of sex, age, education, subjective class, ideology, membership of the Church of Sweden, and the country in which the respondent grew up. We found a strong effect from ideology as well as from membership of the Church of Sweden: right-wing sympathisers and members of the Church of Sweden held the most negative attitudes toward a republican form of government with an elected president. Women, too, were more negative in their attitudes, whereas those belonging to families of salaried employees, particularly those of higher rank, were more positive. On the other hand, neither age, education nor the country in which the respondent grew up had any significant effect.

A comparison shows that there were slightly more positive responses favouring the republican proposal when the additional reference to an elected president was not included. The proportion of negative responses decreased accordingly, although the differences were small. In addition, it should be noted that different people responded to the two questions. The main result is unaltered, however: Swedish people's support for the proposal to establish a republic is limited, and the majority is against it. Even among people very dissatisfied with democracy in Sweden, there is a majority against the proposal.

Journalists and the Question of Establishing a Republican Form of Government

Authors, publicists and researchers have been active in the debate on the governmental system in Sweden. Already at the beginning of the twentieth century the author August Strindberg published very critical articles about the monarchy and, in 1955, the well-known novelist Vilhelm Moberg published the polemical book, *Why I Am a Republican*, which has since appeared in numerous editions (Moberg 1955). An intense debate followed in the 1960s. In the 1964 book *Skall kungamakten stärkas?* (*Should Royal Power be Strengthened?*), Herbert Tingsten, a leading professor of political science and influential chief editor, criticised the lack of correspondence between the mission of the Government Commission on the Constitution, which was tasked with explicitly stating the parliamentary principle in the Constitution, and the Commission's concrete proposals, which, according to Tingsten, strengthened royal power in relation to what had been applicable law for several decades (Tingsten 1964). In their book *Republiken Sverige* [*The Republic of Sweden*], Par-Erik Back, a professor of political science, and Gunnar Fredriksson, a chief editor, presented a proposal for a republican constitution (Back and Fredriksson 1966). From a conservative perspective, the Government Commission on Constitutional Matters was criticised on the grounds that its proposals could possibly facilitate the shift to a republic, and because it reduced the King to the country's foremost PR man (Heckscher 1963; Herlitz 1963). However, the debate ceased after the Torekov Compromise in 1971 and the new Instrument of Government in 1974.

In recent years, a renewed debate on the form of government has emerged. The Swedish Republican Association has worked out a proposal for a republican constitution for Sweden. In the proposal, two alternatives are proposed, 'one implying that the president is to be appointed by the Parliament and the other that the president is to be elected by citizens in free and general elections' (Einarsson and Svensson 2012). The Swedish Royal Association, however, does its work in relative anonymity.

In a joint book, published in 2010, two of the country's leading publicists separately discuss the arguments for and against monarchy. 'Yes, now is the best time for a monarchy' by Anders Linder, and 'No, the monarchy has never been in more danger' by Per Svensson (Linder and Svensson 2010). That same year, Göran Hägg, a Swedish historian and author, published his book, *Utveckla monarkin* [*Develop the monarchy*] (Hägg 2010).

There is no lack of contributions to the debate, both at present and previously, but what are, in general, Swedish journalists' views on the form of government and the head of state? Journalists' opinions on establishing a republic have differed radically from those of the general public. The 2005 Journalist Survey showed that almost half of journalists favoured the proposal to establish a republican form of government in Sweden, one quarter thought it was a bad proposal, and over a quarter did not express an opinion (Asp 2007).

In the 2011 Journalist Survey, a majority of 54 per cent was in favour of establishing a republic and the difference between the Swedish people and journalists had increased. The balance of opinion was −31 for the general public and +31 for the journalists. Among the general public, only 20 per cent approved of the proposal to establish a republic.

Table 9.2 Swedish journalists' and the Swedish people's views on the proposal to establish a republic in Sweden, in 2011 (per cent and Balance of Opinion)

	Very good	Fairly good	Neither nor	Fairly bad	Very bad	Sum	Balance of opinion	N
Swedish Journalists	33	21	23	11	12	100	+31	1336
Swedish People	11	9	29	20	31	100	−31	1370

For the wording of the question, see Figure 9.7. The response alternatives are shown in the table. The balance of opinion is the proportion of 'very good' and 'fairly good' responses minus the proportion of 'very bad' and 'fairly bad' responses.

Source: The 2011 National SOM Survey and the 2011 Journalist Survey.

Table 9.3 Swedish journalists' and the Swedish people's views on establishing a republic in Sweden by party sympathy, for 2011 (Balance of Opinion and Number)

Party sympathy	Swedish People Balance of opinion	Journalists' Balance of opinion	Swedish people number	Journalists' number
V	22	65	73	201
S	−26	28	366	179

(continued)

Table 9.3 *(Continued)*

Party sympathy	Swedish People Balance of opinion	Journalists' Balance of opinion	Swedish people number	Journalists' number
MP	−4	45	162	534
C	−67	−4	78	51
FP	−21	11	101	97
KD	–	–	38	22
M	−50	−22	474	181
SD	−22	–	78	11
Total	−31	31	1370	1336

V=the Left Party, S=the Social Democratic Party, MP=the Green Party, C=the Centre Party, FP=the Liberal Party, KD=the Christian Democratic Party, M=the Moderate Party, SD=the Sweden Democrats. The balance of opinion is the proportion of 'very good' and 'fairly good' responses minus the proportion of 'very bad' and 'fairly bad' responses. Values for groups with fewer than 50 respondents are not shown.
Source: The 2011 National SOM Survey and the 2011 Journalist Survey.

Journalists' political opinions are clearly to the left of those of the general public, with support for the Green Party predominating (Asp 2012b; see Table 9.3 as well). This influences their opinions on the establishment of a republican form of government in Sweden. Among journalists who supported the left-wing parties and the Green Party, there was a clear preference for a republic, and this preference was somewhat weaker among the Liberal Party supporters. Among journalists who supported the Moderate Party and the Centre Party, those opposing a republic were more numerous than those supporting one. In conclusion, then, where the form of government in Sweden is concerned, journalists are not representative of the Swedish population in general. However, it is a newspaper's political orientation that marks the content of its editorial page, although the monarchy versus republic question has less impact than do other political issues.

Members of Parliament and the Question of Establishing a Republican Form of Government

In the 2014 Swedish National Parliament Survey the question of establishing a republic in Sweden was included for the first time (Karlsson and Nordin 2015), which makes it possible to compare the views of parliamentarians with those of Swedish people in 2013. The response rate was very high at 88 per cent; only for the Swedish Democrats was it lower than it had been previously, at 76 per cent. The results provide a representative picture of the opinion of all of the parliamentarians and members of the different parties.

Support for the proposal to establish a republic in Sweden was much stronger among the parliamentarians than among the Swedish people; there were almost as many in favour as against the proposal. The balance of opinion was only −3 compared to −34 among the Swedish people. However, one quarter of the citizens chose the response alternative 'Neither good nor bad' which received a much lower level of response among the parliamentarians.

Table 9.4 The parliamentarians' and the Swedish people's views on the proposal to establish a republic in Sweden (per cent and Balance Index)

	Very Good	Fairly Good	Neither nor	Fairly Bad	Very Bad	Sum	Balance of Opinion	N
Parliamentarians 2014	24	17	15	11	33	100	−3	275
Swedish People 2013	11	9	26	20	34	100	−34	1370

For the wording of the question, see Figure 9.7. The response alternatives are shown in the table. The balance of opinion is the proportion of 'very good' and 'fairly good' responses minus the proportion of 'very bad' and 'fairly bad' responses.

Source: The 2013 National SOM Survey and The Swedish National Parliament Survey 2014.

Table 9.5 The parliamentarians' and the Swedish people's views on establishing a republic in Sweden by party sympathy (Balance of Opinion and number)

Party sympathy	Parliamentarians' Balance of Opinion	Swedish people Balance of Opinion	Parliamentarians Number	Swedish People Number
V	+100	+20	19	107
S	+51	−33	100	501
MP	+70	−17	23	177
C	−37	−53	19	58
FP	+6	−53	16	86
KD	−100	−69	12	69
M	−71	−49	66	390
SD	−94	−36	35	126
Total	−3	−34	290	1637

V=the Left Party, S=the Social Democratic Party, MP=the Green Party, C=the Centre Party, FP=the Liberal Party, KD=the Christian Democratic Party, M=the Moderate Party, SD=the Sweden Democrats. The 2014 National SOM Survey and the Swedish National Parliament Survey 2014.

All of the parliamentarians of the Left Party were in favour of establishing a republic in Sweden and all representatives of the Christian Democratic Party were against it. Even among the Green Party and the Social Democratic Party, there was a majority in favour of a republic. Among the Liberals, too, there was a positive balance of opinion. Among the other alliance parties there was a clear stand against a republic and the Swedish Democrats were found to be strong royalists as well.

The party programmes of the Left Party and the Social Democratic Party have long included a demand for a republican constitution (Wieslander 1974). The Green Party, too, has clearly sided with the establishment of a republic, proposing a motion to this effect during each of its parliamentary terms. Members of the Liberal Party have proposed such motions as well. In the autumn of 2015, a cross-party motion was proposed by individual members of the Left, Social Democratic, Green and Liberal Parties to set up a committee on abolishing the monarchy. This motion was denied, however in the Riksdagen [The Parliament], (Bill No. 2015/16:717).

Aware as they are of the popular support for the monarchy and the fact that the King only has representative and ceremonial functions, even politicians who favour a different form of government may not be willing to pursue the matter, because doing so could lose votes for their political party. The results of the SOM Survey suggest that, thus far, such an assessment has been correct. Introducing the demand to establish a republic would entail a risk of losing voters, thus reducing political influence in more important matters.

Confidence in the Royal House

Now we turn to respondents' perceptions of the functioning of monarchy and the royal house. Since 1986, confidence in the way various social institutions and groups carry out their duties has been investigated in the SOM surveys. In the first year, the respondents were asked to rate their confidence in 11 institutions. In the most recent survey, 21 institutions were included. Confidence in the royal house was high and stable during the period 1995–98. In 1998, only universities and colleges received higher confidence ratings. Later, confidence in the royal house fell for five years in a row, resulting in a seventh place ranking in 2003. In connection with a state visit to the sultanate of Brunei in February 2004, the King, addressing a press conference, made statements about conditions in Brunei that caused an intense media debate. Responding to a journalist's question about whether meeting and negotiating with a leader accused of being anti-democratic and a brutal ruler were problematic in any way, the King answered by talking about the country's great openness and the close contact between the Sultan and his people. This caused all party leaders, several members of parliament and editorial writers to make critical remarks. The royal house pointed out that the statement had been drawn up by the Foreign Office. In addition, the government was criticised for the way in which the state visit had been planned and carried out. One professor of political science spoke of a constitutional crisis (Petersson 2004).

The 2004 SOM Institute Survey marked a strong decline in the Swedish people's confidence in the royal house. It is difficult to find any explanation for this drop other than the King's statement in Brunei and the subsequent media debate. Following the King's much noted January 2005 speech in connection with the tsunami disaster in East Asia, which led to the death of nearly 550 Swedes, confidence in the royal house then increased for two years in a row. Subsequently, however, the decline in confidence resumed, ending up in 2009 at the same low level it was in 2004, in the wake of the Brunei statement.

Confidence in the royal house increased after the Crown Princess's wedding, resulting in a positive balance of opinion of +19 in 2010. There are, however, considerable differences in confidence in the royal family before and after publication of the critical biography *Carl XVI Gustaf: The Reluctant Monarch* (Sjöberg, Rauscher and Meyer 2010). The book critically examined the royal family's ties to German Nazism prior to and during WWII, as well as the King's lifestyle prior to his succession. Prior to publication of the book in early November, the effect of the wedding had been noticeable, resulting in a balance of opinion of +21, which subsequently dropped sharply to +8.[21] All of the positive effects of the wedding had been wiped out, and confidence in the royal house has remained at a low level. Between 2010 and 2011, confidence in the royal house declined more than in any other social institution, and the more recent attention to the birth and christening of Princess Estelle, heir to the throne, has not had any effect. This result was

---

[21] Up to the publication date of this book (November 5 2010), there had been 3923 responses to the question on confidence in the Royal House. After the publication there were 831 responses.

confirmed by the Media Academy's Barometer (*Medieakademins Fortroendebarometer*) for 2012 and 2013 (Holmberg and Weibull 2012, 2013).

Figure 9.9 The Swedish people's, journalists' and parliamentarians' confidence in the way the royal house carries out its duties (Balance of opinion from +100 to −100)

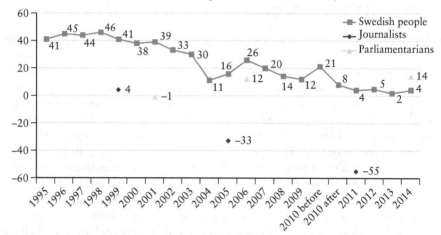

The wording of the question was: 'How great is your confidence in the way the following social institutions and groups (the Royal House) perform their duties?' The response alternatives were: 'very high', 'fairly high', 'neither high nor low', 'fairly low' and 'very low'. The balance of opinion is the proportion of 'very high' and 'fairly high' responses minus the proportion of 'very low' and 'fairly low' responses.
Source: The National SOM Survey for 1995–2014, the Journalist Survey 1999, 2005 and 2011 and the Swedish National Parliament Study 2002, 2006 and 2014.

From being among the top social institutions in the mid-1990s, the royal house now occupies an intermediate level among the 21 institutions examined. Up to and including the year 2009, there was greater confidence in the royal house than in democratically elected – but always more controversial – institutions such as the Parliament, the government, the municipal councils and the European Parliament. In 2010, in the wake of the world financial crisis, confidence in the Parliament and the government increased, causing them to pull ahead of the royal house in the ranking.

In a dimensional analysis, the royal house scores high on the dimension that Holmberg and Weibull refer to as 'the establishment' along with the Church of Sweden, the banks, the top businesses and the armed forces. Of the three power symbols in traditional Swedish society – the throne, the altar and the sword – the throne had consistently been the object of greater confidence than the altar. Since 2011, however, they have been on the same level. There is also a clear and positive relationship between belief in God and church attendance, on the one hand, and confidence in the royal house, on the other.

Journalists and Confidence in the Royal House

Looking at journalists' assessment of their confidence in various social institutions in 1999, the balance of opinion for the royal house was +4. By 2005, it had dropped to −33, which was the lowest value for all of the studied institutions and groups. Considering a comparison between the Swedish people's and journalists' confidence in various social institutions, the royal house shows the most negative discrepancy in assessments made by the two groups (Weibull 2001; Holmberg and Weibull 2006). In the 2011 Journalist Survey, confidence in the royal house had fallen even further, landing at −55 (see Tables 9.6 and 9.7). Of the 13 institutions investigated in the Journalist Survey of 2011, only the banks received lower confidence ratings. Among journalists, 36 per cent had very low confidence, which is clearly the lowest confidence figure for any institution. The youngest, particularly those born in the late 1980s, tended to be less critical. Journalists covering politics and society were less confident than those covering other areas (Weibull 2012).

Table 9.6 Swedish Journalists' and the Swedish people's confidence in the way the royal house carries out its duties, 2011 (per cent and Balance of Opinion)

	Very High	Fairly High	Neither nor	Fairly Low	Very Low	Sum	Balance of Opinion	Number
Swedish Journalists	1	7	29	27	36	100	−55	1370
Swedish People	10	25	35	15	15	100	+5	4150

Source: The 2011 National SOM Survey and the 2011 Journalist Survey.

As noted above, journalists' political sympathies are clearly to the left of those of the general public, with the Green Party predominating (Asp 2012b). This situation also affects confidence in the royal house among journalists. Irrespective of party sympathy, Swedish journalists have a low level of confidence in the way the royal house carries out its duties, with the lowest confidence found among journalists supporting the Left Party and the Green Party. Even for conservative Moderate Party supporters, however, the balance of opinion is negative.

Table 9.7 Swedish journalists' and the Swedish people's confidence in the way the royal house carries out its duties and their Political Party preferences, 2011 (Balance of Opinion)

Party	Journalists, Balance of Opinion	The Swedish People Balance of Opinion	The Swedish Journalists Number	The Swedish People, Number
V	−82	−45	207	227
S	−53	−3	181	1184
MP	−63	−11	541	497
C	−33	+43	53	186
FP	−43	+4	101	287
KD	−	+50	22	123
M	−18	+18	186	1426
SD	−	−6	12	220
Total	−55	+5	1370	4150

V=the Left Party, S=the Social Democratic Party, M=the Green Party, C=the Centre Party, FP=the Liberal Party, KD=the Christian Democratic Party, M=the Moderate Party, SD=the Sweden Democrats.
The balance of opinion is the proportion of 'very high' and 'fairly high' confidence responses minus the proportion of 'very low' and 'fairly low' responses. Values for groups with fewer than 50 respondents are not shown.
Source: The 2011 National SOM Survey and the 2011 Journalist Survey.

In addition, it should be mentioned that confidence in journalists themselves is low. Regional surveys have included questions on the general public's confidence in various professional groups, including journalists. Here, confidence in journalists has been consistently low, with a negative balance of opinion (Nilsson 2010). When the question is differentiated between broadcast journalists and those working in the daily press, confidence in broadcast journalists has consistently been higher (Elliot 1994).

Members of Parliament and Confidence in the Royal House

Previously, parliamentarians have had less confidence in the royal house than the citizens have. In a 2002 research project entitled *Bilder av riksdagen – medborgare och riksdagsledamöter i den representativa demokratin* [*Parliamentary Images – Citizens and Parliamentarians in Representative Democracy*], parliamentarians' confidence in different social institutions was analysed. That year, 30 per cent of all parliamentarians had great or relatively great confidence in the royal house. A comparison of citizens' and parliamentarians' confidence in 21 social institutions revealed that the Swedish people ranked the royal house number four, whereas the parliamentarians ranked it in 18th place, third from the bottom (Brothén 2003). The 2006 Parliament Survey gave a similar picture, where 43 per cent of parliamentarians reported having confidence in the royal house. The citizens ranked the royal house as number seven of the 21 institutions surveyed, whereas the parliamentarians ranked it in 18th place. In 2014, however, confidence was greater among the parliamentarians than among the general public.

Table 9.8 Parliamentarians' and the Swedish people's confidence in the way the royal house carries out its duties 2014 (per cent and Balance of Opinion)

	Very High	Fairly High	Neither Nor	Fairly Low	Very Low	Sum	Balance of Opinion	Number
Parliamentarians	17	27	26	16	14	100	+14	275
Swedish People	9	24	38	14	15	100	+4	5,000

Source: The 2014 National SOM Survey and the Swedish National Parliament Study 2014.

Table 9.9 Parliamentarians' and the Swedish people's confidence in the royal house and political party preferences, 2014 (Balance of Opinion)

Party	Parliamentarians Balance of opinion	The Swedish people Balance of opinion	Parliamentarians number	The Swedish people Number
V	−89	−45	18	303
S	−18	−2	95	1,408
MP	−22	−12	23	396
C	+32	+33	19	320
FP	−28	+16	14	314
KD	+58	+44	12	201

(continued)

Table 9.9 *(Continued)*

Party	Parliamentarians Balance of opinion	The Swedish people Balance of opinion	Parlamentarians number	The Swedish people Number
M	+62	+22	60	1,067
SD	+85	−3	34	442
Total	+14	+4	275	5,000

V=the Left Party, S=the Social Democratic Party, MP=the Green Party, C=the Centre Party, FP=the Liberal Party, KD=the Christian Democratic Party, M=the Moderate Party, SD=the Sweden Democrats.

In parliament, the members of the Left and Green Parties as well as the Liberals had low confidence in the way the royal house performs its duties, while the members of the other alliance parties and the Swedish Democrats had strong confidence in the royal house. There was a much more polarised opinion among the members of parliament than among the people. Within several of the parties there was a great difference between elected members and the electorate.

Members of the Swedish Royal House in a Comparative Perspective

Confidence in the royal house concerns performance, but we will now look at members of the royal house in a comparative perspective. In the European monarchies, opinion polls concerning the position of the monarchy and the popularity of royal personages are carried out reasonably regularly, albeit using different methods and questions (see Roger Mortimore's contribution to this Chapter).

In most monarchies, however, the form of government has long enjoyed widespread support among the general public, particularly in Denmark where the monarchy is in a very strong position (Nilsson 2017). What, then, are the Swedish people's attitudes towards the heads of state in the other European monarchies?

For the 2011 national SOM survey, royalty in four countries were selected: King Carl XVI Gustaf and Crown Princess Victoria of Sweden, Queen Margrethe II of Denmark, King Harald V of Norway and Queen Elizabeth II of Great Britain. The respondents were asked to use a scale to indicate whether they approved or did not approve of these royal figures. The scale has been used since 1986 to assess Swedish politicians.

Table 9.10 The Swedish people's assessments of the popularity of several European royal personages (mean, per cent)

	All Respondents		Monarchists		Republicans		The Individual is not Known to Me
	Mean	Rank	Mean	Rank	Mean	Rank	
Crown Princess Victoria of Sweden	+28	1	+39	1	+3	1	1
Queen Margrethe II of Denmark	+14	2	+22	3	−1	2	12

(continued)

Table 9.10 *(Continued)*

	All Respondents		Monarchists		Republicans		The Individual is not Known to Me
	Mean	Rank	Mean	Rank	Mean	Rank	
King Harald V of Norway	+12	3	+19	4	−1	3	13
King Carl XVI Gustaf of Sweden	+12	3	+24	2	−16	5	1
Queen Elizabeth II of Britain	+4	5	+10	5	−10	4	9

Comment: The survey is based on an 'approval-disapproval' scale, whose values range from −5 to +5. The values were multiplied by 10. The wording of the question was 'This question concerns the extent to which some European Royalties are generally approved of or disapproved of. Using the scale below, where would you place them?'

Practically all respondents were familiar with the Swedish royal family, whereas the sovereigns of the remaining three countries were known by about 90 per cent. Among those rated, Crown Princess Victoria was by far the most popular person. Her value, amounting to +28, was the highest ever for any public personage on record. The Danish, Norwegian and Swedish sovereigns received approximately equal values, between +10 and +15, whereas the Swedish people gave Queen Elizabeth II slightly lower approval scores. Among those in favour of preserving the Swedish monarchy, Carl XVI Gustaf was the second most popular after Crown Princess Victoria. Needless to say, among republicans, the Swedish monarch was the least popular of the assessed royalty. However, even a majority of those in favour of a republican form of government approved of Crown Princess Victoria.

The rating for King Carl XVI was the same as that for the most popular party leader, Fredrik Reinfeldt, in the autumn of 2011; the King was clearly more popular than the remaining party leaders (Holmberg 2012). Assessments of European royalty may also be compared to those of other international leaders. It can be noted that Tarja Halonen, President of Finland at the time of the survey, was known by about 80 per cent of the Swedish public. She received ratings comparable to those for the three Scandinavian sovereigns.

Confidence in the Royal House and Support for the Monarchy

Of what significance, then, is confidence in the royal house for views on the monarchy? Among Swedes who report very great confidence in the way the royal house carries out its duties, over 90 per cent wished to preserve the monarchy. That proportion decreased alongside sinking confidence; among those who reported very low confidence, it was less than 10 per cent. Conversely, the proportion of respondents wishing to abolish the monarchy increased from 1 per cent among those reporting very great confidence to 79 per cent among those reporting very low confidence. Even among respondents reporting fairly low confidence, those wishing to abolish the monarchy were more numerous than those wishing to preserve it. In this group, however, about 30 per cent did not voice an opinion. Attitudes toward the monarchy and willingness to establish a republic are two sides of the same coin. However, the relationship between confidence in the royal house and a desire to establish a republican form of government is weaker. Waning confidence implies being more inclined to want to abolish the monarchy, but doubts regarding establishing a republic remain.

Figure 9.10 Attitudes toward preserving/abolishing the monarchy by confidence in the way the royal house carries out its duties, in 2003, 2010 and 2014 (per cent)

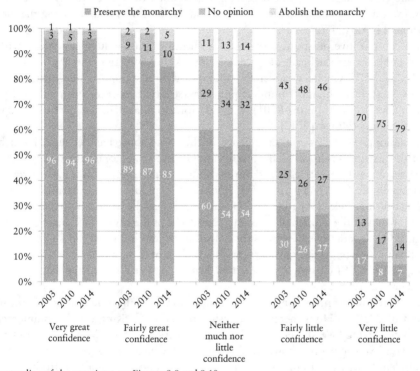

For the wording of the questions, see Figures 9.8 and 9.10.
Source: The National SOM Survey.

Since 1996, the Research Group for Society and Information Studies [*Forskningsgruppen för Samhälls- och Informationsstudier*] (FSI) has followed attitudes toward the Swedish royal house and the Swedish monarchy. The questions and the response alternatives are, however, different from those used in the SOM surveys: 'What is your opinion of the Swedish Royal House?' and 'What is your opinion of the fact that Sweden is a monarchy?' The respondents were asked to respond on a seven-point scale ranging from 'completely negative' to 'completely positive' with a clear middle alternative, 'neither positive nor negative' or 'I know nothing about this'. The main results were the same as those for the SOM surveys: the proportion of respondents who had negative attitudes toward both the royal house and the monarchy increased somewhat, particularly during the period 2005–10 (FSI 2010).[22]

The Swedish People, the Media, the Parliament and the Monarchy

Results from the SOM surveys conducted since 1995 provide a multifaceted picture of the Swedish people's views on the monarchy, the head of state and the royal house. On the principal issue of monarchy-versus-republic, a majority is in favour of preserving the monarchy, whereas only one in five reports wishing to abolish. Likewise, fewer than one in five want to establish a republic, and a majority thinks that changing the form of government is a bad idea.

In a comparative perspective the Swedish head of state is just as popular with the general public as are the heads of state in Denmark, Norway and Finland. In the autumn of 2011, Carl XVI Gustaf was just as popular as the most popular party leader. Crown Princess Victoria is the most popular public person that has ever been assessed in the SOM surveys. In the autumn of 2011, she was more popular than the most admired international leaders (Nilsson 2012).

In the long-term, however, confidence in the royal house has declined. From being one of the institutions in which the Swedish public used to place its greatest confidence – along with universities, colleges and the healthcare system – confidence in the royal house has gradually declined. At present, it is found in the middle of the rankings, along with other institutions belonging to the establishment, such as the banks, major businesses, the armed forces and the Church of Sweden. Confidence in the royal house has been strongly influenced by specific events such as the King's statement in Brunei, his speech following the tsunami disaster, the Crown Princess's wedding and the publication of the critical biography *Carl XVI Gustaf: The Reluctant Monarch*. The effect of these events became very clear in 2010.[23]

At a much-noted press conference in connection with the annual moose hunt in the autumn of 2010 on Hunneberg, a Swedish mountain, the King briefly commented on the debate, saying 'We should turn the page and look ahead' (Magnusson and Ström 2010). The Swedish people, however, did not turn the page. In the long-term, a low level of confidence affects attitudes toward the monarchy and the possible introduction of a republic.

Very few people ever have direct contact with the head of state, and thus the image of the monarchy and the royal house is conveyed by the media. This means that journalists constitute a link between the general public and representatives of the monarchy. However, regarding attitudes toward establishing a republican form of government,

---

[22] At different points in time, various public opinion institutes have posed the same question as the SOM surveys concerning whether the monarchy in Sweden should be preserved or abolished. However, the different survey methodologies used, particularly concerning methods of reporting responses from those who lack an opinion, make it difficult to directly compare these studies to the results from the SOM surveys (Nilsson 2012).

[23] In this contribution the focus is on the years in which data makes it possible to compare the perceptions of the Swedish people, journalists and parliamentarians, but for the attitudes towards the monarchy and establishing a republic the results are almost identical with the situation in 2014. However the confidence in the royal house has gradually increased after 2014 and in 2018 the balance of opinion was +20.

as well as confidence in the royal house, journalists' opinions deviate greatly from those of the Swedish people. Among journalists, there is a majority in favour of establishing a republic, and confidence in the royal house is very low.

At present, the elected members of the Swedish Riksdag, the Parliament, have greater confidence in the way the royal house carries out its duties than the electorate does, but almost as many want to change Sweden into a republic as do not.

The limited confidence in the royal house seen among the Swedish people and above all among journalists constitute potential threats to the monarchy, as does the rather strong support for establishing a republic among parliamentarians and journalists. However, this has not been a problem as long as support for the monarchy has been widespread in the general public.

9.5. THE MONARCHY, 'POPULARITY', LEGITIMACY AND THE MEDIA

Jean Seaton, Professor of Media History, University of Westminster

The Royal Touch

David Nott, a remarkable British surgeon who since his twenties has worked during his vacations in war zones – operating under fire, with inadequate equipment – became a British hero during the war in Syria. When he came back to the ordinary complaints of ordinary patients in London he began to collapse. His diminishing capacity to cope was exposed when he was invited to a private lunch at Buckingham Palace by the Queen, who sat him next to her (the Palace has its ears to the ground). The Queen asked him where he had come from. Wildly he wondered if Hammersmith might be what she was politely asking, but he replied 'Aleppo'. 'Oh' he recounts her Majesty saying, 'What was that like?'

Nott's mind 'filled with images of dust, of crushed school desks, of bloodied and limbless children, of … aid workers horribly executed'. He was on the verge of weeping uncontrollably. The Queen looked at him quizzically and touched his hand. Accounts of the royal touch are very rare. But – like everything to do with monarchy they are also symbolic and important. The Queen's body is seen in quite a unique way. Her Majesty called a footman. A silver box was produced. 'These', her Majesty said, 'are for the dogs'. She broke a biscuit in half, gave one bit to Nott and they both fed the corgis. 'There' said her Majesty. 'That's so much better than talking isn't it?'(Nott 2019)

This might have turned into a bitter diatribe by a brave man railing against the ridiculousness of the monarchy. But that was not his reaction at all. It moved and helped him. The story was highlighted across the press and in all of the interviews with Nott. Why? The anecdote combines the myth and the normal, the absurdity and the compassion, the person and the fable. The 'royal touch' and its capacity to cure ailments was first used and claimed by Edward the Confessor in the eleventh century, and was a feature of the French and English monarchies. In a modern version, the Queen deployed it early in her reign by visiting a leper camp to dispel prejudice; Princess Diana used it equally powerfully to alter public attitudes towards AIDS patients (Pimlott 2012: 12). The royal touch has power. The Queen's body (and touch) remains a peculiar aspect of monarchical power.

Yet the intrusiveness of modern cameras have broached personal space. The fragility of the royal person has a special poignancy in the UK as we watch the moving lesson in gracious mortality she seems to be offering her people. As Sam Knight wrote in a recent piece about what would happen when Her Majesty died, 'The bond between sovereign and subjects is a strange and mostly unknowable thing. A nation's life becomes a person's, and then the string must break' (Knight 2017). As far as one can see the royal touch worked for David Nott. And we know of the power because it has been told.

Monarchy Needs the Media

Communication industries are seen as trivial, vulgar, raucous but irrelevant to more serious issues like 'the Constitution' or 'power' or 'public opinion'. Indeed, political scientists and historians often seem to think there is something shameful in even thinking about 'the media'. This is interesting in itself – and wrong. For no power exists without the means of its projection. Where does the monarchy's legitimacy come from? Public *interest* in the monarchy is the fuel that makes its 'real', serious role possible. You cannot separate the projection and the institution. If the monarchy – according to Bagehot the 'dignified' part of the constitution – is there to 'excite and preserve the reverence of the population', then the ways in which the monarchy is communicated and built into citizens' lives is not separate from the 'efficient parts ... those by which it, in fact, works and rules'. Though even Bagehot argued that they were not 'separable with microscopic accuracy' (Bagehot 1867: 7).

The central paradox is that without the megaphoning of the media, the power of the monarchy fades. The public need to feel an attachment to the monarchy. How can that be maintained – except by public exposure? But the need to feed the monster of publicity and the relentless attention may be damaging for those living in the spotlight. Public 'interest' can be collusive, limiting and self-deluding. There is also a direct link between the performative aspects of monarchy (the fun weddings and the 'happy' families) and the still mysterious ceremonial roles. Yet the institution also needs to be examined and challenged if it is going to survive. The monarchy needs to be reported and questioned. Press secretaries need to like the press. What the public are at times 'interested in' and the 'public interest' can be at odds.

There is not one public but many. Each of these different groups and their attitudes are in part also the product of the media's portrayal of the monarchy. Images, myths, and the framing of stories evolve and change (as do the roles and issues of the monarchy). It is somewhere in the nexus between the soppy, sentimental, nasty, invasive, and hard-headed reporting of the institution and what people think about it that the elusive power lies. The communication is not then separate but integral to the institution itself. There is some kind of battle: that is how it is experienced from inside. So charting the relationships between royal press secretaries and the media is part of the history of the monarchy.

The monarchy has already navigated some of the issues that now seem peculiarly topical to the contemporary media. Private individuals share their most intimate experiences on Facebook and 'curate' their images on Instagram: what is a private life? How are selves composed? The Palace is expert in this dangerous new world.

And fascinatingly, the character, interests, feelings and work ethic of the royal family matter *constitutionally*. The Palace is a functioning and alert bit of the Constitution, yet it works with and projects the human variability and fallibility of real people. You cannot separate public approbation and interest from the individuals concerned. Moreover, the coverage cannot just be turned off. So royal players have to be seen, but a zone of private reality has to be protected. How do royal families relate to the intrusive but necessary coverage they produce? It is like a hall of mirrors: they do things; they project a story and a self; it is reflected and distorted back to them. All lives are performances. Royal lives are performed from birth.

As Ben Pimlott observed in his biography of the Queen, writing about the monarchy was fascinating 'because of the human drama of a life so exceptionally privileged, and so exceptionally constrained; and partly because of the obsession with royalty of the British public, of which I am a member.' It meant that his book was 'about the Queen in people's heads as well as at Buckingham Palace' (Pimlott 2012: 144). When he began his biography of the Queen, he did so against a background of disdain and hostility to the monarchy. For the first time this came both from the right (Mrs Thatcher's reinvigorated conservatism saw the monarchy as 'wet' and part of the enfeebled establishment) and the left – (which had historically dismissed the monarchy as trivial). There were other problems – the monarchy, having proclaimed its role as a 'model' family, was found to be as dysfunctional as most families. The tabloid press displayed this contradiction in salacious detail.

However, in the nineties a new kind of 'left' thinking, led by Tom Nairn's book took the monarchy seriously as a psychological problem. The UK, he argued, was deluded by the glamour of backwardness, and the monarchy was central to this (Nairn 1988: 46). Nairn's barely suppressed anger and excoriating prose (any human decency displayed by royalty was just 'taboo-supported niceness') was also a defence of Scottish nationalism. For Nairn, the monarchy was part of the impediment to the UK becoming a 'modern' country.

Yet 'popularity' was not the only measure of success: in the 1980s the monarchy was not *unpopular*. However, in the words of Ben Pimlott, 'It lost its previous immunity ... the tinsel adulation that accompanied the 1981 wedding (of Charles and Diana) dissolved. It was replaced by a fascinated lip-smacking envy and lust'. The 'ravening' media of the 1980s (and perhaps the ravening public) took its toll: 'Media hunger had turned the bemused, half resisting, half co-operating, ill equipped dynasty into a circus', and brought it close to the point when the only remaining possibility was outright rejection (Pimlott 2012: 502). However, the institution can also recover. The Palace reformed and attended to the problems. Money, marriages and feelings were tackled. After all, the Queen, speaking as a 'grandmother' on television to the nation, mastered and calmed the wrought hysteria of the days after the tragic death of Princess Diana. The acres of royals were trimmed, Prince William and Prince Harry got jobs and they married women resilient to the oppressive intrusions of the media.

The Queen (seen in the 80s as 'frumpy') is now seen as – and indeed *is* – the most elegantly attired nonagenarian in the world, with her own in-house designer. She is also the most hard working. Dresses matter because they feed the media of the day with direct images. No political historian of the reign of Elizabeth I would ignore the immense symbolic and personal importance of the Queen's attire, which both explained and projected her majesty, her virginity, or even her state's omniscience (one famous picture has her in a dress embroidered with eyes). Dresses matter now because they are a means of projecting similarity (royals buy dresses in shops, like you do) and glamour (royals buy dresses in shops of which you could not dream, but of which you approve). A relationship that is direct for half the public (women) can still tell a national story (the UK has an economically important fashion industry and the reach of its soft power as a fashion incubator is wide) and is part of the spectacle of fascination. Without the aid of sumptuary laws to control celebrities' conspicuous consumption there is now a competitive world of image sellers: but monarchies still have an advantage because of their precarious but all important relationship to nations. Thus, being popular again gave the British monarchy greater power. Public opinion shifted because things changed – but it has swung before and will swing again. The monarchy has to use the upswings to reform as a bulwark against the inevitable downswings.

The Media's New Business Models

There is no such thing as 'the media'. Any catch-all phrase that assigns the *Financial Times, Hello Magazine, Mail Online, News of the World*, the *BBC* and *Huffington Post*, and now any number of social media and Facebook pages to the same shared circle of purgatory is absurd. The different aspects of the media play different roles. They differentially represent and shape public opinion in all of its many forms as well.

Understanding the financial systems that different areas of the media live within really matters: media publications and the monarchy are both haplessly shaped by these systems. From the 1960s, tabloid papers found themselves beaten by the UK's public service broadcasters in reporting hard news. They discovered that 'celebrities' were cheaper than news, accumulated circulations more successfully and so maintained advertising revenue. Royal coverage became a staple, and a driver of circulations (see Seaton and Curran 2018). The financial viability of the popular press depended on this kind of content. It was not simply wilful or nasty (though it was sometimes cruel, often but not always untruthful, frequently intrusive and absurd): it was necessary to the survival of these publications, and unconstrained by regulation they felt free to do anything. Kelvin Mackenzie, the editor of the *Sun*, would say to his staff: 'give me a Sunday for Monday splash about the Royals. Don't worry if it is not true' (Chippendale and Horrie 1990: 106).

A shift was accentuated by changes in ownership. Rupert Murdoch's economic model was to have an upmarket paper to influence elite opinion, a popular newspaper to herd audiences and wider opinion and television channels to make money (See Davies 2009; Seaton and Curran 2018: 120–240). The monarchy hunt was unleashed as Murdoch, a republican, was resistant to the lures and honours of the establishment. The combination of a vindictive and prurient mood, a press struggling for circulation and the economic rewards of catching public attention drove the popular press into a new cycle of attention grabbing exposés.

The *News of the World*, the *Sun*, the *Daily Mirror* and the *Daily Mail* (as the Leveson Inquiry showed) began investing heavily in buying stories, bribing, stealing, hacking phones and computers to acquire what had become the main driver of revenue. Leveson concluded that 'There has been a recklessness in prioritising sensational stories, almost irrespective of the harm the stories may cause and the rights of those who would be affected' (Douglas 2012; Leveson 2012). The Palace played a significant part in bringing this illegal, intrusive, and degrading industrial practice to some kind of end. In 2007 the former *News of the World* royal editor Clive Goodman and the private investigator Glen Mulcaire were jailed after being arrested for a trivial story (about Prince William's knee), which the Palace reported to the police. This was a public service, and was a sign of the monarchy's new ability to control the relentless coverage. It was also driven by the intent to create a private space in which to live for the fallible humans at the centre of the hue and cry.

The broadsheets still do some reporting, despite dramatically declining revenues. The business model has collapsed because social media have provided their content for free and usurped their advertising revenues. Nevertheless, they are still vital in setting agendas, including for the broadcasters. However, the broadsheets, released from deference, have often found serious reporting of the monarchy hard to pitch. The *Guardian* adhered to the left-wing view that the monarchy was irrelevant. But in reporting Prince Charles's 'black spider' letters to ministers, it held the monarchy to account. The *Independent* (now only online) began by proudly claiming it would not report on the monarchy, while Murdoch's *Times* and *Sunday Times* opined a good deal about how the monarchy needed to be reformed, and argued that the 'show business side' (which the *News of the World* and the *Sun*, owned by the same proprietor, was promoting) ought to be curtailed. Only the *Times* by the 2020s manages an all too rare combination of lightness of touch with a real understanding of the role of ceremony and history.

Broadcasters: The BBC

If the monarchy, embodied in the Queen, has been the visible guardian of the Constitution, the BBC has been one of the non-visible guardians. Indeed, the monarchy and the BBC have in some ways rather similar roles. Their task, in the words of Sam Cohen (the brilliant press secretary in the 2000s), is 'to take the temperature of the country' and to 'be vigilant to the mood of the people' (Seaton 2012: 302). The BBC and the monarchy share a predicament: to represent the whole nation to itself, including the audiences and groups that are not necessarily powerful, loud, fashionable or of interest to advertisers. There is a geographical aspect to all of this as well: Scotland and Wales, Northern Ireland and English regions are more positively on the maps of the BBC and the monarchy than that of political and economic elites. They both go to them more and have bases in them.

But there has been a paradox: one of the institutions the BBC was there to scrutinise was the monarchy, yet from the very start it has also been charged with voicing the monarchy's functions. In the case of the fraying marriages of the royal children in the 1980s, the BBC failed. Yet this delicacy left the field open to the wolves of the tabloids. By the 1980s the BBC's 'special relationship' with the monarchy was also under competitive threat. Alastair Burnet, the ITN presenter, had developed a closer relationship with the Prince and Princess of Wales. In contrast, Princess Diana's post-divorce interview with Martin Bashir on the BBC was more a confessional than a normal interview, and was watched by a vast worldwide audience.

Later, however, the BBC's coverage of Princess Diana's funeral was perfectly pitched, quiet and considerate. The newsroom chose to relay the public wave of clapping that rolled in from the public screenings in parks that greeted Earl Spencer's speech about his sister. That critical, guilt-ridden, spontaneous eruption was a news event and by including it, the BBC helped resolve the week's tide of emotion.[24] The BBC has often got its coverage of royal affairs wrong. Yet, like the monarchy itself, it has a duty to the whole nation, not just the loud, powerful and rich parts of it. Other broadcasters changed the terms of broadcasts about royal events, but none has as complex a relationship to the monarchy as the BBC.

Viral Social Media

There is, however, a new disruptive way of communicating which is affecting (and will affect) perceptions of the monarchy and its role. The internet and social media are reengineering the world of opinion, behaviour, consumption, politics and social relations in a massive experimental revolution in which profits are derived from attention, and in which the model of viral advertising re-orders everything. The algorithms that monetise online communication supply consumers with more of what they know they like. It is a very damaging model in encouraging discussion about anything collective or important. It takes the tabloid stoking of feeling and righteous indignation for profit to a new level. This time it is the system (not Kelvin MacKenzie) that is the problem.

On one side people 'like' and share things they approve of with people that are 'friends': communication is privatised. It gives the Palace an independent platform which it can use unmediated by 'the media' and the tabloids. The Palace Instagram account, therefore, becomes a potential independent communications force (those dresses again!). Thus, there are advantages to the new media world. However, the architecture of social media means that online communities form very quickly, talk to each other, reinforce like-minded views, and can be extraordinarily vehement and abusive. It is as if people had become their own *News of the World*, normalising outrage, self-righteous indignation, identification and outright hostility to other groups. New 'Kate versus Meghan' groups are forming in this online universe (see Shea 2018; Madormo). They are not pleasant places.

These new media forms, by their very structure, push opinion to extremes. The modern monarchy is not comfortable with extremes. It has become effectively a social democratic instrument, but it must come under pressure from both the rising divisions in society and the virulence of contemporary discourse online. Moreover, leaving the EU has put the UK Union under threat from all sides. How does the monarchy (which somehow unites us) manage this sudden potential dissolution, and what does it say about it to whom, when the media and opinion is so divided? How, indeed, does the monarchy 'manage' the public discussion of its role in the constitutional crisis that is under way?

---

[24] See Seaton 2016 ch 6, which covers a much wider period of BBC and royal coverage.

Then, as if all of that – mediated through silos of opinion and extreme nationalism in the social media world – were not enough, social media has proved to be very easily manipulated. This is not to argue that everything is formed by the media – people have real problems and real discontents. However, these material-based views are peculiarly susceptible to manipulation that is invisible to users. It is not merely that opinion clusters form, but that more personal beliefs crystallise faster and are more resistant to moderation. People 'feel' that they have personal beliefs – even when they have been formed externally by persuasion and targeting.

Typology

Can we crudely typologise the characteristics of monarchical-media relations, taking into account some version of the message the Palace has sought to project – the image and strategy that has guided the monarchy and the 'media' reaction? There have been several large shifts that characterise the longer history of the monarchy, such as the emergence of a 'welfare monarchy' (see Chapter 6). However, it was the *public understanding and admiration* for this shift that made it useful: without the pictures of the monarchs being charitable, the power would have drained away. Another might be how monarchies relate to the recent industrialisation of celebrity culture. It is a crowded market. Yet the UK Monarchy still commands international as well as national attention on a different scale. The paradoxical answer is that monarchs relate to nations: they are different from celebrities because they are royal. The media of the time also needs to be part of the thinking. Pimlott began this typology in the 1990s, but perhaps it can be developed as follows:

Time	The Royal Message.	The Royal/Media Relationship
1950s – 60s.	The Model Family.	The Age of Shintoism

During this period, criticising the monarchy was risky and indeed taboo. The press was controllable, by habit and deference, and television democratised access to state ceremonies (for example the coronation).

1960s – 70s.	Hard Working Modern Professionals.	The Age of Royal Exposure

The Richard Cawston BBC TV Series, *The Royal Family* (when a cautious exploration of the real constitutional work of the Queen and her family became a worldwide hit) was a deliberate attempt by the Palace to show the professional, behind the scenes work of the monarchy. However, by portraying the royal family as real people with character and wit, it broke down a barrier. David Attenborough observed at the time, 'once the tribespeople had seen inside the Headman's hut the mystery would go' (Seaton 2016: 179). It has never been released in full since it was originally shown. The press began to change tone. TV was dominant but was still governed by public service values.

| 1980s. | Fresh, Popular, Glamorous Royalty. | The Age of Stardom |

With the arrival of Princess Diana, the monarchy became glamorous and a trend-setter of fashion. However, the press model had changed. As well as relentlessly attacking Prince Charles, it developed an exploitative relationship with Diana. The press fabricated stories and stole pictures. The monarchy was pursued mercilessly by the press for commercial gain; broadcasting remained important.

| Mid-1980s. | Defensive. | The Age of Pillorying and Ridicule |

Royal marriages fell apart and so did earlier images of the royal family. Royal attempts to use their celebrity value for charitable purposes were occasionally ridiculous, such as the case of the TV game show, *It's a Royal Knock Out*. The rat-a-tat-tat of revelations left little room for real lives at the centre. A new, fashionable form of republicanism developed – Sir David Hare said of the monarchy 'We shall mock them till they wish they had never been born'. This culminated in the *annus horribilis* of 1992 (when Windsor Castle suffered a great fire). The press took the lead not just in prurient intrusiveness into royal feelings but also in holding royal finances to account.

The tabloid press was in the lead. Television remained more balanced.

| 1997. | Diana Princess of Wales Dies (hounded to her death). | The Age of Feeling |

The fortnight after the tragic death was dominated by a national wave of irrational feelings and strange (and indeed troubling) punitiveness. There was a genuine anxiety about public reaction to Diana's death: 'How do you *feel?*' became the only valid media question. But then the Queen's televised speech to the nation, 'as a grandmother' changed the mood. However, there was real insecurity about the capacity of the institution to command public respect.

| 1997–2007. | Getting On With the Job: Green, Useful, 'Normal' People. | The Age of the Right to Intrude |

The most interesting aspect of Palace strategy was not visible in the press because it was aimed at creating a 'private' space for the new generation of royal actors. It involved carefully crafted moments, such as William and Kate's staged 'break up' and getting all the bile out about the Middletons early. There was significant reform: royal finances and royal households were reformed, and the size of the royal family was in effect reduced to key players.

This culminated in a more secure monarchy, with rising levels of public approval, making the first moves against illegitimate intrusion by the tabloid press by taking the *News of the World* to court. This was about re-establishing fair terms (in reality for the public) with the press.

However, this was all designed to deal, as monarchies must, with the private and personal and intimate lives of the players.

2007–18.	Mirroring Modern Britain Back to Itself.	The Age of Inclusive and Diverse Modernity

This period saw the emergence of new players and new stories to tell (about contemporary issues that resonate with the public – mental health, the environment, the Invictus games, bringing up children and grief). Prince William was palpably modest and good at relating to people. It is striking how much of all the reinvention, beginning in this period, has depended on female bodies: new female players, and women who are suitable royal consorts not because they are virgins (as in any previous age of royal wives) but because they have developed the capacity to deal with the media. This period culminated in the wedding of Prince Harry to Meghan Markle, with a gospel choir, a black preacher, and a distinguished young black British cellist. The Queen began a Twitter account; new forms of media are used. The Palace has been more front-footed in beginning to confront media intrusions, such as in the case of online trolling. Television has been important, and has brought a series of ceremonies to a world audience (including the centenary of the end of the First World War). Tabloids continue to stoke division.

2019-?.	The Monarchy Represents the Nation.	The Politics of Political Scandal and Division

Social media, Instagram, chat rooms (some on the dark web). The Press and TV still matter.

For the first time a serious constitutional attack (on the judges and representative democracy, extremists leading both main political parties, and pressures that seem likely to dissolve the Union) has put the political and constitutional role of the monarchy in the spotlight, not personal lives. This has been hard to manage for the Palace. Although social media provides the Palace with an independent voice, this is difficult and improper to use on any except the most accepted parts of the royal job. So, how will it explain its constitutional role? On the other hand, a far wider range of issues have become politicised in new culture wars, so maintaining impartiality will be much harder (see Chapter 4.3). The personal loyalty to the Queen – the *cordon sanitaire* around attacking her – may not pass to the next monarch.

The Monarchy and the New Media Landscape: Protocol Matters

In 2018 President Trump, during an awkwardly crafted visit to the UK, went to see the Queen. A tea and photo opportunity, which Her Majesty apparently hosted without any supporting cast of royal family, was laid on at Windsor Castle. All the king's horses and all the king's men lined up. As the President and the Queen inspected the guard, President Trump strode ahead of the sovereign, thus breaking protocol. Her Majesty – the cameras suddenly zoomed in – a sprightly 93 year old (with no stick) chatting amiably, broke into a trot on a tight corner and got right out ahead of him again. That's our girl, we thought. Protocol in that moment seemed less a fusty thing and more, well, useful. Later during the state visit in 2019 there were no protocol errors, and the Queen was shown warmly chatting to President Trump with every sign of finding it interesting. As it undoubtedly was, getting her measure of the man. The Queen has met every US President since Franklin Roosevelt.

If the popular power of the monarchy comes from being peculiarly chosen by the public as 'special' (sacrificed one might say – though sacrificed with a lot of Givenchy thrown about the shoulders), then the communication of that chosen-ness has to be continually rehearsed. What is different about the monarchy is that it does not present itself *to be* chosen, but is just there. It has a thousand years of history backing up this sense, whilst the Queen has reached a grandly panopticon position in the national family. This 'specialness' is played out in the power to make people, their condition and problems feel known. The sense that monarchy can bring of watching, listening and attending to the mood and temper of the nation has never been more important. This may be the key power to concentrate on, an enduring strength. This is a story that has to be told locally, as well as nationally, which is a challenge when the local media have all but collapsed.

However, 'trust' in all institutions is collapsing. This is not solely a UK problem. What started out as a cheeky lack of deference (which felt democratic) has turned into a flood of deliberate disinformation and a sharing of this as misinformation. The monarchy cannot be immune. This uncertainty has destabilised democracy; the social media algorithms have helped to stoke divisive politics. Are attitudes towards the monarchy – until now a stabilising force – invulnerable to such interference?[25]

External and hostile forces seek deliberately to destabilise secure values and institutions using social media. Clint Watts shows that mere uncertainty is enough to change minds and undermine institutions (Watts 2018). Attitudes towards the monarchy, facts and beliefs are presumably targets for such subversion. The institutional structure that has supported the modern representative monarchy is under severe strain. The UK press, struggling to retain any advertising revenue, has become more shrill and partisan as the personal sensationalism that drove earlier royal coverage has been replaced by political sensationalism, unhinged from reality.

The point of the monarchy has been the nation, but the Union is now more insecure than ever. And after years of a relatively symbolic role in the nation, the Palace may be asked to make real constitutional decisions. Is the Palace impartial about threats to democracy? They are doing this against an unprecedented background of conspiracies, uncertainty, division and misinformation fed by disinformation: quickly metabolised by likes on Facebook and Instagram into your best friend's personal view.

If scandals used to be about frocks and relationships, they are going to be about politics and the Constitution for the foreseeable future.

9.6. CONCLUSIONS

Professor Robert Hazell, Constitution Unit, University College London

A hereditary monarchy is an anachronism in a modern democracy, based upon the principles of equality, and government of the people, by the people and for the people. It is a

---

[25] There is excellent and important research emerging on this – See Moore 2018; Bartlett 2018; and an important report from King's College Media Power Centre, Ramsay and Robertshaw 2019.

paradox which requires explanation and justification. The main justification is that, from the polling evidence, monarchy as an institution clearly still commands – with some variations – enviable levels of general popular support.

Pollsters have suggested that a person's support for the monarchy is a value, not an opinion or an attitude; and as such it is well established and not easily swayed. Support has remained consistently high in most countries, but in others has been more volatile. Support for the monarchy in Sweden has declined in recent years, and Spain has shown big short-term movements in support. The fluctuations in these countries suggest that support is affected by specific events; in Sweden, the King's visit to Brunei, his tsunami speech, and publication of a highly critical biography in 2010; in Spain, the 1981 coup, King Juan Carlos's elephant hunting trip in Botswana, the Nóos corruption scandal involving his son-in-law, and recent allegations that Juan Carlos himself received commission on Saudi contracts.

Jean Seaton vividly describes how the pursuit of the royals by the British tabloid press turned into a witch-hunt. Royal stories sell, however trivial, however false; as do royal photos, however intrusive. But the Spanish case illustrates the proper role of the press in holding the monarchy and royal family to account: the corruption allegations are serious, and King Juan Carlos's son-in-law Inaki Urdangarin is serving a six year prison sentence. The Swedish examples on the other hand show how the monarch can be tripped up by seemingly minor off-the-cuff remarks: diplomatic praise for the Sultan of Brunei on a state visit, and an expressed wish to 'turn the page' when interviewed about the critical biography. To foreign observers neither response seems a major blunder, but the polls showed a sharp fall in confidence in both cases, from which the Swedish monarchy has not recovered (see Figures 9.3 and 9.4).

It is not surprising that, faced by a sharply critical press watching for every false move, the monarchy and their minders have resorted to very tight media management, vetting every phrase in every speech lest it be misinterpreted or taken out of context. The risk is that in so doing royal speeches become bland and uninteresting, and they fail to connect with the public. But different countries seem to allow different degrees of latitude: in Norway the King has made bold statements welcoming foreigners and minorities (see Chapter 8.4), which in Denmark (or in Britain, or the Netherlands) might not be tolerated by right-wing politicians, or sections of the media.

Helle Krunke points to another risk, which is the difficulty of the monarchy being seen to make a useful contribution, while remaining politically neutral (see Chapter 4.3). In an increasingly politicised world, with growing nationalism, identity politics and culture wars, the monarchy is always liable to be criticised. But the solution proposed by some, that the monarchy should be reduced to a purely ceremonial role, is unlikely to remove the criticism. It is noteworthy that Sweden is the one country where the monarch has no political role, but the monarchy is less popular than in all the other countries, save for Spain.

This suggests that the public are not bothered by the monarch still playing a political role, so long as the monarch is responsive to the balance of forces in parliament and observes the conventions. The Easter crisis in Denmark in 1920, and the fate of Grand Duchess Marie-Adélaïde of Luxembourg and King Leopold III of Belgium show what happens when the monarch oversteps the mark politically. What matters is the performance of the individual monarch; popular support has to be regained in each reign, and within the same reign it may have to be periodically renewed. So monarchs have to be perpetually vigilant: one stray remark, one misstep can be held against them for years to come. And in the modern media age it is the image of the monarchy that matters, as much as what they say or what they do: literally in the sense of what they wear (see Jean Seaton on royal dress), and in the carefully staged official photos of the royal family as the model family. Monarchies need the media to publicise what they do; but they cannot control, and do not always welcome, the coverage they get.

Part IV

Conclusions

10

Towards a New Theory of European Monarchy

ROBERT HAZELL AND BOB MORRIS, THE CONSTITUTION UNIT, UNIVERSITY COLLEGE LONDON

INTRODUCTION

A T FIRST SIGHT, the survival of monarchy in some of the world's most advanced democracies seems puzzling. Reliance on a principle of heredity to select a head of state in what is effectively a genetic lottery hardly seems a discriminating and logical system. Isn't monarchy the very antithesis of democracy and its persistence somehow an irregularity which needs to be explained away? As Robert Blackburn has put it: 'Monarchy is essentially a creature of the past and at some point in the future is very likely to collapse' (Blackburn 2006: 139). Others, however, differ: 'In the modern world, constitutional monarchy and democracy are complementary rather than conflicting notions' (Bogdanor 2003).

This chapter attempts to explain the paradox that an ancient, hereditary institution has survived into the modern age, and identify the political mechanisms responsible. The monarchies fall broadly into three historical groups: the older monarchies of Denmark, Norway, Sweden and the UK; the post-Napoleonic settlement monarchies of Belgium, Luxembourg and the Netherlands; and the monarchy of Spain restored in 1976, after almost half a century of authoritarian rule.

All these monarchies, ancient and modern, have witnessed a growing gap between the formal political power conferred on them by the constitution, and the actual power they wield in reality. Allowing their political power to shrink virtually to zero has been the secret of their survival. And as their political power has shrunk, new roles justifying their existence have emerged. After the Second World War the monarchy played an important role in helping countries rebuild, not in the material sense, but rebuilding their sense of nationhood, through the monarchy's classic role of representing unity and national identity, as well as its ceremonial and welfare role, discussed later in this chapter.

What follows revisits the research questions running through this book, about the monarch's constitutional and political role; how much autonomy monarchs enjoy in the exercise of their different functions; how the monarchy is defined and regulated; and the limits to the size of the royal family, and its finances. We then conclude by examining the legitimacy of the monarchy, its unique characteristics and value, the risks and threats it faces, and what lessons may be distilled for the benefit of monarchs and their advisers.

REDUCTION OF THE MONARCH'S CONSTITUTIONAL AND POLITICAL ROLE

Only in Sweden does the monarch have a purely ceremonial role, and the Constitution matches the political reality. This is exemplified in the way the monarch opens parliamentary sessions, but it is the Prime Minister who delivers the speech on the government's programme. The most striking thing in all the other constitutions is how powerful the monarch appears to be, in the formal text of the constitution, as we explained in Chapter 2.

Any stranger reading the Danish constitutional text without getting into detail would gain the impression that the King runs the country. But in Denmark, and the other monarchies, the text has become heavily overlaid with conventions which constrain the monarch to act only on the advice of the government, often through the requirement of a ministerial countersignature to all the monarch's formal acts. This has been achieved in the different countries by formal changes to the constitution, or in legislation, or by changing political conventions, or a combination of these; in all cases the consequence has been a gradual reduction of monarchical power.

Sweden has gone the furthest, in reducing the monarch to a purely ceremonial role in 1974. And in other countries the erosion continues, with further reductions just in the last decade. In Luxembourg the Grand Duke has lost the power to assent to the laws made by parliament; in the UK the Queen has lost the prerogative power to dissolve Parliament.

Yet the monarch still remains the ultimate guardian of the constitution, whose role in an emergency is to safeguard democratic and constitutional values. The most dramatic illustration of that was in Spain in 1981, when King Juan Carlos helped to foil an attempted coup d'état by the Civil Guard. There was a similar episode in Norway, when in 1940 King Haakon VII told his Cabinet that he would rather abdicate than appoint Quisling as head of a new government prepared to collaborate with the invading German forces. A less dramatic example occurred in Denmark in 1993, when the Prime Minister wished to hand over to a Conservative successor, but the new Prime Minister was appointed by the Queen from the Social Democrats, reflecting the new parliamentary majority. In all three countries the action taken by the monarch helped to reinforce the legitimacy of the monarchy as an institution.

The monarch may formally be the guardian of the constitution; but ultimately the exercise of the monarch's reserve powers depends upon popular support. This was evident in the Easter crisis of 1920 in Denmark, when King Christian X lost his Prime Minister and dismissed the rest of the government. The dismissal caused demonstrations threatening the future of the monarchy, and the King was forced to back down. And it was evident in Belgium after the Second World War, when King Leopold III's performance as Commander-in-Chief and refusal to follow his government caused him to spend five years in exile.

The guardian of the constitution must himself observe the constitution. But it may not even require a violation of the constitution; if the monarch by his conduct loses the support of the government or his people, he puts his throne at risk. There have been four examples of this over the last century: in the abdication of Grand Duchess Marie-Adélaïde of Luxembourg in 1919, of the British King Edward VIII in 1936, the Belgian King Leopold III in 1951, and the Spanish King Juan Carlos in 2014. Ultimately, the continuation of the monarch in office, and the monarchy as an institution, depends upon continuing popular support. That is a theme running throughout this chapter.

MODERN MONARCHS HAVE NO POLITICAL POWER, AND ONLY LIMITED INFLUENCE

Constitutional monarchs have little or no discretion when it comes to matters of state; little choice but to approve every action or decision of the government in the hundreds of documents they are required to sign every week. But through Bagehot's trio of rights, the right to be consulted, to encourage and to warn, monarchs can develop influence, even if they do not have a power of veto. The Dutch contributions to Chapter 4 show that a strong minded monarch can occasionally have influence: Queen Juliana in preventing the execution of war criminals, and withholding assent to legislation limiting the size of the royal family; Queen Beatrix in her close interest in appointments.

We can never know the full extent of a monarch's influence; but no one could claim that Queen Beatrix changed government policy through her interest in appointments. Nor has Queen Elizabeth changed British foreign policy through her strong attachment to the Commonwealth. The one exception in terms of influence on foreign policy might be King Juan Carlos in the early years of his reign, when he travelled widely to forge new relationships, and played a significant part in re-establishing Spain's credentials as a democratic state. But once he became a more conventional parliamentary monarch, foreign policy was left more to the elected government (see Chapter 6.5).

A different kind of influence might be psychological rather than political: the potential for the monarch to provide encouragement and support to the prime minister through their weekly meetings. Being a modern prime minister is intensely demanding, and there is often no one in whom they can easily confide. It may be too fanciful to depict the monarch as mentor or coach, but political memoirs show that some prime ministers have clearly valued the opportunity to talk things through with someone above the political fray. At the same time, monarchs will vary in their interest and understanding of political affairs: only those who are conscientious and politically astute are going to be useful sounding boards for their prime ministers.

Monarchs who are too interventionist will encounter resistance and lose their reputation for neutrality. The scope for the monarch to be a neutral actor is shrinking, as traditional areas for royal activity have become increasingly politicised. This can make it harder for the royal family to demonstrate its utility while remaining politically neutral. But when it comes to organising the programme of visits within their own country monarchs still have considerable discretion, in terms of the causes they are seen to support. They also have some limited scope for expressing their own views in their annual Christmas or

New Year message. In some monarchies, such as Norway, the King's speeches on other occasions can generate considerable influence; as can visits such as those following the Breivik massacre. And there is greater scope for the Crown Prince or Princess to support causes which might be deemed controversial or political, on the understanding that when they become monarch, their behaviour will need to become more restrained and strictly neutral.

So far, no other country has followed the example of Sweden, and formally reduced the monarch to a purely ceremonial role. There are three possible reasons why the other countries have resisted the Swedish example. One is simply inertia, and a reluctance by politicians to challenge the powers of an institution which commands strong popular support. A second may be resistance by monarchs themselves. But a final explanation may be the value in a political system of someone who has to be completely neutral: someone above the political fray, with a legitimising role, whose legitimacy derives precisely from their complete neutrality. We return further to the question of legitimacy below.

TIGHT REGULATION OF THE MONARCHY, ITS SIZE AND FINANCES

All the monarchies are tightly regulated by law. Regulation is a series of devices which both control, and preserve the monarchy. Rules laid down in the constitution, and laws passed by parliaments confer legitimacy on the institution, and draw the boundaries for public financial support. There is a common core of matters which are regulated in all countries: the laws of succession, royal marriages, the royal finances. But there is variation between the different countries in who makes the rules defining the size of the royal family, and conferring royal titles. In some countries this is also regulated by the state; in others it is left to the monarch to decide.

The laws of succession are all laid out in the constitution, defining the heir to the throne, and how subsequent monarchs will be identified (see Chapter 2). In the Netherlands and Norway the size of the royal house and royal titles are also regulated by law. In Sweden titles are decided by the King, and in 2019 King Carl XVI Gustaf, in response to growing political pressure, reduced the size of the royal house by removing five of his grandchildren: they no longer have the title royal highness, will not be expected to perform official duties and will not receive public funds. The announcement was made in anticipation of the findings of a parliamentary inquiry into the growing size of the royal family, and concern about its cost: see Chapter 7.4.

At the other end of the spectrum is Luxembourg, where these matters are regulated privately in the *Hausgesetz*, a private family statute of the Grand Duke revised in 2011. It provides for the distribution of titles and of funding by the Grand Duke, and a mechanism to settle inter family disputes. Similarly in the UK, although there is no tradition of *Hausgesetz*, these matters are not regulated by law, but are left to be decided by the reigning monarch. It is the Queen who decides on which members of the family have what title, and how much funding each receives, in a structure which gives a degree of financial resource which allows the monarch to avoid being totally dependent on the government of the day (see Chapter 7.5).

Where official membership of the royal house is defined, it is mainly to determine which members should receive public funding: this is in return for carrying out official duties, representing the nation at home or abroad. In some cases it is kept very tight: in Spain it is only the King and Queen, with the Infanta Leonor (aged 14) just beginning to make some appearances; and in Norway it is limited to just five people – the King and Queen, Crown Prince and Princess, and their 15 year old daughter. But Norway is a country with a population of just over 5 million. The UK has a population of 66 million, so it needs a larger royal family to fulfil all the demands for royal patronage and visits. With a size not legally defined or constrained, there have been 15 members of the British royal family who undertake public duties, and who conducted around 3,800 engagements in 2018 (see Table 6.2). Spain is also a large country, with a population of almost 47 million; it may be that one reason for the low popularity ratings of the Spanish monarchy is its limited visibility – a royal family smaller than that in Norway is serving a population ten times the size. And the Spanish monarchy is doubly constrained, because it also receives far less public funding than the others. Insofar as the published figures are comparable, *pro rata* to population it receives 30 times less funding than the monarchy in Norway: see Table 7.1.

In addition to the tight regulation of the size of the royal family and its finances, there are also the formal and informal constraints on their behaviour discussed in chapter 8. The monarch and close members of the royal family are severely constrained in terms of life choices: their freedom of speech is restricted, some lack freedom to travel, they are not free to marry whom they want, they lack freedom of religion (in Scandinavia and the UK), free choice of career, and the right to privacy and family life which ordinary citizens take for granted. For the heir apparent, and those close in the line of succession, their career choices are limited to public and voluntary service. Marrying, or being born into a royal family thus involves big sacrifices: they lead very privileged lives, but within a gilded cage.

IF THESE EUROPEAN MONARCHS HAVE NO REAL POWER, WHAT IS THE MODERN MONARCHY FOR? WHAT CONCLUSIONS CAN WE DERIVE ABOUT THE ROLE OF MONARCHY IN ADVANCED DEMOCRACIES?

Earlier sections of this chapter described how no European monarch now has any real political power worth mentioning. Formally they still play a central role bestowed upon them by the constitution; but in practice they have almost no discretion in state affairs, and no other choice but to follow the advice of their governments. So the question arises, if they have no real political power, what is the modern monarchy for? Some answers to this question seek to explain the monarchy in terms of its utility, to government, to society, the economy; others seek to explain how the monarchy has survived into modern times through developing its ceremonial and welfare roles.

Monarchies Depend on Continuing Support of Government and the People

Monarchies have survived because of the continuing support of government and the people. The most formal way of testing popular support is to hold a referendum. It is surprising how many referendums have been held in Europe on the future of the monarchy.

Greece held six referendums on the subject in the twentieth century, but was not alone. Eight other European countries have held referendums on the monarchy since 1900, leading to a grand total of 18 referendums, which are listed in Table 10.1. We have simplified the result to being for or against the monarchy; but some of the referendums were about an individual's suitability for the throne, or changing the line of succession, and so were only implicitly about the institution as such.

Table 10.1 Referendums on the monarchy in Europe since 1900

Country	Year	For Monarchy	For Republic	Turnout
Norway	1905	79%	21%	75%
Luxembourg	1919	80%	20%	72%
Greece	1920	99%	1%	n.a.
Greece	1924	30%	70%	n.a.
Greece	1935	98%	2%	n.a.
Iceland	1944	2%	98%	98%
Greece	1946	62%	38%	87%
Italy	1946	46%	54%	89%
Bulgaria	1946	4%	96%	92%
Spain	1947	95%	5%	89%
Belgium	1950	58%	42%	93%
Denmark	1953	79%	21%	59%
Greece	1973	21%	79%	75%
Greece	1974	31%	69%	76%
Spain	1976	97%	3%	78%
Spain	1978	92%	8%	67%
Albania	1997	33%	67%	72%
Denmark	2009	85%	15%	58%

Table 10.2 gives further details of the referendums held in five of the countries studied in this book. In all cases the result of the referendum was in favour of the monarchy, starting with Norway in 1905. That referendum approved the decision to invite Prince Carl of Denmark to become King of the newly independent Norway, after the personal union with Sweden had been formally ended. The next referendum was in Luxembourg after the First World War, approving the succession of Grand Duchess Charlotte after the abdication of Grand Duchess Marie-Adélaïde. The next referendum came after the Second World War, in Belgium, where Leopold III had remained in exile for five years after the war; in a divisive referendum in 1950 the Belgians voted for his return, but only by 58 per cent, and after his homecoming was greeted by widespread protests and a general strike, Leopold announced his intention to abdicate. There was also a post-war referendum in Denmark, approving a new Constitution which retained the monarchy but changed the line of succession by opening it up to women; and a similar post war referendum in Spain,

approving a law of succession to restore the monarchy, followed by two referendums in the 1970s approving the post-Franco monarchical Constitution.

Table 10.2 Referendums on the monarchy since 1900 in Belgium, Denmark, Luxembourg, Norway and Spain

Country	Year	Referendum question	Outcome	Reason for the referendum
Norway	1905	Approve government's invitation to Prince Carl to become King of Norway	Monarchy approved by 79% of voters	Followed dissolution of union with Sweden and the Swedish King Oscar II's abdication as King of Norway.
Luxembourg	1919	Who should be head of state: Grand Duchess Charlotte, or Republic?	Grand Duchess 78% Republic 20%	Monarchy tarnished by behaviour of Grand Duchess Marie-Adélaïde; national self-determination after First World War
Belgium	1950	Are you of the opinion that King Leopold III should resume the exercise of his constitutional powers?	58% voted in favour. Leopold's return was met with protests and a general strike. Within a week he announced his intention to abdicate	King Leopold III's unpopularity following controversial actions during Second World War
Denmark	1953	Approve constitutional reform	79% voted in favour	Abolish Landsting, change line of succession, lower voting age
Denmark	2009	Approve change to Danish Act of Succession	85% voted in favour	To end male primogeniture
Spain	1947	Do you approve of the Law of Succession to the Headship of the State Bill?	95% voted in favour	To provide for the restoration of the monarchy of Spain
Spain	1976	Do you approve of the Political Reform Bill?	97% voted in favour	Desire to move away from the dictatorial powers of the Franco era and turn Spain into a constitutional monarchy
Spain	1978	Do you approve of the Constitution Bill?	92% voted in favour	To ratify the constitutional changes which sought to turn Spain into a constitutional monarchy

Another way of demonstrating that all monarchies depend on continuing support from the people is to observe what happens when monarchs lose that support. The answer is that they are forced to abdicate, and lose their thrones. We have already mentioned the abdication of Grand Duchess Marie-Adélaïde, forced to abdicate in 1919 because of her closeness to the German occupying forces during the First World War; and the abdication of King Leopold III of Belgium, whose unpopularity stemmed from his controversial behaviour in the Second World War, when he insisted on taking personal command of the armed forces, and refused to follow his government into exile. In Britain King Edward VIII was forced to abdicate in 1936 because he would not abandon his wish to marry a twice divorced American woman, Wallis Simpson; and in Spain King Juan Carlos stepped down in 2014 when the opinion polls were showing that two thirds of Spaniards felt he should abdicate.

At a lower level popular support helps to determine the level of state funding for the monarchy, which is a sensitive issue for all governments; and even to decide what titles are deemed acceptable for those who marry into the royal family. It is no coincidence that the Spanish monarchy has much the smallest budget: of all the eight monarchies studied it has the lowest popularity ratings (see Chapter 9.3). And titles for consorts can depend on public acceptability: in 2011 the Dutch Parliament decided that Crown Princess Máxima had earned her spurs, and should be titled Queen when Prince Willem Alexander became King; while in the UK it is still undecided whether it will be acceptable for Camilla, Duchess of Cornwall, to be called Queen as opposed to using some lesser title when Charles becomes King.

Opinion polls may help to decide the eventual answer to whether Camilla is called Queen. Polls provide another means for testing and signifying support for the monarchy. We saw in Chapter 9 how pervasive polling has become in all countries, with questions asking not merely whether people would prefer a republic, but whether they were satisfied with the monarch's performance, is the royal family paid too much, should the monarch abdicate, who is your favourite royal, and so on. Roger Mortimore's analysis shows that support for the monarchy remains high in all countries, with polls regularly showing that between 60 and 80 per cent of the people wish to retain the monarchy, and only 15 to 35 per cent would prefer a republic. Support is highest in Denmark, the Netherlands, Norway and the UK, where it ranges between 70 and 80 per cent; and a little lower in Belgium, Spain and Sweden, at around 60 to 65 per cent. Lennart Nilsson's analysis of Swedish polling (Chapter 9.4) shows that politicians and journalists have stronger republican sympathies than the general population. This helps to ensure the monarchy is kept under close scrutiny, by politicians and the media; it has not yet led a majority of the Swedish population to support becoming a republic.

It may seem surprising that an ancient institution such as a hereditary monarchy can command such high levels of popular support, with opinion poll ratings which elected politicians would die for. That brings us to the arguments which seek to justify a non-elected, hereditary head of state as part of government in a modern democracy. Because monarchies depend on the support of governments as well as the people, it is helpful to consider separately the reasons why governments support having a hereditary monarchy; and the reasons why the people do.

Reasons for Governments to Support the Monarchy

There is a feedback loop between the two. The main reason why governments support a hereditary monarchy is because it has widespread popular support. Even governments with republican sympathies, such as the Socialist Workers Party in Spain or the Social Democrats in Sweden, have not dared to propose abolition of the monarchy, because it would be electorally unpopular. But there is a conditionality in government support: governments support a hereditary monarchy so long as it remains neutral and above politics. Monarchs who seek to intervene find themselves removed or cut down to size. To take just Luxembourg as an example, Grand Duchess Marie-Adélaïde lost the support of the socialists and liberals when she controversially dissolved the Parliament in 1916, leading them later to propose abolition of the monarchy in the week before her abdication in 1919. A century later, Grand Duke Henri lost the right to grant royal assent to bills when he refused to sign a euthanasia bill into law in 2008. Modern monarchs have to remain scrupulously neutral, and above politics; and governments will ensure they are kept in their place. In so doing, governments are helping to safeguard monarchy as an institution: in an age when elected politicians are held in increasing disregard, to be neutral and above politics is itself an advantage. As Vernon Bogdanor has put it:

> A constitutional monarchy settles beyond argument the crucial question of who is to be the head of state, and it places the position of the head of state beyond political competition. In doing so, it alone can represent the whole nation in an emotionally satisfying way; it alone is in a position to interpret the nation to itself (Bogdanor 1995: 301).

Apart from popular support, there are several other reasons why governments may want to support the monarchy. A respected monarchy can lend legitimacy to the other institutions of the state, and bolster the loyalty of citizens to those institutions. And a monarch with no political mandate may be easier to deal with than a president who may have a political past, or claim democratic authority through having been elected or appointed by the government or the parliament. A further small advantage for governments, when politics has become so international, with frequent attendance at international meetings, is being able to despatch the monarch or lesser royals to ceremonial or sporting events, or state funerals and the like. The royal family can help to increase the size of the representational team. And when negotiating trade deals with other countries which are monarchies, such as Saudi Arabia or Morocco, it helps to send a monarch to seal the deal: as the Spanish government has found to its advantage, but at some cost to the reputation of the monarchy (see Chapter 6.5).

As the price of their support, governments have gradually restricted the monarchical sphere. This dilution of constitutional function and power has not, however, led to delegitimisation. On the contrary, a common requirement of neutrality has, with other developments, improved monarchy's position to one of being seen as an impartial guarantor of constitutional propriety, signified amongst other things by granting royal assent to laws and countersigning decrees. In addition, the hereditary principle becomes accepted as a lasting and contrasting counterpoint to the rough and tumble of politics. On the other hand, acceptance of this position depends upon the degree of confidence in whether the monarch is truly impartial. This has led to a gradual disengagement from the process of government formation in some, but not all monarchies. In Sweden and the Netherlands the monarch now has no involvement. But in Belgium, Denmark, Luxembourg and Norway the monarch is still actively involved, although with a degree of political cover in the practice in Belgium and Norway that the appointment of the new prime minister is countersigned by the outgoing prime minister who, on the same occasion, countersigns the dismissal of himself and his own government.

Reasons for the People to Support the Monarchy

We turn next to the reasons why the people might support a hereditary monarchy. For most members of the public the answer lies more in the roles performed by the monarch as head of nation rather than head of state, in the ceremonial roles rather than the constitutional and political functions. Legitimisation has become something based on more than purely constitutional and legal constructs. Even the constitutionally powerless King of Sweden has an important role as the symbol and representative of the nation, and notably exercised it, for example, in a heartfelt and moving speech at a memorial service following the death of nearly 550 Swedes in the 2004 Asian tsunami. Even if absolute neutrality is unachievable, the loss of political authority can enhance monarchical appeal precisely because monarchy is obliged to be disinterested. Furthermore, the 'target area' for objection is reduced: 'The major conundrum facing Swedish republicans ... is that they have been forced to take issue with an institution that their opponents claim lacks political influence' (Åse 2013: 184).

Prominent features of this dimension include the monarchy as a neutral focus of national loyalty, representing the nation abroad, and speaking to and for the nation – at times of crisis and at times of celebration. Regular occasions include monarchical Christmas and New Year broadcasts, which are a feature of all eight monarchies. Examples of the monarch speaking for the nation in times of crisis include the King of Sweden's tsunami speech, mentioned above; Queen Elizabeth's address to the nation following Princess Diana's death in 1997, and her visits to the disasters of Aberfan and Grenfell Tower; and the visits and speeches after terrorist attacks made by the Kings of Norway and of Spain. The existential crisis of the Covid 19 epidemic led all eight monarchs to broadcast special addresses to their nations in the spring of 2020. While encouraging the observance of government preventive policies, they spoke not as head of state but as head of the nation, offering comfort to their people, support for essential public services, and reassurance that the crisis would come to an end.

There are also wider and sometimes more profound features that have become prominent as the result of the development of modern media. Bagehot in 1867 claimed of monarchy, 'Its mystery is its life. We must not let in daylight upon magic' (Bagehot 1867: 53). One hundred and fifty years later, the reverse has become obligatory. Whereas royal marriages in Britain once were private affairs solemnised in the evening in closed chapels, now they are public affairs broadcast to the world. Almost 40 million people in the UK watched the wedding of Prince William in 2011. The same is true of the other monarchies: 25 million Spaniards watched the wedding of Prince Felipe of Asturias in 2004, almost two thirds of the population. Every new royal baby has to be promptly shown off to the media almost regardless of the mother's state of recovery.

Behind such events is the way in which monarchy – performing as an undying family – can represent continuity and stability in a rapidly changing, globalised world. Whereas governments and politicians come and go, the family continues. The result is that all generations can identify with royal family members of their own generation and see reflected their own life experience. Older people can identify with the tradition and history of the nation that monarchy represents. Some may also set store by a monarchy's religious features, above all in the Scandinavian and British monarchies. Royal family presence at national commemorations can focus national feeling in ways that remain unique. Such processes are capable of communicating a sense of affiliation even in those who may object to monarchy in theory.

National commemorations and ceremonial occasions can often contain a religious element. Even though only the UK has a religious coronation, five out of the eight monarchies have a service in the cathedral to bless the start of a new reign (see Table 5.1). Ian Bradley has suggested that it is the ceremonial, and also the emotional and familial elements of royalty (not least as supplied by royal weddings) that primarily appeal to people (Chapter 5.3). Royal weddings take place in church, symbolising the links between church and state and the monarchy, and remind people of the place of religion in society. In the Scandinavian countries and the UK, where the monarch is required to observe the state religion, it might be thought that would be narrow and excluding; but in fact the reverse is the case. Leaders of minority faiths in Britain are defenders of church establishment and the religious character of the monarchy, as a way of keeping religion in the public sphere and national life. In Denmark Queen Margrethe has said something very similar:

> Under the constitution, as the Danish Queen I am bound to the Lutheran faith, but that does not exclude people of other faiths. On the contrary, I believe that the fact that I am religious brings me closer to anyone with a different faith. Besides, I represent all people who are citizens of the Danish nation (Ertel and Sandberg).

And more pithily, King Harald V of Norway (who is also required to be a Lutheran) has said: 'Norwegians believe in God, Allah, the Universe and nothing'. In Sweden, when the Constitution was amended in 2012 to disestablish the state church, the requirement for the monarch to be a Lutheran was kept at King Carl XVI Gustaf's own request (see Chapter 8.3).

Famously, Bagehot suggested that monarchy had survived and indeed thrived by appealing to the heart rather than the head; and it is ceremonial functions, and events like royal weddings, which have the greatest appeal. Some close observers have anatomised interactions between royal family members and citizens to expose how the social rituals work and what they mean. The journalist Emma Duncan, initially sceptical of the value of such events, found herself obliged to follow the Duke and Duchess of Sussex as they performed various royal duties. Noting the professionalism of the royal couple, she also noted the effect that their attention evoked: 'No politician, no other celebs, would bring such undiluted pleasure … There's a lot to be said for an institution that both embodies national values and brings joy' (Duncan 2019). The sociologist Anne Rowbottom followed a group of enthusiasts who regularly attended royal events throughout the country. She concluded that in royal visits 'the civil religion and the legitimacy of the monarchy are being routinely produced and reproduced' (Rowbottom 2002). It seems that, although much of Bagehot's mystery has fallen away, some magic remains. And this despite the slightly more ordinary lifestyle of some royals, like King Olav V of Norway riding the subway to go skiing during the oil crisis in 1973, when private cars were banned on Sundays.[1] Similar processes seem at work in other monarchies. Speaking of Denmark, Louise Phillips has pointed out that

> The royal family is presented publicly as 'ordinary' in Denmark but people identify with them as a result. By this identification, their position as symbol of the nation-state is reinforced, not threatened (Phillips 1999: 226).

Using a theological metaphor, legitimation has shifted from a matter of faith to one of works. This concept lies behind attempts to calculate an economic benefit from monarchy by setting its financial costs against the part played by the royal show of palaces and pomp in boosting national incomes through tourism. Such calculations require ambitious assumptions which means that their findings need not be taken entirely seriously. What is of interest is that they should be thought worth attempting at all.

In the UK 'works' are principally represented by the emergence of what Frank Prochaska has called the welfare monarchy and its effort to encourage charitable endeavour, exemplified in the hundreds of charities with royal patrons, and the large number of visits made by the royal family to charitable and voluntary organisations (see Chapter 6). There appears to be less emphasis on such activities in the Scandinavian monarchies and the Netherlands because of their more extensive welfare states. Accepting the patronage of professional bodies helps to support civil society, and monarchies' role as founts of honour awarding orders and medals extends recognition to citizens in all walks of life to celebrate personal effort and achievement. In various ways the monarch can symbolise and encourage dedication to public service, especially by virtue of its links with the military, but also by visiting hospitals, schools, the police and other public services.

As Table 6.1 shows, the sheer visibility of modern monarchy can bring both attention and glamour to local as well as national events. As we noted above in the comparison between Norway and Spain, there is an equation to be balanced between restraining the size and therefore the cost of a royal family on the one hand and, on the other, limiting too much its capacity to undertake a wide range of the public duties which help to confer legitimacy. Being seen in person is one of the most important sources of a monarchy's popularity because it removes any sense of remote inaccessibility, which media representation cannot alone alleviate.

This is not to argue that none of these features cannot be seen in republics. After all, there is an important sense in which European monarchies *are* republics except for having hereditary heads of state. But republican heads of state lack some of the advantages of monarchs. They have shorter terms of office, will tend to be on the elderly side, will have been elected instead of someone else, and normally have a history of political partisanship which they cannot entirely shrug off. They cannot bring the symbolism of the family to national life, nor can they bring the numbers of a family to the personal encounters that royal visiting can spread across the whole national community; nor can they bring the glamour and stardust of royalty.

---

[1] For a photo of this episode, see https://www.reddit.com/r/pics/comments/3i3edh/king-olav_v_of_norway_riding_the_subway_during/

RISKS AND THREATS

It was said of the pre-revolution French Bourbon monarchy that it had props but few roots. To the extent that traditional forms of monarchical legitimacy are in eclipse, then current monarchies have constantly to rejuvenate their positions. This can happen even within longer reigns, rather than solely in a new reign following accession.

The modern association with celebrity may help confer popularity, but these are shallow and fickle waters which offer insufficient guarantees of permanence. Moreover, celebritisation brings its own dangers. As we saw in Chapter 8, the greatest threat to the monarchy is the loss of privacy: 'The Royals have paid a terrible price for becoming stars on a stage which was not made for this purpose: they now have no privacy and no life of their own' (Williams 1994: 62).

Harassment of the royal family in pursuit of stories about their private lives is worst in the UK, with the phone hacking scandal (see Chapter 9.5), but other countries have also seen flagrant intrusions into their private lives, and those of their children. And it is not just by tabloid newspapers or gossip magazines: harassment is also rife on social media, with wild speculation about the sexual orientation of some of the younger royals, or rival support groups in the UK promoting vicious Kate versus Meghan stories. Such harassment must give serious pause to anyone invited to marry into the royal family: the sacrifice in terms of loss of privacy is immense.

A second threat to the monarchy is simply human frailty. Loyalty now is less to the institution, and more to each holder of the office; and it is conditional on good behaviour. Here one strength of monarchy – undisputed succession and the promise of personal continuity – is also potentially a weakness. The UK is not alone in having had kings who have been mad, bad or stupid. At a time when personality and behaviour are more than ever scrutinised, personal inadequacy can all too easily bring monarchy into disrepute. Elizabeth Longford has disputed this understanding: 'the idea of monarchy has always been more important than the facts of royal lives. Good behaviour gives it strength; bad behaviour of whatever sort has only a passing effect' (Longford 1993: 32). But this view – viable perhaps for kings as bad as George IV or as stupid as William IV – depends in practice on assuming that the social and political climate of the early nineteenth century remains intact when the subsequent changes have been immense. The decline of deference, proliferation of media outlets, and the ruthless competition of modern journalism described by Jean Seaton in Chapter 9.5 have permanently altered the intensity of media exposure which monarchies need to remain visible, but can risk spiralling out of control. Bagehot's mystery has been eclipsed by the modern capacity for investigative intrusion.

Some of the investigative journalism is justified, in holding the monarchy to account. The monarchy is a public institution, which receives significant amounts of public funding, and proper scrutiny of how that money is spent is perfectly reasonable. Investigative journalism has helped to expose corruption scandals, most recently in Spain, where the son-in-law of King Juan Carlos is serving a six-year prison sentence for fraud, embezzlement and corruption. He is not alone: Chapter 4.2 described how in 1976 Prince Bernhard of the Netherlands, the husband of Queen Juliana, was forced to resign as Inspector General of the armed forces when he was found to have received commission from Lockheed on the sale of defence aircraft. Similar allegations have circulated in

Spain about some of the deals negotiated by Juan Carlos with Arab countries, but have never been proved. It was not the only reason for his abdication, but it was one factor in his growing unpopularity.

THE FUTURE FOR MONARCHY

Granted its continuing popularity, European monarchy must be doing something right. Its survival, on the other hand, cannot be taken for granted. For the time being, its power-lessness allows it to remain acceptable to governments and politicians; and at the same time popular with the citizenry for its symbolic national functions, impartial bearing, and the glamour it brings into their lives.

Its room for manoeuvre is, however, increasingly circumscribed by the demands put upon it. Many of these demands are contradictory. Monarchy has to be special, a living fairy tale and an endless source of glamorous images; but its members must also be accessible and ordinary as individuals. We expect them to be interesting and entertaining, to show an informed interest in modern life, to be an inspiration for charitable endeavour and yet always be unimpeachably neutral. Royal families should demonstrate impeccable family values, and yet they are just as human and fallible as the rest of us, with children who go astray, and marriages that break down, but all in the harsh spotlight of relentless publicity.

KEY FINDINGS

To conclude, monarchy may be ancient but it has also proved adaptable in response to enormous social and political change. It continues to possess features of great social value which should not be lightly set aside.

Crucial points to its retaining usefulness and support are:

- It is vital above all that it undertakes its public duties as neutrally as possible and does not abuse its privileged position.
- The size of the royal family needs to be kept as small as possible, but realistically commensurate with the duties to be fulfilled.
- Care should be taken to prepare heirs for succession through higher education (preferably in more than one country) and a wide range of placements in public, military and diplomatic service.
- It must preserve and develop its unique fusion of symbolic state headship with the spectacle of a living family – the modern shape of former magic.
- It must accept a degree of public accountability and transparency – annual accounts signed off by a state auditor, annual reports, and responsive communications.
- Its special place in a nation needs to express monarchy's unique ability to give attention and value to aspects of people's lives which are not normally the focus of government action. In this sense, monarchy should concentrate on what governments cannot do.

Monarchy has weathered severe storms, and survived. Five of the eight monarchies were occupied during World War II and came through even that experience. Many of the previous monarchies in Europe have disappeared following defeat in war, revolution or the collapse of the state. But for those eight monarchies that remain, there seems no reason why they should not continue for many years to come, so long as they retain the support of their governments, and the people.

Bibliography

BOOKS AND JOURNAL ARTICLES

Andersen, P (1954) *Dansk Statsforfatningsret* (Copenhagen, Gyldendal).

Andersen, J (2011) *40 år på Tronen* (Copenhagen, Lindhardt og Ringhof).

Andersson, U (2012) 'Metoddokumentation' in Asp, K (ed), *Svenska journalister 1989–2011* (Göteborgs universitet, Institutionen för journalistik och masskommunikation).

Andeweg, RB, and Irwin, GA (2014), *Governance and Politics of the Netherlands* (Houndmills, Palgrave Macmillan).

Åse, C (2009) *Monarkins makt. Nationell gemenskap i svensk demokrati* (Stockholm, Ordfront).

—— (2013) 'Monarchical Manoeuvres: Gender, Nation and the Boundary Problem in Post-War Swedish Constitutional Development' 21(3) *Nordic Journal of Feminist and Gender Research* 172.

Asp, K (2007) 'Fairness, Informativeness and Scrutiny: the Role of News Media in Democracy' *Nordicom Review* 31.

—— (2012a) (ed), *Svenska journalister 1989–2011* (Göteborgs universitet, Institutionen för journalistik och masskommunikation).

—— (2012b), 'Journalistkårens partisympatier' in Asp, K (ed), *Svenska journalister 1989–2011* (Göteborgs universitet, Institutionen för journalistik och masskommunikation).

Baalen van, C and Brouwer, JW (2005), 'De Toespraken van Beatrix Nader Beschouwd' in Baalen van, C, de Jong, R, Koningin aan het woord, B (eds) *Koningin Beatrix aan het Woord; 25 jaar troonredes, officiële redevoeringen en kersttoespraken* (Den Haag, SDU).

Baalen van, C and Kessel van, A (2012) *De kabinetsformatie in vijftig stappen* (Amsterdam, Boom).

Baalen van, C, Bovend'Eert, PPT et al (1972), *het inkomen van de Koning. De totstandkoming en ontwikkeling van het financieel statuut van het koninklijk huis* (Amsterdam, Boom 2017).

Back, P-E and Fredriksson, G (1966) *Republiken Sverige* (Stockholm, Prisma: Verdandi debatt).

Bagehot, W (1867) *The English Constitution* (Oxford World's Classics, 2001).

Bartlett, J (2018) *The People V Tech* (Harmondsworth, Penguin).

Beckett, I F W (2016) 'Royalty and the Army in the Twentieth Century' in Glencross, M, Rowbotham, J and Kandiah, M (eds) *The Windsor Dynasty 1910 to the Present-Long to Reign over Us?* (London, Palgrave Macmillan).

Behrendt, C and Vrancken, M (2019) *Principes de droit constitutionnel belge* (Brussels, la Charte).

Belmessieri, M (2008) Les pouvoirs réels du monarque constitutionnel en cas de formation d'un gouvernement 12(4) *Chroniques de droit public* 800.

Besch, M (2019) *Normes et légistique en droit public luxembourgeois*, (Windhof, Luxembourg, Promoculture-Larcier).

Besselink, L (2010) 'The Globalizing Turn in the Relationship Between Constitutionalism and Democracy' 3 *Netherlands Journal of Legal Philosophy* 234.

—— (2014) 'The Kingdom of the Netherlands' in Besselink, LFM et al, *Constitutional Law of the EU Member States* (Deventer, Wolters Kluwer).

Bistrup, A (2005) *Margrethe* (Denmark, Politiken Bøger).

Bjørklund, T (2005) *Hundre år med folkeavstemninger: Norge og Norden 1905–2005* (Oslo, Universitetsforlaget).

Bjørn, C (2001) *Blot til Pynt?* (Copenhagen, Fremad).

Blackburn, R (2004) 'Monarchy and the Personal Prerogatives' *Public Law* 543.

—— (2006) *King and Country: Monarchy and the Future King Charles III* (London, Politicos).

Bleich, A (2008) *Joop den Uyl 1919–1987; Dromer en Doordouwer* (Amsterdam, Balans).

Blume, P (1989) *Fra tale til data* (Copenhagen, Akademisk Forlag).

Bramstång, G (1990) *Tronrätt, Bördstitel och hustillhörighet* (Lunds universitet, Juristförlaget).

—— (1994) 'Att vara prins eller inte vara prins – det är frågan' 6 *Förvaltningsrättslig Tidskrift*.

Bogdanor, V (1995) *The Monarchy and the Constitution* (Oxford, Clarendon Press).

Bogdanor, V and Vogenauer, S (2007) 'The Constitution of the UK as of 1 January 2007' in Bryant, C (ed), *Towards a New Constitutional Settlement*, (London, The Smith Institute).

Bomann-Larsen, T (2006) *Vintertonen, Haakon & Maud,* vol 3 (Oslo, Cappelen).

—— (2011) *Æresordet, Haakon & Maud* vol 5 (Oslo, Cappelen).

Bonney, N (2013) *Monarchy, Religion and the State* (Manchester, Manchester University Press).

Bovend'Eert, PPT (1985) 'Koning en Ministers' 39 *Bestuurswetenschappen* 443.

—— (2000) 'Met of zonder Koning' in Prakke, L et al (eds), *Monarchie en Republiek* (Deventer, WEJ Tjeenk Willink).

Bovend'Eert, PPT and Kortmann, CAJM (2018) *Constitutional Law in the Netherlands* (Alphen aan de Rijn, Kluwer Law International).

Bovend'Eert, PPT and Kummeling, HRBM (2017) *Het Nederlandse parlement* (Deventer, Wolters Kluwer).

Bovend'Eert, PPT, Baalen van, C and Kessel van, A (2015) *Zonder Koningin, het Officiële evaluatierapport over de formatie 2012* (Amsterdam, Elsevier Boeken).

Boyce, P (2008) *The Queen's Other Realms: The Crown and its Legacy in Australia, Canada and New Zealand* (Sydney, Federation Press).

Brazier, R (1995) 'The Constitutional Position of the Prince of Wales' *Public Law* 401.

—— (2005) '"Monarchy and the Personal Prerogatives" – A Personal Response to Professor Blackburn' *Public Law* 45.

Bradford, S (1996) *Elizabeth: A Biography of Her Majesty the Queen* (London, Key Porter Books).

Bradley, I (2002) *God Save the Queen: The Spiritual Dimension of Monarchy* (London, Darton, Longman & Todd).

—— (2007), *Believing in Britain: The Spiritual Dimension of Britishness* (London, IB Tauris).

—— (2012) *God Save the Queen: The Spiritual Heart of the Monarchy* (London, Continuum).

—— (2015) 'The Shape of the Next Coronation – Some Tentative Thoughts' 4(1) *Political Theology* 25.

Brendon, P and Whitehead, P (1994) *The Windsors: A Dynasty Revealed* (London, Hodder & Stoughton).

Buys, JT (1983) *De Grondwet, eerste deel* (Arnhem, Gouda Quint).

Bull, T and Sterzel, F (2015) *Regeringsformen – en kommentar* (Lund, Studentlitteratur).

Buttenschøn, C and Ries, O (2003) *Kongemagt og Folkestyre* (Copenhagen, Lindhardt og Ringhof).

Callaghan, J (2006) *Time and Chance* (Politico's).

Cannadine, D (1987) 'The Context, Performance and Meaning of Ritual; The British Monarchy and the Invention of Tradition' in Cannadine, D and Price, S (eds), *Rituals of Royalty: Power and Ceremonial in Traditional Societies* (Oxford, Oxford University Press).

—— (1998) *History in Our Time* (London, Yale University Press).

—— (2008) *Making History Now and Then* (Basingstoke, Palgrave Macmillan).

Carr, W (2002) 'The Intimate Ritual: The Coronation Service' 4(1) *Political Theology* 11.

Chippendale, C and Horrie, C (1990) *'Stick It Up Your Punter': The Rise and Fall of the Sun* (Heinemann).

Chorus, J (2013) *Beatrix; Dwars door alle weerstanden heen,* (Amsterdam, Atlas Contact).

Christensen, J P (1990) *Forfatningsretten og det levende liv* (Copenhagen, Jurist- og Økonomforbundets Forlag).

Conradi, P (2011) *Kungligt. Europas kungahus – släktbanden, makten och hemligheterna,* (Stockholm, Forum).

Corcos, CA (2012) 'From Agnatic Succession to Absolute Primogeniture: The Shift to Equal Rights of Succession to Thrones and Titles in the Modern European Constitutional Monarchy' *Michican State University Law Review* 1587.

Corfixen, K and Thygesen, P (2020) Interview with the Queen Margrethe, *Polotiken,* 11 April.

Cox, J *The Marriage of the Duke of Edinburgh: The Cost of the Royal Household, Royal Annuities and Crown Lands* (London, Truelove).

Cramer, N (1980) 'De Kroon op het Werk van 1813' in Tamse, CA (ed) *De Monarchie in Nederland,* (Amsterdam: Elsevier).

Curran, J and Seaton, J (2018) *Power Without Responsibility: The Press, Broadcasting and Internet in Britain* (Abingdon, Routledge).

Daalder H (2016), *Drees en Soestdijk; De Zaak-Hofmans en andere Crises 1948–1958* (Amsterdam, Balans).

Davies, N (2009) *Flat Earth News* (London, Chatto and Windus).

Dijn de, A (2002) 'A Pragmatic Conservatism. Montesquieu and the Framing of the Belgian Constitution (1830–1831)' 28(4) *History of European Ideas* 227.

Delpérée, F (2017) *Le roi des Belges* (Brussels, L'Académie en poche).

Dimbleby, J (1994) *Prince of Wales* (London, Little, Brown & Co).

Donner, AM (1980) 'Erfelijk en onschendbaar' in Tamse, CA (ed), *De monarchie in Nederland* (Amsterdam/Brussels, Elsevier).

Dooyeweerd, H (1917) *De ministerraad in het Nederlandsche staatsrecht* (Amsterdam, Wed G van Soest).

Drees, W (1980) 'Kroon en ministers' in CA Tamse (ed), *De monarchie in Nederland* (Amsterdam, Elsevier).

Einarsson, M and Svensson, J (2012) *Bara ett penndrag. Förslag till en republikansk författning för Sverige*, (Sweden, Hjalmarsson & Högberg).

Eliasson, I (2013) *Jag vet var jag kommer ifrån* (Stockholm, Albert Bonniers Förlag).

Elliot, M (1998) 'Förtroendet och vårt dagliga möte med samhället' in L Nilsson (ed), *Mångfald. Bilder av en storstadsregion* (Göteborgs universitet, SOM-institutet).

Ergec, R (1990) 'L'institution monarchique à l'épreuve de la crise' *Journal des Tribunaux* 265.

Even, P (2018) 'Der Erneuerte Nassauische Erbverein vom 30. Juni 1783' in Pons, R (ed), *Oranien und Nassau in Europa* (Wiesbaden, Historische Kommission für Nassau).

Fasseur, C (1998) *Wilhelmina: de jonge koningin* (Amsterdam, Balans).

—— (2008) *Juliana and Bernhard; Het verhaal van een huwelijk, de jaren 1936–1956* (Amsterdam, Balans).

Frieden, L (2009) 'Luxembourg: Parliament Abolishes Royal Confirmation of Laws' 7(3) *International Journal of Constitutional Law* 539.

Fulford, R (1976) (ed) *Darling Child: Private Correspondence of Queen Victoria and the German Crown Princess* (London, Evan Bros).

Fusilier, R (1960) *Les monarchies parlementaires. Étude sur les systèmes de gouvernment (Suède, Norvège, Danemark, Belgique, Pays-Bas, Luxembourg)* (Paris, Les éditions ouvrières).

Gallup, G (ed) (1976) *The Gallup International Public Opinion Polls, Great Britain, 1937–1975* (New York, Random House).

Gallup, G and Rae, SF (1940) *The Pulse of Democracy: The Public-Opinion Poll and How it Works* (New York, Simon and Schuster).

Germer, P (1995) *Dansk Statsforfatningsret* (Copenhagen, Jurist- og Økonomforbundets Forlag).

Griera, M, Martínez-Ariño, J and García-Romeral, G (2014) 'Beyond the Separation of Church and State: Explaining the New Governance of Religious Diversity in Spain' 14 *MMG Working Paper* 14.

Goldstein, E (2008) 'The Politics of the State Visit' 3 *The Hague Journal of International Diplomacy* 153.

Gustafsson, N (2018) 'Några anmärkningar om kungens roll för Svenska Akademiens stadgar' 120 *Statsvetenskaplig Tidskrift* 577.

Hägg, G (2010) *Utveckla monarkin* (Stockholm, Norstedts).

Hansen, H (1988) 'Regeringsdannelsen efter folketingsvalget d. 10. maj 1988' 8 *Juristen* 337.

Hardman, R (2018) *Queen of the World* (London, Random House).

Harris, L M (1966) *Long to Reign Over Us? The Status of the Royal Family in the Sixties* (London, Kimber).

Harrison, B (1982) *Peaceable Kingdom: Stability and Change in Modern Britain* (Oxford University Press).

Harrison, D (2006) 'Den kungliga paradoxen – Carl XVI Gustaf i ett historiskt perspektiv' in Ögren, M (ed) *För Sverige – Nuförtiden. En antologi om Carl XVI Gustaf* (Stockholm, Bokförlaget DN).

Häusler, R (1995) 'Der König – ideale Verschmelzung von Mythos und Funktionalität. Der Parlamentarismus als Katalysator für die Transformation der Monarchie zur "psychologischen" Staatsform' 26 *Zeitschreift für Parlamentsfragen* 505.

Heath, E (1998) *The Course of My Life: The Autobiography of Edward Heath* (Hodder and Stoughton).

Heckscher, G (1963) *Trygga folkstyret* (Stockholm, Bokförlaget medborgarskolan).

Henderson, N (1994) *Mandarin: the Diaries of Nicholas Henderson* (London, Phoenix).

Herlitz, N (1963) *1969 års regeringsform? Kommentarer till författningsutredningens förslag* (Swedem, Norstedts).

—— (1969) *Nordic Public Law* (Stockholm, PA Norstedt & Söner).

Heuschling, L (2012) 'Le vol d'Icare du *Fürstenrecht*. L'invalidité des trois décrets du Grand-Duc' 26 *Lëtzebuerger Land* 15.

—— (2012) 'Le *Fürstenrecht* et les mariages princiers au sein de la maison grand-ducale de Luxembourg' 22 *Journal des Tribunaux. Luxembourg* 97.

—— (2013) *Le citoyen monarque. Réflexions sur le grand-duc, la famille grand-ducale et le droit de vote*, (Windhof, Luxembourg, Promoculture-Larcier).

—— (2014) 'Le concept de dissolution, l'histoire des dissolutions de la Chambre des députés du Luxembourg & la coutume' 13 *Jus politicum*.

Heuschling, L and Riassettto, I (2013) 'Les sources autonomes: Fürstenrecht, codes de bonne conduite et normes religieuses en matière financière' in *Quo vadis droit luxembourgeois? Réflexions sur l'évolution des sources techniques et normatives* (Luxembourg, Editions Promoculture-Larcier).

Hill, RJ and White, S (2014) 'Referendums in Russia, the Former Soviet Union and Eastern Europe' in Qvortrup, M (ed), *Referendums Around the World: The Continued Growth of Direct Democracy*, (Basingstoke, Palgrave Macmillan).

Høigaard, JE (2002) *Krisen i Kongehuset* (Copenhagen, Hovedland).

Holm, G (2008) *Hvorfor er feminister så snerpede? 30 spørgsmål om køn og* ligestilling (Copenhagen, Lindhardt og Ringhof).

Holmberg, E and Stjernquist, N (1980) *Grundlagarna med tillhörande författningar* (Stockholm, PA Norstedt & Söner förlag).

Holmberg, E, Stjernquist, N, Regner, G, Eliasson, M and Isberg, M (2012) *Grundlagarna. Regeringsformen, successionsordningen, riksdagsordningen* (Stockholm, Norstedts Juridik).

Huss, A (1962) 'Une institution ressuscitée: la lieutenance en droit constitutionnel luxembourgeois' *Feuille de liaison de la Conférence Saint-Yves* 18.

Huyttens, E (1844/45) *Discussions du Congrès national de Belgique*, (Brussels, Société typographique belge).

Jacobs, G, Kerger, F, Thill, B, Grosbusch, A and Gonner, R (2000) 'Lettre ouverte à toutes les instances de l'Etat' *Luxemburger Wort* 4.

Jansen, E (1921) *Det suspensive lovveto* (Christiania, Grøndahl & Søn).

Janting, J and Tolstrup, T (1999) *Kongehuset i arbejdstøjet* (Denmark, Jyllands-Posten Erhvervsbøger).

Jennings, WI (1959) *The Law and the Constitution* (London, University of London Press).

Jensen, JA (1997) *Parlamentarismens statsretlige betydning* (Copenhagen, Jurist- og Økonomforbundets Forlag).

Jönsson, M and Lundell, P (2009) (eds) *Media and Monarchy in Sweden* (Gothenburg, Nordicom).

Jonsrud, KO (1996) *Monarki og egalitaere verdier – et paradox? En studie av monarkins legitimitet i det* (Norsk teknisk-naturvitenskapelige universitet, Institutt for sociologi og statsvitenskap).

Jørgensen, A (1989) *I Smult Vande, Fra Mine Dagbøger 1975–1977, bind 2* (Copenhagen, Fremad).

Kern, F (1948) *Kingship and Law in the Middle Ages* (London, Basil Blackwell).

Kokonnen, A and Sundell, A (2014) 'Delivering Stability – Primogeniture and Autocratic Dsurvival in European Monarchies 1000–1800)' 108(2) *American Political Science Review* 438.

Kooistra, R and Koole, S (2000) *Beatrix; Invloed en een Macht van een Eigenzinnige Vorstin* (Amsterdam, Bert Bakker, 2000).

Kortmann, CAJM (1987) *De Grondwetsherzieningen 1983 en 1987* (Deventer, Kluwer).

Krag, JO (1973) *Dagbog 1971–1972* (Copenhagen, Gyldendal).

Kranenburg, R (1928) *Het Nederlandsch Staatsrecht, eerste deel* (Haarlem, Tjeenk Willink).

Kuhn, WH (1993) 'Queen Victoria's Civil List: What Did She Do With It?' 36 *Historical Journal* 645.

Larsen, J et al (2010) *Amalienborg* (Copenhagen, Gyldendal).

Linder, PJA and Svensson, P (2010) *Ja. Monarkins bästa tid är nu/Nej. Monarkin har aldrig varit farligare än nu* (Stockholm, Albert Bonniers Förlag).

Listhaug, O (1993) 'Politikk og samfunn' in B Alstad (ed) *Norske meninger 1946–1993* (Soreidgrend, Sigma Forlag).

Longford, E (1993) *Royal Throne: The Future of the Monarchy* (London, Curtis).

Lorimer, D (2004) *Radical Prince* (Edinburgh, Floris Books).

Low, S (1904) *The Governance of England* (London, Fisher Unwin).

Maarseveen van, HTJF (1969) *De heerschappij van de ministerraad* (Den Haag, Staatsuitgeverij).

Mackenzie, J and N (2000) (eds) *The Diaries of Beatrice Webb* (Illinois, Northwestern University Press).

Majerus, P (1990) *L'Etat luxembourgeois. Manuel de droit constitutionnel et administratif* (Editpress, Esch-sur-Alzette).

Marschner, J (2017) *Enlightened Princesses: Caroline, Augusta, Charlotte, and the Shaping of the Modern World* (London, Yale University Press).

Marxer, W (2003) *Das Hausgesetz des Fürstenhauses von Liechtenstein und dessen Verhältnis zum staatlichen Ordnung Liechtensteins* (Liechtenstein, Beiträge Nr).

Matthijs, H (2013) 'De kosten van een staatshoofd in West-Europa' 45 *Tijdschrift voor openbare financiën* 143.

McCombs, M E and Shaw, D L (1972) 'The Agenda-setting Function of Mass Media' 36 *Public Opinion Quarterly* 176.

McClure, D (2014) *Royal Legacy; How the Royal Family Have Made, Spent, and Passed on Their Wealth* (London, Thistle).

Merriënboer van, J, Bootsma, P and Griensven van, P (2008) *Van Agt Biografie; Tour de Force* (Amsterdam, Boom).

Moberg, V (1955), *Därför är jag republikan* (Stockholm, Atlas, 2010).

Modood T (1997) (ed) *Church, State and Religious Minorities* (London, Policy Studies Institute).

Morrah, D (1958) *The Work of the Queen* (London, William Kimber).

Molitor, A (1994) *La fonction royale en Belgique* (Brussels, Éditions du CRISP).

Moore, M (2018) *Democracy Hacked* (London, Bloomsbury).

Mortimore, R (2016) 'Measuring British Public Opinion on the Monarchy and Royal Family' in Glencross, M, Rowbotham, J and Kandiah, M (eds) *The Windsor Dynasty 1910 to the Present – Long to Reign Over Us?* (London, Palgrave Macmillan).

Murphy, P (2008) 'Independence Day and the Crown' 97(398) *Round Table* 667.

—— (2013) *Monarchy and the End of Empire* (Oxford, Oxford University Press).

Nairn, T (1988) *The Enchanted Glass: Britain. And its Monarchy* (London, Verso).

Nergelius, J (2015) *Constitutional Law in Sweden*, (Alphen aan den Rijn, Wolters Kluwer).

Nicolson, N (1971) (ed) *Harold Nicolson: Diaries and Letters, 1945–1962* (London, Collins).

Noelle-Neumann, E (1984) *The Spiral of Silence* (Chicago, University of Chicago Press).

Norton, P (2016) 'A Temporary Occupant of No 10? Prime Ministerial Succession in the Event of the Death of the Incumbent' *Public Law* 18.

Nott, D (2019) *War Doctor: Surgery on the Front Line* (London, Pan-Macmillan).

Nyman, O (1982) 'The New Swedish Constitution' 26 *Scandinavian Studies in Law* 170.

Ögren, M (2006) 'Kort om kungen' in Ögren, M (ed), *För Sverige – nuförtiden. En antologi om Carl XVI Gustaf* (Stockholm, Bokförlaget DN).

Olechnowicz, A (2007) (ed), *The Monarchy and the British Nation, 1780 to the Present* (Cambridge, Cambridge University Press).

Ónega, F (2015) *Juan Carlos I. El hombre que pudo reinar* (Barcelona, Plaza and Janes).

Oud, P J (1967) *Het constitutioneel recht van het Koninkrijk der Nederlanden I* (Zwolle, WEJ Tjeenk Willink).

Parekh, P (2000) *Rethinking Multiculturalism* (Basingstoke, Palgrave Macmillan).

Pescatore, P (1957) 'Essai sur la notion de la loi' in *Le Conseil d'État du Grand-Duché de Luxembourg. Livre jubilaire (1856–1956)* (Luxembourg, Bourg-Bourger).

Petersen, H (2001) 'Monarkiet – en psykologisk statsform i en post-suveræn stat?' in Petersen, H et al (eds), *Staten i Forandring* (Copenhagen, Jurist- og Økonomforbundets Forlag).

Phillips, L (1999) 'Media Discourse and the Danish Monarchy: Reconciling Egalitarianism and Royalism' 21 *Media, Culture and Society* 221.

Pierlot, H (1947) *Pages d'histoire* (Le Soir).

Pimlott, B (2012) *The Queen,* Diamond Jubilee edn (London, Harper Collins).

Poelgeest van, L (1993) 'Een onderwerp van zoo tederen aard' in Heringa, AW (eds) *Verhalen over de Grondwet,* (Den Haag, Boom Juridich).

Pool, A L (1951) *From Domesday Book to Magna Carta* (Oxford, Oxford University Press).

Prochaska, F K (1980) *Women and Philanthropy in Nineteenth-Century England* (Oxford, Oxford University Press).

—— (1995) *Royal Bounty: The Making of a Welfare Monarchy* (Harmondsworth, Penguin).

Range, M (2016) *British Royal and State Funerals: Music and Ceremonial Since Elizabeth I* (Woodbridge, Boydell Press).

Ratcliff, E (1953) *The Coronation Service of Her Majesty Queen Elizabeth II* (London, SPCK).

Redder, G and Palshøj, K (2008) *Frederik. Kronprins af Danmark* (Copenhagen, Høst og Søn).

Richards, P (1995) *Long to Reign Over Us? Fabian Pamphlet 576* (London, Fabian Society).

Roseveare, H (1969) *The Treasury: The Evolution of a British Institution* (London, Penguin).

—— (1991) *The Financial Revolution* (London, Longman).

Ross, A (1983) *Dansk Statsforfatningsret* (Copenhagen, Nyt Nordisk Forlag).

Rowbotham, J (2016) 'The Windsors and Ceremonial Events: State Occasions for the National Family' in Glencross, M, Rowbotham, J and Kandiah, M (eds) *The Windsor Dynasty 1910 to the Present – Long to Reign Over Us?* (London, Palgrave Macmillan).

Rowbottom, A (1994) 'Royal Symbolism and Social Integration' (PhD thesis, Manchester University).

—— (1998) 'The Real Royalists: Folk Performance and Civil Religion at Royal Visits' 109 *Folklore* 77.

—— (2002) 'Following the Queen: The Place of the Royal Family in the Context of Royal Visits and Civil Religion' 7(2) *Sociological Research Online* 1.

Russell, P and Sossin, L (2009) (eds), *Parliamentary Democracy in Crisis* (Toronto: University of Toronto Press).

Samyn, S and Peeters, T (2011), *De gevangenen van de Wetstraat: een reconstructie van zeven maanden onderhandelen* (Ghent, Borgerhoff and Lamberigts).

Schleiter, P, Belu, V and Hazell, R, *Forming a Government in the Event of a Hung Parliament: The UK's Recognition Rules in Comparative Context* (London: The Constitution Unit).

Seaton, J (2012) 'Afterword' in B Pimlott, *The Queen*, Diamond Jubilee Edition (London, Harper Collins).

—— (2016) *'Pinkoes and Traitors: the BBC and the Nation 1974–198* 7 (London, Profile Books).

Seldon, A (1997) *John Major: A Political Life* (London, Orion Books).

Senelle, E, Clément, E and Van de Velde, E (2006) *A l'attention de Sa Majesté le Roi – La monarchie institutionnelle et le régime parlementaire en Belgique* (Paris, Mols).

Shawcross, W (2009) *The Queen Mother: The Official Biography* (London, Random House).

Sjöberg, T, Rauscher, D and Meyer, Y (2010) *Carl XVI Gustaf: Den motvillige monarken* (Stockholm, Lind & Co).

Sørensen, M (1973) *Statsforfatningsret* (Copenhagen, Juristforbundets Forlag).

Shils, E and Young, M (1953) 'The Meaning of the Coronation' 1 *Sociological Review* 53.

Smith, E (2017) *Konstitusjonelt demokrati. Statsforfatningsretten i prisipielt og komparativt lys* (Oslo, Fagbokforlaget).

Smith, S B (2012) *Elizabeth the Queen: The Life of a Modern Monarch* (London, Random House).

Stengers, J (2008) *L'action du Roi en Belgique depuis 1831* (Brussels, Racine).

Sterzel, F (2009) *Författning i utveckling* (Uppsala, Iustus).

Stjernquist, N (1971) 'Grundlagberedningskompromiss i statschefsfrågan' *Statsvetenskaplig tidskrift* 377.

Strong, R (2005) *Coronation* (London, Harper Collins).

Strömberg, H (2001–02) 'Hur fungerar den svenska monarkin?' *Juridisk Tidskrift vid Stockholms Universitet* 721.

Strömholm, S (2006) 'Argument för monarkin' in M Ögren (ed), *För Sverige – Nuförtiden. En antologi om Carl XVI Gustaf* (Stockholm, Bokförlaget DN).

Summers, A (1988) *Angels into Citizens: British Women as Military Nurses 1854–1914* (London & New York, Routledge & Kegan Paul).

Sunnqvist, M and Wenander, H (2018) 'En offentligrättslig korporation under Monarken? Svenska Akademien och kungen i juridiskt perspektiv' 120 *Statsvetenskaplig tidskrift* 559.

Tamse, C A (1991) 'The Question of the Luxembourg Succession and Emma, Queen of the Netherlands and Grand Duchess of Luxembourg' in Tamse, C A et al (eds), *Die Beziehungen zwischen den Niederlanden und Luxemburg im 19. und 20. Jahrhundert* (Den Haag, SDU).

Taylor, J (1996) *British Monarchy, English Church Establishment and Civil Liberty* (Westport, CT, Greenwood Press).

Theroux, P (1983) *The Kingdom by the Sea* (London, Penguin).

Thewes, M (1994) 'Le régime politique du Grand-Duché de Luxembourg' in Guchet, Y (ed), *Les systèmes politiques des pays de l'Union européenne* (Paris, A Colin).

Tingsten, H (1964) *Skall kungamakten stärkas? Kritik av författningsförslaget* (Stockholm, Aldus aktuellt).

Torfs, R (2005) 'State and Church in Belgium' in Robbers, G (ed) *State and Church in the European Union* (Baden-Baden, Nomos Verlag).

Tullock, G (1987) *Autocracy* (Dordrecht, Kluwer Academic Publishers).

Twomey, A (2018) *The Veiled Sceptre: Reserve Powers of Heads of State in Westminster Systems.* (Cambridge, Cambridge University Press).

Velaers, J (2019) *De Grondwet, een artikelsgewijze commentaar,* 3 vols (Bruges, die Keure).

Te Velde te, H (2006) 'Cannadine, Twenty Years On; Monarchy and Political Culture in Nineteenth-Century Britain and the Netherlands' in Deploige, J and Deneckere, G (eds), *Mystifying the Monarch; Studies on Discourse, Power, and History* (Amsterdam, Amsterdam University Press).

Villalonga de, J L (1994) *The King. A life of King Juan Carlos of Spain* (London, Weidenfeld & Nicolson).

Villemann, T (2007) *1015 København K* (Copenhagen, Ekstrabladets Forlag).

Visser, R K (2008) *In dienst van het algemeen belang. Ministeriële verantwoordelijkheid en parlementair vertrouwen* (Amsterdam, Uitgeverij Boom).

Vuye, H and Wouters, V (2016a) *De Maat van de monarchie: macht en middelen van het Belgische koningshuis,* (Antwerp, Friday Publishing House).

—— (2016b) 'Het nieuwe regime van de dotaties van de koninklijke familie. De wet van 27 november 2013 na een jaar proefdraaien' 1 *Chronique de droit public* 2.

Warnling Conradson, W et al (2018) *Statsrättens grunder* (Stockholm, Norstedts Juridik).

Watts, C (2018) *Messing with the Enemy: Surviving in a Social Media World of Hackers, Terrorists, Russians, and Fake News* (London, Harper Collins).

Weibull, L (2012) 'Samhällsförtroende' in Asp, K (ed), *Svenska journalister 1989–2011* (Göteborgs universitet, Institutionen för journalistik och masskommunikation).

Wenander, H (2019) 'The Ghost of the King – Traces of Royal Majesty in the Swedish Modern Constitution of 1974' in Modéer, K Å (ed), *Legal History: Reflecting the Past and the Present* (Stockholm, Institutet för rättshistorisk forskning, forthcoming).

Wieslander, H (1974) (ed), *De politiska partiernas program* (Stockholm, Primasieren).

Wijnen van, H A (2000) *De Macht van de Kroon* (Amsterdam, Balans).

Williams, S (1994) 'A Citizen Monarchy' in Barnet, A (ed) *Power and the Throne* (London, Vintage).

Witte, E (2009) 'The Role of the Monarchy' in Witte, E, Craeybeckx, J and Meynen, A (eds), *Political History of Belgium: From 1830 Onwards*, (Brussels, ASP).

Wolffe, J (2000) *Great Deaths: Grieving, Religion, and Nationhood in Victorian and Edwardian Britain* (British Academy, Oxford University Press).

Zahle, H (2001) *Dansk Forfatningsret, bind 1* (Copenhagen, Jurist- og Økonomforbundets Forlag).

—— (2006) (ed), *Grundloven. Danmarks Riges Grundlov med kommentarer* (Copenhagen, Jurist- og Økonomforbundets Forlag).

REPORTS

Brothén, M (2004) *Förtroendet för riksdagen 2003, Resultat från forskningsprojektet Bilder av riksdagen medborgare och riksdagsledamöter i den representativa demokratin* (presented to the SOM Institute in a seminar 30 March).

Elliot, M (1994) 'Västsvensk tillit och misstro; Förtroendet för yrkesgrupper och medier' in Nilsson, L (ed), *Västsverige i fokus: SOM-undersökningen 1993*, (Göteborgs universitet, SOM-institutet).

—— (1997) *Förtroendet för medierna*, (Göteborgs universitet, Institutionen för journalistik och masskommunikation).

Fabian Society (2003) *Report of the Fabian Commission on the Future of the Monarchy* (London, Fabian Society).

FSI (2010), *Svenska folkets attityder till det svenska kungahuset och till att Sverige är en monarki* (Release ur Kajsa 16 June).

Hazell R and Morris, R M (2018) *Swearing in the new King: The Accession Declarations and Coronation Oaths* (London, the Constitution Unit) www.ucl.ac.uk/constitution-unit/sites/constitution-unit/files/180_swearing_in_the_new_king.pdf.

Holmberg, S and Weibull, L (2006) 'Flagnande förtroende' in Holmberg, S and Weibull, L (eds), *Du sköna nya värld*, (Göteborgs universitet, SOM-institutet).

Nilsson, L (1996) 'Svenska folket och monarkin' in Holmberg, S and Weibull, L (eds), *Mitt i nittiotalet* (Göteborgs universitet, SOM-institutet).

—— (2012) 'Monarkin och statschefen i Sverige – stöd, förtroende och popularitet' in Weibull, L, Oscarsson, H and Bergström, A (eds), *I framtidens skugga nittiotalet* (Göteborgs universitet, SOM-institutet).

—— (2013) 'Svenska folket, journalisterna, monarkin' in Weibull, L, Oscarsson H and Bergström, A, *Vägskäl* (Göteborgs universitet, SOM-institutet).

Petersson, O (1978) *Valundersökningar. Rapport 3. Valundersökning 1976. Teknisk rapport* (Stockholm, Statistika centrålbryan).

Ramsay, G and Robertshaw, S (2019) *Weaponising News* (London, Centre for the Study of Media, Communication and Power). Available at: www.kcl.ac.uk/policy-institute/assets/weaponising-news.pdf.

Vernersdotter, F (2015) 'Den nationella SOM-undersökningen 2014' in Bergström, A, Johansson, B, Oscarsson, H and Oskarson, M (eds), *Fragment* (Göteborgs universitet, SOM-institutet).

Weibull, L (2001) 'Förtroende för samhället – både högt och lågt' in Asp, K (ed), *JMG granskaren. Journalist 2000* (Göteborgs universitet, Centrum för granskning av journalistik och medier).

BLOGS AND NEWSPAPER ARTICLES

Aanmoen, O (2017) 'King Harald – I will not abdicate' *RoyalCentral* (16 February). Available at: royalcentral. co.uk/europe/norway/king-harald-i-will-not-abdicate-76583/.

Addley E and Booth, R (2016) 'Who controls whom? Monarchy vs the media' *Guardian* (8 November). Available at: www.theguardian.com/uk-news/2016/nov/08/who-controls-who-the-monarchy-v-the-media.

Alexander, H and Oscarssen, M (2010) 'Swedes in shock at King Carl Gustav sex scandal' *Daily Telegraph* (6 November). Available at: www.telegraph.co.uk/news/worldnews/europe/sweden/8114740/Swedes-in-shock-at-King-Carl-Gustaf-sex-scandal.html.

Associate Press (2008) 'Luxembourg strips monarch of legislative role' *Guardian* (12 December). Available at: www.theguardian.com/world/2008/dec/12/luxembourg-monarchy.

BBC News (2011), 'Prince Andrew to step down as UK trade envoy' (21 July). Available at: www.bbc.co.uk/news/uk-14235330.

Belga (2013), 'Le futur du roi Albert II et de la monarchie au centre de plusieurs sondages' *Le Vif* (23 May) Available at: www.levif.be/actualite/le-futur-du-roi-albert-ii-et-de-la-monarchie-au-centre-de-plusieurs-sondages/article-normal-85139.html.

—— (2017) 'Une majorité de Belges préfère une monarchie à une république' *La Libre* (22 September). Available at: www.lalibre.be/actu/belgique/une-majorite-de-belges-prefere-une-monarchie-a-une-republique-59c53690cd70a8c26d18c27a.

Berg Eriksen, T (1999) 'Kan Sverige bli mer demokratiskt?' *Dagens Nyheter* (27 May).

Bistrup, A (2010) 'Interview: Dronning Margrethe: Jeg er her jo bare' *Jyllands-Posten* (11 April). Available at: www.jyllands-posten.dk/protected/premium/indblik/article4315554.ece.

Bloxham, J A and Kirkup, J (2011) 'Centuries-old rule of primogeniture in Royal Family scrapped' *Telegraph* (28 October). Available at: www.telegraph.co.uk/news/uknews/theroyalfamily/8854981/Centuries-old-rule-of-succession-in-British-Royal-family-scrapped-by-Commonwealth.html.

Bodry, A (2008) 'Une lecture erronée de la Constitution' *Tageblatt* (4 December). Available at: www.tageblatt. lu/nachrichten/luxemburg/une-lecture-erronee-de-la-constitution-96408758/.

Bogdanor, V (2003) 'Let's be radical and not change the monarchy' *The Times* (16 July). Available at: www. thetimes.co.uk/article/lets-be-really-radical-and-not-change-the-monarchy-qs66wmmjd6x.

Booth, R and Taylor, M (2015) 'Prince Charles black spider memos show lobbying at highest political level' *Guardian*, (13 May). Available at: www.theguardian.com/uk-news/2015/may/13/prince-charles-black-spider-memos-lobbying-ministers-tony-blair.

Bradley, I (2017) 'The Strange Death of Protestant Britain'. Inaugural professorial lecture delivered at St Andrews University, (30 October); shortened version in *The Tablet*, (13 December 2017). Available at: www.thetablet. co.uk/features/2/11857/the-strange-death-of-protestant-britain-the-near-loss-of-religious-sensibilities.

Brekke, A and Skrede, K M (2017) '8 av 10 vil beholde kongehuset: Størst oppslutning blant de unge' *NRK* (18 February). Available at: www.nrk.no/norge/8-av-10-vil-beholde-kongehuset_-storst-oppslutning-blant-de-unge-1.13383378.

Broshammar, M A-J (2010) 'Statschefen bör väljas demokratiskt' *Republikanska Föreningen*. Available at: www.republikanskaforeningen.se/wp-content/uploads/2016/02/Statschefen-b%C3%B6r-v%C3%A4ljas-demokratiskt-opinionsunders%C3%B6kning.pdf.

Cluskey, P (2013) 'Dutch royals search for role as gossip-obsessed media circles new prey' *Irish Times* (30 April). Available at: www.irishtimes.com/news/world/europe/dutch-royals-search-for-role-as-gossip-obsessed-media-circles-new-prey-1.1376870.

Cordsen, C (2010) 'Flertal: Afskaf dronningerunden' *Jyllands-Posten* (11 April). Available at: www. jyllandsposten.dk/indland/ECE4315886/Flertal-Afskaf-dronningerunden/.

Craig, R (2019) 'Could the Government Advise the Queen to Refuse Royal Assent to a Backbench Bill?' *UK Constitutional Law Blog* (22 January). Available at: www.ukconstitutionallaw.org/2019/01/22/robert-craig-could-the-government-advise-the-queen-to-refuse-royal-assent-to-a-backbench-bill/.

Deutsche Welle (2009) 'Denmark votes to change royal succession rules' (9 June) Available at: www.dw.com/en/denmark-votes-to-change-royal-succession-rules/a-4310654.

Douglas, T (2012) 'Leveson Report: Analysis' *BBC News* (29 December). Available at: www.bbc.co.uk/news/entertainment-arts-20541553.

Duncan, E (2019) 'I've learnt the magic of monarchy' *Times* (30 April 2019). Available at: www.thetimes.co.uk/article/i-ve-learnt-to-love-the-magic-of-monarchy-hdt2f2w6z.

Ertel, M and Sandberg, B (2016) 'I Would Not Say We Are a Multicultural Country' *Der Spiegel* (30 September). Available at: www.spiegel.de/international/europe/queen-margrethe-of-denmark-we-are-constants-in-the-world-a-1114542.html.

Fogt, L and Karker, A (2009) 'Bendtsens ven fik ridderkorset' *Berlingske Tidende* (29 March).

Frieden, L (2008) Interview on RTL Television, 2 December, transcription (in Luxembourgish). Available at: gouvernement.lu/fr/actualites/toutes_actualites/interviews/2008/12-decembre/03-frieden-rtl-tele.html.

Gallup (1963), 'Bør Danmark være en republik?' *Aarhus Universitet* (13 March 2014). Available at: danmarkshistorien.dk/leksikon-og-kilder/vis/materiale/gallup-1963-boer-danmark-vaere-en-republik/.

Giertz, E (2017) 'Unik Enkät: Så tycker svenskarna om sitt kungahus' *Expressen* (30 April). Available at: www.expressen.se/nyheter/kungligt/demoskop-kungahuset-2017/.

Glancey, J (2004) 'Life after Carbuncles' *Guardian* (17 May). Available at: www.theguardian.com/artanddesign/2004/may/17/architecture.regeneration.

Goebbels, R (2008) 'Privates Gewissen und staatliche Pflicht' *Tageblatt*, (4 December). Available at: www.tageblatt.lu/nachrichten/luxemburg/privates-gewissen-und-staatliche-pflicht-93308759/.

Grand Duke Henri (2008), 'Message de noël du 25 décembre 2008' partial transcription (in French). Available at: www.gotha.fr/3.aspx?page=9&sr=285.

Guardian (2015), 'Read the Prince Charles "black spider" memos in full' (13 May). Available at: www.theguardian.com/uk-news/ng-interactive/2015/may/13/read-the-prince-charles-black-spider-memos-in-full.

Hazell, R, (2019) 'Holding a Queen's Speech in October risks heaping more embarrassment on the Queen' *Constitution Unit Blog*, (3 October). Available at: www.constitution-unit.com/2019/10/03/holding-a-queens-speech-in-october-risks-heaping-more-embarrassment-on-the-queen/.

Heck van, S (2018) 'Koningsdag enquête 2018: Rapport voor de NOS' *IPSOS* (23 April). Available at: www.download.omroep.nl/nos/docs/18027064_Ipsos_Koningsdagenquete2018_v3.0.pdf.

Herlitz, N (1966) 'Statschefens ställning' *Svenska Dagbladet* (7 April).

Holmberg, S and Weibull, L (2012) 'Förtroendebarometern' *Medieakademin*. Available at: www.medieakademien.se/wp-content/uploads/2019/03/2012_Medieakademin_Fortroendebarometer.pdf.

—— (2013) 'Förtroendebarometern' *Medieakademin*. Available at: www.medieakademien.se/wp-content/uploads/2019/03/2013_Medieakademin_Fortroendebarometer.pdf.

Howarth, D (2018) 'How to change the government without causing a general election' *UK Constitutional Law Blog* (26 November). Available at: www.ukconstitutionallaw.org/2018/11/26/david-howarth-how-to-change-the-government-without-causing-a-general-election/.

Hope, C (2019) 'Queen could be asked to veto John Bercow's attempts to water down Brexit, Government confirms' *Daily Telegraph*, (21 January). Available at: www.telegraph.co.uk/politics/2019/01/21/queen-could-asked-veto-john-bercows-attempts-water-brexit-government/.

Ingvorsen, E S (2016) 'Måling: Kongehuset ligeså populært som for 40 år siden' *DR* (14 November). Available at: www.dr.dk/nyheder/indland/maaling-kongehuset-ligesaa-populaert-som-40-aar-siden.

Ipsos (2018) 'La monarquía española, la menos apoyada entre las monarquías europeas' (14 May). Available at: www.ipsos.com/es-es/la-monarquia-espanola-la-menos-apoyada-entre-las-monarquias-europeas.

Ipsos MORI (2006), 'Monarchy/Royal Family Trends – Queen Camilla?' (24 April). Available at: www.ipsos.com/ipsos-mori/en-uk/monarchyroyal-family-trends-queen-camilla.

—— (2012) 'Monarchy/Royal Family Trends – Most Liked Members of the Royal Family' (19 November). Available at: www.ipsos.com/ipsos-mori/en-uk/monarchyroyal-family-trends-most-liked-members-royal-family.

—— (2016) 'Monarchy/Royal Family Trends – Monarchy v Republic 1993–2016' (15 April). Available at: www.ipsos.com/ipsos-mori/en-uk/monarchyroyal-family-trends-monarchy-v-republic-1993-2016.

—— (2016) 'Monarchy popular as ever ahead of Queen's 90th Birthday celebrations' (15 April). Available at: www.ipsos.com/ipsos-mori/en-uk/monarchy-popular-ever-ahead-queens-90th-birthday-celebrations.

—— (2016) 'High satisfaction levels with Royal Family as the Queen turns 90' (23 May). Available at: www.ipsos.com/ipsos-mori/en-uk/high-satisfaction-levels-royal-family-queen-turns-90.

JessRulz (2017) 'New Polls Illustrate Public Support of Danish, Dutch, Swedish Monarchies' *The Royal Forums* (April 30). Available at: www.theroyalforums.com/63725-new-polls-illustrate-public-support-danish-dutch-swedish-monarchies/.

Le Jeudi (2008) '36% des Luxembourgeois sont républicains' *Le Jeudi* (11 December).

Jyllands-Posten (2010) 'Kan en dronning gå på pension?' (10 April). Available at: jyllands-posten.dk/indland/ECE4315688/Kan-en-dronning-g%C3%A5-p%C3%A5-pension/.

—— (2018) 'Fakta: Sådan er danskernes opbakning til kongehuset' (2 March). Available at: jyllands-posten.dk/indland/ECE10364430/fakta-saadan-er-danskernes-opbakning-til-kongehuset/.

Kalajdzic, P (2014) 'Åtte av ti støtter kongefamilien: – Kan ikke huske å ha sett slik oppslutning' *NRK* (16 May). Available at: www.nrk.no/norge/enorm-stotte-til-kongefamilien-1.11720904.

Karker, A (2018) 'Danskerne: Han bliver en god konge' *BT* (25 May). Available at: www.bt.dk/royale/klar-danskerne-han-bliver-en-god-konge.

Kvalvik (2017) '4 ud af 10 ønsker forandring i Kongehuset' *Altinget* (17 September). Available at: www.altinget.dk/artikel/4-ud-af-10-oensker-forandring-i-kongehuset.

Keeley, G (2016) 'King Felipe takes 20% pay cut and reduces civil list' *Times* (2 June). Available at: www.thetimes.co.uk/article/king-felipe-takes-20-pay-cut-and-reduces-civil-list-h6g7g7k25.

—— (2018) 'Spanish King charms Saudis for arms deal' *Times* (12 April). Available at: www.thetimes.co.uk/article/spain-in-2bn-arms-deal-with-saudi-arabia-vhxmdz0kg.

Knight, S (2017) 'London Bridge is down': The secret plan for the days after the Queen's death' *Guardian* (17 March). Available at: www.theguardian.com/uk-news/2017/mar/16/what-happens-when-queen-elizabeth-dies-london-bridge.

Laws, S (2019) 'The Fixed Term Parliaments Act and the next election' *Policy Exchange Blog* (24 October). Available at: www.policyexchange.org.uk/publication/the-fixed-term-parliaments-act-and-the-next-election/.

Lindblad, K-E (2016) 'Kongehus-spørsmålet som splitter Norge' *Dagbladet* (14 July). Available at: www.dagbladet.no/a/60317753.

Low, V (2018) 'I want a new yacht, Queen told Whitehall in secret letter', *Times* (29 December). Available at: www.thetimes.co.uk/article/i-want-a-new-yacht-queen-told-whitehall-in-secret-letter-pztt0frlh.

—— (2019) 'Prince Andrew quits public life over Epstein scandal' *Times* (21 November). Available at: www.thetimes.co.uk/article/prince-andrew-steps-down-from-public-duties-in-wake-of-tv-interview-over-epstein-links-jt95nqq22.

Lucas-Torres, C (2019) 'La valoración de la Monarquía cae pero mantiene el aprobado' *El Español* (4 January). Available at: www.elespanol.com/espana/politica/20190104/valoracion-monarquia-cae-mantiene-aprobado/365714374_0.html.

Luxemburger Wort (2014), '*Quatre questions à l'ordre du jour: Le référendum aura lieu le 7 juin 2015*' (23 October). Available at: www.wort.lu/fr/luxembourg/quatre-questions-a-l-ordre-du-jour-le-referendum-aura-lieu-le-7-juin-2015-544915f8b9b398870807df36.

—— (2015) '*Sondage sur le Référendum: Le droit de vote des étrangers divise l'électorat*' (6 February). Available at: www.wort.lu/fr/luxembourg/sondage-sur-le-referendum-le-droit-de-vote-des-etrangers-divise-l-electorat-54d4f0450c88b46a8ce53045.

Madden, R L (1976) 'Dutch Prince Was Given $1.1 Million by Lockheed' *New York Times* (7 February). Available at: www.nytimes.com/1976/02/07/archives/dutch-prince-was-given-11-million-by-lockheed-dutch-prince-tied-to.html.

Madormo, M, 'The truth about Kate Middleton and Meghan Markle's relationship' *The List*. Available at: www.thelist.com/110590/kate-middleton-meghan-markle-relationship/.

Magnusson, M and Ström, S (2010) 'Vi vänder blad och ser framåt' *Svenska Dagbladet* (4 November). Available at: www.svd.se/kungen-vi-vander-blad-och-ser-framat.

Marks, S (2019) 'Belgian prince fights own government over Libya cash' *Politico* (19 August). Available at: www.politico.eu/article/belgium-prince-laurent-fight-with-national-government/.

Martínez-Fornés, A (2018) 'El Rey logra la mejor valoración de la Monarquía desde su restauración' *ABC* (6 August). Available at: www.abc.es/espana/abci-logra-mejor-valoracion-monarquia-desde-restauracion-201808052317_noticia.html.

Matzon, M (2019) 'Valgets hemmelige helte' (interview with a.o. Henning Foged) *Djøf bladet*. Available at: www.djoefbladet.dk/artikler/2019/5/valgets-hemmelige-helte.aspx.

McAllister (2006) 'A Woman's Work Is Never Done' *Time* (17 April). Available at: www.content.time.com/time/world/article/0,8599,2050240,00.html.

Nilsson, L (2017) 'Monarkins legitimitet i Sverige och Danmark' *Dixikon* (23 April). Available at: www.dixikon.se/monarkins-legitimitet-i-sverige-och-danmark/.

Norsk Telegrambyrå (2012) '"Alle" liker kong Harald' *Aftenposten* (7 April). Available at: www.aftenposten.no/article/ap-K37BG.html.

—— (2014), 'Sprikende målinger om kongehusets oppslutning' *iTromso* (16 April). Available at: www.itromso.no/ntb/iriks/article9691073.ece.

—— (2016), 'To av tre vil ha monarki' *Stavanger Aftenblad* (17 April). Available at: www.aftenbladet.no/article/sa-Rm28J.html.

NOS Nieuws (2015) '200 jaar koninkrijk ging aan veel Nederlanders voorbij' (25 September). Available at: https://nos.nl/artikel/2059558-200-jaar-koninkrijk-ging-aan-veel-nederlanders-voorbij.html.

—— (2017) 'Meer steun voor de monarchie, vertrouwen in koning gestegen' (27 April). Available at: https://nos.nl/artikel/2170371-meer-steun-voor-de-monarchie-vertrouwen-in-koning-gestegen.html.

Pierce, A (2008), 'Prince Charles to be known as Defender of Faith' *Daily Telegraph* (13 November). Available at: www.telegraph.co.uk/news/uknews/theroyalfamily/3454271/Prince-Charles-to-be-known-as-Defender-of-Faith.html.

The People (1993), 'Charles and Camilla – the tape' (17 January). Available at: www.mirror.co.uk/news/uk-news/how-camillagate-tapes-exposed-secret-10958350.

Petersson, O (2004) 'Kungens kompetens måste ifrågasättas' *Dagens Nyheter* (17 February). Available at: www.dn.se/arkiv/debatt/kungens-kompetens-maste-ifragasattas-grundlagsbrott-att-goran-persson-och-kungen-inte-samtalade-4/.

Politiken (2012) 'Thorning: Statsråd er kommet for at blive' (13 January). Available at: www.politiken.dk/indland/politik/art5040848/Thorning-Statsr%C3%A5d-er-kommet-for-at-blive.

Purves, L (2018) 'A right royal display of tactless ostentation' *The Times* (20 August). Available at: www.thetimes.co.uk/article/a-right-royal-display-of-tactless-ostentation-m3b5l59n7.

Lord Ricketts, Letter to *The Times* (31 January 2017).

Robinson, M (2014) 'Finally Britain and Ireland are reconciled' *CNN* (9 April). Available at: https://edition.cnn.com/2014/04/08/opinion/britain-ireland-visit-robinson/index.html.

Romero, A (2017) 'Felipe VI sitúa a la monarquía en su mejor valoración en 20 años' *El Español* (7 January). Available at: www.elespanol.com/espana/20170101/182732111_0.html.

Rosenbaum, M (2008) 'How to organise a state visit' *BBC Blogs* (15 April). Available at: www.bbc.co.uk/blogs/opensecrets/2008/04/post_21.html.

Sarpsborg Arbeiderblad (2005) 'Ikke helt fjellstøtt' (15 November). Available at: www.sa.no/lokale_nyheter/article1825413.ece?ns_campaign=article&ns_mchannel=recommend_button&ns_source=facebook&ns_linkname=facebook&ns_fee=0.

Shea, C (2018) 'Rumour has it that Meghan Markle and Kate Middleton "hate each other's guts." Is that really the case?' *Chatelaine* (19 May). Available at: www.chatelaine.com/living/entertainment/meghan-kate-feud/.

Shipman, T and Wheeler, C (2019) '"Sack me if you dare" Boris Johnson will tell the Queen, *Sunday Times* (6 October 2019). Available at: www.thetimes.co.uk/article/sack-me-if-you-dare-boris-johnson-will-tell-the-queen-fsbpsnjdc.

Sigma Dos (2014) 'Crece el respaldo a la monarquía tras la abdicación del rey Juan Carlos'. Available at: www.sigmados.com/monarquia-abdicacion-rey-juan-carlos-encuesta-mundo/.

—— (2015) 'Datos de juno de 2015'. Available at: www.sigmados.com/wp-content/uploads/2015/06/Graficos-Felipe.jpg.

Sterba, JP (1971) 'Indonesians, in joy and tears, welcome Juliana as a friend' *The New York Times* (27 August). Available at: www.nytimes.com/1971/08/27/archives/indonesians-in-joy-and-tears-welcome-juliana-as-a-friend.html.

Stickings, (2019) 'King culls Swedish royal family' *Daily Maily* (7 October). Available at: www.dailymail.co.uk/news/article-7547135/Swedish-royal-family-culled-King-Gustaf-strips-five-grandchildren-royal-status.html.

Svenska Dagbladet (2018), 'Kungafamiljen växer – nu måste anslaget begränsas' (15 May). Available at: www.svd.se/kungafamiljen-vaxer--nu-maste-anslaget-begransas.

The Times (9 January 1885). Available at: www.thetimes.co.uk/archive/article/1885-01-09/9/7.html.

Theil, A (2019) 'Unconstitutional prorogation' UK Constitutional Law Blog (3 April). Available at: www.ukconstitutionallaw.org/2019/04/03/stefan-theil-unconstitutional-prorogation/.

Thorning, H (2012) 'Kongehuset har fornyet sig' *Ritzau* (15 January). Available at: www.politiken.dk/indland/art5390434/Thorning-Kongehuset-har-fornyet-sig.

Toharia, J J (2014) 'Un punto y seguido' *Metroscopia* (9 June). Available at: www.metroscopia.org/un-punto-y-seguido/.

TNS Gallup (2013) *Gallup om kongehuset*. Available at: www.webtest.kantargallup.dk/storage/reports/September2019/jAjqnfuKAuvZlAe8hqYK.pdf.

Vernersdotter, F (2012) 'Rekordstöd för kronprinsessan Victoria' *SOM-Institutet* (24 April). Available at: www.som.gu.se/aktuellt/Nyheter/Nyheter_detalj/rekordstod-for-kronprinsessan-victoria.cid1076564.

Walsh, S et al (2017) 'May says Queen invited Trump for state visit' *Reuters* (27 January). Available at: www.uk.reuters.com/article/uk-usa-trump-britain-queen/may-says-queen-invited-trump-for-state-visit-idUKKBN15B21U.

Waterfield, B (2019) 'Belgium's bored Prince Laurent fiddles with his phone through national anthem' *Times* (23 July). Available at: www.thetimes.co.uk/article/belgium-s-bored-prince-laurent-fiddles-with-his-phone-through-national-anthem-hqc2jp2r2.

Weber, P (2017) 'Philippe ou Mathilde? Voici qui les Belges préfèrent' *RTL Info* (23 September). Available at: www.rtl.be/info/belgique/famille-royale/philippe-ou-mathilde-voici-qui-les-belges-preferent-955660.aspx.

Weir, S (2013) 'A monstrous right royal carbuncle' *OpenDemocracy* (12 September). Available at: www.opendemocracy.net/en/opendemocracyuk/monstrous-right-royal-carbuncle/.

Willsher, K (2017) 'Court awards Duchess of Cambridge damages over topless photos' *Guardian* (5 September). Available at: www.theguardian.com/uk-news/2017/sep/05/topless-photos-of-duchess-of-cambridge-were-invasion-of-privacy.

Winchester, L (2015) 'Half of British public now think Camilla should become Queen' *Daily Express* (5 April). Available at: www.express.co.uk/news/royal/568587/Camilla-become-Queen-Consort-half-British-public.

YouGov (2012) 'YouGov/Sunday Times Survey Results. Available at: https://d25d2506sfb94s.cloudfront.net/cumulus_uploads/document/6nces75nwx/YG-Archives-Pol-ST-results-01-050612.pdf.

—— (2018) 'YouGov Survey Results'. Available at: https://d25d2506sfb94s.cloudfront.net/cumulus_uploads/document/m06kzwjbml/InternalResults_180509_RoyalWedding_w.pdf.

YouGov (2018) 'Did you commemorate Remembrance Day? Plus, dementia, and the monarchy results'. Available at: www.yougov.co.uk/opi/surveys/results#/survey/716e3290-e666-11e8-9f57-d37060c36f9b.

YouGov (2018) 'YouGov Republic survey results'. Available at: https://d25d2506sfb94s.cloudfront.net/cumulus_uploads/document/8ts86x0ql0/Republic_MonarchyResults_180511.pdf.

GOVERNMENT AND PARLIAMENTARY PUBLICATIONS

Barber, A (1971) *Commons Hansard* (14 December) api.parliament.uk/historic-hansard/commons/1971/dec/14/civil-list#S5CV0828P0_19711214_HOC_260.

Blackburn, R (2014) 'A New Magna Carta?' *House of Commons Political and Constitutional Reform Committee*, HC 463, July 2014. Available at: www.publications.parliament.uk/pa/cm201415/cmselect/cmpolcon/463/46302.htm.

Belgian Federal Government (2019) 'The King in the new structure of the State'. Available at: www.belgium.be/en/about_belgium/government/federal_authorities/king/new_structure_of_state.

British Embassy Holy See (2019) 'Holy See: Five years since the Papal Visit to the United Kingdom' (15 September). Available at: www.gov.uk/government/news/holy-see-five-years-since-the-papal-visit-to-the-united-kingdom.

Business Sweden (2015) 'State Visit to Lithuania 7–9 October 2015' (5 June). Available at: www.business-sweden.se/en/about-us/news-room/Press-Releases/state-visit-to-lithuania-7-9-october-2015/.

Cabinet Office (2011) *The Cabinet Manual: A Guide to Laws, Conventions and Rules on the Operation of Government* (October). Available at: www.assets.publishing.service.gov.uk/government/uploads/system/uploads/attachment_data/file/60641/cabinet-manual.pdf.

Conseil d'État (2008) 'Avis du 9 décembre 2008 sur le projet de révision de l'art. 34 de la Constitution, parl doc n° 5967-2'. Available at: www.chd.lu/wps/PA_RoleDesAffaires/FTSByteServingServletImpl?path=2338251576BD30543DDDDA4C620CD02FC61C7F6125FA2503160B0E9DD059955B0DCD4DE13189FAAC7CB3F6CA7C4B2789$577DA1C77A3ECEE8FEE8D1F478F0D550.

Commission des institutions et de la révision constitutionnelle (CIRC) (2008) 'Rapport sur le projet de révision de l'art. 34 de la Constitution' 10 December 2008, parl doc n° 5967-3. Available at: www.chd.lu/wps/PA_RoleDesAffaires/FTSByteServingServletImpl?path=7A6684A8268C97E1C1C1D2DAD648CC6B74040AA26A767D3DAD885ADC1AAEA79457AC44FEDFEE4E66116359BF04679229$0407511850A02DAADF77C762F76BE416.

Council of Europe CDL-AD (2002)032-e, 'Opinion on the Amendments to the Constitution of Liechtenstein proposed by the Princely House of Liechtenstein, adopted by the Venice Commission at its 53rd plenary session' (Venice, 13–14 December). Available at: www.venice.coe.int/webforms/documents/default.aspx?pdffile=CDL-AD(2002)032-e.

Eerste Kamer der Staten-Generaal (1996/97), 'Handelingen II 1996/97, nr 5'. Available at: https://zoek. officielebekendmakingen.nl/h-ek-19961997-127-129.html.

Foreign and Commonwealth Office (2016) 'Note by the FCO Protocol Directorate, 22 August'. Available at: www.assets.publishing.service.gov.uk/government/uploads/system/uploads/attachment_data/file/552236/ FOI_0726-16.pdf.

Föreskrifter rörande hovleverantörskap (2015). Available at: www.kungahuset.se/download/18.78ef352d169d87 c34d59f51/1555320328971/Foreskrifter_rorande_hovleverantorskap.pdf.

Het koninklijk huis website (2019) 'Financiën Koninklijk Huis'. Available at: www.koninklijkhuis.nl/ onderwerpen/financien-koninklijk-huis/begroting-van-de-koning.

HM Treasury, *Memorandum of Understanding on Royal Taxation* (March 2013). Available at: www.assets. publishing.service.gov.uk/government/uploads/system/uploads/attachment_data/file/208633/mou_royal_ taxation.pdf.

Houghton, D (1971) 'Memorandum "Proposal to set up a Department of the Crown", *Report of the Select Committee on the Civil List 1972*, Appendix 3.

House of Commons Political and Constitutional Reform Committee (2014–15), *Government Formation Post-Election*, HC 1023. Available at: www.parliament.uk/business/committees/committees-a-z/commons-select/ political-and-constitutional-reform-committee/inquiries/parliament-2010/government-formation1/?type=Oral.

Juncker, J-C (2008) 'Déclaration du Premier ministre sur les implications institutionnelles en cas de refus du Grand-Duc de donner son aval à une éventuelle loi sur le droit de mourir en dignité' (2 December). Available at: https://gouvernement.lu/fr/actualites/toutes_actualites/articles/2008/12-decembre/02-juncker-declaration.html.

Kastrup, M (2008) 'Kulturkamp: Jeg er jo selv vokset op i den kamp' *Berlingske Tidende* (15 June).

Kingdom of Belgium Foreign Affairs, Foreign Trade and Development Cooperation Website (2016) 'Visits of foreign VIPs in Belgium'. Available at: www.diplomatie.belgium.be/en/services/Protocol/visits_and_events_ management/visits_foreign_vips_belgium.

Leveson, B (2012) *The Leveson Inquiry: an Inquiry into the Culture, Practices, and Ethics of the Press*, 4 vols (29 November). Available at: www.gov.uk/government/publications/leveson-inquiry-report-into-the-culture-practices-and-ethics-of-the-press.

Det Norske Kongehus Website, 'HM The King's Speech at the Partisan Building in Kiberg, August 3, 1992'. Available at: www.kongehuset.no/tale.html?tid=30959.

—— (2013), 'The Consecration of King Harald and Queen Sonja'. Available at: www.kongehuset.no/artikkel. html?tid=28733&sek=27278.

Meyers, P H (2009) *Proposition de révision portant modification et nouvel ordonnancement de la Constitution*, 21 April 2009, parl doc n° 6030. Available at: www.chd.lu/wps/PA_RoleDesAffaires/ FTSByteServingServletImpl?path=44E67FD713B985C9EE8D63ED31D1EBD8D0A437BE34 EA18FAC7EB342E336EAF8C3CCAB5EAB903FFE02F4F48F58B9C5144$6630023FBC1727BAFA03C2193C CAAC8E.

Royal House of Denmark Website (2019) 'State Visits'. Available at: kongehuset.dk/en/the-monarchy-in-denmark/state-visits.

—— (2019) 'The Royal Yacht Dannebrog'. Available at: kongehuset.dk/en/palaces/the-royal-yacht.

Royal House of Norway Website (2019) 'State Visits'. Available at: www.royalcourt.no/seksjon.html?tid=1025 26&sek=102525.

Royal Household of the Netherlands Website, 'Incoming State Visits'. Available at: www.royal-house.nl/topics/ state-visits/incoming-state-visits.

Royal Household of the UK Website, 'State Visits'. Available at: www.royal.uk/state-visits-2.

—— 'The role of the Royal Family'. Available at: www.royal.uk/role-royal-family.

Royal Norwegian Embassy in Cairo Website (2016) 'Speech given by His Majesty The King' (1 September). Available at: www.norway.no/en/egypt/norway-egypt/news-events/news2/speech-given-by-his-majesty-the-king/.

Royal Yacht Britannia Website, 'History'. Available at: www.royalyachtbritannia.co.uk/about/history/.

The Sovereign Grant and Sovereign Grant Reserve (2019) 'Annual Report and Accounts, 2018–19' (25 June). Available at: www.royal.uk/sites/default/files/media/final_sovereign_grant_for_website.pdf.

StartupDelta Website, 'Constantijn van Orange'. Available at: www.startupdelta.org/constantijn-van-oranje/.

Swedish Royal Court Website, 'Duties of the Monarch'. Available at: www.kungahuset.se/royalcourt/ monarchytheroyalcourt/dutiesofthemonarch.4.396160511584257f2180003302.html.

—— 'Ekonomi'. Available at: www.kungahuset.se/monarkinhovstaterna/ekonomi.4.7c4768101a4e888 3780001030.html.

—— 'State Visits'. Available at: www.kungahuset.se/royalcourt/monarchytheroyalcourt/dutiesofthemonarch/royalvisits/statevisits.4.396160511584257f2180006113.htm.

—— (2011) 'A State Visit: How it works'. Available at: www.kungahuset.se/royalcourt/latestnews/2011/2011/astatevisithowitworks.5.40e05eec12926f26304800021306.html.

Turnbull, A (2011) *Lords Hansard*. Available at: publications.parliament.uk/pa/ld201011/ldhansrd/text/111003-0001.htm.

Tweede Kamer der Staten Generaal (1979/80), 'Kamerstukken II 1979/1980, 16 035, nr 3'. Available at: www.repository.overheid.nl/frbr/sgd/19791980/0000172397/1/pdf/SGD_19791980_0006465.pdf.

—— (1980/1), 'Kamerstukken II 1980/1981, 16035, nr 8. Available at: www.repository.overheid.nl/frbr/sgd/19801981/0000161212/1/pdf/SGD_19801981_0003372.pdf.

—— (1980/1), 'Handelingen II 1980/1981'. Available at: www.repository.overheid.nl/frbr/sgd/19801981/0000158333/1/pdf/SGD_19801981_0000540.pdf.

—— (1999/2000), 'Kamerstukken II 1999/2000, 27 409, nr 1'. Available at: https://zoek.officielebekendmakingen.nl/kst-27409-1.html.

UK Trade and Investment (2015) 'Chinese state visit: up to £40 billion deals agreed' (23 October). Available at: www.gov.uk/government/news/chinese-state-visit-up-to-40-billion-deals-agreed.

LEGISLATION

Bet. KU 1973:26 Förslag till ny regeringsform och ny riksdagsordning m.m (Sweden).

Bet. 2004/05:KU20 Granskningsbetänkande (Sweden).

Bet. 2013/14:KU1 Utgiftsområde 1 Rikets styrelse (Sweden).

Bet. 2004/05:KU20, 88 (Sweden).

L 109, 26 June 1998, session 1997–98 (Denmark).

L 85, 13 November 1998, session 1998–99 (Denmark).

Lagen (2002:1022) om revision av statlig verksamhet m.m (Sweden).

Loi de révision du 12 mars 2009; parl doc n° 5967 (Luxembourg).

Prop. 1973: 90 Med förslag till ny regeringsform och riksdagsordning m.m. med förslag till ny regeringsform och ny riksdagsordning m.m (Sweden).

Riksdagen, Motion No 2015/16:717 (Sweden).

SOU 1972:15 Ny regeringsform. Ny riksdagsordning (Sweden).

CASES

von Hannover v Germany European Court of Human Rights [2004] EMLR 379; (2005) 40 EHRR 1.

ARCHIVAL MATERIAL

Documents from the National Archives, UK: Government finances/Personal and family papers (BA), Welsh Office (BD), Cabinet Office (CAB), Colonial Office (CO), Foreign and Commonwealth Office (FCO), Prime Minister's Office (PREM), The Treasury (T).

Royal Archives, GV/CC 47/672.

Telegram from British Embassy, Washington, to FCO, 18 November 1988, Thatcher Mss: uncatalogued, Churchill Archive Centre.

Table of Monarchs
and their Close Families

Index

CPSIA information can be obtained
at www.ICGtesting.com
Printed in the USA
LVHW061000030421
683363LV00003B/123